Georg Popp
Juma Al-Maskari

Oman

Jewel of the Arabian Gulf

ODYSSEY BOOKS & GUIDES

Regional Studies

Traveling in Oman

The Green Pages

Welcome

"Why Oman?"

That's the question I've been most asked since my first trip to the Sultanate in 1992. At that time it was difficult to think of a more remote corner of the world. Just booking a flight proved to be an adventure. The travel agent obstinately persisted in trying to sell me a ticket to Amman in Jordan. No one knew what the booking code for Muscat was. Looking back it seems that my landing there was a result of a mixture of personal providence and Omani politics - or maybe it was the will of Allah.

My personal journey to Oman began back in 1983 and was entirely accidental. It was then that my girlfriend was looking for a room in a student home. The only place on offer with a waiting time of less than a year was the International House. When she moved in she was warmly welcomed by an Arab in nickel-framed glasses: Juma Al Maskari from Oman. As there was no university in the Sultanate at that time, students were all sent abroad to study. For personal reasons most opted to study in Arabic or English speaking countries. In those days only four Omanis chose the more difficult option of Germany. Juma wanted to go there, especially, because as a child he had been captivated by German children's television programs shown in Oman. He was a devotee of classical music.

Oman is not a land of spectacular sights but makes many unforgettable impressions

From the initially casual contacts a close and deep friendship developed between us. Being subjected to the many questions that he and the other Omanis put to me concerning the culture of their host country forced me to reflect more critically on my own personal preferences and on our local customs and religion. They were deeply shocked on first being confronted with a south German baroque church with bones laid out as relics in side altars and lovingly detailed depictions of saints being tortured. "So you pray to old bones? How can your children sleep after going to church. Is this the religion of brotherly love?" And then on weekends there was always the Omanis' wish to visit a river with a waterfall and simply to stand and look into the raging waters. Juma's numerous photos gave me another way of looking at our daily life.

At the time that I finished my studies at the Academy of Fine Art, Oman had just issued the first tourist visas. Now was my chance to discover a new world. What was originally planned as a three-week holiday turned into a project which, years later, shows no sign of coming to an end. All my attempts to prepare for the journey failed because of the complete lack of serious travel literature. So I set about learning Arabic, only to find out on the first day that Juma's family preferred to speak Swahili - the family came from Zanzibar. Almost as soon as we arrived, Juma's brother Salim, a field geologist, packed us into his car and drove us through deserts and wadis. I was immediately captivated by the colors of Oman and began to search out pigments. Salim had a thorough knowledge of all the stone and rock in Oman but had never viewed them from the point of view of an artist. Together we explored the country according to color, making expeditions to regions of red, violet, black, white and yellow. Just as Juma had set about thoroughly investigating Germany, so I began to want to know more and more about this fascinating land with its endearing people. In 1993 we organized a large exhibition in Muscat. Juma showed his personal impressions of Germany and I mine of Oman. Following this I was invited to write the first German travel guide about Oman.

That I was able to complete this task, thanks are due above all to Juma, his brother Salim and the whole Al-Maskery and Al Harthi families, who all supported my work with advice and practical assistance. For their understanding for my journey into another world thanks are also due to my wife and family.

Oman at a glance

	Area in km^2	Population in million	Density people/km^2	Gross Nat. Prod. per capita*
Oman	**309,500**	**2.74**	**8.8**	**21,160 US$**
Saudi Arabia	2,240,000	23.12	10.3	23,834 US$
Yemen	536,869	20.98	39	2,412 US$
UAE	77,700	4.53	58	38,830 US$
Iran	1,648,000	68.25	41	11,250 US$
United Kingdom	244,110	58.8	241	36,523 US$
Germany	357,021	82.5	231	35,442 US$
France	543,965	59.1	108	34,208 US$
USA	9,363,364	270.26	28.9	46,859 US$

Population: Alongside the 1.92 million citizens there are over 800,000 foreigners in Oman. Life expectancy is about 74 years and baby and infant mortality, at 1.03%, is relatively low.
Language: The official language is Arabic. Among the minorities Iranian, African (e.g. Swahili) and Indo-Aryan (e.g. Urdu) languages are spoken. English is widespread as a language of trade and commerce.
Religion: The state religion is Islam. Along with the 85% Muslims there are 13% Hindu (mostly among guest workers) and small Christian minorities.
Politics: The Consultative Council (82 members) is appointed every three years by the Sultan from among 182 elected representatives. A Council of State (Majlis al Dawlah), comprising 41 members appointed by the Sultan, was also created as an upper house of the Oman Council to discuss policy issues. The voting age is 21. There is universal suffrage.
Economy: 37% of workers are employed in agriculture, which, however, only accounts for about 2.5% of the Gross Domestic Product. The majority of the GDP (49.3%) comes from the service sector. Imports stand at 2.3 billion US dollars with exports of 4.3 billion US dollars, of which 77% is made up of oil and 12% of industrial products (machinery and transport.) Tourism plays a minor economic role.

*All statistics are taken from the Fischer World Almanac 2007, mostly based on the year 2005 and own research.

Images of Oman

Oman – a Gulf State?

Who can think of the Gulf Region without media images being brought to mind? They are stamped on our memories. In the mind's eye we see unending deserts with ghostly towers of oil derricks emerging from the shimmering heat. Now and then the barren landscape is enlivened by a "ship of the desert," a camel rising from the emptiness only to sink back into the emptiness. Crippling temperatures, extreme dryness, burning oilfields: seemingly a hell on earth. Such images hardly stir one to make a holiday trip to Oman. More enticing are thoughts of the fairytale wealth of the oil sheikhs and their magnificent modern cities on the Arabian Gulf. But even these fantasies have lost much of their original allure.

A glance at the map shows that the term "Gulf State" for Oman, viewed geographically, applies only in a very limited sense. The territory of the Sultanate that is in the Gulf Region is reduced to the northern tip of the Musandam Peninsula, which separates the Arabian Gulf, also known as the Persian Gulf, from the Gulf of Oman. In the 1980s, after the Islamic revolution in Iran and the overthrow of the Shah (1979), this small exclave on the Strait of Hormuz, cut off from the state of Oman by the emirates Ras al Khaymah, Khawr Fakkan and Al-Fujayrah, became one of the strategically most important regions for the supply of energy to the industrial nations. Overnight the focus of western oil interests shifted to Musandam and the hitherto unknown and uninteresting country of Oman. The peninsula is an inaccessible, rugged and wild mountain landscape, crisscrossed with deep fjords. Musandam became known as the "Norway of the Middle East." From this cliff fortress the Omanis control the entire tanker traffic in the Gulf. This function as "Guardian of the Gulf," together with the exploitation of its own oil resources, led to the Sultanate being labelled a "Gulf State," but this label is hard to apply to the whole country. The area which most fits the notion of a Gulf State landscape is an area called the "Central Plains," a flat and stony desert, some 500 kilometers long and almost devoid of people, which makes up the large central area of the country. It separates the Al Batinah coastal plain and the dry north of the Sultanate, with its massive up to 3000-plus meter high Hajar Mountains, from Dhofar in the south, which, during the monsoon season, is partly green and tropically humid. In the middle of this desert, far from any human settlement

In Oman women play a siginificant role in society.

or road, is Fuhud, one of the centers of Omani oil production. Here temperatures of over 45°C in the rarely to be found shade are not unusual. There is no trace of luxury to be found. The adjacent part of the vast Saudi Arabian desert is not called Rub al Khali, the "Empty Quarter," for nothing. Oman counts as one of the oil-exporting nations of the Middle East, but its oil production of 278 million barrels a year (2008) is only 15 percent of the Saudi Arabian oil production.

The identity of the Omani people is not based on the possession of oil but on its renowned age-old tradition as a trading and sea-faring nation.

The Sultanate of Oman - a Tale from 1001 Nights?

If you want to do the Omanis justice and get a good feel for the Sultanate, then you can do no better than to take down *The Thousand And One Nights* and read the tales of Sindbad the Sailor, perhaps in the celebrated English translation of the 19th century scholar and explorer, Sir Richard Burton. A picture of the magnificence of the Orient quickly unfolds before the mind's eye. Colorful and fantastic scenes arise - pictures of the choicest goods heaped up in the narrow, winding alleys of the oriental markets: the suqs. Exotic spices, gorgeous carpets, gold, pearls, and precious silverwork attract the eye. Haggling traders, storytellers, coffee sellers, breathtakingly beautiful women, striking visages from all corners of the world fill the streets with bursting, sensual life. The fragrance of sandalwood and frankincense. Enormously rich merchants dwelling in fairytale palaces. In glaring contrast to this we have the pictures of arduous and adventurous sea voyages to unknown, dangerous realms filled with the promise of wealth. Over the centuries these fairytale visions of the Orient have inspired artists. Their imagined world, depicted in such a realistic style, has so impressed itself upon the western mind that the boundaries between fantasy and reality have become blurred beyond recognition. The European picture of the Orient is often, if not always, based on these fantastic inventions of the 19th century artistic imagination. It is better to trust in the pictures conjured up in one's own mind by reading the tales.

As with most legends that of Sindbad the Sailor has its roots in history. This is not necessarily in the Baghdad of Haroun Ar- Rashid as the story recounts, but may well have been in 9th century Oman.

The ancient port of Sohar lays claim to being the home port of Sindbad. In its day this settlement on the fertile Al Batinah coast of the Gulf of Oman was the largest and most important seaport of the Islamic world. Al-Muqaddasi, a chronicler of the time, described Sohar as the "gateway to China and warehouse of the Orient." It was renowned for its innumerable merchants and businesses - and for its legendary wealth.

Already in the 8th century the fame of the Omani seafarer Abu Ubaida bin Abdullah bin Qassim had spread throughout the then known world. He had made a 7000 kilometer adventure-filled sea voyage over the seven seas from Sohar as far as Canton in China. In doing so he laid the foundations of modern scientific navigation and grounded many a legend. Many skillful and daring Omani Sindbads followed his example and within 200 years they had woven a trading network spanning the Arabian Gulf, the Indian Ocean and its coastal seas. In the center of this profitable network lay the port of Sohar, hoarding its wealth. The volume of goods apparently far exceeded all the descriptions of the later tales. Here the finest porcelain and the most expensive silk, musk and jewels from China were traded. Spices and precious woods came from India and Malaysia. In those days the merchants of the Gulf Region offered not black gold but white gold: pearls. Tortoise shell, leopard skins, ivory and slaves were brought from East Africa to add to the fame and wealth of Sohar.

This state of paradise lasted until 1507, when the Portuguese conquered all of the Omani coastal towns and demanded a share of the flourishing trade in the Indian Ocean. Ironically these devastating attacks could only have been a result of Oman's internationally admired prowess in navigation. In 1498 Vasco da Gama had rounded the Cape of Good Hope and discovered the long sought-after sea route from Europe to India, with its promise of great riches. Apparently da Gama had hired the famous Omani master navigator Ahmad bin Majid in Malindi in East Africa to show him the way to the East, which had already been sailed by the Omanis for 700 years. Contemporary sources speak of an Arabic "master navigator." It seems unlikely that such an experienced man should not have realized the significance and possible consequences of his act. Oman was to lose its independence.

Over the centuries the importance of its economic and geopolitical situation was repeatedly to prove too tempting for world powers to allow Oman to develop without foreign interference. The Portuguese managed to maintain their rule for 150 years. They were then forced first out of Oman and then later out of all their East African possessions by Sultan Saif Al Yaruba with his powerful fleet.

The victory over the Portuguese colonial power was the birth of Oman as a great Arabic maritime trading power.
The Omani empire quickly regenerated and flourished more magnificently than ever. At its zenith in the first half of the 19th century, based on trading contacts, the Omani Sultan Said was effectively ruler over the Arabian coast from Shatt Al Arab ("Stream of the Arabs," a river in southeastern Iraq) to Aden, and over the East African coast from the Horn of Africa to northern Mozambique. His influence stretched far into the interior of Africa, up to the East African lakes. His commercial connections stretched from China across Europe to America. As in the times before the Portuguese interlude of the 16th and 17th centuries, all the most precious commodities of this earth were traded. Slaves were as significant a commodity as cloves, dates, and the legendary native produce which the Omanis sold successfully and high priced from antiquity onwards: frankincense.
From 1784 the capital of this empire was the port of Muscat, protected by mountains. Alongside goods from all over the world, the Persians, Turks, Indians, Chinese, Africans and Europeans gave

Omani women love to wear colorful clothing, not just on National Day.

the town a cosmopolitan flair. However the jewel in the crown was Zanzibar, that mystical island off the coast of Tanzania, whose very name conjures up images of paradise. This fertile island with its pleasing climate became the residence of the Sultan and the center for the nobility of this fabulous Sultanate.

Weapons have only a symbolic significance in Oman today.

Following the death of the majestic Sultan Said the kingdom began to fall apart and Oman slowly sank into oblivion, a long process which would end in total international isolation and backwardness. All that remained were the legends of Sindbad the Sailor and the unbelievable wealth of the Orient. A journey to the Sultanate brings to life many of the lost images of the Orient. So much that was fabulous from the ages of commerce and seafaring is here still reality. The Orient lives on in Oman, not in photogenic productions for tourists but as an essential part of the nature of the people of this land.

The Sultanate of Oman – a Model State for the Arab world?

Looking back, the most important day in the long, rich history of the Sultanate is July 23, 1970. Following a palace coup, Sultan Said bin Taimur, who had kept the country in none too splendid isolation, was replaced by his son, the European-educated Qaboos bin Said Al-Said. This was the beginning of Oman's remarkable development from a loose medieval federation of tribes to an ultra-modern 21st century state.

At the time of Qaboos's seizure of power there was no idea of the size of the country or of its population. In the whole of Oman fewer than 10 kilometers of roads had been built. The transportation of goods was as it had been for centuries - either coastal shipping by dhow or overland by camel caravan. The remaining infrastructure consisted of a post office, a clinic and three boys' schools. All routes to and from Oman had been barred for 40 years. Trade had been suppressed and even music, as an expression of *joie de vivre,* was frowned upon. Oman was one of the most underdeveloped countries on earth.

This restrictive framework did serve, however, to protect the unique ancient Arabic social structure of Oman. Exactly as Sultan Said bin Taimur had intended, all western forms of culture had passed it by. However, many of the liberal-minded Omanis were unable to identify with Said's policies. They left the country - at that time an illegal act. Omanis who had remained in the former possessions of the erstwhile trading power, above all in East Africa, saw nothing to tempt them back to the Sultanate. Oman had nothing to offer its exiles. The situation changed instantly with the change of rule. Sultan Qaboos requested all Omanis living abroad to return. Their experience, connections, diplomatic skills and above all their often internationally top-level education, together with the boosting of the oil industry, were to be the foundations for the planned rebuilding of the country. Many people took up the call and brought the characteristics and languages of their host countries with them, together with their know-how. Oman is once more a melting-pot on the Indian Ocean. Alongside the official languages of Arabic and English, Urdu and Hindi are used and also Swahili is to be heard. Among the tribes living in the less accessible mountain areas of the south other languages are spoken with roots in Sabaean (i.e. the language of the kingdom of the Queen of Sheba in the 10th century BC), which still has no fixed written form.

Today Oman is a country in the early stages of a new era. However, modernization at any price is not the order of the day. The utmost care is being taken to bring together the old, traditional ways of life with the inevitable demands and standards of a modern, competitive economy. The pitfalls of industrialization in the west and other developing countries are to be avoided. Protection of the cultural heritage, nature and ecology is not just a matter of lip-service in Oman, but is a genuine political aim.

Unlike in almost all other countries, a portion of the rather modest oil revenues (only some 40% of the production level of Great Britain) is put aside for further development of the country. Modernization has been concentrated in the new capital region, known as the "Capital Area," on the south eastern edge of the Al Batinah coastal plain. Along a 50-kilometer stretch of coast a modern city has emerged from nothing. There is an airport here but also a large, accessible nature reserve for butterflies, sea-snails, mussels, birds and plants. Meanwhile, well-constructed asphalt roads connect all the larger towns in Oman. By 1986 the construction of basic infrastructure was largely finished.

A young country with a young population: over half of Omanis are under 18.

Development has been breathtaking, especially in regard to the health service: in 1970 there were only 100 health workers in the whole country and only one hospital clinic, run by American missionaries in Mutrah. In 2007 the official statistics show 59 modern hospitals and 140 clinics, with 17,780 health employees of which 4908 are doctors. 58% of health workers are Omanis. It was only in 1993 that the first doctors to be educated in Oman graduated from the University of Muscat. The average life expectancy in 1970 was 49.3; it is now 74.3.

The UN considers this non-aligned country to be a "model pupil" among nations. Nowhere else have so many of the recommendations of the United Nations and World Health Organization been carried out. In 2001 the WHO report on the efficiency of health systems throughout the world ranked Oman at number one. In four decades child mortality had been reduced from 310 per 1,000 births to just 10.

Oman has developed into a politically stable and reliable partner in the midst of a crisis region. Tolerance and liberalism are the hallmark of the current climate in the country. Although Omanis are devout Muslims, there is religious freedom and there are churches of all confessions. Unlike in Saudi Arabia, where women are not permitted to work alongside men or to drive cars, in Oman women are employed, occupy several seats in the Consultative Council and fill official posts even at the rank of Minister and Ambassador. The current ambassadors to the USA, Germany and Netherlands are all women. In 1996 the Sultan introduced the Basic Law, effectively an Islamic constitution guaranteeing a measure of freedom of the press and sexual equality under the law. Omani women are not compelled to wear the veil. If they do so, it is because they themselves have chosen this form of dress as a sign of religious devotion.

Of the numerous schools of Islamic belief and law, the majority of Omanis belong to Ibadhiyah, a branch of the faith which is marked by its tolerance as well as holding firm to the basic tenets of Islam and, although it goes back to the year 700, it could serve as a model for modern times.

Omanis have always been merchants, and have always understood how to make a profit. The traditional markets, the suqs, are once again full with wares from the world market. To make a visit to a suq in Muscat is to enter an Aladdin's cave overflowing with goods of every kind. Alongside the traditional products of frankincense, spices, textiles, silverware and dates, one finds the complete range of mass produced products from the far east - and the most expensive perfume in the world, an Omani creation called *Amouage*, which can be bought in gold bottles for between 2500 and 3000 US-dollars. You can buy replicas of Indian gods as well as Christian devotional items here. Or "Rat-Glue," a special glue which you smear on floorboards - anyone or anything that treads on it becomes stuck fast.

In its early years the modernization of Oman was almost totally dependent on the skills provided by foreign experts and advisors at all levels. Now as a generation of educated Omanis has grown up and is in a position to take over the reins, these foreign experts are gradually being replaced by younger, home-grown experts.

"Omanization" and the reduction of the dependency on oil as sole source of income through economic diversification are the challenges of the new millennium. If these astute political policies are continued, Oman has a great future in store for itself. The Sultanate has awoken from its sleep and no Arab state is better prepared to face the challenging demands of the future.

Along with its breathtaking landscape and the marks of its adventurous history, Oman embodies an exciting symbiosis of the traditional Arab way of life and the most modern technology. Progress does not have to go hand in hand with complete loss of cultural identity and humanity. Oman is making its own way into the new millennium with the self-confidence of a country with a great past.

Rugged mountains and extensive oases characterize northern Oman.

Omani Landscapes

The official statistics of the Sultanate of Oman declare the size of the country to be 309,500 square kilometers. Some western publications still speak of only 212,000 square kilometers. Not an insignificant difference. The main reason for the different estimates is certainly the long unclear question of borders.

The line of demarcation with Saudi Arabia was only officially established in 1990. Until then the Saudis had always placed the border much further to the east. Negotiations with Yemen were completed in 1993, resulting in an exchange of frontier areas, and a boundary agreement was ratified with the United Arab Emirates in 2003. With a population of 2.743 million (2007) Oman remains an extremely sparsely populated land. The population density is between eight and nine inhabitants per square kilometer. The way the various forms of landscape influence the people is one of the most striking features of the Sultanate.

Just a few kilometers outside of the towns one is confronted with expanses of nature which remind the European traveller of primeval or lunar landscapes. Faced with such vast dimensions, man and his technology shrink into insignificance.

Arriving at the airport in As Seeb, you land on the border between two geographically completely different worlds, the Al Batinah Plain and the Hajar Mountains. The **Al Batinah Plain** stretches 270 kilometers along the coast northwest of As Seeb to the border with the United Arab Emirates. The average width is 10 to 30 kilometers and on the coastal side there is an up to 3 kilometer wide fertile strip which is farmed the whole year round. Plantation follows plantation. Date palms, limes, bananas, mangoes and papayas flourish luxuriantly here in "nature's hothouse." The majority of the population lives here on the Al Batinah Plain.

The plain is surrounded by the great rocky **Hajar Mountains** (*hajar* is Arabic for "rocky"), which run parallel to the coast and form an insurmountable wall to the interior. The mountain chain stretches in a wide, 650 kilometer long curve from Ras Al Had, the most easterly point of Oman, to the most northerly, the tip of the Musandam peninsula, at the entrance to the Arabian Gulf. These rugged fold-mountains rise to a height of 3,075 meters in the massif of **Jabal Al Akhdar**, the "Green Mountain." Rain falling on the high flanks of the mountains supplies an artificial system of irrigation canals, known as the *aflaj*, providing hundreds of mountain oases with water. Oasis settlements and countless fortresses, evidence of a turbulent past, are scattered over the whole length of the range. The Sumail Gap splits the mighty mountain chain in two: the Western Hajars (or **Al Hajar al Gharbi**) and the Eastern Hajars (or **Al Hajar ash Sharqi**.)

An endless, rock-strewn plateau runs 500 kilometers south from the foothills of the mountains. This is the **Jiddat al Harasis**, once more home to the great white oryx. To the west of this hostile region is the even more inhospitable, seemingly unending central Arabian desert, the **Rub al Khali**, or Empty Quarter, with its high dunes. As if this landscape were not forbidding enough, 200 kilometers south of the Hajar Mountains bordering Saudi Arabia is the **Umm as Samim** ("mother of poison"), an area of about 6000 square kilometers of treacherous drifting sands and salt flats, where only a few Bedouin dare venture. However the desert regions of Oman are the gateway to riches - the oilfields are here. South of Ash Sharqiyyah, the Wihibah Sands stretch 200 kilometers by 80 kilometers wide along the coast. With its rolling sand dunes this is the archetypal desert formation. These sands form the northern frontier of the 650 square kilometer coastal district **Barr al Hikman**, or **Al Huqf**, an area predominantly made up of salt flats, called *sabkhas*.

The most southerly province is **Dhofar** which, with its 100,000 square kilometers, makes up a third of the country. Dhofar has a varied terrain. As well as the high dunes of the Empty Quarter

Fascinating graphic design: dunes in the Wihibah desert

there are unexplored caves and numerous sinkholes in the steep mountain valleys. However, most people mean the mountains and coastal strip when they speak of this area.

Near the south coast the rocky plateau rises to a mountain region, the **Nejd**. Between June and September the south coast is washed by the monsoon (or *khareef*) rains, giving a tropical fecundity to the eight kilometer wide band of coastal plain near Salalah, the second largest city of Oman, and the southern slopes of the 1500 meter high **Jabal Qara**. During these months the whole region is enveloped in heavy fog and drizzle. While the rest of the Arabian peninsula is wilting under the most extreme heat, here temperatures rarely exceed 35°C. This mountain range is the historical source of frankincense.

Separated from the rest of the country by the United Arab Emirates is the **Musandam Peninsula**, the northernmost extremity of Oman. At the Strait of Hormuz, the cliffs of the Hajar Mountains fall steeply into the sea. The name Musandam actually refers to an island to the extreme north of the peninsula but has come to be used for the whole area. Its wildly fissured fjord-like landscape has led to its being called the "Norway of the Middle East." Omanis know it by the name *ruus al jibaal*, "head of the mountains." The traditional way of life of the indigenous people is semi-nomadic, in the summer living along the coast and in winter in the mountains.

Oman - the Presence of the Past

A great part of Oman's attraction is that everywhere you feel the presence of the past. To understand everyday life it is necessary to have some historical background. Until very recently the area that is currently Oman did not exist as a state in the modern sense. Social life was determined by tribal structures. To make the history simpler and more accurate we will rather speak of "Omanis" when discussing people who occupied the area that is now known as Oman.

Homeland of Merchants and Seafarers

From the late Stone Age, clusters of population had existed in the area. In about 200 AD the Arabic Al-Azd tribe migrated from Yemen. Up until this time our knowledge of the people and their way of life is scant. There are several reasons for this. The first is that up until 1970, when Oman opened itself up to the world, it was one of the most unexplored regions on earth, a *terra incognita*. Systematic archaeological excavations only began in the Seventies; because of the often inaccessible nature of the country they have been slow and laborious. Much has been discovered, but there's certainly much more lying hidden in the mountain landscape of the north or beneath sand dunes and scree. Up until 1975 there was war in southern Oman and large expanses were covered in landmines. The American archaeologist Andrew Williamson was killed when his vehicle drove over a mine. He was one of the pioneers of field research in the early years of archaeological research in Oman and his death was a heavy blow for all researchers in the country. His work was successfully continued by the Italian Paolo Costa who published the results in the *Journal of Oman Studies*.

All along the coast traces of Oman's seafaring history can be seen, as here in Bander Al Jissah.

The second reason for this scant knowledge is that most relics from the Stone Age are simple tools such as hand-axes and scrapers made out of quartz or flint; these tools are to be found throughout the land but because of the lack of other evidence, for example traces of settlements which can be dated, they are difficult to place in the periods of Stone Age civilization. Their age is estimated as being from 70,000 to 10,000 years BC, which would be in line with the last ice age. The end of the Stone Age in Oman has been dated as about 5000 BC but stone tools were still in use up to 500 BC. Between 1982 and 1985 the remains of a settlement and burial ground were uncovered on the Ras Al Hamra peninsula near Al Qurm. These finds showed that the place had been occupied continuously between 3500 and 2800 BC. and that the people lived from fishing and hunting. Interestingly the remains of large fish were discovered, which could only have been caught at sea by boat. Boatbuilding must have played a significant role even at this time. These conclusions were confirmed by similar finds by French archaeologists in Ras Al Jinz in 1993.

The clearest signs of early settlement are to be found in tombs erected in the foothills of the mountains. Known as beehive tombs because of their shape, these tombs were built throughout eastern Arabia from the middle of the fourth millennium BC. This kind of tomb is characteristic of the **Hafit Period** (3500 to 2700 BC), named after a mountain near Al Buraymi on the northeastern frontier of the United Arab Emirates, where these structures were first discovered. The tombs had long since been plundered and all that was found were ceramic vessels, apparently worthless to tomb robbers. These show a distinct similarity to vessels of the same period from Mesopotamia ("Land Between the Rivers"); one must assume that at this time there was already trade with the area between the Tigris and the Euphrates.

In the 1950s Danish archaeologists had already made a discovery some 15 kilometers north of Abu Dhabi on the small island of Umm-an-Nar: a settlement and a graveyard with large, round tombs in the form of towers of up to thirteen meters diameter from between 2700 and 2000 BC. These extensive finds differ significantly from those of the Dilmun civilization which then extended from Kuwait to Qatar. The researchers suspected an independent civilization spreading eastwards to Oman; this was named the **Umm-an-Nar civilization**.

This theory was confirmed by the finding of similar beehive structures, graves and settlements in the northern Omani mountains at Bat near Ibri, and in Hili at the Al Buraymi oasis. The tombs at Bat were the second site in Oman to be listed by UNESCO as a World Heritage Site. According to UNESCO's World Heritage List, together with the neighboring sites, it forms the most complete collection of settlements and necropolises from the 3rd millennium BC in the world. At the beginning of the 1990s a helicopter pilot, flying over a 2000 meter high plateau near Wadi Tiwi in the eastern Hajar Mountains, spotted 60 tower tombs, up to eight meters high and some in excellent condition and probably dating from the same

period. In addition to ceramics from Mesopotamia and the red jugs typical of the Umm-an-Nar civilization, with their wonderfully executed black, geometric motifs, archaeologists found soapstone vessels and beads crafted from carnelian, gold and silver.
The signs of well-organized settlements and successful integration in a national trading network lead one to conclude that the Umm-an-Nar civilization represents one of the high points in the history of the region. The story of how this peak of civilization was reached remains to be unearthed in the Omani mountains.

Magan, Land of Copper

The term "Magan" (or "Makkan") first appears around 2300 BC in the writings of King Sargon of Akkad. This Mesopotamian ruler describes ships from Dilmun, Magan and Meluhha, with their various cargoes being unloaded on the quays of Akkad. Trade with these regions clearly flourished at this time.
In 2200 BC Sargon's grandson, Naram-Sin, reported his victory over the king of Magan. He commemorated his triumph in a masterpiece of Mesopotamian sculpture, the Naram-Sin stele, his own portrait carved from diorite. Alabaster bowls were found nearby in which Naram-Sin had had the words "Spoils from Magan" engraved. Tablets from the period, inscribed with administrative texts, mention the occurrence of copper in Magan for the first time and also the importing of ivory, semi-precious stones, wood for building and furniture, along with diorite, all in exchange for silver, textiles, wool and furs from Mesopotamia. In the 1930s cuneiform tablets were discovered in Ur which verified a vigorous trade between Mesopotamia, Magan and Dilmun in the period between 2500 and 1500 BC. "Dilmun" is now the island of Bahrain in the Arabian Gulf. This was further verified by the excavations of Danish archaeologists in the 1950s. The island's freshwater springs led to Dilmun becoming an important supply port as well as transfer depot for goods. "Meluhha" was the Sumerian term for the Mohenjodaro civilization of the Indus basin. The geographical location of Magan remained a puzzle.
In 1974 Canadian geologists prospecting for minerals in the Hajar Mountains came across numerous traces of copper mining and processing from days long gone. Following this the German Museum of Mining in Bochum (Germany) set up a five-year research project, which began in 1977. The idea was to demonstrate that the historic Magan is identical with present-day Oman.

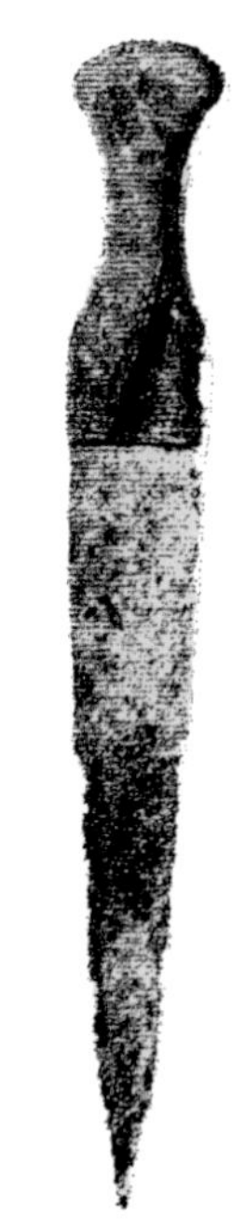

Dagger from a tomb near Al Wasit, 2000 – 1200 BC.

Investigations of copper objects found in Oman, Bahrain and Iraq formed the basis of this theory. All of these samples apparently stemmed from the same unknown source. The Hajar Mountains form part of an oceanic ridge which stretches from the Omani island of Masirah, through Iran as far as Cyprus. Geologically speaking it is comprised mostly of *Samail ophiolite*, a rock stratum of volcanic origin between 94 and 98 million years old in which there are beds of sulphide ore deposits from which the metal can be won. In the course of the research project 150 historic copper workings were located scattered across the mountains in Oman.

Seal from the Magan period, found in Al Moyassar

To the great disappointment of the researchers the first finds dated not, as hoped, from the Bronze Age, but from the early Islamic (9th - 10th century) and middle Islamic (12th - 19th century) periods. As copper extraction in the Orient during this period was as little known as in historic Magan, they widened the area of their investigations. Further excavations soon solved the puzzle. Copper production in Oman took place in the same locations over centuries and millennia. The early copper workings lay buried beneath the later ones. Because of the intensive use of the terrain, no traces of the earlier building structures of this era could be found. What did remain from the Bronze Age were immense slagheaps and vast quantities of clay shards with a thin vitrified coating, probably fragments of the oldest generation of smelting furnaces.

These finds gave a good picture of the scale of copper extraction during the Bronze Age. Dating revealed that the peak of this production phase must have been between 2200 and 1900 BC, in other words during the Umm-an-Nar period. The 10,000 tons of slag found mainly in the hinterland of Sohar indicate the production of 2000 to 4000 tons of copper. The quality of the copper was improved by repeated smelting, but because of its impurities it was known as black copper. Its composition is identical to finds in Ur, Sumer and in the Indus basin. Experts no longer doubt the identification of Magan, the land of copper, with Oman. Its territory may have extended to the area of Iran on the opposite side of the Strait of Hormuz, but this has yet to be proven.

Copper production reached its peak during the early Islamic period. Improved know-how in the area of copper working was introduced to Oman either by the Persian occupiers or via the sea routes from Persia or Azerbaijan. This transfer of technology led to a substantial stepping up of copper extraction in Oman. The quality and quantity of the copper could be greatly increased through pre-processing of the ore in roasting sheds as well as the construction of larger, more efficient smelting furnaces. Between 40,000 and 150,000 tons of slag have been found at workings such as Lasail, Arjah, Semdah,

Al Moyassar, Raki and Tawi Raki. Altogether some 600,000 tons of slag from the early Islamic period have been found in the Hajar Mountains, evidence of the extraction of between 48,000 and 60,000 tons of copper. From the Bronze Age to the Middle Ages, Oman was the greatest center in the Middle East for the production and exporting of copper. The glory days of copper production came to an abrupt end in the 10th century. The reason was probably political unrest and/or an acute shortage of fuel wood resulting from over-exploitation of trees.

The form of the up to 8 meter high tower structures of Shir in the Eastern Hajar Mountains connect the beehive tombs of the Hafit period with the charnel-houses of the Umm-an-Nar period. They stem from the 3rd millennium BC.

After an interruption of 200 years, about the time it would have taken the forests to regenerate, copper production was taken up again and has continued into modern times. However the great age of copper was over – the demand continuously fell and other goods took over in importance. The introduction of simple kilns was a backward step technologically, caused by the long period when there had been no production. Mining of copper ore was halted. Instead, the slag from the previous centuries, still high in copper content, was simply re-smelted. The metal thus extracted was of a lower quality. It is hardly surprising that over the next 700 years only 25,000 tons of new slag was created, and because of inefficient technology only 5% of the early Islamic production was attained. The country's oldest tradition was brought back to life in 1983 with the opening of an ultra-modern copper works at Lasail in northern Oman. The Oman Mining Company produces copper of 99.9% purity, mostly used in the export of certain cathodes. In 1992 it seemed that the copper ore deposits in the region had all been exploited and with further falls in the price of copper, the plant was threatened with closure in 1994. However the discovery in 1993 of new deposits of 8.4 million tons secured production well into the new millennium.

Construction of Copper-smelting Furnaces in Oman

It is difficult to reconstruct completely a Bronze Age smelting furnace. In Sohar's hinterland large quantities of two to four centimeter thick, slightly curved clay shards were found. Covered in a thin vitrified coating, they are fragments of the interior of furnaces. If one tries to assemble these shards into a whole the result is a pear-shaped construction with an average height of 50 centimeters and a diameter of 40 centimeters. One of these furnaces would have a capacity of 10 to 15 liters. Using a bellows a temperature of 1150°C could be reached. Stones were used to break the ore into small lumps which were then mixed with charcoal and poured through the open neck of the furnace. The process was repeated several times until the final product was the so-called black copper, which, in its molten form, would be run off into a small gulley, or slag-pit, in the ground in front of the furnace. It is not possible to extrapolate further technical details from the remains which have been found.

In the early Islamic period copper production was based on a cylindrical shaft furnace with a sloping floor. This type of furnace was always built against a rock and was made up of rough stones held together with mortar. The shaft itself was about one and a half meters high with a diameter of 60 centimeters. To reduce heat loss it was tapered towards the top. The inner surface was plastered smooth with mortar. The bottom half of the furnace's front had a thin wall. This had a small opening through which air could be pumped with a bellows and at the base there was an opening through which the cinders and the copper could be run off into a prepared gulley. To renew the oven it was only necessary to knock out and replace the thin walled front.

In 1997 the National Mining Company, a privately-owned concern based in Muscat, was set up to explore for copper and gold in the Oman ophiolite. After extensive geological exploration they reckon on annually extracting 22,000 tons of copper and 8,000 ounces of gold. In 1995 the non-oil minerals sector accounted for 0.6% of the economy. It is believed that by 2020 it will account for 2%. This is vital for the continuance of a new town built along with the copper works between Sohar and the industry park and bearing the symbolic name of "Magan." As long as copper is mined in Oman, Magan will live on.

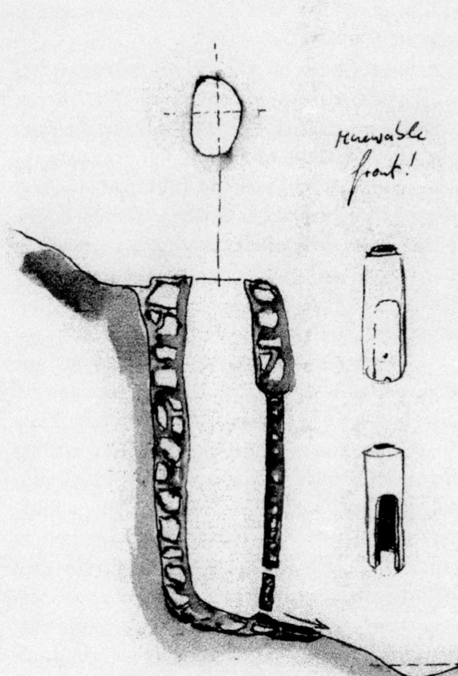

This type of furnace was highly efficient and would be in service until the slagheaps produced from it reached some 6,000 tons at which point the location would have to be moved for lack of space.

Copper extracted in this fashion was 60% pure, better than the earlier black copper. This was a result of the new smelting furnaces and above all the repeated pre-processing of the ore in roasting furnaces. The spherical stove furnaces used from the 12th century were technically very simple in comparison. They had a diameter of 30 to 40 centimeters and were half-buried in soft earth. This meant that one had to destroy the whole furnace in order to retrieve the molten ore at the bottom.

This technological deterioration was the result of the two-hundred year interruption in copper production in Oman.

Drawing after The Journal of Oman Studies, Vol. 10

Dhofar, Land of Frankincense

Around 1800 BC the invasion by Indo-Germanic tribes completely wiped out the flourishing Indus civilization. The fortunes of Magan's Umm-an-Nar civilization, which had been based chiefly on trade from India to Mesopotamia, began to sink. About 700 BC a new Indo-Germanic culture emerged around the Indus and maritime trade between India and Arabia revived but Oman did not regain its international importance and fame until the beginning of classical antiquity. During this period the frankincense extracted in Dhofar in southern Oman became the most expensive raw product in the world, as valuable as gold. It brought southern Arabia legendary wealth and the not unenviable name of *Arabia Felix*, or "happy Arabia." Varieties of wild frankincense trees can be found in very small areas from Somalia through Yemen to Dhofar in Oman. They are mainly to be found in southern Arabia. The resin of the *Boswellia sacra,* which is found in Dhofar, is regarded as the finest of all and in those days was the most in demand as well as the most expensive.

In the ancient world the use of frankincense for cult purposes was extremely widespread. We know from Herodotus that in the 6th century BC more than two and a half tons of the valuable resin were burnt in the Babylonian Temple of Baal alone. From the 5th millennium BC frankincense had been used in Mesopotamia and Egypt to create an atmosphere redolent of the divine presence. The gifts that the Three Kings from the Orient brought for the infant Jesus were frankincense, myrrh and gold, precious gifts probably sent by the ruler of the land of frankincense.

This symbol stands for one of the most expensive scents of the world, the frankincense based perfume Amouage.

For the funeral of his wife Poppaea Sabina, the Roman emperor Nero had an entire year's producion of frankincense from the Arabian peninsula burnt in Rome as testimony to his love. Up till today the resin has also had its use as a medicinal remedy. Pliny the Elder described the characteristics of good quality frankincense and mentioned it as an antidote to hemlock poisoning. In its solid form it is taken against stomach complaints. The ethereal vapors that are given off when it is burned demonstrably relieve breathing difficulties and the resulting phenols act as a disinfectant. Through the centuries one comes across mentions in literature of the mind-altering and intoxicating effects of the fumes. It is only recently that the Austrian chemist, Georg F. Friedrich, showed that when the resin is burnt THC (tetrahydro-cannabinol), the active ingredient in cannabis, is given off. This phenomenon was doubtless well-known to the priests of antiquity.

The ports of *Samharam*, known to the Greeks as "Moscha," described in 150 AD by the cartographer Ptolemy of Alexandria as "Omanum Emporium," and *Saffara Metropolis* enjoyed legendary wealth as centers of the frankincense trade. The remains of Samharam were identified in the 1950s on the southern coast of Oman, near modern day Salalah. The other two towns were apparently located with the help of imaging from the Challenger space shuttle. The various historical descriptions of the wealth of Ubar - or Irem, (the City of Pillars), as it is called in the 89th Sura of the Quran in which the town is described as the image of paradise - were so mythically excessive that for a long time there was serious doubt that it really was anything other than a legend. T. E. Lawrence (1888 - 1935), better known as "Lawrence of Arabia," had searched for Ubar and referred to it as the "Atlantis of the desert."

Today frankincense is still harvested as it was thousands of years ago: the bark is cut and the exuded resin is scraped off.

In 1981, looking at satellite images of southern Oman, American hobby archaeologists had already noticed ancient caravan routes in the desert which had been covered over with sand in the course of millennia and had now been made visible from space by the latest camera and film technology. Excavations of a watering place near the main intersection of all the old routes, 200 kilometers northwest of Samharam at Ash Shasir on the edge of the Empty Quarter, seemed to quickly confirm the truth of the legend.

The excavations which were subsequently carried out, with the backing of Sultan Qaboos, soon demonstrated that the fabulous city had not, in fact, been discovered. Ubar had to return to the realm of legend. A historically important resting place at the junction of several caravan routes had been found, but it had definitely not been a town. The area was simply too small. The variety of artifacts from around 2000 BC which were brought to light bore witness, however, to ancient trade routes. The ceramics which were found came from Syria, Rome, Greece and even China. Finds of stone tools showed that the spot had already been settled from 5000 BC onwards.

Probably the world's oldest surviving chess game, from the 5th century AD was found in Ash Shasir along with early Semitic writing tablets of a kind hitherto unknown. It may be that with the completion of the excavations the history of Arabia will partly be seen in a completely new light. Archaeologists suspect that an excavation site near the southern Oman coast east of Salalah is the remains of Saffara Metropolis.
Caravan routes were the main means of transport for the costly frankincense. Due to the wind conditions and threat of pirates in the Red Sea, the sea route along the coast of Yemen and through the Red Sea presented no real alternative to land transport. The main frankincense route began in Samharam, continued to Ash Shasir, through the Yemeni Hadramaut mountains to Marib, and then turned northwards and forked in Najran.

The Fragrant Realm

Unlike in the West, where frankincense still fulfils a liturgical function, in Oman it is not put to any religious purpose at all. The sacrificial offering up of frankincense is seen as a relic of pre-Islamic or "heathen" cultures and as such is frowned upon. The main use for frankincense in Oman is domestic, as a perfume.
Men and women like to hang their clothing on a pyramid-shaped wooden stand, some 60 centimeters high, beneath which the resin is burnt in a clay incense burner. The fabrics fumigated in this way absorb the ethereal scent and then slowly exude it in the course of the following days. In hot, sweat-inducing desert climates this is, especially for men, a far pleasanter way of surrounding themselves with a pleasant protective odor than applying deodorants directly onto the skin.
On festive occasions rooms are also scented. People prefer to make their own individual mixtures, called *bokhur*, from frankincense, myrrh, musk, rose petals, sandalwood and other pleasant-smelling substances, which are first dried, then ground and then laid on the burner to slowly smolder. The clay burners, giving off their scented clouds, are handed around among the guests so they can perfume their beards and hair. In the kitchen frankincense is used

The basis of most incenses is the resin of the Boswellia tree.

One route went northeast across the deserts of the Arabian peninsula to the Arabian Gulf and Mesopotamia, and the other followed the Red Sea via Jiddah to Petra in Jordan. From there one route led to Alexandria and the other to Mesopotamia. Most of the caravans started out from Dhofar for Jiddah after the harvesting of the frankincense in October. 150 to 400 camels were loaded up with some 50 tons of frankincense. The domestication and breeding of camels were prerequisites for these arduous journeys across parched wastes.

Modern research shows that camel breeding began in the hinterland of the Dhofar mountains around 1500 BC and the tradition continues today. The abundant finds of artifacts from distant cultures found in Ash Shasir and dating to before 1500 BC raise the question of how they were transported if not by camel.

to cover smells after frying fish, or to flavor water. This latter is done by setting a large, upturned earthenware jug over a smoking incense burner. The vessel is thus impregnated with the smoke and is then filled with water and stored overnight in a cool place. This valuable water is only prepared in summer and serves as the ultimate thirst-quencher. The taste is reminiscent of holy water, except that the Omanis use a much higher quality of resin, which improves the taste.

Armed with the injunction to spare no expense in creating "the most valuable perfume in the world," French Master Parfumier, Guy Robert set about his task to find the earth's most precious ingredients that would fulfill his dream. In creating the prize-winning scent *Amouage*, Robert used over 120 natural ingredients from around the globe. From Oman he took the finest silver frankincense of the Dhofar and Rock Rose from the secret, forbidding mountains of Jabal Al Akhdar. To these unique and classic scents he added a subtle range of other ingredients, with top notes of rose, jasmine, lily of the valley, heart notes of myrrh (Zanzibar), patchouli, orris and sandalwood, and base notes of ambergris and civet. The result was the most expensive perfume in the world, macerated and matured at the Perfumery in Muscat and then hand-bottled in gold- or silver-plated lead crystal flasks.

Frankincense and scents mixed from various ingredients like sandalwood, myrrh and flower oils are a part of everyday life in Oman and can be found in every household and suq. A journey to Oman is a journey to a culture of fragrances. Although perfumes from all over the world can be bought in Oman, women continue to prefer to mix their own individual scents from all the available oils. Western perfumes are often too pungent for the sensitive noses of the Omanis. For this ancient and sophisticated art of perfumery there are specialized shops, for example in the suqs of Mutrah and As Seeb. They are easy to spot from the shelves of glass bottles filled with the most various perfumes and the windows filled with various scented woods. Oman is full of aromas, providing a wonderful opportunity to re-educate your sense of smell.

The fabulous wealth brought to *Arabia Felix* by the frankincense, and the duties raised on the trade between south Asia, east Asia, Africa and the ancient Mediterranean cultures, naturally provoked the Egyptians as well as the Romans and Persians. The locations of the valuable frankincense trees were kept secret. All attempts by other nations to find and subjugate the land of frankincense, known to them as "Sakalan," came to nothing. The Sabaean empire, made up of vassal states, ruled over Dhofar until it collapsed amid the struggles of the individual states for power and control of the trade routes. In 120 BC the Parthians, who then ruled over Persia, succeeded in invading Dhofar from the east and keeping control for a century before the Himyarite rulers of Yemen regained power. When the Sabaean empire collapsed in the 6th century AD and it became a province of the Sasanians, the known history of the land of frankincense came to a temporary stop.

The women of Dhofar are famed for their incense mixtures of scented wood dust, frankincense, myrrh and essential oils. The recipes are secret and only exchanged within the family.

The resin still played a role in the maritime trade of Oman and south Yemen right up to the 20th century, above all in the trade with India. At the end of the 19th century 460 tons were exported yearly. In ancient times this could have been about 5000 tons, but exact figures are not known. When India gained independence in 1949 high import duties brought an end to trade with the subcontinent. The proclamation of the People's Democratic Republic of Yemen in 1967 was the final blow for the frankincense trade. The resulting closure of the port of Aden, the main shipping port for the frankincense from Dhofar, and the Dhofar war from 1965 to 1975 meant a temporary cessation to this ancient trading tradition. At the beginning of the 3rd millennium, the building up of the infrastructure and the consequent improvements in living conditions have given a fresh impulse to the frankincense trade. The raw material is gaining importance and is once more exported, albeit in meager quantities in comparison to ancient times. The price for the resin has meanwhile become affordable. Entire suqs in Salalah are now dedicated to the sale of frankincense and perfumes based on it such as *bokhur* and *attar*. Frankincense is a thriving cottage industry in the area. The Dhofar municipality established a purpose-built Frankincense Suq in Salalah. Run by Omanis who have been in the trade for generations, blending an astonishing variety of *bokhur* fragrances, the recipes for which are closely guarded trade secrets, it is a must for most visitors.

As a source of revenue frankincense plays only a very minor role today and the harvest is mainly marketed within Oman itself, being bought by both Omanis and visiting tourists.

100
Avanti

Water and Maritime Trade

A resource more precious than frankincense or gold has always been fresh water, especially in a land such as Oman with its harsh terrain and fierce temperatures. While the mountainous regions have abundant rainfall vast tracts of the country remain parched. A simple but ingenious means of distributing water to people around the country was hit upon, legend has it, by King Solomon.
Some 2500 years ago, according to ancient and still often recounted legends, the fabulous King Solomon flew over Oman on his flying carpet. He was accompanied by several *Jinns*, or genies. For Oman it was a time of unspeakable hardship: there was great drought, harvests were devastated and the people were starving. Solomon saw this and was overcome with pity. He asked the people how he could help them and they simply asked for water. Solomon then ordered his *Jinns* to lay a network of irrigation canals, often running underground, across the whole country - the *falaj* water distribution and irrigation system.
Since then the system has been overhauled and extended many times and in many places in the mountain region of northern Oman it is still the basis of rural water supply. Scientists of course would not accept the truth of the legend, regarding it as a mere fairy tale. However, there is a grain of truth in the legend: the system stems from this period. The irrigation method of *aflaj* (plural of *falaj*) is first described in the 6th century BC and developed in the highlands of Persia. It may have been Persians who introduced the system to Oman or it may have been Omanis who introduced it to Persia. Around 563 BC Cyrus the Great conquered northern Oman. The highest quality underground canals, called the *qanat-aflaj*, derive from the time of his reign. The Persians maintained their dominance over the coastal area of the Hajar Mountains during the entire period of the Achaemenid, Parthian and Sasanian dynasties (i.e. from 563 BC to 637 AD.) Knowledge about this period in Oman's history is patchy. In the *Periplus Maris Erythraei*, ("Circumnaviga-tion of the Erythrean Sea" [i.e. the Red Sea]), an anonymous Greek travel book written in the 1st century AD, Oman is described as a Persian province. Around the 5th century BC a maritime settle-ment "Mazun" developed in the vicinity of today's Sohar. By the 3rd century AD this was one of the most important ports. During the pre-Islamic era Daba in Musandam was also a port of great significance for Oman, conducting trade with Sindh (a province of Pakistan), India and China.

Since the arrival of the Persians maritime trading had slowly developed between the northern coast of the Indian Ocean and East Africa. The exploits of the Persians, followed by the rapid conquests of Alexander the Great, were to boost Oman's mercantile fortunes. These were later adversely affected by the establishment of new trade routes between Egypt and India around 100 BC. However this was compensated for by the opening of new markets further east and south along the east coast of Africa. Indonesian traders shipped cinnamon from China and Java to Madagascar and the Zanzibar region and thence northwards to Arabia. This connection with East Africa would come to be of key importance in the history of Oman.
Around the beginning of the 3rd century AD the Mediterranean area fell into economic decline and this, too, adversely impacted Oman's trade. In 330 AD the refounding of Byzantium, which the emperor Constantine I renamed as Constantinople (today's Istanbul), as the capital of the eastern half of the Roman Empire and the establishment of Christianity as the official religion affected the trade in spices and aromatics. Ancient burial rites had depended heavily upon these products, but they were not so significant for the newly-founded Christian empire.
At the beginning of the 6th century increasing numbers of Arab settlers from the south, the Azdi, and from the east, the Nizari of the Najd region, eventually drove out the Persians. In 570 AD the Persians managed to reoccupy a part of the coast and Sohar became the residence of the Sasanian viceroy. The land was divided by treaty between the Arab Al-Azd King Julanda and the Persians, Sasanian rule being restricted to the region around Sohar, the rest of the country being held by the Al-Azd.

The *aflaj* system:
A spring or a natural reservoir is excavated in a mountain or on a slope.
A tunnel is dug which is just large enough for a man to crawl through with shafts every 20 meters.
The water flows along this slightly inclined tunnel to the edge of the area to be irrigated where the well is and from where the water flows above ground through irrigation canals.
These *aflaj* can be from a few hundred meters long to 80 kilometers and even pass over or under wadis.

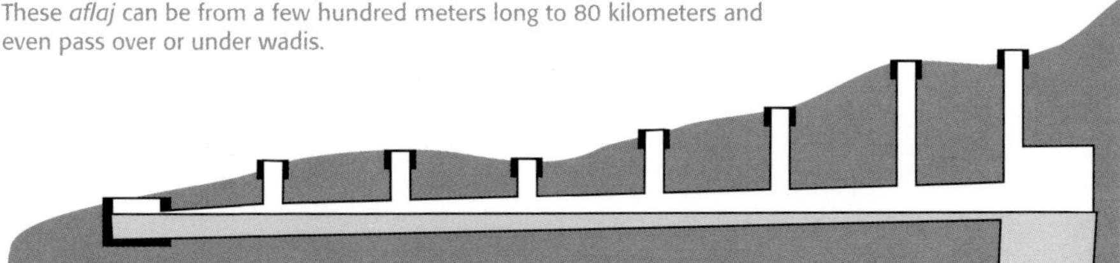

Under the Sign of the Crescent

Neither Sword nor Flame - a Letter

Islam is all too often presented to Western audiences in terms of conflict, especially in the years following September 11, 2001. The media presents us an image of hard, unyielding fanatics, who espouse violence as a justified means of dealing with their opponents; Islam is often felt to be a threat to Western values. This hostile image, while easy to grasp, does scant justice to a highly-civilized religion, practiced peacefully by millions of believers the world over. "Islam" is Arabic for "self-surrender" and etymologically is closely related to *salaam*, meaning "peace." Muslims greet one another with the words *as salaam ´alaikum*, "peace be upon you."

The notion, widespread in the West, that Islam only spread through the use of violence is contradicted by the example of Oman. During Mohammed's lifetime (570-632) the coastal region of Oman was under Persian Sasanian rule while the Al-Azd tribe governed the interior.

Ibadhi mosques are noted for their simplicity; only sometimes the qibla wall (the one facing Mecca) is decorated with richly detailed ornament.

Legend has it that the first Omani to become a Muslim was a certain Mazin bin Ghadhuba from Samail in the Hajar Mountains. He had heard of Prophet Mohammed and his teachings and rode straight to Medina to visit him. Here he was converted by the Prophet himself. Back in Oman he began to preach the gospel of one God to the people in his neighborhood.

According to this legend the mosque in Samail is the oldest in the country. More historically certain is that another Omani scholar, a Christian, was sent as an envoy to Medina to find out more about the prophet. He converted and returned to Oman completely persuaded of the truth of the Prophet.

So there were already Muslims in Oman when a merchant from Mohammed's tribe (the Quraish), Amr bin Al-As, brought a letter from Mohammed to the ruling sons of King Julanda bin Mustakbar, Abd and Jaifar. It was 630 AD in the western calendar. The letter matched those sent by Mohammed to the rulers of Byzantium, Persia, Ethiopia, Egypt and Yemen. In it he called upon the regents to acknowledge him as God's prophet and to convert to Islam.

After consulting the envoys, who had already converted to Islam, and the tribal elders and legal scholars, the two princes, Abd and Jaifar, took up Mohammed's offer and joined his movement. On hearing of this Mohammed is reported to have said, "God bless the people of Ghubaira. They believe in me without having seen me." ("Ghubaira" is an old name for Oman, still used in Zanzibar.) The 4000-odd Sasanians who had come from Persia and settled the coastal towns were called upon to do likewise. When they refused they were driven out of the country. Amr bin Al-As remained in Oman as a teacher of Islam for two years until the death of Mohammed in 632 AD. By the time he left many Omanis had followed the example of the tribal elders and joined the Muslim congregation. Abd Al Julanda and other princes of the Azdi tribe accompanied Mohammed's envoy back to Medina where they were welcomed by Mohammed's successor, Abu Bakr, the first caliph, with a speech in which he once more praised the peaceful conversion of Oman. However, even during his reign and that of the Omani princes, war was to break out over the "right" religion for Oman. Dhu't Taj Lakit, like Abd and Jaifar a member of the Azdi tribe, instigated it by declaring himself to be the true prophet. Abd and Jaifar withdrew to the mountain region of Jabal Al Akhdar, the caliph Abu Bakr sent reinforcements, and in the resulting battle near Daba in northern Oman the Muslims were victorious. The heathen was finally vanquished in Oman.

The Al-Azd sent troops to Basra, in what is today southern Iraq, to join the campaigns of conquest of the first two caliphs, Abu Bakr and Umar. Because they had not been forced to submit to the new religion but had converted to Islam from conviction, Omanis were regarded as the most important pillars of the Islamic movement in the early centuries. The Islamic metropolis of Basra became a second home for many Omanis.

The Ibadhis - the first Democrats of Islam

During the controversial rule of the first Umayyad caliph Muawiyah from 683 AD, the Islamic scholar Abdullah bin Ibadh worked in Basra. He took the position that the Muslim congregation should return to the original values of the time of Mohammed and the caliphs Abu Bakr and Umar. Together with the highly respected scholar Abu Shaatha who came from near Nizwa in Oman, he developed a new Islamic doctrine, Ibadhism, some hundred years before the establishment of the well-known Sunni schools of law and theology.

Ibadhism, as a politically, philosophically and theologically defined branch of Islam, is based on the principle that every theologically trained Muslim believer is a potential candidate for the office of Imam, the religious and administrative head with complete authority to govern. In the eyes of Ibadhis the Imam is the "first among equals," just as man is God's creature among all God's chosen

creatures. The *umma*, the community of Muslims, elects from within its own ranks an educated believer whom they think best suited for the office.
On the other hand, Ibadhis do not require that there always be a head of the community - a major difference to the Sunni schools of thought. If no one is considered to be fit for the high demands of the office of Imam, then the post remains temporarily unfilled. An elected Imam who fails to live up to expectations can be voted out of office.
Moderation and tolerance are hallmarks of Ibadhi teaching. Ibadhis reject any use of force as a means of propagating Islamic principles. Differing opinions and interpretations must be taken into account. The shedding of blood between believers on account of theological differences is considered shameful by Ibadhis. This point differentiates them fundamentally from the Kharijites (or Khawarij), an Islamic sect with whom they are often associated. What they share with this group of religious fanatics is their absolute rejection of the arbitration between Muawiyah and Mohammed's son-in-law, Ali, which resulted in Ali's losing his power as caliph. As supporters of Ali's cause, the Kharijites also hold that the *umma* should elect the Imam. Like the Kharijites, the Ibadhis were mercilessly persecuted and had to flee from Basra to their original homelands, which, for the north Africans, were Libya, Algeria and Tunisia. However the majority fled to Oman and withdrew to the rough Hajar Mountains near Nizwa, from where the religion that now dominates the country spread. British observers of Omani rule in East Africa remarked that Ibadhis are the least fanatic and sectarian of all Muslims, openly praying side by side with Sunni Muslims. Hostile action is reserved for just one type of person: the unjust ruler who refuses to reform or relinquish his power.
In theology the Ibadhis reject a literal interpretation of simplistic anthropomorphic descriptions of God, denying the possibility of seeing God in this life or the afterlife. According to the Ibadhis the principles of the Islamic faith must always be considered in the light of changing cultural and historical circumstances. Only by doing this can Islam retain its strength and relevance. On the one

Mohammed's letter to Abd and Jaifar Al Julanda

In the name of God, the all merciful, the all good. From Mohammed, God's messenger, to Jaifar and Abd, the two sons of Julanda. Peace be upon those, who follow the right path!
I call upon you with an invitation to Islam. If you recognize Islam you will be safe, for I am God's messenger to all people, to warn all living, and to fulfill the word to the unbelievers. If you turn to Islam I will be your friend. If you refuse, you will lose your power, my horsemen will occupy your land and my prophecy will prevail over your kingdom.

(sealed with "Mohamed, God's messenger")

hand the Ibadhis are purists of Islamic orthodoxy; on the other they are extremely progressive in their readiness to interpret the Quran in the light of the here and now. With their basic liberal position they are fundamentally democrats. They adhere strictly to the basic message of the Prophet Mohammed.

The visitor to Oman will be quick to note the successful efforts made to strengthen the position of women within society and to extend their rights. The western nightmare image of a fanatical Islam in which women have no rights, are kept hidden, or are forced to conceal themselves behind shapeless black robes has no basis in the reality of Oman. In their brilliantly colored robes the women exude self-confidence. Women have technical occupations as well as holding leading positions in administration, business and government. Women are as established in society as men. They receive pay equal to men's for the same work.

International Women's Day 2004 was marked by the appointment of the Oxford-educated Dr. Rawyah bint Saud Al Busaidi as Minister of Higher Education. Meanwhile four Minister posts have been held by women within the same time. Sultan Qaboos has been a firm believer that women have as much to offer Oman as men: "We call upon Omani women everywhere, in the village and the cities,

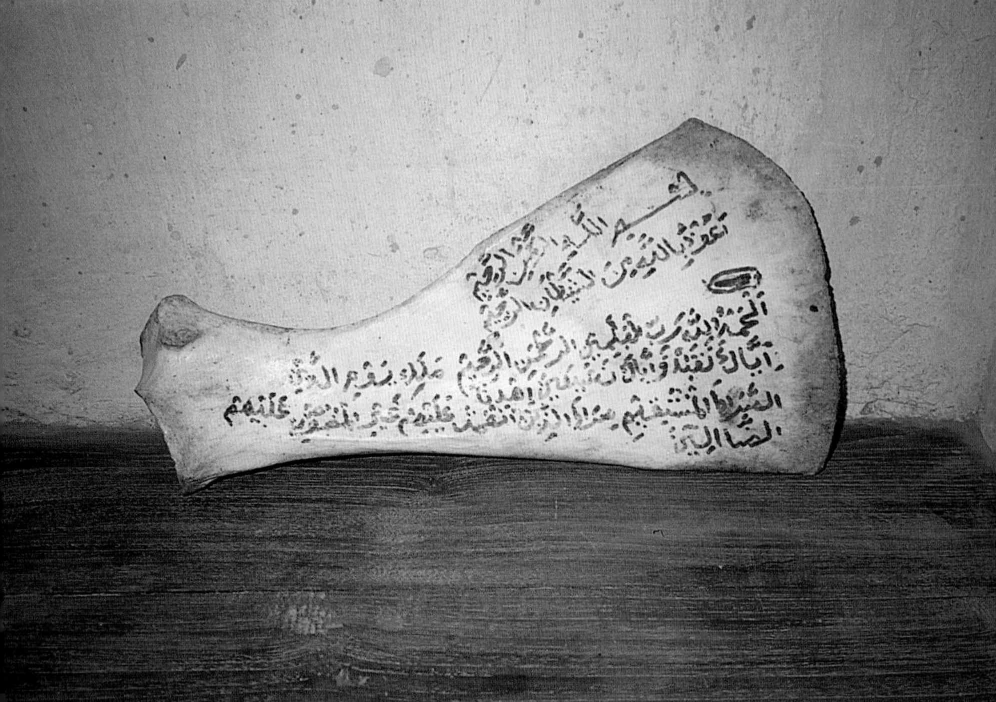

Camel's shoulder blades were used in Quran schools instead of paper. They were cheap and durable.

One of the many country mosques in simple Ibadhi style.

in both urban and Bedu communities, in the hills and mountains, to roll up their sleeves and contribute to the process of economic and social development - everyone, according to his capabilities, experience, skills and his position in life."

Ibadhis reject all forms of excess, especially in religion. Due to this "puritanism," their mosques lack adornments and are mostly simple, bare rooms, the wall facing Mecca fitted with a prayer niche, or *mihrab*, which is occasionally ornately decorated. To Ibadhi eyes an elaborate minaret is also unnecessary; it is sufficient to have a few steps up to the roof of the mosque, from where the *adhan*, or call to prayer can be made.

The Omani historian, As-Salimi, made the most fitting description of Ibadhi history. He compared it to a bird, the egg of which was laid in Medina, which hatched in Basra and which then flew to Oman and settled there. Of course not all Omanis are Ibadhis; in the coastal regions there also live many Shi'ites and Sunnis. Although in some places highly decorated new mosques dominate the townscape, life in the country is marked by the fundamental tolerance that is the spirit of the Ibadhis. In Oman you can see Muslims of various persuasions going to pray together in the mosque; fanatics have no place here.

Sunni and Shi'a – Division in the Islamic Brotherhood

Since every religion addresses a collectivity with varying psychological and spiritual temperaments, it must possess within itself the possibility of different interpretations. By bearing within itself, providentially, several modes of interpretation of the same truth, it is able to integrate a multiplicity into unity and to create a religious civilization. In traditional and pre-modern Christianity one finds the Catholic and Orthodox churches, not to speak of the smaller eastern churches such as the Coptic and Maronite. [...]

Whether Sunni or Shi'ite: in all schools of Islam the muezzin calls believers to prayer.

In Islam, which is a worldwide religion meant for various ethnic and racial types, there also existed from the beginning the possibility of two different perspectives. Sunnism and Shi'ism are both orthodox interpretations of the Islamic revelation contained providentially within Islam in order to enable it to integrate people of different psychological constitutions into itself. [...]

To say that Sunnism and Shi'ism were meant for different spiritual temperaments should not, however, be interpreted strictly in a racial or ethical sense. One should not think that a particular people has always been solidly Sunni and another Shi'ite. Of course, today the Persians are nearly all Shi'ite while most Arabs and Turks are Sunnis and these ethnic divisions do have a relation with the present distribution of Sunnism and Shi'ism in the Muslim world. [...]

In order to understand the Sunni and Shi'ite perspectives it is necessary to glance at the religious history of Islam, the development of these two dimensions from their common origin and their subsequent history. From an external point of view the difference between Sunnism and Shi'ism concerns the problem of "successor" to the Prophet as the leader of the community after his death. The two schools may thus be said to have begun as distinct entities when the Prophet finished his earthly career, because it was precisely at this moment that difference of opinion as to his successor arose. A small group believed that such a function must remain in the family of the Prophet and backed 'Ali, whom they believed to have been designated for this role by appointment (*ta'yin*) and testament (*nass*.) They became known as his "partisans" (*shi'ah*) while the majority agreed on Abu Bakr on the assumption that the Prophet left no instruction on this matter; they gained the name of "The People of tradition and the consensus of opinion" (*ahl al-sunnah wa'l-jama'ah.*) But more generally the Shi'ah of 'Ali, in the sense of those who backed and followed him among the companions, already existed during the Prophet's lifetime and there are several references to them in prophetic sayings. Only with the death of the Prophet did they become crystallised as a group distinct from the Sunnis.

But the question also involved the function of the person who was to succeed the Prophet, for surely such a person could not continue to possess prophetic powers. Thus Sunnism considered the "successor"of the Prophet to be his *khalifah* or caliph only in his capacity as the ruler of a newly founded community, while the Shi'ites believed that the "successor" must also be the "trustee" (*wasi*) of his esoteric knowledge and the interpreter of the religious sciences. That is why, although the difference between Sunnism and Shi'ism appears to be only a political one, it is, in reality, more than that. It is also theological. There is a question of both political succession and religious authority. [...]

The often richly decorated prayer niches in mosques always face Mecca.

An important aspect of Sunnism, especially as far as its comparison with Shi'ism is concerned, is political theory. All Sunnis accept the first four caliphs, Abu Bakr, 'Umar, 'Uthman and 'Ali as true vice-regents (*khalifah*) of the Prophet who fulfilled this function in its fullness so that they are called the "rightly-guided caliphs" (*al-khulafa' al-rashidin.*) With the establishment of the Umayyad caliphate the name of the institution of caliphate was continued, but in reality the Islamic caliphate was transformed into an Arab kingdom.

That is why later Sunni jurists accepted only the first four caliphs as full embodiments of the ideal of the caliphate.

The political theory of the caliphate was, however, elaborately developed [...] When discussing the theory of the caliphate, the Sunni political theorists usually referred to it as the imamate by which they meant the office of the person whose duty it was to administer the *Shari'ah* and act as judge. But since this term is particularly associated with Shi'ism, it is better to refer to the Sunni institution as the caliphate and use the term imamate in connection with Shi'ism to avoid confusion.

(Seyyed Hossein Nasr, *Ideals and Realities of Islam*, p. 141 - 147.)

Ramadan and the Eid Festivals in Oman

During the Muslim fasting month of Ramadan (the ninth month in the Muslim calendar), believers must refrain from eating, drinking, smoking and sexual pleasures from sunrise to sunset. Children under twelve and the sick do not have to fast. If giving birth during Ramadan women may abstain from fasting for two weeks but should make up this time later. People who are allowed to eat and drink during Ramadan may not do so in public. Opening times for government offices and for shops are restricted, with daytime activities being mostly avoided. During Ramadan no bills may be collected. This goes for private businesses as well as state-owned ones. For example a telephone company can only cut service on account of an unpaid bill when Ramadan is over.

Life takes place at night. Then one meets with neighbors, friends and acquaintances for great feasts to which each brings a dish. Youths play football or volleyball until midnight on the numerous small floodlit sports grounds. People pray together in the mosque and afterwards sit outdoors conversing. In Oman Ramadan is a time for communication, for renewing old acquaintances and for forming new ones. Attention is not concentrated on daily work but on one's fellow man. Before dawn breaks, usually between three and four in the morning, the *suhur*, or night meal, is eaten alone.

The 27th night of Ramadan is the "Night of Power" (*laylat al qadr*), the night when, by an act of revelation, Mohammed received the first verses of the Holy Quran from Allah. Prayer is especially effective on this day. According to tradition and to the Quran itself, God counts the "Night of Power" as more than a thousand months so on this date one prays even more than in the rest of Ramadan.

The first day of the month following Ramadan, Shewal, is the **Eid al-Fitr**, also known as the "little festival," and signifies the end of the fasting period. In many Islamic countries Eid al-Fitr has the same social significance as Christmas in traditional Christian countries and is usually celebrated for three days. Many travel to Dubai in the United Arab Emirates to go shopping in style. The children receive presents from their parents (but not vice versa!.) There are great celebrations and people wish one another "Eid mubarak" - a blessed festival.

On the ninth of Dhu al-Hijjah, the twelfth month of the Islamic calendar, the "big festival" begins, the **Eid al-Adha** which represents the day when Abraham was ready to sacrifice his son in the name of God.

These two depictions of the holy cities of Mecca (above) and Medina (below left) are from 1900. Then as now tents are seen everywhere in Mecca during the time of pilgrimage.

The festival follows much the same course as the "little festival" but goes on for a week and is the traditional time for inner reflection and the pilgrimage to Mecca.

During festival times especially, everyone should show support for the poor and the needy. This form of voluntary charity (*sadaqah*) - the amount of which the individual decides for himself - is in addition to the compulsory donations of *zakat* and *sadaqat al-Fitr*, the proceeds of which benefit the poor and needy at the time of *Eid al-Fitr*. The *zakat* (literally purification) is a duty for every Muslim believer who has more than a certain level of wealth, and is up to 10% of annual income. This ancient form of social security is based on the Islamic injunction of brotherhood. At the same time the property of the rich is "purified" of that part to which they are not entitled according to the will of the Quran. The coordination and distribution of the alms is dealt with by the prayer and congregation leaders in the mosques, the imams as well as the Ministry of Endowments and Islamic Affairs. They advise as to who can be helped and what form this assistance should take. The donations often consist of long-lasting foodstuffs such as rice, fat, sugar and salt which are then given in large quantities directly to the recipient by the donor. The needy could be large families with low incomes or families that have gotten into difficulties through accident or illness.

Because of the enormous social importance of *zakat* it belongs to the **Five Pillars of Islam**. The Five Pillars of Islam are:

shahada, the belief in the one true God;
salat, the prayer ritual to be performed five times a day;
zakat, giving alms to the poor;
sawm, fasting during Ramadan; and
hajj, the pilgrimage to Mecca.

Departures for New Shores

In the 7th century the hitherto scattered peoples living in the deserts of Arabia came together under the banner of Islam to form a religious and national entity with a vast potential of energy and creativity. The Arabs describe the pre-Islamic period with the word *jahiliyah* (i.e. Age of Ignorance), denoting a time of barbarism and lack of culture. Islam was the source of a new self-confidence which found expression in expansionism. Before then Arabia was a political no-man's land, fought over in turn by Assyrians, Babylonians, Egyptians, Persians, Parthians, Greeks and others. Shortly after the death of Mohammed, it was now the turn of the Islamic movement to overcome the neighboring cultures. In 635 Damascus fell. In 638 Jerusalem capitulated and in 642 Alexandria. In 710 Arabs landed for the first time in Spain. By 714 large parts of the Iberian peninsula were under Islamic rule.

The Arabs laid down new benchmarks of civilization and culture. They can justifiably be seen as the most important influence in the development of Europe in the Middle Ages. At a time when Arabs were at their cultural, scientific and political height, they reintroduced to the west the long forgotten (or suppressed by Christianity) learning of antiquity, fostered new forms of architecture, taught modern science, hygiene, literature, music and other arts as well as a hitherto unknown tolerance towards people of other beliefs. What are held as virtues of western civilization and which have been promoted as such with missionary zeal over the centuries now have their roots in Arabia of the Middle Ages.

Chinese porcelain was highly valued in Oman - it is integrated in the ornamentation of religious architecture. In trade with China it was often exchanged for dates.

Up until 750 Damascus was the center of Arabic culture and the Islamic empire, under the rule of the Umayyad Dynasty. From then to the 13th century it was Baghdad under the Abassids. The demand for exquisite luxury items in these centers of the empire was as great as their wealth. Many of the goods necessary to maintain a high standard of living had to be brought in from the East, above all precious woods, spices, ivory, gemstones, silver and precious metals. The main shipping ports for these goods were Basra and Siraf (modern Taheri.) This was when the Omanis came into their own. It was as if they were predestined to profit from the lucrative intermediate trade - no other people at this time were so well-situated. They already had three thousand years of experience in maritime trade, and had also learned much from the Persians. They had extensive knowledge of shipbuilding and navigation which had enabled them to trade regularly with China from about 660. Omani sailors were the best of the age. Since the collapse of the

Muslim community, the *umma*, in 658, the Omanis identified less with the Islamic world to their west and gradually withdrew from the wars of conquest and theological conflicts with their fellow believers, the Hajar Mountains providing them a perfect natural barrier. They concentrated successfully on developing trade with the east, although their activities were often disrupted by the Abassids and the Ismaili Qarmatian sect, a radical Shi'ite grouping. The first "legitimate" Imam was elected by the Omani Ibadhis in 751. Just a year later the first Abassid caliph responded by sending a punitive expedition. The first Ibadhi Imam, Julanda bin Masud, died in the conflict.

At the same time the Omanis exploited their unique geographical position to build up a vast trade network covering the Indian Ocean and its neighboring seas. Oman's eastward-facing situation on the extreme edge of the Arabian peninsula had climatic advantages during the golden age of sail: Oman lies on the edge of the equatorial monsoon zone. If the merchants began their long journey in Basra on the Arabian Gulf during September or October using small coastal sailing craft, in November they could catch the beginning of the northeast monsoon to continue the journey from Sohar or Muscat in the direction of East Africa or southern India in larger seaworthy ships. The long and dangerous journey from India to China was made using the southwest monsoon from the beginning of April. To sail from Oman to Canton on the south China coast took seven to eight months. Ships returned from India using the northeast monsoon and from East Africa using the southwest monsoon. It was using these trade routes that the compass was introduced to Arabia from China in the 11th century and from there to Europe about two hundred years later.

The chief Omani ports at this time were Muscat and Sohar. Muscat was the last opportunity to take on fresh water before the crossing to southern India. From the 9th century Sohar had been the richest and most important port in the Islamic world. The port flourished to become the leading trade center for luxury goods and slaves. Frankincense, myrrh, dates, copper and slaves were exported from Oman and pearls, gemstones, porcelain, precious woods, spices and scents, textiles and weapons-grade steel were imported to Arabia. Via Oman's widespread trade contacts and settlements Islam was to spread peacefully to far off regions such as China, Malaysia or Madagascar. At a time when such travels took months or years, interracial mixing between Omanis and their host peoples was inevitable and accepted on all sides.

In 878 trade with China was abruptly broken off. Several thousand foreigners were killed during an uprising in Canton. Nevertheless trade with Chinese merchants continued on the neutral soil of Malaysia. Chinese ports were re-opened to foreign trade in 979. In 929 the Qarmatians overran Oman and for 35 years exacted tribute money. Surprisingly this did not lead to a diminution of trade. During this period Oman was no longer subject to the caliph, the ruler of the Arab world. The new rulers tolerated the teachings of the Ibadhis. This period of foreign subjection was extremely peaceful and economically successful. The Omanis felt themselves so strong that in 943 they dared an attack on Basra with their fleet. The conquest of the town itself failed but Ubullah, the harbor of Basra, was occupied for a time. When, ten years later, the Omanis once more attacked Basra, they went too far. The caliph of Baghdad dispatched a naval force which attacked Sohar in 965 and laid waste to the flourishing town, sinking the entire Omani fleet, consisting of 79 ships. The naval power of Sohar was destroyed at one blow and the ports of Basra and Siraf no longer had to suffer Omani competition.

The following three centuries are marked by various invasions with their inevitable consequences. First the country was occupied in 1064 for about 80 years by the Seljuks from the steppes of central Asia; later they were conquered by Ghuzz Turks and Muzaffarid from Fars in Persia. For the years from 1153 to 1406 there is no evidence of an Ibadhi Imam, a clear sign of the unrest during this period. Omani maritime trade lost its importance and Hormuz took over the role of Sohar.

Around the middle of the 12th century the port of Qalhat, to the southeast of Muscat, became a new economic center for Oman. Towards the end of the 13th century the Emir of Hormuz, Mahmud bin Ahmad al Kusi, landed here and conquered parts of Oman. Qalhat became a flourishing dependency of Hormuz. The world travellers Ibn Battuta (1304-1377) and Marco Polo (1254-1324) visited it and wrote enthusiastic reports of life there. In the 15th century the flourishing town was largely reduced to rubble by an earthquake.

What remained was completely destroyed by the Portuguese in 1507. Qalhat was never built up again and today all that remains is a vast, impressive expanse of rubble. The outer walls of the mosque are the only bit of building to have survived - in the eyes of many Omanis a sure sign of the true God.

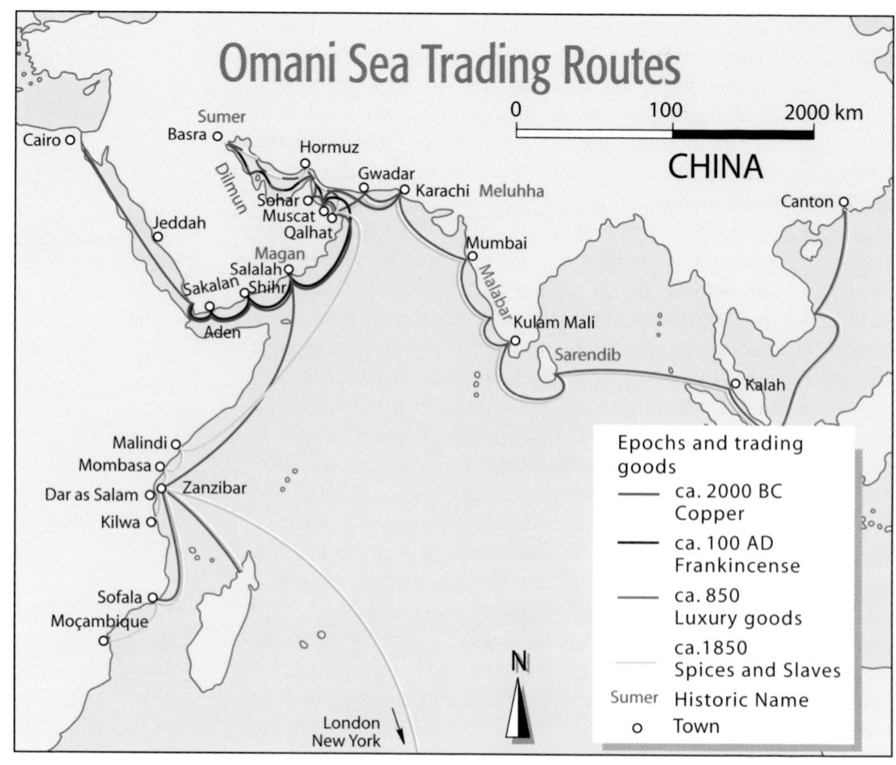

On the Trail of Sindbad

Even from today's standpoint it is not hard to imagine what an adventurous undertaking a sea voyage from Oman to China must have been in the early Islamic period.

The tales of Sindbad the Sailor were spun from sailors' yarns. Whether he really existed or just represents the personification of all these sailors' stories is impossible to say. What is certain is that there were merchants from Sohar at this time whose bold journeys to China made them the equals in every way of the legendary Sindbad. In Sohar today it is still said that he was a citizen of the town.

In 1979 the Irishman Timothy Severin decided to travel the traditional sea route from Oman to China in an exact replica of a merchant ship of that era. He managed to get the enthusiastic backing of Sultan Qaboos and the Minister of Culture for his idea.

Oman took over the complete financing of the project. In 1980, after difficult preparations, a traditionally-built, seaworthy dhow of the boom type was once more to be seen in Sur. This ancient type of ship is still in use today in parts of the Gulf region.
The most striking thing about the method of shipbuilding at this time was the complete avoidance of any type of metal. The planks of the ship were not nailed together but stitched together with cord made from coconut-husk fiber. This resulted in a hull that was elastic and could give way against the beating of the sea, without warping or springing leaks.
This laborious and time-consuming process changed with the arrival of the Portuguese. The Omanis took over the European technique of using nails and the broad, flattened stern replaced the traditional narrower pointed stern. These changes also allowed for the new weaponry, cannon, which required a different structure of ship.
After a great deal of exertion and with the help of craftsmen from the Lakshadweep islands off the Indian Malabar coast and the few remaining shipbuilders in Sur, Severin finally succeeded in building a ship more than 20 meters long completely out of original construction materials and stitched together using traditional techniques. The launch took place as planned on the 10th National Day, November 1980. At the Sultan's request the ship was named "Sohar." The core of the mixed European and Arab twenty-man crew was made up of eight Omani sailors, among whom was an old man who went back to the time of the Omani sailing fleet and had practical experience of sailing a boom.
The "Sohar" took seven months to sail from Sur to Canton. Severin precisely followed the old Arab route which led to China via the Lakshadweep islands, the Malabar Coast, Sri Lanka, Sumatra, the Strait of Malacca, and the China Seas - even today an adventurous journey of over 6000 miles and filled with danger. Illness, shortage of water and provisions, doldrums, pirates, heat, a broken mast and fearful storms accompanied and threatened the journey just as it would have done the sailors 1000 years previously.
In his account of the journey, *The Sindbad Voyage*, Severin attempts to place Sindbad's adventures geographically. The "Island of Diamonds" could well have been Sri Lanka, still rich in diamonds, or Serendip as it used to be named in Arabic. The "Old Man of the Sea" of the 5th voyage could have been an orang-utan or "man of the forest," as the inhabitants name this primate. Severin impressively describes the hardships and labors of his undertaking as well as one of the most interesting and important aspects of the journey, the navigation.

Timothy Severin on Ahmad bin Majid's Art of Navigation

The navigation of *Sohar* was an essential element in the whole Sindbad Voyage. One of the objectives of the project was to find out if the early Arab navigators had succeeded in finding their way to China. It was a stupendous achievement: they had sailed nearly a quarter of the way round the world at a time when the average European ship was having navigational problems in crossing the English Channel, and the Arabs had steered their routes, not by luck but by careful calculation. The earliest Arab texts gave a few hints as to how they had managed this feat. They stressed that they used the stars, not the sun, to fix their position; and there were a number of vague references to charts and pilot books which seem to have been carried on board, and which had been compiled from the experience of senior navigators. But no early Arab sea charts have survived, and not until the 15th century did a book appear which began to lift the edges of the veil of mystery which surrounded Arab navigation. Suitably, the book was written by an Omani. He was a master navigator from Sur, by the name of Ahmad bin Majid, and he was one of the most renowned seafarers of his time. Fortunately his writings had been translated and painstakingly annotated by an English scholar Gerald Tibbetts. I had taken a copy of Tibbetts's edition of Ibn Majid's book with me aboard *Sohar*, and now it became my manual in trying to test out the methods of early Arab navigation.

It was a difficult manual to follow, not least because Ibn Majid had written it in verse. [. . .] Just how did an early Arab navigator measure his position? How did he [Ahmad bin Majid] lay off his course? The instrument he used was no more than a wooden tablet about 3 inches wide with a hole in the middle of it; through this hole ran a piece of string with a knot in it. The navigator placed the knot between his teeth, stretched out the string until it was taut, and closing one eye held the tablet so that one edge of it touched the horizon. He then checked the height of the Pole Star against the side or the upper edge of the tablet. It seemed devastatingly simple.

I cut a simple tablet out of a piece of cardboard, pierced a central hole, rigged the knotted string, and went on deck to try out Ibn Majid's instructions. He had advised the navigator to wash his eyes with cold water before taking an observation, to adopt a firm stance, and to avoid looking upwind if possible so as not to make the eyes water. The best time to take an observation, he said, was when there was a clear horizon. The moonlit night was perfect, and after a few moments of waving the tablet unsteadily I got the knack and found I could measure the height of the Pole Star. Then I took a star sight with a modern sextant, worked out *Sohar's* position, and made a note of the result. The following night I repeated the experiment, and saw how the position of the Pole Star had altered against the side of the cardboard tablet. I consulted my copy of Ibn Majid's manual, and compared his data with a set of modern navigation tables. The relationship was obvious, though Ibn Majid did not use degrees and minutes for his measurements, but calculated the height of the Pole Star in finger widths, which he called *isba*. By the third night I was able to judge the height of the Pole Star accurately enough to plot the ship's latitude position to within a variance of 30 miles using only a bit of cardboard and a string with a knot in it! I was only a beginner, yet already I could have navigated *Sohar* to any selected point on the Indian coast a good 500 miles away from *Sohar*'s present position. All I needed to know was the height of the Pole Star in finger breadths at that location, sail south until I counted the same number of finger breadths aboard *Sohar*, turn east and keep the Pole Star at the same height until I made my landfall.

It is a technique now known as 'latitude sailing,' but what made Ibn Majid's achievement much more impressive was that he claimed to know how to calculate his latitude not just by the Pole Star, but by a whole series of other stars which he used when the Pole Star was invisible. He produced lists of stars whose altitude, if measured at the right time, could be substituted for Pole Star altitudes. Some of the stars were easy enough - he used the stars in the Southern Cross, for example - but others had to be measured in pairs, when they were in a particular relation to one another, and in a certain lunar month. Thus Ibn Majid's knowledge of the constellations and their movement had to be encyclopedic. [. . .]

Ahmad bin Majid also knew what to look for when he made his landfalls. He knew the distinctive outlines of particular hills and headlands, and he gave a whole list of the *isba* positions of the most important ports. Little wonder that Ibn Majid had been considered a *mu'allim*, the highest grade of navigator. [. . .] The mu'allim had to be able to navigate his ship at all times out of sight of land, from any port to any port, using only the stars and his fund of experience, and never losing his way even if buffeted by storms or carried off his track by the current. [. . .]

It was formerly claimed that he [Ahmad bin Majid] was the same Arab pilot who had shown Vasco da Gama the route from Africa to India. Having rounded the Cape of Good Hope and sailed up the East African coast, Vasco da Gama hired this pilot to lead his Portuguese ships to Calicut on the Malabar coast of India, because the Arab and Indian *mu'allims* had been making the same ocean passage for centuries. Thus what was a voyage of discovery to the Portuguese was a regular routine for Arab *mu'allims.*

The star-reading tablet and string, known usually as a *kamal*, worked for me.

(Timothy Severin, *The Sindbad Voyage*, p. 91 - 94. The "Sohar" has found a final resting place on a roundabout by the Al Bustan Palace Hotel.)

Portuguese Intermezzo

Up until about 1500 trade in luxury goods from East Africa and the Far East was in Arab, for the most part Omani, hands. As the Middle Ages came to a close, these expensive wares found an increasing market in Europe, where overseas merchants established themselves as a new social group. They sold goods from the east, above all spices and textiles, making enormous profits in the process. Through their financial strength they soon established themselves as forces to be reckoned with at home. Politics in Europe was now determined by families such as the Medici in Italy and the Welsers and Fuggers in Germany.

As the market for these goods grew, the great mercantile houses became increasingly concerned to cut out the Arab middleman and to buy goods directly and as cheaply as possible. India, then an unknown and almost mythical land, became the imaginary aim of many an important expedition. Marco Polo started out from Venice with his father and uncle to chart the Silk Road and returned in 1295, reporting strange and exotic worlds with untold riches. The Portuguese determined to find a sea route to India.

At the beginning of the 16th century the Portuguese built the fort of Sohar on the foundations of a fortress they had destroyed during the conquest.

The people of the Iberian peninsula had early become accustomed to the lifestyle introduced by Arabs and had come to treasure the small but expensive comforts of the good life. When, with the fall of Granada in 1492, the Arabs lost their last foothold in Spain, the Portuguese took this as the signal to expand into Arab territories and to seize the lucrative trade with the east. Six years after Columbus' first voyage to America, Vasco da Gama succeeded, in 1498, in circumnavigating Africa. In Malindi, in East Africa, da Gama hired the famous Omani navigator, Ahmad bin Majid, who showed him the route to Calicut on the Malabar Coast of India. From then on there existed a direct trade route between Europe and India. Beginning in 1503 the Portuguese conquered the Arab settlements in East Africa. Zanzibar had to pay tribute money for 25 years. In 1506 Admiral Alfonso de Albuquerque laid siege to the island of Socotra in the Gulf of Aden with a fleet of five ships. The knowledge of a sea route to India had to be turned to a profit and he was under orders to block the trade route with the East via the Red Sea that was used by the Venetians and Egyptians. In addition he was to take possession of the important Arab trading posts and found colonies. In his pocket he carried a decree from King Manuel pronouncing him Governor of the still unconquered colony of India. The intention was to establish a Portuguese colonial empire in the Indian Ocean. This seemed well within the realm of

possibility, their cannon making their ships far superior to anything the Arabs had to offer in defense. In order to control trade with the east they simply had to block the two narrow entries of the old routes: the entries to the Red Sea and to the Arabian Gulf.

Up until 1508 the Portuguese moved up the Omani coast in the direction of Hormuz. Although strongly impressed by the towns with their flourishing business life and magnificent gardens, they left behind a trail of destruction and death.

The ports of Qalhat, Qurayyat, Muscat, Sohar and finally, on the other side of the Strait, Hormuz, at that time held by Omanis, were reduced to ruins. Any inhabitants who showed the slightest resistance were killed and any ships crossing their path were sunk. Tolerance and magnanimity in regard to foreign cultures and religions were not the order of the day in the Europe of this time – it was the age of the Inquisition. The Portuguese introduced taxes and duties and built the first large fortress of the Gulf Region at Hormuz. In 1515 Admiral Albuquerque died in Goa, in India, having realized his dream.

Although the Portuguese now appeared to have gained complete control of the profitable trade route, in fact they never fully succeeded. The trading centers of the Indian Ocean were scattered over thousands of nautical miles, and the number of occupying forces was far too small to provide an effective defense against foreign powers. The Ottoman Turks had ruled Egypt since 1517. In 1538 they reacted against the blockade of the Red Sea by sending a battle fleet. Up until the middle of the 16th century the Ottomans succeeded in pushing back the Portuguese, finally gaining Muscat, but they were unable to hold it. Their attempt to capture Hormuz failed. From about 1580 other European powers became involved in the Indian Ocean. They also wanted to secure a part of the lucrative spice trade.

The English, the Dutch and the French each established East India Companies. The English East India Company, founded in 1600, was responsible for the fall of Hormuz in 1622. In 1623 the Dutch established the "Verenigde Oostindische Compagnie" (United East India Company) in Bander Abbas. The French "Compagnie des Indes" (Company of the Indies) was active from 1664. By the beginning of the 17th century, Portugal's power was past its zenith. National sovereignty had been ceded to Spain and control of trade in the East lost to England and the Netherlands.

Alfonso de Albuquerque (1453–1515) the conqueror of the Omani coastal towns.

The Yaruba Dynasty

Resistance to the weakening colonial power of Portugal also increased in Oman's interior. In 1624 the Imam Nasir ibn Murshid of the Yarub tribe succeeded in uniting more tribes into a force to be reckoned with. Because the Portuguese at this time did not want to risk any military action, they made a treaty with the Imam, in which they agreed to pay him a yearly tribute, to evacuate Sohar and to guarantee the Omanis free access to Muscat. Muscat and Mutrah were no longer threatened.

In 1634 the Imam finally conquered the occupied towns of Sur and Qurayyat. He was a popular personality of great personal integrity and his style of rule was repaid with universal respect. He died on April 22, 1649, with his soldiers laying siege to what remained of the Portuguese forces in Muscat.

After Nasir ibn Murshid's death his cousin Sultan bin Saif was elected Imam by popular acclaim. (Note: in Oman "Sultan" is not only a ruler's title but also a normal first name.) This was to prove an inspired choice. He had been a great supporter in the reunification process of his predecessor and had distinguished himself in the struggles against the occupiers at Sur and Qurayyat. As was to be expected he continued Oman's liberation struggle. The tribes buried their internal disputes and rallied behind Sultan bin Saif. By 1650 the Portuguese were completely driven out of Oman. In January 1650 he drove the Portuguese out of Muscat, which gained him the greatest respect among the tribes.

The Portuguese were the last official foreign occupiers of the country. Imam Sultan bin Saif used the mood now prevalent across the country to call for a Holy War, or Jihad (which actually means struggle in defense of Islam) against the Portuguese and pursued them into the Indian Ocean. With his fleet of wooden dhows he chased them as far as Goa on the western coast of India as well as bombarding their settlements on the east coast of Africa.

A new golden age of Omani sea power began, although they were never able to win back their previous monopoly on the Indian trade because of the strong European competition. Imam Sultan's political aim was to drive the Portuguese out of as many as possible of the former Arab trading posts in India, and above all East Africa. With this aim he built up his own merchant and battle fleets. Having defeated the Portuguese in several sea battles, he captured many of the better-equipped Portuguese vessels and was able to lay the foundations of a powerful Omani navy.

The ships he built differed in construction from traditional Arab

ships in that they combined Arab elements, such as speed and maneuverability, with European preferences for increased storage capacity and weaponry, into a new type of ship. In 1652 the Omanis conquered Zanzibar and in 1655 Bombay was taken and sacked. Omanis were once more a significant force in the trade of the Indian Ocean. The economy markedly improved. The profits were used to renew the aqueduct between Izki and Nizwa and over twelve years a fortress was built at Nizwa.

Imam Sultan was succeeded in 1668 by his son Bilarub who continued his father's expansionist policies and in 1670 conquered Diu in the Indian province of Gujarat. He built his palace in Jabrin, southwest of Bahla, and moved the capital here from Nizwa. Bilarub's rule was challenged by his brother Saif and ended after a short civil war in 1692 and Bilarub's suicide.

Saif forced back the Portuguese along the coast of East Africa as far as south of Cape Delgado in today's Mozambique; Pemba, Zanzibar, Kilwa, Mombasa and Patta all came under Omani rule. Their trading activities concentrated increasingly on East Africa; the main commodities were iron for weapons from the hinterland of Mombasa and gold from Zimbabwe which was exported to India from the port of Sofala. Another lucrative commodity was the increasing number of slaves. This maritime success filled the country's treasury as well as the ruler's private coffers. He ordered the construction of new *aflaj* and the renovation of older canal systems. He attempted to use the new wealth to build up agriculture and had thousands upon thousands of date palms planted, 30,000 at the Barka oasis alone.

At the end of the 17th century Imam Bilarub ibn Sultan Al-Yaruba surrounded himself with scientists and artists in Jabrin castle.

According to European figures the Omani navy in 1715 consisted of one ship with 74 cannon, two with 64 cannon, one with 50 cannon, 18 with from 12 to 32 cannon and a number of row boats, each with between 4 and 8 cannon. All countries that traded in the Indian Ocean at the beginning of the 18th century felt their own interests to be threatened by Omani ships which attacked towns and increasingly after 1704, English seafarers. Persia, the Netherlands and Great Britain planned a combined retaliatory action but this was not carried out due to the death of Imam Saif, whose son and successor, Imam Sultan bin Saif II, limited his attacks to Persian and Portuguese shipping.

The death of Saif II in 1718 marked the beginning of the end for the Yaruba dynasty. The rule of the Yaruba Imams had been based on support from tribes in the country's interior with their main towns and centers of power being Ar Rustaq, Al Hazm, Jabrin, and Nizwa in the Jabal Al Akhdar region. The dynasty and the personal enrichment of the Imams through trade became increasingly a thorn in the flesh for the Ibadhis. With the defeat of the Portuguese the two great tribal confederations, the Hinawis (who claimed descent from an eponymous ancestor of northern Arabian origin) and the Ghafiris (who claimed descent from an eponymous ancestor of southern Arabian origin), previously united against this common enemy, had nothing to keep them together and old rivalries soon broke out.

Saif bin Sultan II, the son and dynastic successor to Imam Sultan bin Saif II, was still a minor but was nonetheless elected by the *umma* to be Imam. In a surprise action he was replaced by Muhanna bin Sultan. The coup was the result of a selection made by a leading group of elders and scholars, the *ulema*. They had always favored Muhanna as more suited to the office than a minor, but had not had the chance to push their favorite at the official election. Imam Muhanna tried to win the trust of the people but reaped only mistrust and animosity. Yarub bin Bilarub, son of the deposed Imam Bilarub, led the movement against Muhanna. He besieged Muhanna in the stronghold of Ar Rustaq, lured him out of the fortress with false promises, and murdered him. Yarub then expressed contrition for his act, himself accepted the office of Imam and returned to Nizwa. This in turn angered the people who wished to see the legally elected boy as Imam. It resulted in a new uprising which quickly escalated into a full-scale civil war between the Hinawis and the Ghafiris. The struggle lasted a quarter of a century, both parties proclaiming their own Imam, and the now grown Saif became a political football in the power game between the two tribal confederations.

The conflict took on a new dimension when Saif requested military aid from abroad. He first brought mercenaries from Baluchistan and then asked the Persians for assistance. In 1736 the first Persian troops arrived, the transport of soldiers and horses having been undertaken by the Dutch. In 1737 nearly 7000 Persians sent by Nadir Shah were fighting in Oman, but not out of altruistic motives, as Saif realized when it was too late. They used the power struggle to re-establish themselves in Oman. In 1743 the two opposing Yaruba pretenders to the imamate died. By this time the Persians had the whole of the Al Batinah coast, the heart of maritime commerce, in their own hands. Only Sohar, under the leadership of Ahmad ibn Said, put up a bitter resistance against the attempted conquest.

The Al-Bu-Said Dynasty

The resistance of the governor of Sohar, Ahmad ibn Said, was a reason for the Hinawis and the Ghafiris to once more join forces to fight against encroachers from outside, this time the Persians. Ahmad ibn Said gained universal respect and authority over the two hostile factions through a spectacular action. After the deaths of Saif and Sultan, the Persians had lifted the siege of Sohar and agreed with Ahmad ibn Said to withdraw to Muscat. He then invited the Persian officers to a ceremonial banquet at Barka. During the meal a signal suddenly sounded, a call to vengeance on the foreign invaders. This massacre, in 1747, ended the last attempt by Persians to establish themselves in Oman. Ahmad ibn Said became a people's hero and was elected to be the new Imam. He thus founded the dynasty of Al-Bu-Said which rules to this day. At the beginning of his period of office there were often conflicts between the rival groups and also between his sons, Saif and Sultan, but he finally succeeded in re-establishing peace after the long period of civil war. In spite of all the internal conflicts the country remained a significant power in the Indian Ocean, thanks to its large fleet. Omani support was increasingly solicited in the region. When the Persians besieged Basra in 1756, the populace asked Imam Ahmad for aid and he sent ten ships to end the blockade. After many such skirmishes the Omanis established control over maritime trade in the Arabian Gulf and Bander Abbas near Hormuz. The British, above all, made great efforts to win over the Omanis as allies in their disputes with France and the Netherlands in the Indian Ocean. In 1798 Imam Sultan bin Ahmad became the first Arab prince to sign a treaty with the English crown. It forbade French and Dutch merchants from having offices in Muscat or even anchoring in the bay. Frenchmen in the service of the Sultan were let go. The British thwarted Napoleon's attempt to establish contact with Muscat after he had occupied Egypt.

In 1752 the Imam signed a treaty with Portugal to delineate their spheres of interest in East Africa. Cape Delgado, south of Zanzibar, became the demarcation line. All areas to the north were left to the Omanis. Omanis managed to avoid being drawn into conflicts with the European interests about trade with India by increasing their activities in East Africa and Baluchistan. In 1792 the Omanis took over Gwadar on the Pakistani coast and held it until 1958. While the Omanis increasingly busied themselves with foreign affairs, at their back a serious threat arose, one which they initially greatly underestimated: Wahhabism. In 1744 the unpopular Basra religious reformer Muhammad bin Abdul Wahhab had found refuge with the Al-Saud family at the Diraiya oasis in the central Arabian Najd. Like Abdullah bin Ibadh, Abdul Wahhab propagated a return to Islamic fundamentals with a belief in the one true God - not unreasonable at a time when idol worship and belief in spirits were prevalent in many areas of the Arabian peninsula. He viewed himself as the leader of a new religious community and condemned all who refused to join him as heretics and unbelievers. Their lives and possessions were then considered forfeit to him and his followers.

The sheikhs of Al-Saud united under this doctrine and swore to establish the new teachings in all lands governed by them. This immediately resulted in the first campaigns of conversion, which, in view of their intolerance towards Muslim brothers, were effectively wars of conquest.

By the time of the founder's death in 1792 the whole of central Arabia was already Wahhabi. The new Imam of the movement was the leading Sheikh of Al-Saud, Abdul Aziz I. In 1802 the Wahhabi conquered Karbala in Mesopotamia and in 1803 Mecca. After these successes in the west, they turned east in the direction of Oman. Ports and access to the ocean offered a great attraction; they only had indirect access through the Arabian Gulf in the north and the Red Sea in the south. These sea passages, as the Portuguese had demonstrated, were easy to blockade and to control, a great strategic problem, even today. In 1800 the Wahhabi, together with the Qawasim from the Ras al-Khaimah region, occupied the Omani oasis Al Buraymi. Their preparations to conquer Oman were interrupted by the murder of Abdul Aziz I. The threatened campaign did not take place and Imam Sultan bin Ahmad offered to make tribute payments to the Wahhabi.

In spite of this, fights and tensions between the two parties frequently arose, which is why the Omanis intensified their relations with the British, who had been gaining in influence in the Indian Ocean. The two countries had interests in common. The most important common interest shared by Oman and Great Britain was the suppression of piracy in the Arabian Gulf, which had assumed hitherto unknown proportions with the spread of Wahhabism.

The tribes on the north coast of Oman, known to the British as the Qawasim, had come under the influence of Wahhabism and found in its ideology a legitimation for all attacks in the form of Holy War (Jihad) against unbelievers. Thus the number of attacks on ships in the Gulf increased and this coastal region quickly became known as the "Pirate Coast."

These incidents affected not only British merchant and war ships but also Omani interests, which led to a number of punitive ex-

The modern state of Oman is grounded in its history as a successful seafaring nation. Naval pageants remind the youth of Oman of this tradition.

peditions. In 1804 Imam Sultan bin Ahmad was killed in one of these actions. The Wahhabis exploited the squabbling between his sons Said, Salim and Badr bin Saif over their inheritance to bring Muscat under their control. According to reports from Italians residing in Muscat and French agents, Badr, ruling with backing from the Wahhabi, was murdered by Said in 1807. Afterwards Said let it be known among the Arab tribes that the murder was the act of Wahhabi troops, who were then defeated by an outraged mob outside the fortress of Barka. According to other sources, Badr was killed in unexplained circumstances in the fortress of Nakhl when he and the brothers were trying out weapons.

From 1802 Said was the official ruler of Oman for 52 years. Like his predecessors since 1779, he attached no great importance to the spiritual worth of being Imam. He called himself "Sayyid" (Lord.) The Europeans addressed him with the monarchical title of "Sultan." Under Said Oman's expansionist commercial policy reached its historic high water mark.

Sultan Said and Zanzibar

Like his father, Sultan Said decided on a policy of collaboration with the British. The most important aims were to control piracy and to stop Wahhabi expansion. After the Wahhabi had already been driven out of the coastal town of Barka and the Omani region of Sur, they suffered a calamitous defeat when Turks attacked the Diraiya oasis in the heart of their domains. The leaders of the movement were taken to Constantinople, where Emir Abdullah was publicly executed. This signified the end of the first Wahhabi empire. The Omanis and British used this opportunity in 1819-20 to deal a heavy blow against the "Pirate Coast." The tribes there were defeated and bound by treaty to keep the peace. Piracy in the Gulf was not completely eradicated but was considerably reduced.

The Wahhabi regrouped within a few years and once more threatened the ports of Oman. They found allies in Oman among the tribes of Bani Bu Hasan and Bani Bu Ali from the Ash Sharqiyyah region. Oman's new position as a British protectorate made little impression on them, but at least put a barrier in their path. The threat to the country from the Wahhabi, and the military confrontations that this led to, are at the root of the tensions between Oman and Saudi Arabia, which were finally eased by the signing of the frontier treaty in 1990.

Successful export of the 19th century: cloves from Omani Zanzibar

Sultan Said's chief concern was to secure and expand the economic interests of Omani possessions in the Indian Ocean, the Gulf Region, southern Persia, Baluchistan and the coast of East Africa as far south as Cape Delgado and Madagascar. However he failed in his repeated attempts to bring Bahrain under his control. By marrying the daughter of the Prince of Shiraz in1827, he secured the possessions of Hormuz, Qishm, Bander Abbas and the Henjam islands in the Strait of Hormuz.

The East African bases had served the Omanis as depots for thousands of years. From here ships were loaded with ivory, wood, iron, gold and other wares from the interior such as slaves, a particularly lucrative line of goods. In 1828 Said for the first time visited the Omani settlements in East Africa and immediately felt at home. He moved his court from Muscat to Zanzibar so that he could personally oversee economic development in the region. The personal presence of the ruler was a demonstration of power over the Omani governors who had hitherto tended to act as independent powers. The economic development of Zanzibar and the other East African possessions was marked by the demands of the European colonial powers and the still young USA for luxury goods, cheap raw materials and labor. In the first half of the 19th century Zanzibar developed into an economic empire reaching deep into the interior of East Africa as far as Lake Victoria. The rise of Zanzibar was built above all on trading in cloves, slaves and ivory.

In 1812, in order to develop the agricultural potential of this fertile island, cloves were introduced from Indonesia and cultivated in plantations. Sultan Said's investment paid off. By 1850 the Omanis produced three quarters of the world's cloves production and effectively held a monopoly. The wealthy classes of the colonial powers increasingly demanded more luxury goods, among them ivory and cloves. In parts of Europe a cottage industry developed in working ivory, for example in Odenwald in Germany. The more ivory that was bought from Africa, the rarer the natural commodity became and the higher the price - all to the profit of the Omanis. Industrialization in Europe and America was based on the capitalist rule of maximizing profit through as cheap as possible means of production. In other words: wealth was based in many cases on slavery. Slaves were required especially for the cultivation of sugar cane, cotton and other plantations of America, the Caribbean islands, the Antilles, Mauritius and Reunion. Reliable figures on the size of this trade in human misery are hard to ascertain; the epoch remains one of the darkest chapters of history. In his study *Slaves, Spices and Ivory in Zanzibar*, the historian Abdul Sheriff of the University of Dar es Salaam writes of a French slave trader who made a trip to Zanzibar in 1775 and bought 1625 slaves from the Omani middlemen.

The Sultanate of Zanzibar had a red flag and minted coins based on the silver Maria Theresa thaler. The Order of the Shining Star was only bestowed upon Europeans.

The majority of these slaves came from Kilwa on the East African coast. In the following year the Frenchman signed a 100-year contract with the Swahili Sultan of Kilwa. He could thus cut out the commission paid to the Omanis. The contract guaranteed that 1000 slaves would be bought annually. The price per head was to be independent of gender and age and a price of 22 piasters, including tax, was fixed. The contract lapsed in 1780 with the death of the Frenchman and the price per human soared to 40 piasters. The Omanis made sure that they would never again be excluded from the trade. The most active buyers continued to be the French. French captains often complained of the long waiting times due to bad organization in preparing the "goods" for departure. The role of Europeans in the international slave trade was at least as significant as that of the Omanis. It was the colonial powers who controlled the international shipping routes.

There are several reasons for the disparaging image of the "Arab

Omani dhows plied the Indian Ocean from China to East Africa for a thousand years ...

slave driver." Around the end of the 19th century the first European racist ideologies emerged. Omanis, who had intermingled with Africans over the centuries, became judged as second class people due to their lack of racial purity and their Islamic belief. Another is that Omanis increasingly used slaves themselves on the clove plantations, themselves adapting to Western means of production. Their largest plantations had up to 12,000 clove trees and required 1500 laborers for the harvest. Another reason for the disapproval may well have been envy, which grew proportionately with the profit and wealth of the Omanis.

Sultan Said was fully aware of the expanding power of the British in the Indian Ocean and the potential consequences - especially for the lucrative slave trade - this carried for the Omanis. In 1822 he agreed with the British, who wanted to abolish slavery in their colonies, to stop the human trafficking. However this had no impact on the flourishing trade. In 1839 the ban of 1822 was modified and slave trading was declared to be piracy. Merchant ships had to allow their holds to be inspected on demand by the "Bombay Marine."

The "Bombay Marine" was the battle fleet of the British East India Company, which in 1798 had been given the task of protecting British colonial interests in the Indian Ocean. By reducing the slave trade the British were able to weaken the economic power of both the Omanis and the French, and their influence in the Indian Ocean grew steadily. Sultan Said's practice of only traveling from Zanzibar to Muscat every two years accelerated the process. Already by 1840 the British were dominant in the north of the Indian Ocean. In 1848 the Sultan agreed to a general ban on slavery in return for compensation from the British. In 1856 Sultan Said died a natural death at sea when returning from Muscat and he was buried in a palace garden in Zanzibar.

For more than a hundred years Zanzibar remained the residence of the Sultan of Zanzibar and the home of many Omanis. In January 1964 a revolution took people by surprise, and was followed by pogroms which left many Omanis dead. After only one hundred days a Zanzibar devoid of Arabs united with Tanganyika to form the state of Tanzania.

...but today only a few majestic old hulls litter the shores of the island of Muhut off the eastern coast of Oman.

Memoirs of an Arabian Princess

Salme, a daughter of Sultan Said ibn Sultan, fell in love with the German representative of the Hamburg-based Zanzibar trading house Hansing & Co., Heinrich Ruete, who lived in the immediate vicinity. After the Sultan's death there were disputes over the inheritance between his sons Majid, his deputy in Zanzibar, and Thuwaini, his deputy in Muscat, who had been born there and had never journeyed to Zanzibar. In this unsettled time the Princess, born in 1844, decided to flee and, with the assistance of the British, travelled by steamship from Zanzibar to Aden, where she had herself christened Emily and in 1867 married her German beloved who had followed six months later. The newlyweds then travelled to Hamburg, where the Princess bore two daughters and a son, Rudolph Said Ruete. Tragically Salme's husband died just three years later in an accident. Not having found acceptance among the people of Hamburg the young widow moved to Dresden with her children, then to Rudolfstein and finally to Berlin where she was received warmly and felt comfortable.

This unusual life story of an Omani princess found literary expression in her memoirs in which she describes in detail life in the Sultan's palace in Zanzibar. The book is a unique document about the end of the Omani trading empire and life in the Sultan's palace, a place from which Europeans had always been excluded and which they could only imagine. What was the reality behind the pictures of their imaginations? What made up the everyday life of a princess? Salme bint Said ibn Sultan provided a singular insight into this world in her memoirs published in German under her married name of Emily Ruete. The perspective is that of the German empire at the turn of the last century.

She saw the basic difference in attitude to life and work between a middle European and an Oriental as resulting from the differing climatic conditions and their immediate consequences. Because of the cold weather, for example, the Hamburger has to hoard great numbers of possessions. He needs a roof over his head, rooms that can be heated, different clothes according to the season. He has to put by supplies for the winter, or at least get over this season of scarcity through trade. The loss of energy due to the colder environment requires a diet rich in calories. For him possessions are a question of survival, which means he is constantly on the go. He has to work for all this. The Oriental, on the other hand, is in a position to lead a much more pleasurable life. The climate is warm all the year round so there is no fear of freezing or starving: water, a few dates and a shirt are all that he needs to survive. Bursts of activity are soon slowed by the high temperatures. Anyone who has experienced summer in Oman without an air conditioner can vouch for how crippling the heat can be. Salme describes a day in the Sultan's palace as follows:

"Extravagant habits may be met with in every country. Those who possess both inclination and means will never lack the opportunity of gratifying the one and spending the other to the fullest, whereever they may be. Indeed, I do not intend to enlarge on this subject, but merely draw comparisons between the respective requirements of different countries. Countless objects are needed in this country to protect the frail life of a newborn child against the effects of an ever-changing temperature, while the Southern baby is left almost naked, and sleeps in a draught of warm air. Here a child of two years – from the richest to the poorest–cannot do without shoes, stockings, drawers, a dress, petticoats, gloves, bonnet, ties, gaiters, fur muff, and muffatees – their sole difference being quality; while there, all the clothing the son of a prince requires consists of two articles–a shirt and the kofije.

Now, I ask, is the Arab mother, who wants so very little for herself and for her child, to work as hard as the European housewife ? She has not the slightest idea what is meant by darning stockings or mending gloves, or of any of those numerous trifles that a nursery entails; and as for that important and troublesome domestic item, a washing-day, it is a thing to us unknown; our linen is washed daily, and dried in little more than half an hour, smoothed flat (not ironed), and put away. We do not use, and are therefore spared the anxiety of those useless ornaments called muslin curtains. The garments of an Eastern woman, those of the greatest lady included, require an incredibly small amount of attention and mending: this is easily explained, as women move very little either indoors or out, and have fewer dresses.

All this helps to render life to Eastern women, without distinction of station and rank, much less complicated. But to become properly acquainted with, and to get initiated into all these minor details of household life, it is necessary to have been in the East, and to have lived there for a considerable time. No reliance is to be placed on the reports of travellers, who stop for a short time only, who are unable to gain an insight into all these details, and maybe obtain all their information from hotel waiters. Foreign ladies even, supposing they have actually entered a harem either at Constantinople or Cairo, have never seen the inside of a real harem at all, hut only its outside, represented by the state rooms decorated and furnished in European style.

Our climate, moreover, is so splendid and productive that it is hardly necessary to provide for the coming day. I do not deny that our people, taken as a whole, are averse to "flurry;"but it will be easier to realize the effects of a tropical sun, if one only considers how very trying a hot July or August in Europe can be sometimes. [...]

In this way life in the East is less laborious and more peaceful: it was this that I wanted particularly to point out and to prove before entering on a more minute description of the daily life in an Arab household. Let me, however, state expressly that I am only speaking here of things referring to Oman and Zanzibar, which, in many respects, differ from those in other Eastern countries. The hours of prayer regulate the daily life of every Mahometan; they are said five times a day, and if this be strictly observed, as is ordained by the holy book, including ablution and changing of dress, they take up three hours at the very least.

Persons of rank are roused between four and half-past five o'clock a.m. for the first prayer, and return to sleep afterwards; devout people wait for sunrise at six o'clock a.m. before doing so; the lower classes begin their daily task immediately after the first prayer. All persons in our house could live just as they pleased, provided they followed the regulations set down for devotions and for the attendance at the two principal meals.

The majority slept till eight o'clock, when the women and girls are gently roused by a slave, who begins to rub and knead them all over, which produces a very agreeable sensation. In the meantime the bath has been filled with fresh spring water, and the garments - on which jessamine and orange blossoms have been strewn during the night - are fumigated with amber and musk before they are put on.

About an hour is spent with the toilet, after which everybody has to wish our father good morning before sitting down to breakfast, the first of our two daily meals. Though a copious and very abundant repast, it took us very little time to get it over, as all the dishes had been prepared and placed on the table in readiness.

After breakfast everybody is at liberty to employ his leisure as he likes. The gentlemen get ready to go to the audience-chamber; the women, who have no work on hand, sit down at the windows to look out into the animated streets, or watch for a stealthy glance from the flashing eye of a belated noble hurrying to the *levée*, until, alas! The voice of an apprehensive mother or aunt calls the unhappy girl away from the gay scene below. Two or three hours are thus rapidly passed away. Meanwhile the gentlemen call upon each other and send word to the ladies whom they wish to visit in the evening. The older women, who take no pleasure in all this lively stir, retire to their rooms, alone or in company, to take up some fancy work, to embroider their veils, shirts, or drawers with gold thread, or cambric shirts for their husbands and sons with red and white silk–an art which requires considerable skill. Others, again, read novels, visit the sick in their rooms, or employ themselves with their own private affairs.

At one o'clock the servants announce that it is time for the second prayer. The sun is now in full blaze, and after prayer all escape gladly to some cool place to dream away an hour or two upon handsomely plaited soft mats, into which sacred mottoes are woven, or to chat and eat cakes and fruit.

The third prayer is said at four o'clock p.m., and then we dress in our more elaborate afternoon costumes. Again we call upon our father, wishing him "good afternoon" – our grown-up brothers and sisters are allowed to call him father, the little children and their mothers only address him as hbabi (sir.)

Now followed the liveliest time of the day: we sat down to our principal meal, at which all members of our large family met together for the second time. After the meal the eunuchs placed European chairs on the grand piazza in front of my father's apartments for the grown-up people. While we little children remained standing in deference to old age, which is, I believe, nowhere honored to that degree. The numerous family grouped round our usually grave father, the trim and well-armed eunuchs being ranged at some distance in rank and file along the gallery. Coffee and all kinds of French fruit-syrups were handed round, of which we children partook freely. Conversation was carried on accompanied by the tunes of a mighty barrel-organ (the largest I have ever seen), or, for a change, by some large musical box; sometimes a blind Arab woman, called Amra, who possessed an exquisite voice, was called in to sing.

An hour and a half later we all separated, and employed ourselves as we liked. Some chewed betelnut, which is a Suahely habit, and not liked on that account by Arabs born in Arabia proper. Those, however, among us who had been born on the East coast of Africa, and were brought up together with negroes and mulattoes, rather fancied this habit, notwithstanding the disapproval of our Asiatic relations, though we never indulged in it in our father's presence.

Not long afterwards, gunshots and the beat of drums of the Indian guard announced sunset and the time for the fourth prayer. Not one of our daily devotions was performed faster, everybody seemed in a hurry to get it over. For those who did not wish to go out themselves (we and our mothers always required a special permission from our father or from his representative, which was rarely refused), or those who did not expect visitors, were sure to be invited by some one in the house, or received visits from brothers and sisters, stepmothers, stepchildren, or from other people. Coffee and lemonade, fruits and cakes were freely partaken of. There was a great deal of merry joking and laughing going on; some read aloud, others played at cards (never for money, however), or sang, or listened to Negroes playing the sese, or sewed, embroidered and made lace.

It is, therefore, quite a mistake to suppose that a great lady in the East does absolutely nothing. It is true she does not paint, nor play, nor dance (according to Western notions.) But are there no other amusements to divert oneself with? People in our country are very temperate, and they are not given to a feverish pursuit of everchanging amusements and pleasures, though from the European point of view Oriental life may appear somewhat monotonous.

Our own personal attendants were, of course, all women ; the menservants were dismissed every evening to their homes and families, and the eunuchs slept also outside the house. Oil lamps are kept burning all night in the rooms and passages, but no candles are allowed after bedtime. Children above the age of two are no longer put to bed at a certain hour, they are left to themselves until they are tired. It frequently occurs that the children, overcome by fatigue, lie down anywhere and fall asleep, and then they are generally picked up carefully by some slaves and carried to their couches, sometimes a long way, without awaking to the fact.

Those people who have not gone out or received visitors generally retire about ten o'clock. On moonlight nights many take a walk on the flat housetops, which was a very delightful airing.

The fifth and last prayer ought to be said at 7.30 p.m., but as many are prevented at this time, it may be left unsaid until midnight or bedtime.

At bedtime all ladies of rank are waited upon by their female slaves, whose business it is to watch the falling asleep of their mistresses. One of them repeats the kneading process of the morning, while another fans gently, until they too may retire. I have mentioned already that all women go to bed fully dressed, and with all their jewels."

(Emily Ruete, *Memoirs of an Arabian Princess*, p. 49 - 56, 1888 translation)

The Fall of the Omani Commercial Empire

In the second half of the 19th century, Oman's commercial empire became enmeshed in a tangle of European colonial interests, technical innovations and internal intrigue. The death of Sultan Said was followed by a power struggle between his sons, Majid and Thuwaini, who had been his representatives in Zanzibar and Muscat. In 1861 the British stepped in as mediators, resulting in a treaty by which the empire was divided. The wealthy Sultanate of Zanzibar undertook to financially support the relatively poor Sultanate of Muscat. Great Britain acted as guarantor of these payments. The opening of the Suez Canal in 1869 was a severe blow to Oman's position in world trade. The ports on the Gulf of Oman quickly lost importance in favor of Aden and the entry to the Red Sea. The emergence of steamships accelerated this decline as the Omanis were not in a position to develop this technology. Sail continued to play a role in trade with India, but it had become a minor one. The economic decline led to further concessions to the British. In 1873 and 1884 the existing treaties regarding the slave trade were tightened up. Tanganyika sought foreign protection to shelter the slave traders, receiving it from Germany in 1885. In 1890 the Germans ceded all demands on Zanzibar to the British in exchange for the strategic North Sea island of Helgoland. By the end of the century the slave trade had come to a complete stop, Zanzibar discontinued payments to Muscat and both Sultanates became increasingly dependent on Great Britain.

At first the Omanis could make up for the loss of income from the slave trade by engaging in the international arms trade. They soon became the dominant force in the arms trade in the Indian Ocean, which disturbed the British more than the slave trade had. The main purchasers of the weapons were all potential opponents of British colonialism, especially in India. In 1898 the British replied with a ban on the Omani arms trade with India and Persia. The sinking profits from trade led to dissatisfaction in the north with the Albusaidi sultans.

As early as 1868 resistance against the Sultan of Muscat had begun to form and Salim, the grandson of Said, was driven from his royal seat. The temporal dynasty of the Sultans had for long been a thorn in the flesh of the country's religious leaders. Azzan bin Qais, the leader of the resistance, was elected Imam. Alongside the Sultanate there was once more an Imamate in the country. In 1871 and again in 1877 and 1883 the British reverted to their tried and tested "gunboat diplomacy" in order to maintain an Albusaidi in power by force. Having a Sultanate and an imamate alongside one another meant a split in the country between the coastal area and the interior. Heavy duties imposed by the Sultan led to the reduction of trade between the two areas of influence. English goods were free from duty. Oman had effectively become a British protectorate. The rebellions reached a climax in 1915 when Imam Salim bin Rashid was able to unite the two tribal confederations, the Hinawis and the Ghafiris, against the Sultan. With the aid of the British the Sultan managed to retain Muscat and, as a result of the fighting, the Treaty of As Seeb was signed on September 25, 1920 between the Imam, Muhammad al Khalili, the tribes of Oman and a representative of the Sultan. The Sultan's jurisdiction was thereby limited to the coastal towns and the Imam controlled the interior, although without actual sovereignty. The British now dominated the Sultan, who ruled by their grace and favor, and the French had to close their consulate in Muscat. The treaty had effected the division of the country and the lack of backing for the Sultan in his own country was shown by the number of opposing tribal leaders who signed. The treaty secured peace in Oman up to the death of the Imam in 1954. In the meantime the world outside of this now isolated country had changed radically. After two world wars two implacable superpowers with a fearful arsenal of nuclear weapons confronted one another. The accelerating industrialization of the west had increased its dependency on fossil fuels. The Arabian peninsula had become the industrialized nations' lifeline; without oil, technological development could not be maintained. In earlier times the wealth of Arabia had been guaranteed by frankincense, silk, spices and ivory - in the 20th century it could be guaranteed by energy in the form of oil. Two groups had an interest in the possible discovery of oil in Oman. The new Imam, Ghalib bin Ali, tried to establish his territories as an independent sovereign state and disputed the Sultan's right to give exploration rights to British companies. Ghalib was backed by the Saudis, who once more occupied the Al Buraymi oasis in an attempt to establish their territorial rights in Oman. In 1955 the Sultan reacted by sending troops, supported by British officers, into the interior of Oman. They met with barely any resistance and Imam Ghalib bin Ali fled to Saudi Arabia. The Sultan occupied the imamate.

The offense to tribal sovereignty led to a powerful reaction. This time the disaffected groups united under Suleiman bin Himyar, Nasir al Nabhani and Talib bin Ali, the Imam's brother. In 1958 the tribes in Jabal Al Akhdar rose against the Sultan. This latest

attempt to rebel openly against the powerful alliance of the Sultan and the British was defeated by an attack of the British Special Air Service (SAS) regiment on Tanuf, the center of the resistance. Tanuf was completely destroyed and the ringleaders escaped to Saudi Arabia. Sultan Said bin Taimur appeared once again to be ruler of a united Oman. However within a few years, on the other side of the borders which he had himself closed, a new alliance formed against him.

The Secret War

The lack of backing for the Sultan among the people, his dependency on Great Britain, his tendency to isolationism and his outdated, inefficient army, provoked his opponents and communist groupings to attack. As early as 1962 the first armed incidents took place. In 1965 Said's opponents formed the Dhofar Liberation Front (DLF), an alliance of disparate dissident groups under the leadership of Mussalim bin Nufl, a former gardener at the Sultan's palace in Salalah. They carried out small attacks in Dhofar on police stations at Thumrayt on the road to Muscat. The Sultan had particularly neglected this region in the south. Quite a few Dhofari worked illegally as foreign workers in the oil fields of Saudi Arabia and the gap between the medieval conditions of their home life and the ultra modernity of their working life was painfully apparent to them. The people there were receptive to political and ideological agitation calling for the liberation of Oman from the restrictive Sultan Said. On April 28, 1966 members of the DLF who had infiltrated the Sultan's army and were serving in his personal bodyguard made an attempt to assassinate him. He escaped unharmed but immediately took punitive measures which only served to increase his unpopularity in the region. He imposed a severe economic blockade on the mountain area of Jabal Al Akhdar, from where the would-be assassins had come. Whole communities who had had nothing to do with the attempt on the Sultan's life suffered as a consequence and many hitherto loyal Dhofari soldiers were dismissed from the army. Said bin Taimur seemed only to be able to react with savage reprisals, never attempting to tackle the root causes of discontent, and treating the troubles as if they were simply a tribal issue. After the assassination attempt the Sultan isolated himself even more and finally withdrew to his palace, where he remained for the last years of his reign, protected by his Baluchi Guard.

When Sultan Said bin Taimur had come to power in 1932 the coun-

The only remaining building in Tanuf after the defeat of the Jabal Al Akhdar uprising was the mosque and then only the outer walls.

try was steeped in debt. Within a few years the debts had all been cleared but he continued with his financial stringency long after it was strictly necessary and his conservatism became an obstacle to economic and social development. After oil was discovered in the region it became clear to people that there were alternatives to backwardness and poverty.

On November 27, 1967 a Democratic People's Republic was declared in neighboring Yemen. The British colonial powers were violently expelled and the government became increasingly dependent on support from Moscow. In 1968 the communist-oriented sections of the liberation front DLF also gained the upper hand in Oman and liberation from the imperial rule of the west became the new avowed aim. The organization was renamed the Popular Front for the Liberation of Oman and the Arabian Gulf (PFLOAG) and subsequently received intensive support from Moscow, Peking and Iraq. They denounced Sultan Said bin Taimur as a stooge of British imperialism and their rhetoric became increasingly Marxist and Maoist, with both China and then Russia vying for influence among revolutionaries in the region. The days in which Britain could openly operate militarily in a foreign country were long gone - the British Empire was in retreat and the army could not be deployed at will to maintain the *Pax Britannica*.

Under these conditions the Sultan could never settle the Dhofar war in his favor. Contemporary estimates in 1969 put the number of PFLOAG guerilla fighters at 5,000 against Omani government forces which never exceeded 1,000. The government forces' military equipment was also hopelessly outdated, whereas the PFLOAG were in receipt of sophisticated weaponry supplied by Moscow in an attempt to counter Peking's influence. At the beginning of 1970, the PFLOAG held the mountains and large parts of the coast of Dhofar under their control. Salalah was cut off and victory for the guerilla troops seemed to be only a question of time. In northern Oman a new revolutionary group had emerged, the National Democratic Front for the Liberation of the Occupied Arab Gulf (the NDFLOAG.) This had its origins among Omani dissidents in Baghdad. In June 1970 they attacked the military camp of Izki, southwest of Muscat and then went on to attack Nizwa. The insurgents were defeated and the NDFLOAG was dissolved and subsumed within the PFLOAG. However the spread of the troubles to the north of the country greatly exacerbated the feeling of instability within the whole region and had a great psychological impact on the military in Oman. Plans were also hatched for attacks to be made within Muscat itself.

It was in this situation that the liberal forces gathered around

Qaboos, the son of the Sultan, who had been living under virtual house arrest in Salalah since his return from abroad. On July 23, 1970 there was a successful palace coup. Sultan Said had to step down and immigrated to England where he took up residence at the Dorchester Hotel in Park Lane, London. He died as the result of a heart attack in 1972.

On July 29, 1970 the British government formally recognized Qaboos as Sultan of Oman. On July 30th Sultan Qaboos addressed the nation in a broadcast:

"I promise to proceed forthwith in the process of creating a modern government. My first act will be the immediate abolition of all the unnecessary restrictions on your lives and activities.

I will proceed as quickly as possible to transform your life into a prosperous one, with a bright future. Every one of you must play his part towards this goal.

Our country in the past was famous and strong. If we work in unity and cooperation we will regenerate that glorious past and we will take a respectable place in the world. Yesterday it was complete darkness and with the help of God, tomorrow will be a new dawn on Muscat, Oman and its people. God bless us all and may He grant our efforts success."

Sultan Qaboos bin Said stood at a crossroads: a victory meant the possibility of a fresh beginning, a defeat would mean the end of the state of Oman after a century of steady decline. To ward off this defeat, the young Sultan immediately announced an amnesty for all Omanis fighting on the side of the PFLOAG. Whereas his father had reacted to opposition with angry intransigence, Sultan Qaboos set about regaining control over the country with characteristic tact and diplomacy. His promise to open up and develop the country satisfied the wishes of many of the Omani guerilla fighters. They were prepared to put their trust in Qaboos because his mother was from Dhofar, he had been born there, and had gone to school there and had spent the years before the coup in the crisis region. Spiritually and ethnically he counted as one of them and had demonstrated this by his offer. In August the first 200 fighters changed sides.

The dispute had developed a new dimension with the change of power. It was no longer to do with the liberation of Oman from western imperialism but with the protection of Oman, now an oil-producing state strategically placed at the entrance of the Arabian Gulf, from a communist takeover. Seen under this aspect it was easier to find allies from abroad. The conflict became an international one. At the request of the Sultan, Great Britain sent a 90 strong special unit, the "British Army Training Team" (BATT.) These were actually members of Britain's elite fighting force, the Special Air Service (SAS), although this was never aired in the House of Commons at the time. Its main task was the strategic leadership and military training of the Jabali, the mountain farmers of Dhofar. They helped to train and organize the irregular tribal militia force, the *Firqat*. The operation of the troops was kept secret for two years in order to avoid difficulties with the UN, becoming dubbed in the press as "Britain's secret war." This military assistance certainly improved the position of the Omani forces but the number of soldiers was in itself too negligible to assure victory.

The oil crisis starting in October 1973 finally confirmed the dependency of the industrial nations on Arabia. Control of the entrance to the Arabian Gulf by a communist-ruled country was not only a nightmare scenario for the western states but also for the Shah of Iran. At the beginning of 1973 Qaboos had already received Iranian military aid in the form of nine helicopters, and in December a further 1500 men of the "Imperial Iranian Battle Group" arrived. Egypt provided political support, whereby the other Arabian countries kept their distance in so far as they did not directly support the PFLOAG. An exception was King Hussein of Jordan who sent a special unit to Oman in February 1975. Step by step the guerilla fighters were forced back into the mountains of Dhofar and their sphere of action became increasingly limited.

Many Omani families still possess old sea chests. In former times all one's worldly goods would be packed into these heavy, lockable chests and taken on the long sea journeys from Muscat to Zanzibar. The chests are often richly decorated with rivets and sheet brass.

At 12 noon on December 2, 1975 Qaboos received the news from John Akehurst, the commander of the British "Dhofar Brigade" that Dhofar was now a safe area and the civil development of the region could begin. On December 11, 1975 the Sultan declared victory. The Sultanate of Oman could proclaim its existence.

Oman Faces the Future

Sultan Qaboos bin Said Al-Said

Everywhere you go in Oman you'll see the Sultan. His portrait decorates banks, homes, offices and shopping centers. At first sight you might take this to be characteristic of the personality cult of a dictator. But in Oman this interpretation would be quite wrong. These depictions are not standardized but are quite varied in their execution, more like folk art. Most of the portraits show a thoughtful, gentle man, who possesses determination and power but doesn't feel the need to make a show of them. Anyone who stays in the country a bit longer soon comes to appreciate that the relationship between ruler and subject is not characterized by power but is rather one of affection and respect. For Omanis the Sultan has become a caring father figure – the personification of the oriental ideal of the good and just ruler.

Qaboos is the eighth Sultan in the direct line of the Al-Bu-Said dynasty. He was born in 1940 on November 18th, now celebrated as Oman's National Day, in Salalah in Dhofar, where he spent his childhood and received his early education. His love of nature and genuine concern for ecological matters has its roots in his childhood idyll in Dhofar. His beloved mother, Mazoon bint Ahmad, was from the local fishing village Taqah. Qaboos was to maintain close ties with the people of the region. This was to prove invaluable in reuniting the country after years of civil unrest.

Sultan Qaboos

His early years having been spent in relative seclusion, in 1958 his father, Sultan Said bin Taimur, sent him to have his education finished in England. He first attended a private school in Suffolk and in 1960 entered the Royal Military Academy at Sandhurst. After serving six months with the British Army of the Rhine in Germany, he studied administration for two years in England. Back in Salalah he followed this up with a six year study of Islam and the culture and history of Oman. In July 1970, at the end of this period of studies and training, the now 29 year old son of the Sultan saw a chance to open up the country. His father was overthrown in a palace revolt and he took over the reins of government.

The Foundation of a New State

In order to turn the medieval tribal society into a modern national state it was first necessary to overcome a century of stagnation. Oil resources, which were already known about at this time, would provide the financial basis for this task. The first thing Qaboos did was to lift bans and cancel decrees that his father had made and which were out of date. Wearing sunglasses was now permitted and the enjoyment of music, which had up until then been suppressed, was encouraged by the Sultan himself. Muscat's city gate now remained open after sunset. Controls on trade were lifted.

Together with a committee of experts from the United Nations, plans for the country's development were drawn up. The main problem was the illiteracy rate of over 90%. The level of education was extremely low. The Omanis then living in the country could only do simple laboring jobs. Educated people had long since turned their backs on the Sultanate because of the lack of prospects. They had built new lives for themselves all over the world. On taking up office, the young Sultan appealed to Omanis around the world to help him with the difficult task of reconstruction. Omanis living abroad had faith in Sultan Qaboos and the possibilities the new country could offer. At the beginning of the 1970s many gave up their secure jobs abroad in order to help with the task. Experts in medicine, law and economics, along with professors from such renowned universities as Harvard and Oxford, were among those who returned.

The demand for a skilled work force and for experts was still greater, so experts were brought in from abroad. Qaboos took care to take these from various countries. He wanted to avoid individual countries or cultural groups having a dominant influence. The strongest influence during the early phases continued to be that of the British, who had already cooperated closely with the rulers of Muscat in the 19th century. In addition consultants and skilled workers were taken from other European countries as well as Egypt, Morocco and the Sudan.

The development plans worked out by the United Nations and the forming of effective teams of experts were the *sine qua non* for the

The National Flag of Oman

The new national flag of the Sultanate was first hoisted on December 17th 1970.

It signified a new political start for the country. The flag carries an emblem of two crossed swords and the Omani curved dagger, a *khanjar*, with a belt. The colors have a symbolic meaning: white stands for peace and prosperity, red for the struggle for freedom and unity and green for the Islamic belief and the fertility and beauty of Oman.

For the 25th national jubilee the proportion of the colors, the size of the flag and the height of the flagpoles in relation to buildings were officially regulated.

country's new beginning. Another fundamental requirement was to be the stabilization of internal affairs.

By allowing tribal leaders and bitter opponents of his father a place in government, Qaboos succeeded in preventing the renewal of old disputes. With the ending of the civil war in the border area with Yemen in 1975, the weapons finally fell silent in Oman, and the internal peace necessary for real progress was established.

The increasing of oil production capacity provided the financial basis for the investment necessary to build up the country. The credit initially required to develop the oil fields was gladly provided by the west; the shock following the oil crisis of 1973 was deep-seated and they were keen to gain the trust of a prudent and energetic statesman. Oil exporting countries friendly to the west were courted at this time. Oman's strategic importance on the Strait of Hormuz for ensuring the supply of oil was finally realized by western states in 1979 when the Shah of Iran was toppled. A politically stable and reliable Sultanate became important to the industrialized countries. Oman was chosen to be the "Guardian of the Gulf."

The Islamic ideal of equality finds expression in Omani dress code: all men wear full-length robes, *dishdashas*. This goes for farmers and fishermen as well as for ministers and other notables.

The Conception of the State

In 1970 Sultan Qaboos bin Said became head of state under an ancient Arab system of rule, in which the Sultan has the role of father to the people. His subjects can approach him directly with problems and petitions. The Sultan is both the highest judge in the land and a trusted advisor. Such a system can only work to everyone's satisfaction when the ruler is educated, well-informed and his subjects not too numerous. And this is how it is in Oman. Sultan Qaboos keeps to as much of the traditional style of rule as possible - an important means of maintaining cultural identity in a country subject to rapid change. During the unsettling times of his country's development he has remained the calm in the eye of the storm. If, for example, someone feels he has been treated unfairly by the administration or has a serious problem, he doesn't need to go through the complicated and wearing stages of judicial appeal, but can turn directly to the responsible minister and demand a ruling. In eastern fairy tales the Sultan is accustomed to mix with his people incognito. Qaboos has his own way of doing this: he drives through the town at night to see that everything is in order. Once a year Qaboos undertakes a month-long "Meet The People Tour," as it is officially called. This tour covers every region in the country. He is accompanied by ministers and other decision mak-

ers. So that the members of the government, who normally reside in the modern city of Muscat, do not lose touch with the modest living standards of the people, the whole retinue spends the nights in spartan military camps. Water is rationed and wood for burning is brought on the journey. Audiences are held at regular intervals. Everyone can discuss his problems, complaints and ideas face to face with the Sultan himself. The government members responsible for the individual cases are called upon and everything is settled on the spot.

But for Qaboos the days of the traditional Sultanate appear to be numbered. Unlike other Middle Eastern rulers he has not announced a definite successor. The people are being gently led towards democratic responsibility for their own affairs.

The achievements of the modern state are often condensed into symbolic plaques.

The political development of Oman has not always been welcomed by the Arab world. The Omani model is a thorn in the flesh for many Islamic fundamentalists. In 1994 plans to assassinate the Sultan during his appearance in Nizwa for the National Day celebrations were discovered during a raid in Egypt. The plot was foiled and the people were in suspense to know how the ruler would react. Qaboos disappeared from the scene for a long period - most suspected somewhere in the desert - and then reappeared at the Nizwa celebrations with a moving speech. Part of his speech ran as follows: "Extremism, under whatever guise, fanaticism of whatever kind, factionalism of whatever persuasion would be hateful poisonous plants in the soil of our country which will not be allowed to flourish."

"Almighty God has sent down the Holy Quran with wisdom and clarity. He set out in it the general principles and Laws of Jurisprudence, but he did not express these in details which might differ from place to place and time to time. He did so to enable us to interpret the Law of Islam according to its basic principles and the requirements of life. [...] Obstinacy in religious understanding leads to backwardness in Muslims, prevalence of violence and intolerance. This, as a matter of fact, is far removed from Islam which rejects exaggeration and bigotry, because it is the religion of liberality."

The assassination attempt made it clear that Oman was not a *Shangri-la* isolated from the rest of the world. Political development is going ahead at full pace and is susceptible to unexpected violent attacks. It was with this background that the November 6, 1996 constitution of Oman and the establishment of the Omani Council (*Majlis Oman*) should be viewed.

The Council, made up of an appointed upper chamber (*Majlis al Dawla*) and elected lower chamber (*Majlis ash Shura*), helps with the decision processes and ensures cooperation between government and the people. Following Saudi Arabia's declaration of a constitution in 1992, Oman had been the only Arab state without its own constitutional foundation.

In the following years the Majlis system, geared to tribal customs, was gradually further democratized by extending the voting franchise. In the summer of 1994 the voting right for the *Majlis ash Shura* was extended to women in the capital region of Muscat and they could also sit in this forum. For the election of October 2003 this right was extended to all women in Oman over the age of 21. The term of office in the *Majlis al Dawla*, the upper chamber, is four years and can be renewed. In 2003 it had 53 members of whom 5 were women. The members are nominated by the Sultan and must be at least 40 years old and Omani citizens. They may not be elected to the *Majlis ash Shura*, the lower chamber, and may not hold any other public office.

The *Majlis ash Shura*, the State Consultative Council, has the task of advising the government on affairs which affect Omani society. It is made up of 82 elected members who are independent representatives of the people in the various *wilayat* (regions.) The term of office is four years and a member cannot be elected for a third term. The Sultan is leader of the cabinet and appoints and dismisses the deputy prime minister, ministers and state secretaries. He is responsible for the calling of a state of emergency, general mobilization, declarations of war and ratifying international treaties and agreements, and the passing of new laws. The political reality is that Oman is well on the way from a Sultanate ruled by decree to becoming an independent constitutional monarchy with an Islamic democracy. The driving idea of Sultan Qaboos bin Said is always to sensibly combine the traditional and the modern. In 1971 the Sultanate of Oman ordered the construction of a naval training ship in Scotland. It was called "Shabab Oman" ("Youth of Oman") and has been seen around the world taking part in tall ships races, winning the Cutty Sark trophy in 1996 and 2001. The latest victory was the spectacular winning of the 2009 iShares Cup by the trimaran *Oman Sail Masirah*.

Another project that calls to mind the great seafaring heritage and openness to the world of the Omani people is the construction of the *Jewel of Muscat*.

This project is a historical and cultural initiative launched by the governments of Oman and Singapore that involves the original reconstruction of a 9th century ship based on the design of the archaeological findings of the Belitung Wreck, which was discovered in 1998 in Indonesia. Once built, the ship is expected to sail from Oman to Singapore. The journey is expected to begin in February 2010, with the ship reaching Singapore by June of that year.

The 1996 Constitution

The Sultanate of Oman's constitution lays the foundation for legal procedure as well as the procedure for the election of a successor. Some western observers were disappointed that it was not as progressive as had been expected. Others pointed out that rapid social development could not be expected to succeed without some basis in tradition. The constitution is divided into seven parts. The following selection serves to give a flavor of the spirit of this Basic Law of the State with its 81 articles.

Part 1: The State and the System of Government

Article 2 [Religion]: The religion of the State is Islam and the Islamic Shariah is the basis of legislation.
Article 5 [Form of Government]: The system of government is an hereditary Sultanate in which succession passes to a male descendant of Sayyid Turki bin Said bin Sultan. It is a condition that the male who is chosen to rule should be an adult Muslim of sound mind and a legitimate son of Omani Muslim parents.
Article 6 [Succession]: (1) Within three days of the position of Sultan becoming vacant, the Ruling Family Council shall determine upon who will succeed to the Throne. (2) If the Ruling Family Council does not agree upon a successor, the Defense Council shall confirm the appointment of the person designated by the Sultan in his letter to the Family Council.
Article 7 [Oath of the Sultan]: Before exercising his powers the Sultan shall swear the following oath at a joint session of the Oman and Defense Councils: "I swear by Almighty God to respect the Basic Law of the State and the Laws, to fully protect the interests and freedoms of the citizens, and to preserve the independence of the country and its territorial integrity."
Article 9 [Substantive State Principles]: Rule in the Sultanate shall be based on justice, Shura Consultation, and equality. Citizens shall have the right to take part in public affairs, in accordance with this Basic Law and the conditions and circumstances defined in the Law.

Part 2: Principles Guiding State Policy

Article 10 [Political Principles]: [...] Laying suitable foundations for the establishment of the pillars of genuine Shura Consultation, based on the national heritage, its values and its Islamic Shariah, and on pride in its history, while incorporating such contemporary manifestations as are appropriate. Establishing a sound administrative system that guarantees justice, tranquility and equality for citizens, ensures respect for public order and safeguards the higher interests of the country.
Article 11 [Economic Principles]: The basis of the national economy is justice and the principles of a free economy. The State encourages saving and oversees the regulation of credit. All natural resources are the property of the State. [...] Public property is inviolable. [...] Private property is protected. [...] Confiscation of property is prohibited and the penalty of specific confiscation shall only be imposed by judicial order in circumstances defined by the Law.
Article 12 [Social Principles]: Justice, equality and equality of opportunity between Omanis

are the pillars of society, guaranteed by the State. [...] The State guarantees assistance for the citizen and his family in cases of emergency, sickness, incapacity and old age in accordance with the social security system. It also encourages society to share the burdens of dealing with the effects of public disasters and calamities. The State enacts laws to protect the employee and the employer, and regulates relations between them. [...]

Article 13 [Cultural Principles]: Education is a fundamental element for the progress of society which the State fosters and endeavours to make available to all. Education aims to raise and develop general cultural standards, promote scientific thought, kindle the spirit of enquiry, meet the needs of the economic and social plans, and create a generation strong in body and moral fiber, proud of its nation, country and heritage, and committed to safeguarding their achievements. The State provides public education, combats illiteracy and encourages the establishment of private schools and institutes under State supervision and in accordance with the provisions of the Law. The State fosters and conserves the national heritage, and encourages and promotes the sciences, literature, and scientific research.

Part 3: Public Rights and Duties

Article 16 [Deportation, Right of Entry]: It is not permitted to deport or exile citizens, or prevent them from returning to the Sultanate.

Article 17 [Citizen Equality, No Discrimination]: All citizens are equal before the Law, and they are equal in public rights and duties. There shall be no discrimination between them on the grounds of gender, origin, color, language, religion, sect, domicile or social status.

Article 18 [Personal Freedom]: Personal freedom is guaranteed in accordance with the Law. No person may be arrested, searched, detained or imprisoned, or have his residence or movement curtailed, except in accordance with the provisions of the Law.

Article 20 [Personal Integrity]: No person shall be subjected to physical or psychological torture, enticement or humiliating treatment, and the Law lays down the punishment for anyone who is guilty of such actions. No statement shall be valid if it is established that it has been obtained as a result of torture, enticement or humiliating treatment, or threats of such measures.

Article 22 [Presumption of Innocence, Due Process, Personal Integrity]: An accused person is innocent until proven guilty in a legal trial which ensures him the essential guarantee to exercise his right of defense according to the Law. It is prohibited to harm the accused either bodily or mentally.

Article 27 [Home]: Dwellings are inviolable and it is not permitted to enter them without the permission of the owner or legal occupant, except in the circumstances specified by the Law and in the manner stipulated therein.

Article 28 [Religion]: The freedom to practice religious rites in accordance with recognized customs is guaranteed provided that it does not disrupt public order or conflict with accepted standards of behavior.

Article 29 [Expression]: Freedom of opinion and expression, whether spoken, written or in other forms, is guaranteed within the limits of the Law.

National Organization

Oman is an Islamic state. Everyday life follows the rhythm of Islam. The legal system is founded on the shariya (shariah), the law of Islam. The development of the country follows five year plans. Each year, on the other hand, has its special emphases, which the Sultan announces on National Day (November 18th/19th.) For example the themes for 1988 and 1989 were agricultural development, in 1991 and 1992 promoting industry, 1993 youth, 1998 the private sector of the economy, and 2001 and 2002 were years of the environment. On the global stage, UNESCO has instituted the 'Sultan Qaboos Prize for Environmental Preservation,' to be awarded every two years to recognize outstanding contributions by individuals, groups of individuals, institutes or organizations in the management and preservation of the environment, consistent with the policies, aims and objectives of UNESCO. Sultan Qaboos is not just paying lip-service when he talks of environmental concerns but is putting a lifelong passion into practice as head of state.

The seventh five year plan (2006-2010) emphasied education, the creation of jobs and social aid programs as well as the expansion of industry, tourism and fishing.

Muslims view each other as brothers and consider that property should be fairly distributed. For the country's development this means that from the very beginning the revenues from the 50% state-owned oil company PDO have not primarily flowed into private hands, but have been invested in community projects. The first major aim for development was the establishment of a modern infrastructure and effective, comprehensive education and health systems. Extensive capital outlay and concentrated organization made the impossible possible: by 1986 all the targets for these sectors had been met, only 10 years after the first five year plan. A few examples serve to illustrate the sheer scale of achievement in terms of development: in 1970 there was only one asphalt road in the whole of Oman and that was shorter than 10 kilometers. It connected Muscat with a landing strip in Ruwi. The main means of transport were ships along the coast and the camel caravan in the country's interior. Today the road network in Oman consists of 20,161 kilometers of asphalt roads and more than 25,000 kilometers of unsurfaced roads. Anyone who has driven a car in Oman will appreciate what a technical achievement this was in the almost inaccessible mountain regions of the country. Oman boasts one of the most modern telephone networks in the world, built by Siemens and Ericsson. The postal service covers the whole country and is fast

and reliable. In 1970 there was a single hospital worthy of mention, located in Mutrah. This has grown into a comprehensive health service with more than 18,000 healthcare employees. Medical care is now provided to nearly 100% of the population. Compared to the original 3 boys' schools there are now 1187 schools for boys and girls. The educational system combines elements of the English school system and the German technical schools, and also includes Quran schools, adult education institutes and technical colleges.
In 1986 a university was opened in Muscat with faculties of mathematics, information technology, biology, geology, Islamic studies, education and medicine. In 1990 the first students were graduated from a university in their own country, and in 1993 the first medical students qualified. The primacy given to education has paid off. A skilled foreign workforce, in particular teachers and workers, is increasingly being replaced by Omanis. This policy of "Omanization" is being pursued in all areas. The Ministry of Foreign Affairs and the police force are staffed exclusively by Omanis.

A network of modern public telephones gave everyone the possibility of contact with the outside world, even in remote areas already before the widespread use of cell phones.

The high standard of education for all is not just a prerequisite for the successful Omanization of business and administrative life in Oman; it is also the key to economic diversification. It is increasingly recognized that in the modern world a country's greatest assets are its human resources and that an individual's greatest resource is his intelligence. With the global impact of information and communications technology, knowledge has become the key to success and Oman is positioning its people to take a full and active role in the building up of a successful "knowledge economy," able to respond rapidly to the change-driven demands of the modern technological world.
Of course some mistakes have been made in the detailed planning of this rapid development drive and some things get sacrificed on the way to these achievements. It would be impossible to do this without any problems arising and there is inevitably an impact on society. The idea behind development has always been to keep the unavoidable changes to the people's way of life within manageable bounds.
Witness the new metropolis of Muscat: if you land at As Seeb expecting an ancient Arab town with narrow winding streets, you're in for a shock. As you drive the more than 50 kilometers through the Capital Area you pass row upon row of new buildings, and the highway will be packed with traffic. It is not the longed-for Orient you were fondly imagining.
The city of Muscat is the heart of a modern nation, a planner's dream of a city for motorists, and a nightmare for pedestrians. Here you'll find the ministries, administrative centers, shopping centers,

an international airport, oil refineries, innumerable company offices, harbors - in short, everything that you would expect from a competitive capital region. But it is only in historic Muscat that old buildings have been sacrificed to make way for progress and modern architecture. Apart from that the new capital is literally built on sand, something unavoidable in this country.

As such "progress" was initially concentrated in the area of Muscat, the rest of the Sultanate was spared any direct negative consequences from this leap forward. No great culture shock materialized.

Muscat's new "great city gate"

Of course people in the interior no longer live as they did in the middle ages and they drive utility vehicles instead of riding camels but the rhythm of life and cultural integrity have been preserved. It is this cultural integrity which makes Oman such an attractive destination for an increasing number of tourists from both east and west. Tradition and modernity have been reconciled, enabling the tourist to experience at firsthand a highly-developed culture with customs extending back for thousands of years, yet not for the lack of modern amenities.

Considerable efforts also had to be made in the field of diplomatic relations. In 1970 there was virtually no contact with the outside world. For a country to become an equal member of an international community, it first needs to establish a diplomatic presence abroad. Guidelines for foreign policy need to be drawn up and entry to the great international organizations must be considered. All of this happened very quickly: as early as 1971 Oman joined the United Nations, the World Health Organization and the International Monetary Fund. Membership in UNESCO, Interpol and the Arab League followed in 1972. Oman joined the Non-aligned Movement in 1973. Today the Sultanate is a full member of more than 100 international and regional organizations, but is not a member of OPEC.

Oman's foreign policy is based on good relations with its neighbors, shunning involvement in the internal affairs of other countries and recognizing international law and practice. As a non-aligned country the Sultanate works for the preservation of peace. For instance, Iran and Saudi Arabia resumed their broken diplomatic relations after a meeting brokered by Oman in Muscat in 1990. Along with Sudan, Oman was the only Islamic state that did not break off diplomatic relations with Egypt following the Camp David treaty with Israel. The Sultanate condemned the September 11th terrorist attacks on New York and Washington. Addressing the Oman Council on September 25, 2001, His Majesty Sultan Qaboos stated: "All types of terrorism, regardless of who practices it, constitute an attack on the peace that all nations aspire to, and on the international stability and security that we work with other countries to achieve. Therefore, we condemn terrorism, demanding an end to terrorism and for its causes to be resolved. We support international measures to fight terrorism that do not harm nations or cause innocent people to pay for practices not related to them in any Arabic or Islamic country." Sultan Qaboos continues to use his influence to promote peace and stability in the area: "Peace is the objective of the state. It is one of the principles of our internal and external policies. It is a strategic objective we endeavor to achieve for the sake of security, stability, development and prosperity."

Sultan Qaboos commands a respect which enables him to play the part of a trusted peacemaker, able to strengthen relations between the Arab world and the West. A country dedicated to peaceful coexistence with the rest of the world, Oman provides a politically and economically stable location, an oasis of peace and prosperity. So it is no wonder that in 2007 Sultan Qaboos has been awarded two peace prizes: The "Peace Prize of the Russian International Association" and the "Jawaharlal Nehru Award for International Understanding" of the Indian Council for Cultural Relations, both in recognition of his contribution to the cause of peace, co-operation and international understanding.

In 2009 the Sultan was ranked by the World Islamic Encyclopedia among the top ten of the 500 most influential leaders in the Arab and Islamic world. The reason it cited for selecting Sultan Qaboos included his adherence to Islamic values and virtues, his supreme ability to combine Islamic values with the benefits of modern life and his tolerance towards other religions. It pointed out that under his leadership Oman had liberated itself from the burden of foreign debt and managed to build up a solid state reserve fund to serve as a cushion in times of crisis.

Chronology

70000 – 5000 BC
Stone Age in Oman

3500–2700 BC
Hafit Period, first beehive tombs

2700–2000 BC
Umm-an-Nar civilization, large circular communal graves

2500–1500 BC
Land of copper, Makkan: copper exports to Dilmun, Mesopotamia and the Indus basin; shipbuilding in Oman; Dhofar under Sabaean rule

700 BC–300 AD
Heyday of the frankincense trade with Mesopotamia, Egypt, Greece and Rome

120 BC–20 AD

Dhofar ruled by Parthians, then the Himyarites until the 6th century AD, thereafter the Sasanians

563 AD
Persian King Cyrus the Great conquers northern Oman, Persian rule lasts until the end of the Sasanian empire in 637 AD

before 570 AD
Persians driven out of Oman by Arab tribes; in 570 regain a foothold in Sohar; Sohar becomes the residence of a governor and a Nestorian bishop

1st century AD
Maritime trade between the northern coasts of the Indian Ocean and East Africa

622 (0 Islamic calendar)
Hegira: Mohammed moves from Mecca to Medina; start of the Islamic calendar

630 (8)
Islamization of Oman by Amr bin Al-As; return of Mohammed from Medina to Mecca

658 (37)
Battle of Siffin between supporters of Ali and Muawiyah; division between Sunni and Shi'ite

ca. 660 (39)
Beginning of trade with China

683 (62)
Abdullah ibn Ibadh, the founder of the Ibadhi school of thought, active in Basra

751 (133)
Election of the first Ibadhi imam

752 (134)
Punitive expedition of the Abassid caliph against the Ibadhis

878 (264)
Uprising in Canton, abrupt cessation of trade with China; trade continues with Malaysia, Sri Lanka and Indonesia as intermediaries

892–965 (278–353)
Heyday of Sohar

979 (368)
Chinese ports reopened

10th–13th century
Various invasions by Seljuks, Ghuzz Turks and Muzaffarid

1498 (903)
Vasco da Gama reaches India with Omani assistance

1506–1508 (911–913)
Portuguese destroy the Omani ports of Qalhat, Qurayyat, Muscat and Sohar and conquer Hormuz in present-day Iran

1550–1581 (956–988)
Turks repeatedly plunder Muscat

1640–1643 (1049–1052)
Imam Nasir ibn Murshid Al-Yaruba expels the Portuguese from Muscat and Mutrah

1649 (1058)
Imam Nasir dies, beginning of the Yaruba dynasty

1650 (1059)
Imam Sultan ibn Saif expels the Portuguese from Oman, construction of the Omani fleet

1650–1718 (1059–1130)
Further establishment of Omani naval power in the Indian Ocean, conquest and pillaging in East Africa, India and Persia

1719–1747 (1131–1159)
Civil war in Oman, Persians called in to assist the Omanis re-occupy parts of the country

1747 (1159)
Ahmad ibn Said defeats the Persians and is elected imam, founding of the Al-Bu-Said dynasty

1752 (1165)
Treaty with Portugal, division of spheres of interest in East Africa, boundary is Cape Delgado

1806/09/19 (1221/1224/1234)
Punitive expeditions together with the British against the Qawasim on account of their piracy

up to 1828 (1243)
Development of naval power in the Indian Ocean, sphere of influence from Mogadishu to Cape Delgado, Gwadar in Baluchistan (now Pakistan) and Bander Abbas in Persia

1828 (1243)
Sultan Said ibn Sultan moves his residence to Zanzibar

1856 (1272)
Death of Sultan Said, succession conflict

1861 (1277)
Separation of the Sultanates of Zanzibar and Muscat. Zanzibar becomes a British protectorate

1871 (1288) onwards
Economic decline, tribal uprisings against the Sultan, the Sultan's power base reduced to the coastal area

1913 (1331)
Imam elected by tribes rebelling against the Sultan

1920 (1338)
Treaty of As Seeb, division of Oman into a Sultanate on the coast and an imamate in the interior

1955 (1374)
Sultan Said bin Taymur uses military force to expel the Imam to Saudi Arabia

1958 (1377)
Gwadar returned to Pakistan

1959 (1378)
End of the Jabal Al Akhdar rebellion

1964 (1383)
Revolution in Zanzibar, Sultan and Omanis expelled from Zanzibar

1964–1975 (1383–1395)
Dhofar conflict: civil war between socialist oriented rebels and the western oriented government of Qaboos (after 1970)

1970 (1390)
Qaboos takes over power, establishment of a national state

1971 (1391)
Oman becomes a full member of the United Nations

1972 (1392)
"Trucial States" (states under the protection of Great Britain) gain independence as the United Arab Emirates

1990 (1410)
Border treaty with Saudi Arabia

1992 (1412)
Border treaty with Yemen

1993 (1413)
Oman elected to Security Council of the United Nations

1996 (1416)
Declaration of the first constitution of the state of Oman

2002 (1422)
Universal suffrage introduced for citizens over 21

2003 (1423)
For the first time in the history of the Gulf States a ministerial post held by a woman: in Oman.

Life in Oman

The Date Palm, Oman's Tree of Life

Following an age-old tradition many Omanis still plant the shoot of a date palm to commemorate the birth of a son. The child's personal tree grows alongside him, providing many of life's necessities. The lifespan of a date palm is about that of a man and having a personal tree is a guarantee against starvation. It is a traditional form of life insurance. The climate in the mountainous north of Oman provides the perfect living conditions for the *Phoenix dactylifera*, as the date palm is known among botanists. (*Phoenix* refers to the Phoenicians who are supposed to have been responsible for the spread of the tree and the specific name *dactylifera* comes from the Greek word for date *dactylos* and *fero* meaning "I bear," hence date-bearing.) The summers are long, hot, dry and windy, the winters short, and now and then there are thunderous downpours of rain. Date palms are cultivated in an area of 35,000 hectares between Musandam in the north and Sur in the south. The desert-like plains south of Sur are too dry. Dhofar, on the other hand, is too wet on account of the monsoon rains. About half of the land suitable for cultivation in the Sultanate is taken up with date plantations. 50 to 60 % of the plantations are in the fertile Al Batinah Plain. However the best dates are harvested in the regions to the west and east of the Hajar Mountains. The total number of date palms in Oman is estimated to be in the region of eight million, approximately four trees for each inhabitant. Date pits from archaeological excavations show that the *Phoenix dactylifera* has accompanied the inhabitants of the land throughout their eventful history from the Bronze Age through to the present. There are several reasons for this.

For centuries dates were the staple foodstuff of Oman.
Statistically there are four date palms for every Omani inhabitant.
Trees intended to produce good crops cannot be grown from pits but only from offshots.

The consumption of only fifteen dates satisfies the daily requirements for essential vitamins, minerals and other trace elements of an adult person. Stored in clay vessels dates keep for several years. They constituted the most important part of the diet of those Omanis who were traveling in inhospitable regions, in deserts and on the oceans. Thanks to dates and dried lemons Omani seamen were protected from the scourge of western sailors - scurvy - which was endemic due to vitamin deficiency. Sea journeys lasting several months could be made with no medical problems due to lack of proper nutrition. This was assuredly a significant reason for the success of Omani maritime trade in centuries past. Even today a strict diet of dates is considered a key to longevity and to remaining fit both physically and mentally.

Dates were always one of the most important exports in the trade with India and China. The extensive trade relations in the early Islamic period also led to the spread of the teachings of the Quran, in which dates are given an important ritual function during the fasting month of Ramadan. The Prophet Mohammed recommended that the fast be broken at sunset by eating dates when possible. In order to observe this ritual people in China were prepared to pay large sums of money or to exchange "white gold," porcelain, for dates. A large quantity of antique Chinese porcelain found its way to Oman where it can be seen today in abundance in the museums of old forts or in the private households of traditional merchant families. The significance of the date for Omani maritime trade can be judged by the fact that the capacity of a ship was measured according to the number of sacks of dates which it could hold.

The *Phoenix dactylifera* serves not just as an important source of nutrition but also, after about 50 years, when the crop of fruit begins to diminish, as a source of raw materials for house building and handicrafts. Before the introduction of electricity in the 1970s, in coastal areas houses known as *barastis* were built from the branches of palm trees, a means of construction ideally suited to the climate. The necessary building materials for this type of house are all obtained from the palm tree. Beams are sawn from the trunks of aging trees to make the timber frame which is held together by cords made from palm fiber. A *barasti* traditionally consists of several single room units within a fenced-in area. The house includes storerooms, lavatories, cooking and washing areas as well as summer and winter quarters. Palm fronds serve as material for rain-proof roofs, for the windproof walls of the winter quarters and for the outer fence. Other walls are required to let air through so that in coastal areas the land-sea breeze phenomenon can be used as a natural air conditioning system. These walls consist of mat panels which are made from the stalks of the palm fronds. The construction of the *barasti* reached its apogee on the Al Batinah coast. Today, however, such buildings are often being replaced with concrete buildings with electric air conditioning and may well disappear within the foreseeable future. You'll come across them most often in the interior of the country, albeit in the architecturally insignificant form of animal sheds, outhouses or the movable Bedouin dwellings.

Phoneix dactylifera

The leaf fronds which spread out from the stalks are a favorite raw material for basketry and wickerwork. Variously colored, they are used in the manufacture of mats, bird cages, fish traps, pyramid-shaped stands for drying and perfuming clothing, fans, bags and all sorts of baskets. Up until twenty years ago even the 3 meter long fishing boats known as *shashah* were made from palm sticks bound together with coir.

Date palms are also used in the traditional clay buildings. The ceilings of the houses consist of rafters made from palm wood covered with palm matting. This basis is then covered with a roughly 30 centimeter thick layer of clay, which is itself reinforced with several layers of palm leaves. This not only strengthens the ceiling but also serves to make its construction lighter. Clay is often reinforced with palm fibers as well as stones. This increases the stability of the outer walls. Doors and window frames are made out of palm wood and often decorated with artistic carvings.

With modernization the date palm lost much of its traditional and economic standing. Many plantations were neglected or were cut down for wood. There was a danger that the date palm would degenerate into a symbol for social backwardness. This tendency was set into reverse by a nationally sponsored project, the Date Palm Improvement Project (DPIP.) Within the framework of this project cultivation methods have been rationalized, new marketing strategies developed and new date products created. Production plants for date vinegar, date syrup, bars of date chocolate and date yoghurt have been set up. Date honey and date sugar are made from the juice of fresh dates. The sap from some date trees can be made into a fermented beverage and date palm flour is made from the pith of the tree. The dates can be used to make wine and date oil is obtained from the seeds and used for soap manufacture. Date sugar is of great economic significance.

Overleaf:
Today Omani children, like these in Musandam grow up without tribal conflicts.

The fruit contains up to 80% sugar and is markedly healthier than other sorts of sugar. The amount of sugar produced, per hectare, compares favorably with that of sugar cane and is higher than sugar beet. The marketing strategists of the DPIP have promoted its use as a sweetener for the food industry, especially in products for diabetics. With such versatility the date palm is set to continue its vital role in Omani life.

Tribal Society in Oman

When Sultan Qaboos came to power in 1970 he became the ruler of a "living museum." Outside of the Sultanate the national governments of other Arab states had long since broken the political power of the tribal princes. Not so in Oman. The old tribal structures were alive and powerful in Oman as nowhere else in Arabia. In order to establish a new state Qaboos first had to peacefully unite the tribes, put an end to ancient feuds and persuade the leaders of the individual groupings to hand over their traditional powers to the Omani state and to actively cooperate in the building up of the new country - a difficult task for a young ruler if ever there was one. The head of the tribe is the eldest of the tribe, the sheikh, which literally means "old man." He shares this title with the remaining elders of the tribe, who have gained this distinction through their experience of life and through the respect that comes naturally with age. As "sheikh" can also denote any man of honor, sometimes younger people are also addressed as "old man." As a group of tribal members of rank and honor the sheikhs make up the council or *Majlis*. The head of this tribal council is *primus inter pares*, first among equals, who draws his authority from age, respect and competence.

Some Omani tribes elect their chiefs. If the candidate holds himself aloof from the nomination this is taken as a sign that he is prepared to accept the election and also possesses the moral qualities necessary for the office. The good and bad qualities of the candidates are minutely weighed against one another in heated discussions until agreement is reached as to who is best-suited to lead the tribe. He is confirmed in his office as sheikh by the personal agreement of the tribal members. In the past it sometimes happened that no agreement could be arrived at when one part of a tribe could not be persuaded to subject itself to the favored candidate. In such cases the tribe would split. The individual groups would then join up with other tribes which would require an oath of allegiance in return for offering them protection. The leading sheikhs of such tribal groups are called *Tamima*. Among the Bedouin the individual tribal branches are led by a *rashid*. Members of the tribal councils in towns and communities are called **wali**. Jurisprudence is administered regionally by the *wali*, in conjunction with the **qadi**, a judge who has attained that position either by graduating from an Islamic law college or by taking advanced study with local religious experts. The *Majlis* system is of primary significance for the modern Omani state because it represents a form of democratic direct representation due to its nearness to the people. Everyone with a problem has the right to speak directly to his sheikh, who will then bring the matter before the next higher tribal council. In this way the problem is passed through a hierarchy of *Majlis* to the level at which justice can be dispensed. The supreme sovereign, the Sultan, is the ultimate guarantor of this hierarchical system. This is also the key to understanding how a loosely coupled confederation of tribal areas could be united into a national state. It is not for nothing that the political organization of modern Oman contains elements of this traditional *Majlis* system.

Oman's populace is made up of two groupings. In the 2nd century AD parts of the Al-Azd tribe from the wadi Jawf in east Yemen under the leadership of Malik bin Faham migrated into Oman. This migration went on for over 200 years. These people apparently left their former settlement in Marib as a consequence of the collapse of a dam. The bulk of the tribe migrated in the direction of Mecca and Medina. The home of the Yemeni migrants was to be called "Oman," named after Oman bin Ibrahim al Khalil or Oman bin Saba bin Yafthan bin Ibrahim, a descendant of Abraham. Later the Nizari moved into Oman from central Arabia. In the first quarter of the 18th century the two ethnic groups polarised into the political factions of the Hinawis, named after Bani Hina of Yemen and the Ghafiris, named after Bani Ghafir of the Nizaris.

Each of the country's forts is watched over by a guard, fitted out with the insignia of bygone days.

This division is eclipsed by a tension which is completely independent of tribal affinity. While the people of the interior tended towards isolationism, the occupants of the coastal regions, especially the wealthy port towns, demonstrated an openness to the outside world. The deep-rooted, highly complex conflict between the two groups can be starkly simplified as a division between the desert tribes, the Bedouin, and the city tribes, the Hadr - a conflict between settlers and nomads, rich and poor, town-dwelling confinement and the limitless freedom of the desert.

These conflicts stretched well into the twentieth century, tribes often changing their positions, collapsing into tribal offshoots or forming alliances under the leadership of an Ibadhi Imam against outside aggressors, whether Portuguese, Persians, Sunni caliphs, Qarmatians, Wahhabi or British. An atmosphere of tension lasted over centuries during which the structure of society was constantly changing. Geographical isolation led to the continuance of feuds which lasted for generations.

The Al-Harithi and the Al-Maskery were shooting at each other in Ibra up until 1970. Rights to a well were the basis of this ancient dispute. The fighting was interrupted for a few hours each day to allow both sides to go shopping in the communal market. Even

Watchtowers cover the area around Ibra.

today the old town displays signs of the division of the settlement. In the 1980s there was a marriage between members of the two tribes – a kind of Romeo and Juliet story with a happy ending. The union was respected by both sides and today the family lives peacefully with its children in As Seeb.

The everlasting and senseless feuding proved too much for many Omanis and many emigrated to East Africa, Baluchistan or to other regions, mostly to places where Omanis had long had trading relations. They first returned to their land of origin after 1970, when it was possible to make a new beginning in peace. All tribes are represented in the current government in the form of a *Majlis* system and Oman has become a country remarkable for being peaceable. Weapons principally have a symbolic and aesthetic value. One has the impression that after centuries of fighting the Omanis would now like to enjoy at least as long a peace.

Ethnic Groups in Oman

A centuries' old tradition of trade has left unmistakable traces in today's society. Alone the skin color of Omanis ranges through all shades from black to white and bears a telling and unmistakable witness to Oman's cosmopolitan past.

Alongside the descendants of tribes of northern and southern Arabia, the majority forming Hinawis and Ghafiris, there live today many Omanis in whose veins African blood also flows. They are generally called Zanzibaris and because of their educational advantages they formed the majority of the technocrats within the newly-modernized state. Many Zanzibaris studied in universities in Great Britain, the USA or in British East Africa (Kenya, Uganda and Tanzania.) The East African Bantu tongue Swahili is still spoken among Zanzibaris and is kept alive in Oman.

The inhabitants of the remote fishing village of Kumzar on the Strait of Hormuz, the Kumzari, are probably immigrants from Baluchistan and speak a Persian dialect.

Baluchistanis served as mercenaries in Oman and played an important role in the army until the change of power in 1970. But also as ordinary workers they found they had better earning potential here than at home on the Makran coast of Pakistan. The Baluchistanis speak Urdu.

Along the Al Batinah coast several Indian communities have been established over time. In the past Indian merchants, Banyans, played a central role in exchanging goods and were involved in most trade with or via India. The Banyans have been settled in Oman from at least the 16th century and have preserved their Hindu beliefs and language.

The Khojas, also successful Indian merchants, live in Mutrah in a part of town completely cut off from its environment. Until 1970 it was forbidden for outsiders to enter their part of town. Today the gate is always open and their dress and speech is no different than that of Omanis but sightseers are still not welcome in their small walled-in world.

Numerous other Islamic and Hindu communities have found their home in Oman. Today what binds the many ethnic groups together is the abstract notion of "Omani citizen," the most important foundation for a modern nation state.

Eating with Tradition

Originally the country's bare, dry earth was able to offer little to the Omani kitchen. Some ingredients have always had to be imported. Until recently dates, lemons, a few vegetables, rice, water and bread formed the basis of the Omani diet in the impenetrable interior of the country. On festival days a goat would be slaughtered and sometimes merchants would bring dried fish to the oases by camel. On the fertile coast the menu was enriched with fresh fish, fruit and goods imported by sea. Nutmeg and other spices and fruits from India, East Africa and the far east were imported to Oman and found their way into the country's kitchens.

Culinary culture has to be seen with the historic background and current social structure in mind. Even the way tea is drunk separates Omanis from other Arabs. Omanis drink tea with a lot of milk, sugar and spices such as cardamom and cloves. In winter fresh ginger is added so that the tea has a more warming effect. This manner of preparing tea is typical of the Indian subcontinent and is seen by many other Arabs as a crime against their national drink.

The Omani kitchen has a variety of ways of preparing dates; dried, they can be kept for long periods. Asian guest workers prefer piquant dried pepper pods. Fish is eaten grilled.

If you are invited to eat in a traditional Omani household, you will be received at the appointed time in the reception room, the *Majlis*. You sit comfortably on the floor with a glass of juice and talk about family, God and the world; you make conversation before the meal. A large tray is brought in with fresh fruit, which the host has cut into mouth-size pieces and hands out to the guests. Because you eat with your hands, you always wash them first in a bowl of water which is handed around the circle. As a rule each time the tray is passed around there is a lengthy dispute as to who should receive the first piece of fruit. The host would always like it to be the eldest. The eldest would like the honor to go to the rare guest, who of course tries to refuse with exaggerated gestures, which means that the whole ritual has to begin again from the start. The key word is always "*fadall*," "help yourself."

For the main course there is almost always rice which has been spiced with cloves, cinnamon and cardamom. It is served on a large plate placed on the floor in the center of the group. More bowls contain various dishes from which you take something and place before you on the large communal plate. A chicken is often served, roasted or boiled with tomatoes, onions, garlic and vegetables (*chicken saloona*); lamb with dried lemons, onions, tomatoes and green peppers, cardamom and cinnamon (*maqboos*) or fish in coconut milk and turmeric (*samak pablo.*)

The following dishes are also original Omani: *Laham haris* is

a wheat and meat paste which requires the cook to pound the wheat–which has been soaked overnight–till it turns mushy and then boil with lamb for several hours. It is handed around at the end of a meal. *Kabouli* consists of rice with pine kernels, cashews, cinnamon, cardamom and dried lemons with lamb or goat meat. By far the most time-consuming dish from the Omani kitchen is *showa*. A lamb is strongly spiced, wrapped in banana leaves and laid in an earth oven over charcoal. Cooking time varies according to the size of the animal and can be between 20 hours and 3 days. This elaborate dish is a favorite at Eid festivals. With every meal there is salad with tomatoes, cucumber, onions, paprika and spring onions. A favorite side dish is pickled lemon. Less often you may find dried shark with onions. The main dish is followed by fruit and then dates. As a sweet dessert there is a confection of boiled dates, clarified butter and sesame seeds, or *halwa,* the national sweet made of sugar caramelised in clarified butter and starch. Halwa's flavor can be refined with cardamom and saffron. At the end of the meal you perfume your hands with rose water or another scented water and drink coffee before taking your leave.

Unfortunately you're only likely to receive such a traditional Omani meal if invited to an Omani household. Hotels and restaurants tend to feature Indian, Chinese or European menues. Real exceptions that are to be recommended are the Bin Atiq restaurants in Salalah and Muscat and the Seblat Al Bustan, an "authentic Omani nighttime Bedouin tented dining experience" provided by the award-winning Al Bustan Palace hotel in Muscat. The latter may sound like the usual gaudy tourist trap but is actually completely authentic when it comes to the food and music that is on offer. After initial difficulties with his own cooks the hotel's French master chef commissioned women from the neighboring village of Al Bustan to take care of the menu and its preparation. The dishes, served in tents in the open air, are both substantial and superb. Here you will not just be among tourists - Omanis themselves are also clientele.

The numerous small restaurants are usually Pakistani or Indian and generally frequented by guest workers. Omanis like to cook with spices from the far east but are not great fans of very hotly-spiced food. The Indian restaurants in which Omanis can be found have spicy food which is not so hot. A standard menu in small restaurants consists of soup of the day, mixed salad and rice with a side dish, usually cooked vegetables in a small bowl or fried pieces of lamb, fish or chicken. This is followed by fresh dates or melon. This rice dish is known throughout the country under the Indian description *Biryani*.

Omanis seldom go out to eat and their private menus have other influences. As a result of the enormous economic boom of the last thirty years almost every middle-class household employs a housekeeper from southern India or the Philippines. They ensure that there is always something to eat readily available. Indian cooking can be found everywhere, especially curry and coconut in all varieties as well as unleavened bread, *chapattis*. Eggs and chicken are other essential ingredients in the Omani kitchen. A normal breakfast consists of an omelette with paprika and tomatoes, tea and *chapattis*.

The extension of agricultural production, the revival of trade and the variety of groceries of all kinds that are available today, combined with personal prosperity after so many years of isolation and privation, have unleashed a wave of consumption across the country, comparable to that in Europe after the end of the Second World War.

The country is once again prosperous and one can enjoy the fruits of the years of reconstruction. A diet increasingly rich in calories and cholesterol increasingly worries doctors in the country. Ever more Omanis suffer from hitherto relatively unknown illnesses and symptoms such as high blood pressure and high levels of cholesterol, diabetes and obesity.

The Greening of Oman

Until 1970 Oman was completely cut off from the industrial and economic developments of the modern world. Up to this point life in Oman had been pre-industrial and, seen from today's point of view, completely environmentally friendly. The only chance people had to survive was to suit their way of life as naturally and closely as possible to the extreme climatic conditions in which they found themselves. Modern ecologists might view Oman's way of life as having been in a state of prelapsarian paradise. At the same time the lack of any infrastructure and industry offered an ideal basis for the building up of a modern nation. There were no obstacles in the form of contaminated countryside or decaying industries to clear up, no workforce whose existence would be threatened by the latest technologies. Modernization would not have to cope with the ravages of outdated industry - rather with an unspoilt environment and culture.

The greatest achievement of the rapid development of the country since 1970 is that from the very beginning Sultan Qaboos recognized the immense importance of keeping Oman's environment intact and took measures to ensure environmental protection. Oman was the first Arab country to pass environmental protection laws, in 1974, even before the development of the first of Oman's five year plans. As Oman became ever more developed, so the efforts to conserve the natural environment were stepped up.

In 1979 the Council for Conservation of the Environment and Prevention of Pollution was established with Sultan Qaboos himself as chairman. Laws proposed by this council were enacted in 1982 and ensured that environmental issues should be addressed in the planning of all new projects. In 1984 the Ministry of the Environment was established with the responsibility of implementing the national plan for the environment and the Law for the Conservation of the Environment and Prevention of Pollution.

In October 1990 a seven-year coastal zone management project was completed in response to the threat posed by rapid urban development. The project covered the entire 1,700 kilometer long coastline of Oman. New species of fish and corals were discovered as well as hitherto unknown breeding and feeding sites of turtles and birds. All of the findings from the various disciplines of biology, ecology and geology were logged and stored in a comprehensive environmental database. The study formed the basis for licensing all future investment measures in the coastal areas.

The data from this study and from others in the country's interior were used by the International Union for the Conservation of Nature (IUCN) for the setting up of nature conservation areas and sanctuaries. Step by step their suggestions have been implemented, for example through the process of Integrated Coastal Area Management (ICAM) to ensure biodiversity. Environmental protection measures are not just confined to selected nature reserves but include all parts of the country. However small a development project, before it can be carried out it requires the blessing of the Ministry of Regional Municipalities, Environment and Water Resources (MRMEWR) in the form of a "No Environmental Objection" certificate. Such a certificate is only given out when the builder can demonstrate that the plant, for example, will be built and run using modern environmentally friendly materials and technology.

The once normal practice of watering fields and plantations by temporary flooding went against the modern ecological ideas of agricultural production on account of the concomitant high expenditure of water, the rapid evaporation and the resulting increase in the salinity of the soil. New, more economical methods of irrigation were propagated and promoted by the government. In the larger settlements irrigation is now done by a method known as "dripping," whereby perforated pipes are used to supply water

drop by drop direct to the plants' roots, thus greatly cutting back on the consumption of that most precious commodity.

Nowadays the rainwater from the mountains is dammed and then channeled into the groundwater table.

Today the drinking water in the Capital Region is provided by seawater desalination plants. To improve the taste this is mixed with fresh water so that what comes out of the tap is 80% desalinated water and 20% fresh water. All along the coast more desalination plants driven by natural gas are being constructed.
These measures should ensure adequate water supplies for future generations. Due to the intensification of agriculture the water table level in the Al Batinah Plain had dropped markedly by the mid 1990s.
In order to make the maximum use of the sparse rainfall recharge dams were built in several of the narrow mountain valleys of the Hajar Mountains. Bore holes in the reservoir floors allow the torrents of water from thunderstorms to run down and recharge the underground aquifers within a few hours of the precipitation. The success of recharge dams is most marked in the region around Barka. In recent years the soil of the date plantations here had become salty due to the sinking water table and most of the palms had stopped producing fruit or had died off. Today the trees once more put on a lavish display of succulent green.
The effects of these measures to conserve water were made more

pronounced through a phenomenon with which no one had reckoned. Since 1996 each year there have been strong and sometimes lasting precipitation over the country. At the beginning of 1998 the region around Al Qabil on the edge of the Wihibah desert was beset by a hail storm lasting for several hours. In places the ice was knee-high. The Al Qabil Guesthouse was in need of complete restoration after the storm.

For some time they had noted an increase in the temperature of seawater and a shift of the monsoon zones in the Indian Ocean as a consequence of climatic change. In temperate regions the effects of climate changes are barely perceptible, but in areas of climatic extremes even small changes can have overwhelming results.

Evidence for this was provided by the immense, and completely unforeseen, damage caused by Cyclone Gonu in June 2007. Within a few hours undreamt of masses of water rained down over the mountains between Muscat and Sur, and with elemental force burst a way through the wadis to the coast. Afterwards many places looked as if a war had been visited upon this peaceful country. Roads lay in ruins across the landscape. Houses, villages and entire valleys were laid waste. No one could remember such an event happening before.

In the autumn of 2008 the next natural disaster followed, From Musandam to Al Ashkarah on the edge of the Wihibah desert a carpet of algae several nautical miles wide and several meters deep – known as "red tide" – spread along the coast. During almost the entire season sea bathing, snorkeling and diving along this enormous stretch of coastline were all but impossible. The algae absorb the oxygen in the water resulting in the death of many fish and those that did survive were in such a state of confusion that nocturnal fish became active during the day and diurnal ones slept.

Both the cyclone and the algae blooms which have affected Oman are a result of climate change. In future the country would like to increase its own contribution to climate protection. With this in mind the Oman Green Energy Company is constructing Oman's first bio refinery in Sohar. Soon ethanol will be extracted from vegetable raw materials, principally from the regenerable organic waste from the country's more than eight million date palms. In the coming years a network of biodiesel filling stations is planned. This "green" diesel will be markedly cheaper than normal petrol. The target is to cut Oman's carbon dioxide emissions by 20 percent by 2020. 80 percent of the ethanol production will be for export.

Oman and the Solar Age

At the moment it is hard for anyone in the country to conceive of a surfeit of water. However, the state has become increasingly conscious of the abundance of wind and solar energy. Over 1700 kilometers of coastline could offer a rich harvest of wind energy and the potential for solar energy is unsurpassed anywhere in the world. As early as 1992 the United Nations published a study of the usage of renewable energy. Step by step the suggested measures have been put into practice.

Although the country has oil and natural gas at its disposal, in many parts of Oman sun and wind can be cheaper than fossil fuels because they can be used locally without any centralized organization. The laying of electric cables and gas pipelines across vast stretches of desert and through rugged mountain terrain in order to reach all small mountain villages is all but impossible to finance. Heavy rainfalls and thunderstorms make it difficult to provide these places with energy because the torrential floodwaters regularly wash everything before them into the alleys below, including roads and utility pipelines. Solar plants for heating water and for photovoltaic electricity production offer a good solution to local needs.

Since 1996 panels of solar cells are ever more frequently to be seen along roadsides. Remote crossroads are often lit at night using solar energy which has been collected during the day. All 62 of the country's television and radio transmitters are now powered by solar energy as opposed to diesel generators. Because most of them could only be reached by helicopter their upkeep had previously proved intolerably expensive. Solar cells reduced running costs significantly; they are almost maintenance free and no longer require to be refueled.

Early in 1998, following UN recommendations, a Japanese company made the first survey measurements in Thamrait in southern Oman for the construction of a wind-driven power station. In Muscat the Ministry for Electricity and Water follow all developments in the area of solar energy with the greatest of interest. Alongside solar heating and electricity it is hoped that soon an efficient solar system for the desalination of seawater and above all for air conditioning will be developed; nothing requires so much electricity in this country as air conditioning. In contrast to its oil-rich neighbors Oman's energy costs are high. Wasting finite resources of fossil fuels is not permissible.

Oil – but what next?

In 1967 Oman first began to export oil in very small quantities. By the mid 1970s output was a modest 300,000 barrels per day, which rose to some 900,000 barrels per day by the end of the 1990s. In the early years of the new millennium output sank by some 10%. Profit from the sale of oil made undreamt of progress possible but at the same time created its own economic problems. The effect of economic dependency on foreign market conditions and the international price of oil was clearly felt by Omanis in the years from 1986 to 1988. During these years the price of oil fell from 30 to less than 10 US dollars a barrel. Oman was fortunate; the fall in the price of oil did not happen during the delicate start-up phases of reconstruction - the infrastructure, education and health systems were largely in place by 1986.

The first Gulf War saw the price of Omani crude oil rapidly rise to over 30 dollars. The war had another economic effect: Omani ports grew in importance. Because they lay outside of the potential danger zones of the Gulf trouble spots, the shipping insurers did not require surcharges on their premiums due to the extra risk. As a result the freight traffic of Omani ports rose, a tendency which has continued ever since.

The high oil prices, however, did not last. In July 1997 a barrel of Oman crude fetched barely 20 dollars and in July 1998 only 12 dollars. In the same period - only one year - the budget deficit rose from 110 to 275 million dollars. The heavy dependency on the international price of oil, combined with Oman's comparatively limited oil reserves, forced the country to think about alternative means for the future. Since 2004, due to the Iraq war, the crisis of the Russian oil company Yukos, the weakness of the US dollar and other factors, the price of a barrel of oil rose to 65 dollars in 2007 for the first time, reaching its peak with an average price of 101 dollars in 2008 and dropping to 65 dollars in September 2009. According to the Minister of Oil and Gas, Oman needs an oil price of at least 55 dollars per barrel to balance its budget.

Compared with the oil reserves of other Arab states, Oman's estimated 5,8 billion barrels is decidedly modest. The government reckons that supplies could be exhausted in some 20 years. The United Arab Emirates, on the other hand, have reserves for at least another 100 years. Particular attention is now being paid to economic development in areas that are independent of the oil sector. In 1991 oil's share of GDP fell significantly below the 50% mark to 42.1%. In the north the millennia old tradition of copper production has been revitalised using ultra-modern technology. Two cement factories, several grain mills and a textile factory concentrate their production mostly on exports. In Rusayl an industrial estate for light industry has been established. Large plants for processing polyolefin and aluminum are being set up in Sohar. Increasingly the most important form of energy both at home and for export is natural gas. In 2003 reserves of natural gas stood at 25 trillion cubic feet, and new reserves are still being discovered. Power stations, desalination plants and energy intensive industries are gradually turning to natural gas as the preferred fuel. In 2000, on the coast between Qalhat and Sur, the largest liquefied natural gas (LNG) plants in the world went into service. The plant is served by its own transport terminal.

In 2002 6.5 million tons of liquid gas were exported from there. The main customers for the gas are South Korea, Japan, Spain and the USA. The dependency on oil is to be further reduced by developing other branches of the economy and thereby increasing their share of the national income. To this end investment is being made in agriculture, fishing, light industry, mining and service areas. The intention is to make the country as self-sufficient as possible. With new jobs for a well-educated youth the dependency on foreign experts will also be reduced. Here the emphasis is on skilled trades and technical jobs. 80% of a company's training costs are met by the state. The founding of new companies is also being promoted.

The days of the oil derricks are numbered

The main emphasis for investment, however, is on the opening up of the country's interior. The marked discrepancy between development in the area around Muscat and the rest of the country is to be reduced by major capital investment. The planned investment in less developed regions of the country, although undoubtedly important, makes some Omanis thoughtful. The contrast between the land's interior and the coastal towns is a fundamental part of the national identity. Modernization entailing a change in cultural values is something that has to be handled extremely sensitively.

The sixth Five Year Plan (2001 - 2005) based sustained development

increasingly on the private sector. As opposed to the fifth Five Year Plan, the share of private investment was to rise from 37.7% to 53.9%. The main emphasis of the sixth plan was on increasing the number of jobs for Omanis, guaranteeing stable personal incomes, increasing the number of students at universities and technical colleges, pursuing a sustainable financial policy and the promotion of economic diversification and expansion of the private sector.
The main areas for investment were the extension of the road network and further development of ports, energy and water supplies, home-building and tourism. The tourist trade was to be built up. Large new holiday resorts were planned or under construction. But the world economic crises also affected the Sultanate and some of those ambitious projects.
The Seventh Five Year Development Plan (2006-2010) aimed to speed up the process of diversifying the sources of national income by increasing non-oil activities. The development of human resources was another major priority of the Seventh Plan. Accordingly, major importance is being attached to education, health, the

"Beautification" is in the Eye of the Beholder

Whoever visits the country for the first time and drives the first hundred kilometers on one of the newly built highways which cross the land outside the Capital Region may be overwhelmed by Oman's countryside, by the elemental beauty of the strange rock formations, the colored rock deserts, the views of the sea or palm forests. But even at the start of the highway at the airport the visitor meets the first products of an artificial beautification program: alongside the highways and on the central areas of roundabouts can be seen decorative works in the form of fixed street furniture in which items of the country's folklore are either enlarged, shrunk, or copied to scale: concrete palms with concrete flower containers hanging from them, life-sized naturally-colored Arabian horses with bridles, long-spouted coffee jugs and curved daggers - *khanjars* - as big as a man, mounted on cubic or cylindrical plinths, a painted jug alone in the desert or a composition made up of fountains. Incense burners, wells complete with draught-oxen, native animals like the newly-reintroduced oryx antelope - all made out of concrete or plastic. On a rock plateau between Mutrah and Muscat can be found the *fata morgana* of a spaceship - snow-white between red-brown rocks above the blue-green sea in the Riyam Park. What reminds the European visitor of a recently landed UFO is actually a watchtower in the form of an incense burner. Here the principle of "beautification" has gone beyond the roadside and has created something to catch the eye for miles around. There are similar monumental showpieces in the middle of roundabouts in the Capital Region which serve to help one creation of employment opportunities for nationals and the further development of Omanization programs. It also aimed at the development of the information technology (IT) sector, the expansion of research and development to cover most sectors of the national economy, and further support for the Scientific Research Council . Omanis are rightly proud of their cultural and natural environments, which are not only sources of self esteem but also vital resources for the future of the country once the oil boom is over. Oman's tourism concept of quality rather than quantity aims at cultural tourism supported by educational travel. This concept could be endangered by investors simply interested in turning a quick profit. The quick money to be made by mass tourism has already seduced many elsewhere and led to the undermining of cultures. A seaside paradise on the Indian Ocean might be a worthy dream for many but could be a nightmare for Oman and its culture. However, as long as oil and gas can be exported and trade in the Capital Area flourishes, the tourism resource does not have to be exploited to the full extent.

Overleaf:
The mostly hand-embroidered caps, called *Kumma*, are only worn by Omanis living in villages and towns, not by Bedouin.

get one's bearings - in their eclectic mix of modern building materials and traditional motifs they make the Westerner think of postmodern design. Comparable motifs can be found along American highways or in museums: as western Pop Art.

Another form of "beautification" seems to be in pursuit of an age-old dream of paradise, the effect of which seems the more luxurious, the more remote it is from its surroundings of rock, sand and heat. The lifeless countryside is artificially brought to life. Water systems, installed and maintained by countless Indian laborers, allow strips of luxuriant vegetation to flourish alongside the highways between the surrounding karst and the asphalt surface. Here and there a man collects litter from the roadside. A waterfall gushes from a rock wall, triumphing over the crippling heat. Not far from the road is a ring of white limestone rocks forming a magic circle around stems of stunted acacias which have managed to survive in the rocky waste. And if someone has begun to build a house on a plot of land parallel to the road there will be a fence made up of white, door-shaped panels screening the building site.

The official decoration of the roadways is part of the state beautification program of the Diwan, the Sultanate's central authority which coordinates and finances such activities. On National Day in particular each town in which the ceremony takes place receives a beautification boost. Individual regions display motifs typical of the area. Sometimes in wide open countryside there may be nothing other than a fortress folly in miniature: a piece of wall between two turrets. It marks an old tribal frontier.

Prof. Dr. Thomas Zacharias

Traveling in Oman

Traveling in Oman you should always be prepared for the unexpected. If you go through the land with your senses alert, not constrained by the corset of a too rigid itinerary, but allowing yourself the leisure to encounter the small, apparently trivial things in daily life, then the country will make its own unforgettable impression on you. But if you race from sight to sight following a tight timetable and cut yourself off from the small details and everyday things happening around you, then you are bound to be disappointed. The most significant archaeological sites are hard to reach, being far away from the asphalt roads. The few finds that are easy to get to can hardly fulfill high expectations - in comparison with internationally renowned sites they stick out on account of their plainness. The ancient Omani architecture does not have the variety or magnificence of the Yemeni - it has a stark simplicity.

The culture of Oman lacks all grandeur, arrogance and brashness. But it is just this which makes the country such an unusual destination, giving the visitor the chance to escape the world of hectic activity and striving to once more feel human, to appreciate the world with sharpened senses. To be in Oman is to see colors and to smell scents, to sense the horizon, to physically experience extreme contrasts, to get the feeling of losing oneself in unending landscapes. The fine sense of feeling in the fingertips, almost atrophied for many Westerners, can be brought back to life. Civilized eating with the fingers is an unimaginably difficult art for most people. But many things taste better if the fingers have first felt what the tongue and stomach are about to receive.

Oman exudes inner calm, composure and an openness to what is foreign; these characteristics offer a great incentive not only to travel around unknown Oman but also to really experience the life there. If you have an interest in ecology and natural habitats you will be pleased to know you share one of Sultan Qaboos's abiding childhood passions. The needs of natural conservation have been embedded in the country's laws and Sultan Qaboos also sponsors the prestigious Sultan Qaboos Prize for Environmental Preservation awarded yearly by UNESCO. Nature reserves have been established in Oman's many varied habitats and Oman is a favorite destination for bird spotters the world over, due to the many species of migratory birds stopping off in the lagoons of southern Oman before completing their journeys between Europe and Africa. The excellent roads and hotels allow the modern traveler to explore the various regions of the country without danger. Road signs are almost always in two languages, Arabic and English. The English spelling of streets and villages used in this publication in general follows the newly approved names list of the National Survey Authority (N.S.A.) which reflects the most accurate transliteration of Arabic names. These may differ slightly from the actual spellings seen on street signs or other maps. Examples for this are "Al Udhaybah" and "Ras Al Jinz" (the approved spellings) which are seen on signposts as "Azaibah" and "Ras al Ginz."

As you drive along you will note that places of tourist and cultural interest are indicated with brown road signs, and it is often warranted to spontaneously stop at these sites to investigate further. As every wise traveler knows, serendipity is the greatest reward. However, getting off the beaten track and into areas which are difficult for strangers to visit is not a prerequisite for a happy adventure, and you don't have to risk hair-raising tours to remote deserts and wadis to get to know Oman. The principle roads may lead to the various regions of the country, and each region may be a world unto itself, but the daily life and landscapes one encounters in the least accessible areas of the country are barely different from those in the more accessible areas. You just need to keep your senses alert and be prepared to make your own discoveries wherever you happen to be.

On the Road in the Sultanate

In many respects Oman is a fascinating country. It is a land of strong contrasts. Omanis have to be alert to maintain the careful balancing act between the traditional and the modern. Foreigners can come to understand and experience this situation if they are prepared to put themselves in the current, none too easy, position of Omanis. This is possible if they concern themselves not just with what is photogenic, but also with the achievements of a young country in becoming modern and its attendant problems. Behind the modern facades of new houses much of the old, traditional community way of life has been preserved - especially in rural areas. Omanis are very friendly in their manner and are very open to the few tourists who visit their country. They will often greet the visitor with a raised open hand, the ancient sign for peaceful intent (i.e. showing that they are not holding a weapon.) They expect a similar greeting or gesture in response - a first, and important, step in approaching the culture in which one is a guest. Refusing a greeting is understood as a deliberate act of rejection and is taken as a personal insult. Up until the change of rule in 1970 foreigners

were the sole source of information from the outside world. Even now news conveyed by individuals is valued more than the reports of the mass media. After the usual courteous formalities, the "How are you?" and the "Where do you come from?" often comes the seriously-intended question, "What's new in the world?" Even in remote areas there is a great interest in foreign affairs. Answering such questions seriously is a sign of courtesy and respect. You may then be pleasantly surprised to be invited to an extended chat and offered coffee and dates.

There are particular rules of conduct associated with the ancient rituals of hospitality of which the visitor is well to be aware. You sit together on mats on the ground, either in the open air or in the reception room of the house. As a rule you should remove your shoes before entering an Arabic home, however luxurious or simple the household may be. How you sit on the floor is unimportant but you should be careful not to present the soles of the feet to another person as this is considered most impolite. Coffee is drunk out of small porcelain cups with just enough for a good mouthful. A European who is used to drinking a liter of coffee each day will be tempted to take ten or more of these mini portions. Etiquette decrees however that you should stop after no more than three cups, and emphatically refuse further offers by saying "No, thank you – la, shukran" and by shaking the cup as you give it back. Any further offers to take another cup are purely rhetorical. Another *faux pas* to be avoided is asking to see the other rooms of a house. The purpose of a reception room consists in keeping guests from invading one's private sphere. To be shown around the house is to be taken into the family. If you are invited to eat then the rule is to eat with the right hand. Left-handed people can declare themselves an exception and reverse the rule. Anyone familiar with Arabic lavatories will know why the left hand is considered unclean.

Even though many places appear abandoned and deserted, you will meet people everywhere.

If you are traveling in the country's interior, please be sure not to wear clothing offensive to Muslims, only photograph people after obtaining their express permission, do not leave litter anywhere and above all do nothing that could pollute any of the water distribution channels. In Oman water is the source of life. It is used for irrigating fields, for drinking and for cooking, for ritual cleansing before prayer and for washing and bathing. Fresh water is a most precious commodity in a land with little rainfall.

If you are tactful in your curiosity and encounter this many-faceted culture with sensitivity and respect, then this Islamic land, like many others, will be an enriching experience.

Muscat – the Capital Area

The region known today as the "Capital Area" covers a length of 50 kilometers from As Seeb in the west to the Shangri-La's Barr Al Jissah Resort & Spa in the east. The built-up areas are bounded to the north by the coastline and to the south by the Hajar mountains, whose cliffs reach to the sea in the east. In a small bay, boxed in by sheer cliff-faces, is the historic port of Muscat which has lent its name to the whole area. Up to 1970, together with Mutrah, situated in the adjoining bay, and a few small, insignificant oases, this was the only inhabited part of the current Capital Area. After the change of government, the area was developed at breakneck speed from a desert landscape with bays and cliffs to a modern capital city. This transformation has been chronicled by the German Professor of Geography, Fred Scholz. In minute detail he and his students documented every change, every reform and every deviation from what was originally planned. The countless details found their way into his monumental book, *Muscat*, a 500-page study of the development of the Capital Area after 1970.

The Sultan Qaboos Grand Mosque is one of the highpoints of architecture in the country.

The first tentative development plans had been made under Sultan Said bin Taimur at the end of the 1960s, after the first modest oil revenues began to flow in. These plans had little in common with what was set in train after 1970. The old building regulations allowed for the reconstruction of damaged or collapsed houses, so long as they were rebuilt using the original materials and rejected any more radical urban regeneration. The coastal settlements were still to be characterized by palm branch huts.

This changed almost instantly with the change of government in 1970. Before the year was out the English firm of John R. Harris, Architects, Design and Planning Consultants, had presented a plan for land utilization for the Capital Area, which, apart from a few changes in detail, was for the most part realized. Today Muscat is seen as a unique example of modern town planning and by the end of the 20th century it had been transformed from a medieval port into a modern metropolis ready for the twenty-first century. Problems resulting from such a rapid development are of course unavoidable, but these only demonstrate that a town is a living organism, developing organically, and not a vast, sterile, architectural model.

Muscat is a child of the 1970s, with all its enthusiasm for the automobile. Alongside the construction of a car-friendly metropolis, the number of cars registered in Oman rapidly rose from 9726 in 1975 to 87,582 in 1983. This expansion has continued unbroken right up to the present day. Between 1975 and 2007 Toyota sold more than 700,000 vehicles in Oman. In 2005 not only were 40,000 new driving licenses issued, but also 9247 accidents involving injury to persons were registered, half of these in greater Muscat alone. In 2008 Oman had the world's highest per capita mortality rate for automobile accidents in the world. Sadly traffic jams and accidents are now part of daily life on the roads of Oman's capital. This should be taken into account when planning journeys where appointments have to be kept, or for instance when reckoning the time it may take to get to the airport. In order to mitigate the situation a number of new roads and several new highways are currently being built, which makes it easy to lose one's bearings, even for natives of the city.

The various town districts line the main highway, the Sultan Qaboos Road, as in an oversized street village. Every 5 kilometers or so a roundabout provides an opportunity to leave the highway, change direction, or to get the feel of one's location in the town. The roundabouts are an important means of orientation within Muscat. Each one has its own name and its own visual characteristics. Filled with enthusiasm for the car, no one spared even a thought for the pedestrian. Guest workers and poorer people who cannot afford their own car use bus taxis. They let the driver drop them near one of the large shopping centers, for example the Al Harthy Complex at the Al Qurm roundabout, and then in order to get there they first have to cross four lanes, packed with fast-moving traffic: the Omani version of Russian roulette. The highway is 50 kilometers long with very few underpasses and bridges for pedestrians.

The architectural development of this huge area is by no means finished, and new buildings are constantly edging into any remaining open spaces, slowly but inexorably. At the beginning of the 1970s the buildings had a somewhat improvised quality. Many *barastis*, the palm huts, were replaced by cement houses or corrugated-iron huts. Returning exiles from all over the world were accommodated in uninspiring small prefab houses. In the mid-1970s came the first buildings to reflect traditional characteristics of Omani architecture. The traditional clay architecture with its rounded walls, embrasures, latticed windows, courtyards, roof terraces and reception rooms, called *majlis*, was adapted and re-interpreted using modern building materials.

This basic idea of architectural quotation also found its way into the new building regulations which are still in force today. Builders are given considerable latitude in the matter of design. The only requirement is that they include "elements of traditional style." This regulation allows the most varied interpretations and combinations of materials, forms and colors. In Muscat a nation is playfully seeking a modern language of form which nonetheless relates to native tradition. Meanwhile, some elements and buildings have been copied throughout the country and so set a trend for the future, while others have remained one-offs, bearing witness to the builder's individual imagination. The colorful mixture of historicized new buildings is certainly not to everyone's taste. It does, however, reflect the varied and imaginative ways in which a people are setting about creating a national identity, and is a noble experiment in times characterized by bland mass architecture.

The Capital Area is certainly the product of urban planning ambition, but the underlying principles are not always clear. Topographical givens, already existing buildings, and the various interests of the decision-makers require accommodation rather than the enforcement of fixed ideas. Nonetheless some principles can be discerned: the Capital Area runs along an axis between the historic towns of Muscat in the east and As Seeb in the west.

In Muscat there is the Sultan's palace and in As Seeb another of the ruler's estates. At both of these termini industrial and trading areas are situated leading towards the center. In the west there is the airport and in the east the ports for goods and oil. In the center residential and governmental districts mingle with industrial and business estates.

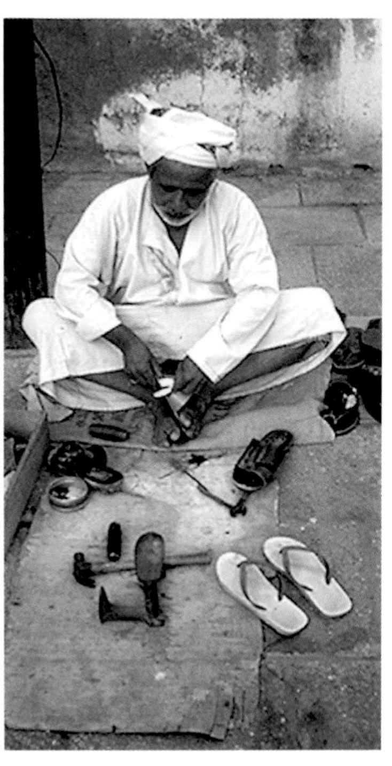

Cottage industry: a cobbler in the As Seeb suq.

The Capital Area combines the most varied aspects of life in Oman, for example leisure, business and administration, with coming to terms with its own history. In the following chapters, a closer look at the individual districts will throw light on their differences and functions. The contours of the town, too large to be taken in as a whole on a common city map, will become clearer, allowing the visitor to fully appreciate what he is seeing.

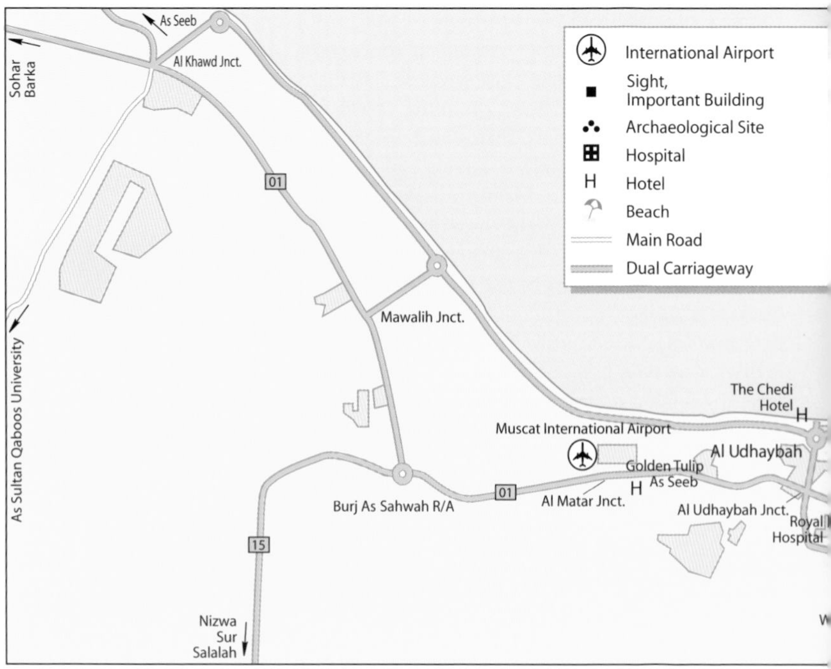

A Trip to As Seeb – Getting Your Bearings

At the start of a stay in Muscat, it is worth taking a trip from Ruwi in the east to As Seeb in the west. This will help you to get your bearings within the Capital Area and give you a feel for the distances and contrasts within the country. The excursion will also give you a first overview of the various parts of the Capital Area and their characteristics. The liveliest is the small village of As Seeb, the highpoint of the excursion when, in the late afternoon or on Friday morning, the suq is most frequented. Coming from the east on the four-lane city highway, regardless which direction you take from the Ruwi roundabout, you will reach Al Qurm after making a large loop around the Ruwi Heights. The northern route brings you via the Bayt al Falaj roundabout, past the Mutrah turn-off, to the oil port of Mina al Fahl, north of the highway, where the company grounds of "Petroleum Development Oman," PDO for short, are located.

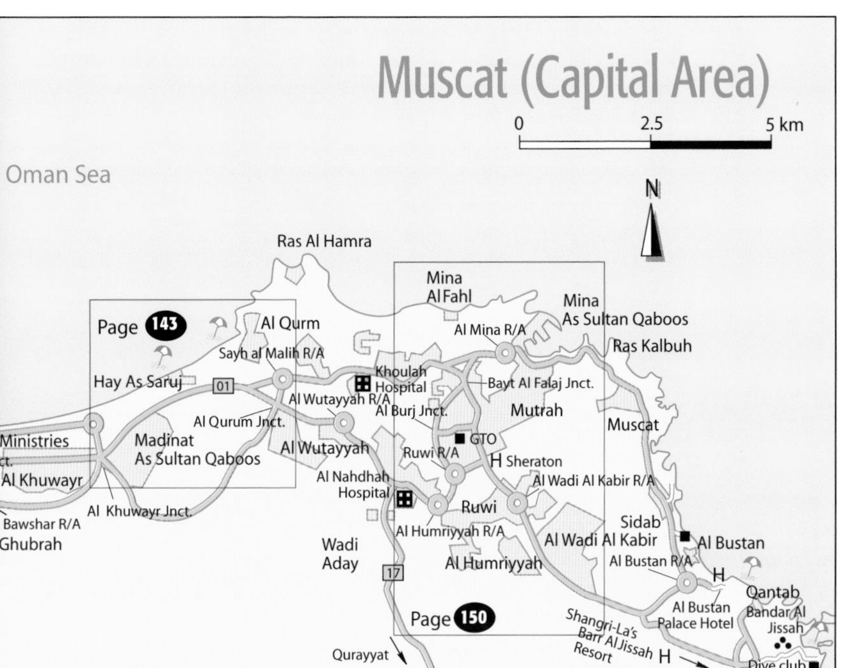

Next comes the residential area of the Al Qurm Heights, one of the most sought-after addresses. At the Sayh al Malih roundabout, you can turn off to Al Qurm's nature reserve, park and beach. The landscape of the southern route from Ruwi to Al Qurm is not so attractive. It leads past the turn-off to Qurayyat, the Wadi Adaj roundabout, to the Al Qurm roundabout where the largest cluster of shopping centers is located. The northern and southern routes join after the Al Qurm roundabout. Another two kilometers beyond the entrance to the Muscat Intercontinental Hotel, to the north of the main road you can see two dome-shaped buildings, one of which is the **Children's Museum**. The Al Khuwayr roundabout has exits to the new highway to Ghala and for the government ministries, the embassy quarter, the new Grand Hyatt hotel and the popular beach promenade of Shati Al Qurm. In recent years Muscat's most exclusive quarter has developed alongside this promenade. The buildings are in modern Arabic style and are well worth a closer look. West of the roundabout, on the north side of the city highway, the government ministries are strung like pearls. Each bears its individual architectural stamp. The **Natural History Museum** is located within the Ministry of National Heritage and Culture complex. It provides a good insight into the flora, fauna and geology of Oman. In the autumn of 2007 the **Sayyid Faisal Bin Ali Museum** was sensitively integrated into a former theater on the same site. A small space is cleverly used to host a display illustrating the development of weaponry in the country from the Stone Age up to the 20th century, as well as an overview of the most important of the clay fortresses.

Northwest of the Al Ghubbrah roundabout, near the coast, you can

The Sultan Qaboos Grand Mosque

Built alongside the main road, the Sultan Qaboos Grand Mosque is today one of the most important monuments in the country. In 1992 the Sultan ordered the building of a mosque, which should be the largest in the land. In 1993 the contract was awarded to the team of architects Mohamed Saleh Makiya and Quad Design (London and Muscat.) Building began in the spring of 1995 and the building was officially opened on May 4, 2001. The site of the mosque covers an area of 416,000 square meters and stretches for one kilometer along Sultan Qaboos Street. Along with the buildings there are also beautiful gardens with fountains which are a delight to the eye. Following ancient Omani tradition, the complex is built on raised earthworks so that the base of the building is above the neighboring ground level. The main entrance is to the south and leads through three tall arches to the main minaret. The perspective - looking through the arches, following a line of dark marble set in the ground - has the effect of making the minaret seem even higher than its 91.5 meters. The remaining four minarets, each with a height of 45 meters, complete the symmetry at the corners of the rectangular complex. The five minarets symbolize the five pillars of Islam.

The visitors' entrance leads through a block, to the left of which is the Islamic Studies Center with its extensive library. Next to this is a large court where the main building stands. During the Eid festivals and the fasting month of Ramadan up to 14,000 believers can pray here in the open air. Non-Muslims are only allowed into the main prayer building to the left of the atrium and some of the foyers. Please ensure you pay attention to the notice boards and only enter the mosque with covered arms and legs. Women should wear headscarves. The main prayer hall is entered through a square atrium at the foot of the main minaret. Before entering shoes should be removed and placed on the racks provided at the side of the entrance. Passing through an immense wooden portal, you come into what must be the most aesthetically impressive room in Oman. The hall, 61 by 71 meters, can hold 6000 believers at prayer.

see the large seawater desalination plant, the heart of Muscat's water supply system. West of the Al Udhaybah roundabout, the newly-built **Sultan Qaboos Grand Mosque** reaches up to the heavens. It is the only mosque in Oman which is open to non-Muslim visitors. It took six years to complete the mosque and a visit is definitely a highlight of any journey to Oman.

Beyond the airport and the Al Sahwa roundabout, with its imposing clock tower, the main road makes a wide curve to the north. This roundabout also serves as the most important entry point to the interior of Oman. The road which branches off here leads to Nizwa, the

The floor is covered in a carpet which is 4263 square meters in size, a masterpiece of Persian carpet weaving, both a logistic and an artistic triumph.

The design and preparatory work alone took 15 months. 600 weavers from the east Persian province of Kurashan worked for a further 27 months to complete the 58 sections made up of altogether 1.7 billion knots. The detailed finishing work and the fitting of the 21 ton carpet took another four months. The floral and geometrical pattern combines the stylistic traditions of Tabris, Isfahan and Kashan. The wool was dyed with plant extracts mixed according to traditional recipes.

The precious carpet has its optical counterpart in the wooden ceiling, decorated lavishly with calligraphic designs and arabesques. The room is crowned by a 34 meter high dome, the splendor and elegance of which is unsurpassable. In the center hangs a chandelier made of Swarowsky crystal, its 1122 lamps lending the dome a magical aura. The chandelier has a diameter of eight meters, is 14 meters high and, together with its gilded steel frame, weighs eight tons. It is made up of individual pendants which mirror the form of the whole chandelier and which, despite its immensity, give an impression of lightness. It was designed by the Munich company of Faustig.

The pillars and walls of the hall are in plain white and grey marble, making a discreet setting for the splendor of the stained glass windows and the prayer niches, or *mihrabs*, with their painted tiles.

Apart from the prayer hall it is worth taking a stroll along the covered walkways. These have niches explaining the various stylistic motifs drawn from the whole Islamic world. You can also marvel at the richly ornamented designs of the exterior walls of the various buildings. The quiet but richly detailed architecture manages to take the highly differing styles of Islamic tradition from various epochs and integrate them into a harmonious whole. This design principle of the Sultan Qaboos Grand Mosque is symbolic of an ideal of Omani society: to bring the various Islamic traditions under the roof of Ibadhism, and to do this peacefully.

(open Saturday to Thursday Mornings, from 08:00 to 11:00)

ancient royal seat, to Sur in the east, and to Salalah in the south. All the bus taxis also go from here to the country's interior. After the Al Mawalih roundabout you pass the residential area of Al Hayl. The mountains recede into the distance to the south, the Al Batinah coastal plain gradually opens up, and the land becomes more fertile. Sea breezes provide a welcome coolness. The Al Khowd roundabout is also known locally as the "University roundabout;" here a road branches off to the Sultan Qaboos University. Continue along the main road to the northwest and follow the Al Batinah coastline, through Barka, to Sohar. Turn off to the right towards the northeast, and after a few kilometers along Al Adiyat Road, you reach the small coastal town of As Seeb.

The road to As Seeb winds past extensive, wall-enclosed plantations. The largest belongs to the Sultan, who, in addition to his palace in Muscat, has an estate here in As Seeb. Follow the road straight ahead, past a roundabout, past the royal stables on the right-hand side to a T-junction. Turn right here and Wadi al Bahais Street leads to **As Seeb**. As you enter the town you will see many shops, furniture dealers and restaurants. The further you enter into the town, the busier the streets and squares become. Here, at the western extremity of the Capital Area, As Seeb has developed into a lively local center. People here are not so dependent on the motor car, and the town lends itself to exploration on foot.

Vegetables
in the As Seeb suq.

The large **suq**, with its lanes, is not so enclosed as the one in Mutrah. It runs between the main thoroughfare and the coast. Its atmosphere permeates the whole area, especially in the late afternoon, evening and on Fridays, when the market takes place. In small restaurants you can eat simple and good grilled dishes. Glance over at the frame makers with their well-sorted stock of art prints, among them Black Forest landscapes, clowns and, of course, numerous portraits of Sultan Qaboos. Behind them plumbing merchants have a fascinating and exotic selection of sinks and tap fittings on show. Traders sit in any free space in the suq with a variety of wares: *khanjars,* the Omani curved daggers, tobacco, vegetables, even rifles. Cobblers carry out major repairs on the spot; while you wait they simply lend you a pair of sandals so that you can continue shopping. Near the street and the great mosque, haberdashers and tailors ply their trade; next to them are shops dealing in groceries, spices and household goods. The resident butchers and fruit and vegetable traders occupy their own walled area.

On Friday mornings the square in front of it, near the coast, is taken over by small traders offering a range of goods from vegetables to cows and dried fish. Until 1996 the returning fisherman would unload their catch directly onto the beach in front of the

market. Today, about half a kilometer north of this spot, there is a newly-built fish market. The fishermen sell their catches here. The market is tiled and each noon, after closing time, the tiles are spotlessly cleaned. The new market has led to a marked improvement in hygiene.
If you don't wish to travel by highway, then return to Muscat along the newly built roads running alongside the Indian Ocean. They lead from the market area to the new As Seeb Corniche, past the airport to Al Udhaybah and from there to the ministries in Al Khuwayr and further on to Al Qurm.

Al Qurm – from the Stone Age into the Oil Age

Leave the main road at the Al Qurm roundabout, head north in the direction of the coast, and after a few hundred meters on the left you reach the entrance to **Al Qurm Park**. Like all the green areas in the capital, this public park is a popular destination for Omani families on weekends, i.e. Thursday and Friday, and on warm evenings. The boating lake with its magnificent fountains in the middle of the park and Waterfall Hill make up the main attractions. Both are at their most impressive at night, when they are colorfully illuminated. For desert dwellers this is undoubtedly a spectacular sight. Visitors from Europe and the United States are more impressed by the **Al Qurm Nature Reserve**, directly adjoining the park to the west.
The Al Qurm Nature Reserve comprises extensive wetlands at the mouth of Wadi Aday. Densely populated with mangroves, the area is green all year round, and lends itself to the name of the district: "Al Qurm" means "fertile garden." The protected area itself cannot be entered but follow the road to Al Qurm Beach and by taking a stroll along the coast road at ebb tide you will get an interesting view of the biotope.
The wetlands are made of clay and mud from the country's interior which have been deposited here in the estuary area and augmented by lime from seashells and sand. Before plants can colonize the mud, biological processes have to convert algae and bacteria into a culture or medium suitable for growth. These processes release fermentation gases which visitors with sensitive noses will immediately detect. At low tide, around each mangrove you can see a thick network of tubes rising vertically out of the mud. These 'snorkels' provide the roots, hidden in the mud, with oxygen. Keeping quiet

PDO – Petroleum Development Oman

The oil business is still the driving force behind the development of the Sultanate of Oman. In 2005 oil revenue constituted 70 percent of the state's income, even if its share of the Gross Domestic Product was "only" 40 percent. Petroleum Development Oman Ltd. (PDO) first discovered oil in commercially significant quantities in 1964 near Fuhud, close to the Saudi Arabian border. As early as 1925 the Iraq Petroleum Company had received a concession from Sultan Taimur. In 1937 the concession was transferred to the PDO, the main shareholder of which was the Royal Dutch/Shell group. Other major shareholders were the Compagnie Française des Petroles (later TotalFina-Elf), the Anglo-Persian Company (later BP) and Partex. In 1974 the Omani state became the main shareholder, acquiring a 60 percent shareholding. In recent years the granting of concessions to Elf Aquitaine (France), Occidental (America) and Japex (Japan) has weakened PDO's monopoly, but only moderately. In 2001 the PDO accounted for 90 percent of the daily production of 840,000 barrels (1 barrel is 159 liters, or 35 imperial gallons.) Output was reduced during the following years by about 10 percent. This was partly due to technical problems but also due to diminishing stocks. By 2010 the old production rates should be reached as a result of new old fields expected to be found through increased exploration. The main customers for Omani oil, of which 90 percent is exported, are Japan and China; the rest is also exported almost without exception to Asian countries such as Taiwan, Korea and Thailand.

The oil is pumped through a central pipeline from the country's interior and from south Oman. The pipeline ends in the port of Mina al Fahl in Muscat. The precious raw material's route takes it across the entire country. In addition to covering enormous distances, the pipeline has to overcome the massive natural barrier of the Hajar Mountains, following the Sumail Gap along the road to Nizwa. Near Muscat it climbs the mountains and is stored in large tanks whence it flows under its own power to the loading stations in the harbor. PDO not only guarantees the greater part of the state's income but also provides support for the Sultan's educational policies. It is own educational institution guarantees the rapid Omanization of the company. On average some 700 of the company's Omanis participate in various educational programs both at home and abroad. In 1993 Omanis made up 65 percent of the staff: 45 percent in management positions. Today some 90 percent of the workforce is Omani.

and exercising a little patience, you can watch the varied fauna of the nature reserve. Male fiddler crabs, with one oversized white claw, resurface from their burrows in the tidal zone. During the mating season they give any approaching female an unmistakable wave with their imposing claw.

The wetland biotope also serves as a nursery for numerous birds, fish and insects, among them butterflies. Numerous species of mussels and oysters are also native to this habitat. More than 5000 years ago this source of food also attracted another creature - man. This has been confirmed by archaeological finds on the neighboring peninsula. Today the Muscat Crowne Plaza Hotel, surrounded by numerous other new buildings, dominates the peninsula of Ras Al Hamra. In 1977 and in the early 1980s, during the various building operations, archaeologists found about 10 heaps of shell fragments, ashes, bones and sand: prehistoric "rubbish heaps" which had grown over hundreds of years. In the adjoining settlements post holes were found in the ground, relics of buildings on stilts, as well as many graves. The scientists established seven distinct layers covering the period between 3500 BC and 2800 BC. Together with the latest finds south of Sur, these are the oldest traces of human settlement in Oman. In the simple, oval graves the researchers found the remains of eighty people buried lying on their right sides with drawn up legs. Simple burial objects in the form of necklaces, earrings and armbands, made from shells and steatite, accompanied the dead. No traces of ceramics were found. The number of fragments of turtle shells and turtle bones lead to the conclusion that these creatures played a role in a cult of the dead. Stone tools and fishhooks fashioned from seashells provide an insight into a simple hunter and gatherer way of life based around these mangrove swamps. Today almost nothing remains to be seen of these excavations, the whole site having now been almost completely built over.

Follow the same road back in the direction of the roundabout and, shortly before it, bear left into Seih Al Malih Street and at the end you will come to the main gate of the half public-owned Omani oil company "Petroleum Development Oman" (PDO.) To the right of the gate a comparatively small but excellently-presented and very informative company museum is to be found in the **Oil and Gas Exhibition Center**. It provides information about the history of oil production in Oman, oil processing and about "black gold" itself. Next to the Exhibition Center is a **Planetarium**, inaugurated on the occasion of Oman's 30th National Day.

A visit is only possible by prior arrangement by telephone. *(Movie screening: Wednesday 17:00, Thursday 10:00 and 11:00, Tel.: 24675542)*

If you want to experience more about the life of people in this country, it is worth making a visit to the newly redesigned ethnographic **Museum of Omani Heritage**, formerly known as the Oman Museum, which is situated three kilometers southwest of the Al Qurm roundabout on Al Alam Street behind the Ministry of Information. The ground floor outlines the development of the traditional ways of life of fisherman, craftsmen and farmers. The numerous exhibits - archaeological finds, photos and graphics, all

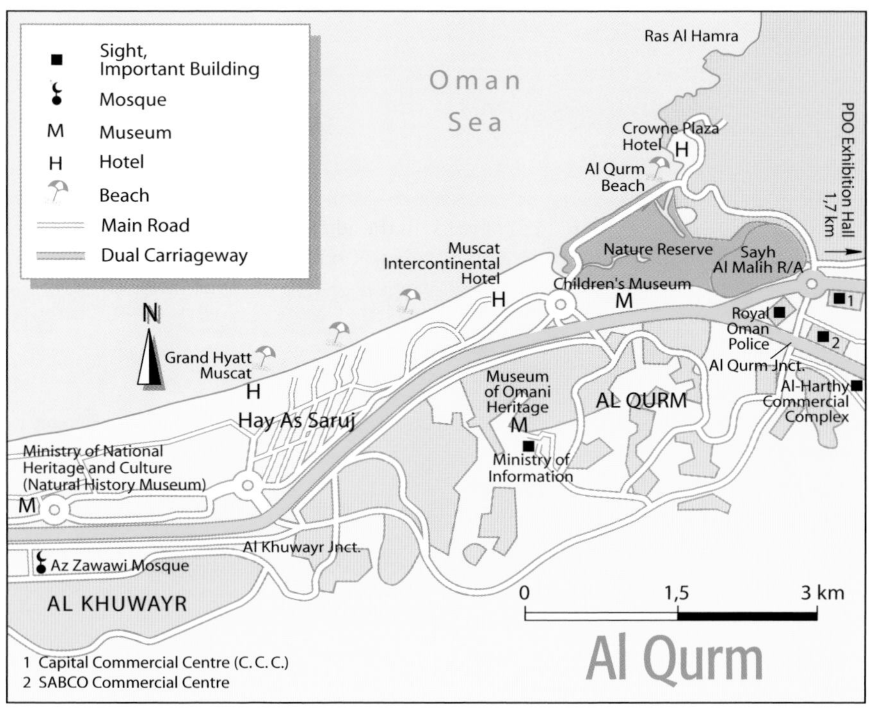

accompanied by short but informative texts in English - together form a collection which provides an impressive picture of living conditions in Oman over the last 5000 years.

The rooms on the first floor focus on private life - you wander through the lifecycle of people in this country from birth to old age, experiencing much about the rituals and customs on life's journey and you can familiarise yourself with the associated symbols and artifacts. Much of what the traveler in this country experiences as strange and unknown, but also as seemingly familiar, is described and explained in this museum. *(open Saturday to Wednesday 8:30-13:30, October to March also 16:00-18:00)*

144/145: Modern Arab architecture at Al Qurm.

At the next roundabout, the Al Khuwayr roundabout, turn off in the direction of the coast, and you'll come to the most luxurious district of Muscat, Shati Al Qurm, and to the Muscat Grand Hyatt, which is well worth seeing.

The Fairytale Palace of Sheikh Ahmad Farid

For five years there was an enormous construction site, with a multi-storeyed building between the luxurious villas along the beach at Shati Al Qurm. Progress was slow but steady and gradually the building grew to completion. In its drive to expand, it subsumed the extant roads leading to surrounding buildings. Suddenly you would find to your consternation that a concrete wall was now barring what had till now been a through road. Everybody felt that something huge was emerging but no one knew exactly what. All that was certain, was that it had something to do with a hotel. After its completion in 1998 the Sultanate of Oman was richer to the tune of one luxury hotel, a dream palace with a fairytale story. Construction consumed the unheard-of investment sum of more than 125 million Euros. However this is not, as some might suspect, the result of an oil state's showy extravagance. The Grand Hyatt Muscat, run by the Hyatt Regency hotel group, is to date one of the largest privately-funded investments made in Oman. It is a clear sign that the wealthy of Oman are prepared to invest their profits not abroad, but in their own country. This was one of the main demands of Sultan Qaboos when he designated 1998 the "Year of the Private Sector."

With its 280 rooms it is one of the largest hotels in the country. It is the dream palace of Sheikh Ahmad Farid made real. Sheikh Ahmad Farid is himself not an Omani but stems from the ruling house of Yemen, where he was born. The monarchy in Yemen came to an end with the victory of the communist-leaning groups in the civil war between North and South Yemen in 1969.

It was at this time that Ahmad Farid fled to Oman. After completing his studies at Cambridge, he enlisted in the Omani army, then engaged in fighting in Dhofar against communist guerrilla troops from Yemen.

After the war in Dhofar came to an end, he remained in Oman, founding a construction company, which in the following years developed into the largest and most profitable in the region. Having sole responsibility for all decisions, the Sheikh was able to ensure that his personal vision was realized. No shoddy compromises between competing property developers had to be arrived at. The singularity of his vision is clearly apparent.

His intention was to combine the cultural characteristics of Yemen with those of Oman without detracting from the placement of both cultures in the global context of the outgoing millennium.

Stylistic features of both cultures meet in the external façade. Colossal reliefs of Omani silver jewelry are embedded in the sandstone façades with their typically Yemeni white, stepped walls decorating the roof edges. Enter the building through the main entrance and you will hardly believe your eyes. Compared to the splendor and opulence of the lobby, the lobby of the Al Bustan Palace, the government-built hotel and Oman's previous fairytale palace, seems like the sober nave of a gothic church. There is not a single square meter which is not decorated in one form or another. The richly ornamented treasury of motifs covers all surfaces, whether in white and gold stucco work, as paintings or in the variegated marble inlaid flooring. Guests sit at small tables under palm trees and canopies resembling Bedouin tents, drinking the best Italian cappuccino and nibbling at select homemade Swiss confectionery. The room is dominated by the heroic statue of an Arab rider with a falcon surrounded by fountains. The product of an Italian sculpture studio, your eye is continually drawn to it without your being able to explain why. Only after some time do you realize that the statue is not in fact static but is almost imperceptibly rotating so that its aspect is slowly but constantly changing. The sky, as represented in the gold-decorated dome changes gradually from black to deep blue with twinkling stars. A vast glass frontage gives an unbroken view over the hotel grounds to the sea beyond. Even this is decorated at the edges with motifs from the treasure chests of both countries, done in lead glazing. At its foot are more fountains with a row of life-size bronze heads of oryx antelopes.

Bronze bowls of fire atop pillars line the way to the outdoor pool and to the entrance gate. Wherever your gaze roams it alights upon an abundant show of splendor and magnificence, which is almost overwhelming. Happily the client for whom the building was made had the courage to employ an Italian firm for the interior decoration which has balanced oriental opulence with modern Italian art and design.

Apart from the obligatory portrait of the Sultan, the colors of which harmonize wonderfully with the rest of the room, the paintings are restricted to contemporary abstract and graphic works which provide a welcome contrast to their environment and allow for an interesting cultural interplay. The high quality of the selected works makes the Grand Hyatt the only "museum" of contemporary European art in Oman. Italian design is also on show in the very spacious hotel rooms.

The walls are decorated with contemporary art and splendid small format black and white photographs with Omani themes. Italian designer lamps illuminate the rooms.

The cupboards, tables and chairs combine wood and metal and were designed in Italy especially for the building. Small formal details of Arabic ornamentation combine with the overall concept to give the rooms the unity of complete works of art.

The hotel's decoration gives an insight into the world of Sheikh Ahmad Farid's imagination. The hotel bar "John Barry" reflects his hobby, treasure hunting. The USS John Barry was a liberty ship sunk by a U-boat off the coast of Oman in 1944, and alleged to have silver treasure aboard. An account of the event is given in the book "Stalin's Silver" by John Beasant. The Sheikh financed the finding and raising of the ship in the mid 1990s. The treasure really was on board and consisted of silver coins which had been minted in America for the Saudi ruler Abdul Aziz bin Saud. A number of the recovered coins were laboriously worked into the bar's wooden counter and covered with plastic resin to prevent theft. The reception for the official opening with guests from all over the Gulf region caused something of a scandal. The coins were engraved with a symbol for Mecca. The Saudi Arabian guests were shocked to see such a religious symbol in such close conjunction with high proof alcohol. So the coins were even more laboriously extracted from the bar and replaced with international small change, giving quite a strange impression. In a small room adjoining the bar the guest can find more pictures and newspaper cuttings about the successful salvage.

The lobby of Sheikh Ahmad Farid's hotel palace has to be seen to be believed.

The Royal Oman Symphony Orchestra

Sultan Qaboos loves classical music, above all Mozart, so it is hardly surprising that by 1985 he had already decided to found a national symphony orchestra. However he didn't simply engage foreign music professionals, but decided to establish an orchestra made up of Omanis - still unique in the Arab world. At this time, however, there was simply no one in the whole country who could play a suitable instrument, even rudimentally. The first step was to scour the country and seek out musically gifted children and give them the opportunity to attend a boarding school where, alongside normal lessons, a musical instrument would be taught. After graduating from school those who had really developed into musicians were not sent to Europe or America for further studies but were taught by highly-qualified teachers specifically brought to the Sultanate for the purpose. The intention was to prevent the young musicians spending their most impressionable years abroad and thus running the risk of losing touch with their own culture. Over the years the children of 1985 and thereafter have grown into an orchestra fit to be taken seriously. The first performances took place in the Sultan's private circle - he even liked to conduct them himself - before they ventured before the Omani public. The concerts given in the Al Bustan Palace Hotel were primarily attended by foreigners living in the country. At the beginning of the new millennium there followed appearances in the Gulf Region and in 2006 before invited guests of UNESCO in Paris. In 2007 the orchestra performed for the first time in front of the critical and musically pampered followers of classical music in Europe at the Young Euro Classic festival as part of the European Music Summer in Berlin.

August 10, 2007 was to be a memorable day for both musicians and public. The Berlin Konzerthaus was full to the rafters, with *Deutschlandradio* broadcasting the event live. As the orchestra took up their positions the public first saw female musicians in Omani national costume - bright green dress, red headscarf and gold head jewelry. It may also have been a novelty for many that the young women were represented in all sections of the orchestra including percussion. They were not restricted, as in many European orchestras, to string instruments, flutes and harp. Women even made up the majority in the brass section.

The initial nervousness of the musicians before the gigantic backdrop of the full concert hall was soon replaced by the sheer joy of performing as they registered that the audience were responding to their playing with increasing fascination and enthusiasm. The program was carefully chosen. Shostakovich's *Festive Overture* in A Major Op. 96 was followed by the *Andalusian Suite* for oud and orchestra by Marcel Khalife, who himself performed as soloist. The work, composed in 2002, uniquely combines the western tradition of classical music with Arab lute playing.

After the interval came *Shanti Priya* for Indian violin and orchestra composed and performed by Dr. Subramaniam, the Paganini of Indian classical music. Spellbound, the auditorium followed his virtuoso violin playing, which he performed not standing but sitting cross-legged on the floor, the body of the instrument tucked under his chin and the neck of the violin propped on the floor of the podium.

Impression taken at the concert in Berlin in August 2007.

The work mostly used ragas of southern Indian musical tradition, which combined with the orchestra, were woven into a musical structure.
As if the evening hadn't offered enough in the way of novelty and excitement, the official part of the concert was brought to an end with a composition by the young Omani Hamdan Al Shuaily, *The Blessed Renaissance*, in which he used musical means to reflect the rapid development of the state of Oman from 1970 to the present day. The work, written for a large symphony orchestra with great feeling, combines traditional Omani folk music with Western compositional techniques.
The music critic of the German daily, the *Berliner Zeitung*, summed up the evening: unanimous applause - enraptured applause going on for several minutes - continuous applause with cries of "Bravo!" at the end - a thunderous, passionate standing ovation from the audience.

Currently a large concert hall and opera house is being created next to the Intercontinental Hotel in Al Qurm, between the Omani Ministry of Foreign Affairs and the Sultan Qaboos highway. If all goes well from 2010 one will be able to listen in Oman itself to regular performances of this unique ensemble. The orchestra also has its own Internet presence in Facebook.

Ruwi and Mutrah – the Old and the New Business Centers

It is hard to believe that what is today one of the most densely built-up areas of the Capital Area was until 1970 almost completely unsettled: the **Ruwi** basin, Muscat's modern business center. Ruwi is visually dominated by two tall buildings which soar high above all the others. The northern part of the district is marked by the radio and television broadcasting tower, known as the **GTO Tower**. Embellished with historical towers and battlements, the foundations support a tall broadcasting mast, useful as an orientation point when trying to get your bearings in the city. At the foot of the tower is the main post office. The banking and business quarter, known as the **Central Business District**, spreads south from here along Markaz Mutrah al Tijari Street, where most of the airlines have their offices. The street follows what was once the runway of the Ruwi airfield. You can see remains of this in the open spaces to the south in the wadi, which are now used for car driving practice. South of Al Jaame Street the Central District is bounded by the Ministry of Commerce and Industry and the tower of the Sheraton Hotel, another recognizable feature of Ruwi's skyline. To the west Al Jaame Street runs into the Ruwi roundabout. You can find the central bus station just to the north of the street, before the roundabout. Both sides of Ruwi Suq Street are packed with shops selling all conceivable wares. This is Muscat's main shopping center. On weekends thousands of guest workers throng the street in search of bargains, to meet and talk, or simply to stroll around. Ruwi also accommodates the collections of the **National Museum** and the **Sultan's Armed Forces Museum**. The term National Museum may raise expectations in the visitor of a diverse display of rich cultural heritage - these expectations may not be completely met. The building in Al Noor Street has several storeys. Only one room, however, is dedicated to the exhibition, laid out in thematically arranged niches. The museum's days are numbered as it is planned to build a new museum which will justify the name National Museum on the site of the Ministry of Heritage and Culture.

What is really worth seeing is the military history museum, the Sultan's Armed Forces (SAF) Museum, in Bayt Al Falaj, north of the GTO Tower. The collection is housed in a historical 18th century fort, which was supplied with water from its own *falaj* - hence the name. The fort played an important role in the defense of Oman against the Imam's troops at the beginning of the last century and today it serves also as a barracks. The well laid-out exhibition

The panorama of Mutrah bay seen from the fish market.

rooms are spread over two floors and provide a thorough survey of Oman's military history, with uniforms from several epochs, an overview of the various military divisions and their weapons, as well as materials relating to the Jabal Al Akhdar rebellion and the Dhofar war *(Saturday to Thursday mornings, 8:30 - 13:30.)*

In contrast to Ruwi, **Mutrah**, the harbor town to the north, is a historical settlement. Open to the hinterland and thus without natural protection from attack, it never gained the importance of the neighboring harbor of Muscat, completely screened on the land side by mountains. Unlike Muscat, Mutrah is seldom mentioned in historical sources. The Portuguese marked the place on their maritime charts, thereby giving it a certain significance, and built the fortress overlooking the harbor. Today it has been largely restored but is not accessible to the public.

Another protective fort to the western end of the bay had to give way to the new port of Mina As Sultan Qaboos. In 1648, after heavy fighting, the Portuguese yielded the town, which they had occupied for a century, back to the Omanis, who once more gained control of a seaport. Up until the mid nineteenth century overseas trade was dominated by neighboring Muscat. Only in the second half of the nineteenth century did what had been seen as Mutrah's strategic disadvantage come to be seen as a decided economic advantage. By

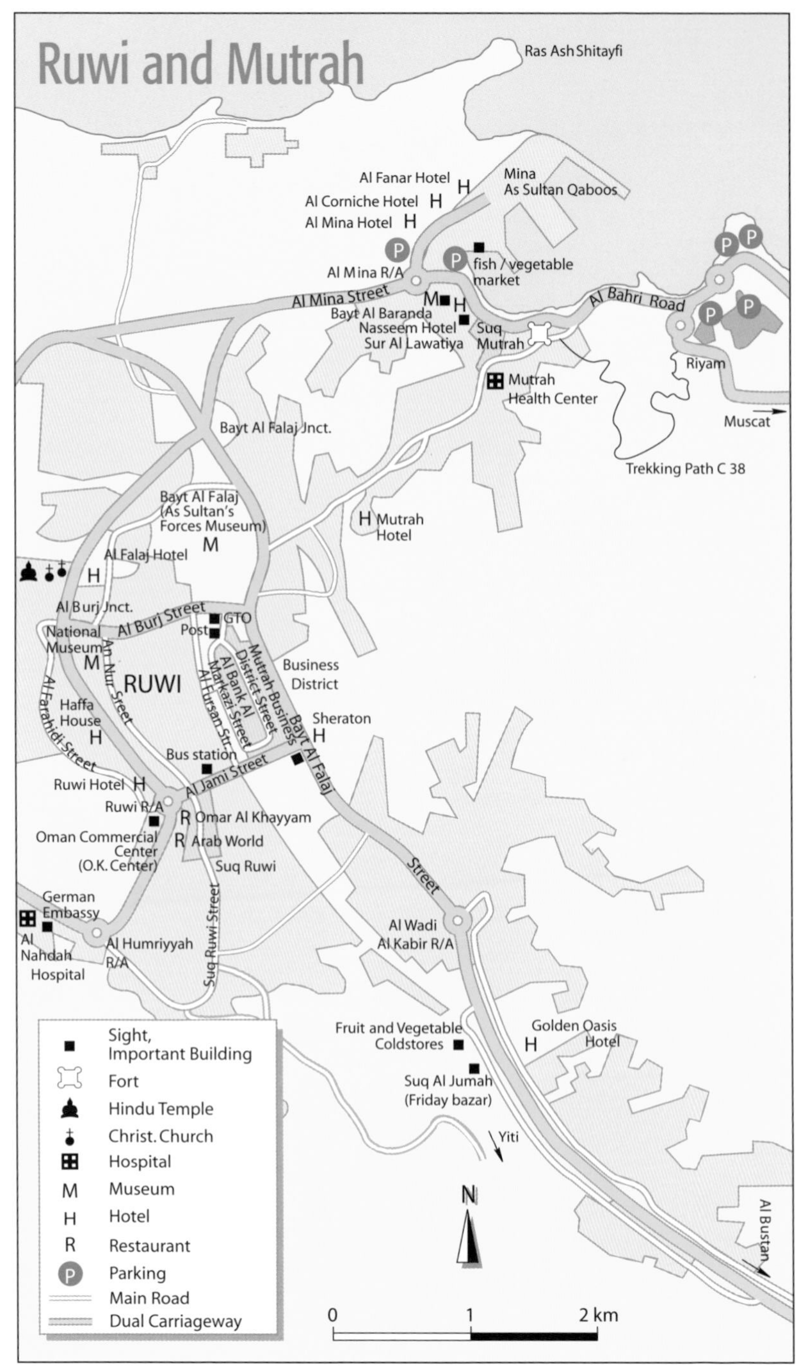

Ruwi and Mutrah
Ras Ash Shitayfi
Mina
As Sultan Qaboos
Al Fanar Hotel
Al Corniche Hotel
Al Mina Hotel
Al Mina R/A
fish / vegetable market
Al Mina Street
Bayt Al Baranda
Nasseem Hotel
Sur Al Lawatiya
Suq Mutrah
Al Bahri Road
Riyam
Mutrah Health Center
Muscat
Trekking Path C 38
Bayt Al Falaj Jnct.
Bayt Al Falaj (As Sultan's Forces Museum)
Mutrah Hotel
Al Falaj Hotel
Al Burj Jnct.
Al Burj Street
GTO
Post
National Museum
An Nur Street
RUWI
Al Bank Al Markazi Street
Al Fursan Str.
Mutrah Business District Street
Business District
Haffa House
Al Farahidi Street
Sheraton
Bayt Al Falaj Street
Bus station
Al Jami Street
Ruwi Hotel
Ruwi R/A
Omar Al Khayyam
Arab World
Oman Commercial Center (O.K. Center)
Suq Ruwi
German Embassy
Al Nahdah Hospital
Al Humriyyah R/A
Suq Ruwi Street
Al Wadi Al Kabir R/A
Fruit and Vegetable Coldstores
Golden Oasis Hotel
Suq Al Jumah (Friday bazar)
Yiti
N
Al Bustan
0
1
2 km
Sight, Important Building
Fort
Hindu Temple
Christ. Church
Hospital
Museum
Hotel
Restaurant
Parking
Main Road
Dual Carriageway

1900 the port had developed into a bustling trading metropolis, protected from the interior by defensive towers and walls.
Mutrah's importance did not change after the change of rule in 1970. The town expanded further and planning strategies designated it to become the main maritime trade and transshipment center for north Oman. On the northern side of the bay the large container port **Mina As Sultan Qaboos** was built, together with a new **fish market** and associated processing plants and parking places, of which there is a distinct shortage in Mutrah. Each morning the fishermen moor their boats directly next to the market and sell their colorful bounty. No visitor to Oman should miss a morning visit to this market.

Fresh fish in all shapes, sizes and colors are on offer every morning in the fish market.

The new coastal road, the **Corniche**, opened in 1972, leads from the fish market to Muscat. In modern times new buildings shot up everywhere, leaving only a few towers of the old fortifications with a chance to survive into the 21th century. These remains can be seen on the summits of the surrounding mountains.
By no means has everything in Mutrah had to yield to progress. At the beginning of the Corniche, tucked away behind the school and the Nasseem Hotel, is one of the most beautiful of the preserved traditional houses of Muscat, the **Bayt Al Baranda**. It was used from 1909 to 1933 by the American Mission as a clinic. Today this museum provides information not only about the geological emergence of the Hajar mountain range and the early days of settlement of the Capital Area, but also an outstanding overview of the eventful history of the town and how world travelers of past centuries viewed and described it. *(Opening times Saturday to Wednesday, 09:00 to 13:00 and 16:00 to 18:00, Thursdays 09:00 to 13:00 only.)*
In the southwest curve of the bay, directly overlooking the coast, a number of imposing 19th century houses remain and they are stylistically unlike any other buildings in Oman. Airy, richly ornamented balconies and large, arched windows decorate the white facades. The architecture is light and playful, waking associations with Indian and Pakistani houses with good reason. They form the harbor frontage of the **Sur al Lawatiya** quarter, inhabited by the Shi'ite Khodja religious community. The Khodjas, originating mostly from Hyderabad in India and from Pakistan, are today among the most successful merchants in Oman. The first indications of their immigration come from the end of the 18th century. In Mutrah the new arrivals built their own small new world in the style of their homeland. The houses then stood directly on the beach. Foreigners were not allowed to enter this part of the town, a rule that is still respected. Today the completely enclosed area has

an entrance gate on the harbor side, but next to it is a sign saying "Residential Area," indicating that onlookers are still not welcome in the domestic area of the Khodjas. Since 1997 a magnificent mosque with a blue dome enriches the skyline of this unique architectural ensemble. To the east of this quarter is the **Mutrah suq**, the largest and most important in the country.

The fabric of the buildings is new but in no other shopping district is there such an old-fashioned oriental spirit of trade. Through a gate from the Corniche you enter the Khore Bamba, the covered main artery of the market, which is criss-crossed with narrow alleys. In the suq you will be met by the most unbelievable contrasts. Scenes from times believed to be long gone exist side by side with the modern. Ancient Omanis sit motionless in front of their tiny shop fronts and sell even older-seeming ropes, pots, screws and nails. These traders spread an aura of timeless calm over the market throng, appearing to have been left over from an earlier age. Directly next to them a business-minded Indian loudly extols his astonish-

Guest Workers

The building up of the modern state of Oman required the help of guest workers, just as it had with Oman's maritime empire. Now, as then, migrant workers come from Asia. The majority (59 percent) of the over 800,000 foreigners come from India and are employed in commerce, construction and the service industries. The remainder of the army of guest workers come from Pakistan, Bangladesh, Sri Lanka, and the Philippines. The conception and planning of the reconstruction, on the other hand, is firmly in European hands. Around two thirds of the over 3000 European experts in the country come from Great Britain. The well-paid experts have to give 10 percent of their salaries towards financing the Omani education system. If originally there were too few qualified native workers, the situation has changed radically within the last twenty years. The population exploded from an estimated 650,000 inhabitants in 1970 to over 2.5 million in 2005, of whom 668,000 (26 percent) were foreigners, most of them being guest workers. In the Muscat region the proportion, at 47 percent, was significantly higher, whereas on the Al Batinah coast it was only 15 percent. To compare: in the United Arab Emirates fewer than 20 percent of the workforce are natives; in Germany, with its fear of being overwhelmed by foreigners, over 95 percent of the total population are German citizens.

Meanwhile all young Omanis have access in at least some areas to a very good education, and their wages are thus markedly higher than those of Asians, who for many years have occupied many of the available posts, above all in commerce. In the past many Omani employers have profited from this cheap labor. In the retail trade, especially, there was often just one Omani, who was in the position of manager but never actually present.

ingly varied collection of thermos flasks, which are all decorated with oriental designs. Alongside these he has on offer inflatable dinosaurs, plastic dolls and flowers, and even Leonardo da Vinci's Last Supper, in bas-relief pressed into a plastic sheet and mounted with a clock: European renaissance art meets the oriental bazaar! The suq is divided up along traditional lines with individual zones for the sale of particular types of goods. You will find silversmiths and goldsmiths along the Sur al Lawatiya. Well worth noting is the shop belonging to **Ismail Yousuf Sumar & Partners**, the oldest silversmith's business in Mutrah, where modern Omani silver jewelry is on offer from their own workshops. The textile traders sit in the small alley running parallel to the Corniche near the entrance. Shops selling all manner of household goods, writing materials, and Omani and Indian handicrafts can be found along the main alley which forks off through the middle of the suq. The rattle of sewing machines fills the area east of the main alley - the tailors are at work here. All sorts of magnificently colored materials

Although a single manager can thus "manage" a number of businesses, this type of management means that in the long run he is actually in danger of losing control over the business's turnover. Over time such lack of supervision can lead, here as indeed anywhere, to embezzlement, corruption and the development of alternative mafia-like structures. The government reacted against this way of doing business with drastic measures. If the success of the educational sector was not to be carried to absurd lengths, something needed to be done. A new law was passed in order to clear up this appalling state of affairs. Since 1994, throughout the country the aim has been to replace foreign workers with Omanis. A work permit for a foreigner is only issued when it can be proven that there is no Omani available who could carry out the job. Every business owner must be personally present. Police make spot checks to ensure that these laws are respected. As one might have expected, these measures could not be carried out overnight without crippling the economy. Today, happily, you will see a young Omani in almost every shop. Even the service industries, such as working at a petrol station or a grocery store, which were long held to be beneath the dignity of Omanis, are no longer taboo. Particular favorite jobs such as fisherman, taxi driver and policeman were already exclusively in the hands of Omanis. Whether in the future Omanis will so enthusiastically take up less attractive jobs in the construction and service industries remains to be seen. This change to the Omani social structure, however, seems inevitable given that over 50 percent of the population is under 18 years old. Creating work for this large number of Omanis is one of the greatest challenges facing the government in the near future.

burst out of the small windows and pile up in front of the shops, an orgy of color beyond compare. At the southern end you leave the covered suq, again through a gate. There is a small vegetable market here, a main meeting point for Indian workers on Friday evenings, the Islamic weekend. The locals vanish in the general hubbub; Oman seems far away and India ever closer. To Omanis the square is known as "little Bombay."

If you're good on your feet and have brought a pair of stout walking shoes with you, you can try the **hiking path C38** which will give you a unique view over the harbor and its bay. The path starts at the end of the parking area beneath Mutrah fort and runs over the rugged mountains in a bow leading back to the bay. The path ends in Riyam park. The route takes about two hours. As with all hiking in Oman, it is essential that you take an adequate supply of water with you.

The Mutrah suq is renowned for the number of textile and small tailors' shops.

Historic Muscat

Follow the Corniche from Mutrah eastwards and you come directly to neighboring bay of Muscat. On the way, on high ground to the right, you will be struck by a strange object, looking to western eyes as though a UFO has just landed: this is the lookout tower of **Riyam Park**, which offers a fascinating view over the bay of Mutrah and the small fishing settlement of Kalbuh. The spontaneous association with a UFO is quite wrong and one that no Omani can understand. The tower has the characteristic form of an outsized incense burner, which every Omani child would recognize instantly. Especially during Ramadan and in the summer the park is a favorite place for family excursions and sporting activities. Shortly after the bay the road is crossed by a new city gate, which also accommodates the **Muscat Gate Museum**. The city's lively history is recounted on large, very informative display boards with fascinating old photographs and maps *(open Saturday to Thursday 9:30 - 12:30 and 16:30 - 19:00.)*

Muscat itself is made up mostly of one way streets. It is best to leave the car in one of the parking-lots and explore the town on foot. For the young Sultan Qaboos, old Muscat symbolized a period of isolation and backwardness which it was his task to overcome. It was here that he was to begin with the country's renewal. Here it should be apparent to everybody that modernization was the order of the day.

In the eyes of many Omanis the ruler overshot the mark. Of the town's original building fabric, only a handful of houses survived this development. A centuries old, lively port on the Indian Ocean was transformed into an administrative district, smartened up but somewhat lifeless.

The suq (which had occupied the largest part of the town center), a business quarter of mostly Indian tradesmen, the church built by the Portuguese, a small boatyard for fishing boats, the old Sultan's palace, large merchants' houses and warehouses, two Hindu temples, a residential district inhabited by a multitude of ethnic groupings (Persians, Baluchistanis, Nubians, Abyssinians, Khodjas and Yemenites), a small hospital and extensive *barasti* settlements outside the city gates - all these witnesses to a great seafaring nation have vanished. The old Sultan's palace had to give way to the new Al Alam Palace, the suq to large administration buildings and palace offices, and the old city wall to a new one with car-friendly gates.

Undoubtedly the most attractive place in the new town is west of the Sultan's palace on the coast. Here, at the foot of Fort Mirani, you have a magnificent view from the sea over the palace, over Jalali fort and the impressive bay of Muscat.

Muscat's beginnings are still unresearched. According to legend the town was founded by Himyarite merchants from present-day Yemen, but hard historical evidence for this is lacking. The town is first mentioned in the 10th century by the Arab geographer, Ibn Al Faqih Al Hamadani. The famous traveler Ibn Battuta describes it in the 14th century as a fishing port.

Muscat's prominence as a maritime port is first mentioned by the famous Omani seafarer Ahmad bin Majid at the end of the 15th century. The town's heyday seems to have started at the end of the Middle Ages, when the geographical advantages of Muscat's protected harbor and supply of fresh water was recognized and it was understood how to put this to use.

In 1507 Alfonso de Albuquerque of Portugal conquered Muscat, which was then flourishing under the rule of the kingdom of Hormuz, and he destroyed 34 ships in the harbor. The European colonial powers knew how to prize the strategic advantages of Muscat. By means of a supply running directly from the mountains down to the harbor, ships were able to replenish their vital stores of fresh water before resuming their long journeys. The harbor was one of the safest of the time. The cliffs running down to the sea kept the strong winds at bay and the ring of mountains protected the town from attacks from the country's interior. In 1550 and 1581 Turkish fleets attacked the town, inflicting heavy losses on the Portuguese. As a result the colonial rulers pushed ahead with the construction of the **Mirani** and **Jalali forts** on either side of the entrance to the harbor. They were completed in 1586 and 1588 respectively. (These forts are not open to the public.) At the beginning of the 17th century more fortifications were erected on the land side and the harbor increased greatly in military worth. When, in 1622, the Portuguese lost Hormuz to the Persians, they transferred the main naval base for their fleet to Muscat. However, in 1650, after several sieges and heavy fighting, they were also driven out from here by Imam Nasir ibn Murshid.

Jalali fort, built by the Portuguese.

The increased importance of the port within the rapidly expanding Omani trading empire resulted in 1779 in Ahmad ibn Said transferring the royal seat from Ar Rustaq to Muscat. The civil war and the associated Persian occupation of the town from 1737 to 1741 had not managed to slow the rise of Muscat and it became the military, economic and political hub of the Indian Ocean. The great powers of France and Great Britain both courted the Omanis' favors, looking for ways of increasing their influence, and opened diplomatic legations and trading branches. The harbor controlled almost all of the shipping - even boats putting into port in Muscat on their way to other destinations paid customs dues. Ships' crews left their "autographs" on the rocks at the bay's entrance. In letters that are up to five meters high you can read ships' names and their dates of arrival immortalized in the cliff face.

A prestigious palace was required to reflect the increased power of Muscat. For a long time the imams had resided in the Portuguese built church. The building of a palace was apparently begun around 1800 under the rule of Sultan bin Ahmad and was later continually extended. In the 20th century a conglomeration of buildings grew directly alongside the harbor, taking up some 300 meters of the waterfront. This tendency of prestigious buildings to proliferate is also to be seen in Sultan Qaboos's new **Al Alam Palace**, built on the same site but starting with a ground area five times as large. Designed and built by an Indian architect at the beginning of the 1970s it was already being extended in the 1990s. A large guesthouse was built near the Mirani Fort. To the east of the bay near the Palace and the Palace Guard was the no less magnificent residence of the British Embassy. In 1994 the Embassy had to move to the diplomatic quarter. This freed up the site for another extensive expansion of the palace as the complete area around the embassy was cleared along with two of the few remaining trading company houses.

The slow decline of the town as a maritime metropolis began around 1820. The Omani overseas traders received increasing competition from European as well as Arabic quarters. Piracy had been successfully defeated resulting in a decrease in the importance of having a protected harbor and in 1828 Said ibn Sultan transferred the royal seat to Zanzibar. Muscat lost its importance as a transshipment center in favor of East Africa.

Only a few buildings of typical Arabic construction have survived from Muscat's heyday in the 18th century. They were simply called *bayts* (houses.) The most impressive buildings consist of two storeys and have a flat roof which was used as a sleeping place in early summer. The head of the household would receive guests in a special room on the roof of the house. The large windows, which reached down to the floor, served the same function as air conditioning. The small windows on the ground floor often served as embrasures from which one could shoot if the building was attacked. Stables, storerooms and the kitchen were usually located on

A Woman's Rule

You'll find little mention in historical writings of the fact that, before the rule of the famous Sultan Said whose rule began officially in 1804, the fate of the town of Muscat lay in the hands of a woman. She is still held in high respect be the Omani people. A detailed report of this unusual regency is given in the memoirs of Princess Salme, the daughter of Sultan Said ibn Sultan:

"My grandfather, the Sultan Imam of Mesket, in Oman, left at his death three children: my father Said, my uncle Sâlum, and my aunt Asche. My father was only nine years old at the time, and a regency had to be established. Contrary to all custom, my great-aunt at once declared in the most decided manner that she would carry on the government herself until her nephew was of age, and she suffered no opposition. The ministers, who had never anticipated such a thing, and who had already in secret congratulated themselves on the prospect of ruling the country for some years, could do nothing but submit. They had to make their reports to her, and to receive her instructions and commands every day. She watched closely and knew everything, and nothing could remained concealed from her, to the great vexation and annoyance of all the disloyal and idle officials ...

Her courage was soon put to a very severe test. Not long after she had taken up the reins of government a very serious war broke out – unfortunately a frequent occurrence in Oman. Some of the next of kin had thought it an easy affair to overthrow the government of a woman, to extinguish our house, and possess themselves of power. Their hordes ravaged the country with fire and sword, and advanced close to the gates of Mesket. Thousands of country people from the sacked provinces had already fled for shelter and protection into the city, leaving all their goods and chattels behind.

the ground floor. The living quarters on the upper floor had tall, narrow, arched windows which allowed in plenty of air and light. Protection against direct sunlight was provided by artistically carved wooden shutters on the windows and balconies. The outline of a *bayt* is almost always square, with the rooms arranged around an inner courtyard with a gallery.

You can view the inside and outside of **Bayt Nadir** in the west of the town and Bayt Fransa in the southwest. Their architecture is perfectly suited to the extreme climatic conditions of Muscat. **Bayt Fransa** formerly served as the French Consulate. Since 1992 it has housed the **Omani French Museum**, which documents a difficult past alongside the cordial relationship which currently exists between the two countries. The exhibition is not particularly interesting but the architecture and the building itself well reward a

Mesket is strongly fortified and well able to stand a siege, but of what use are the strongest walls when provisions and ammunition are exhausted?

But in this terrible distress my great-aunt proved herself equal to the occasion, and she even gained the admiration of the enemy. Dressed in men's clothes, she inspected the outposts herself at night, she watched and encouraged the soldiers in all exposed places, and was saved several times only by the speed of her horse in unforeseen attacks...

The situation grew, however, to be very critical at Mesket. Famine at last broke out, and the people were well-nigh distracted, as no assistance or relief could be expected from without. It was, therefore, decided to attempt a last sortie in order to die at least with glory. There was just sufficient powder left for one more attack, but there was no more lead for either guns or muskets. In this emergency the regent ordered iron nails and pebbles to be used in place of balls, the guns were loaded with all the old iron and brass that could be collected, and she opened her treasury to have bullets made out of her own silver dollars. Every nerve was strained, and the sally succeeded beyond all hope. The enemy was completely taken by surprise, and fled in all directions, leaving more than half their men dead and wounded on the field. Mesket was saved, and, delivered out of her deep distress, the brave woman knelt down on the battle field and thanked God in fervent prayer. From that time her government was a peaceful one, and she ruled so wisely that she was able to transfer to her nephew, my father, an empire so unimpaired as to place him in a position to extend the empire by the conquest of Zanzibar. It is to my great-aunt, therefore, that we owe, and not to an inconsiderable degree, the acquisition of this second empire. She, *too*, was an Eastern woman!"

Emily Ruete, *Memoirs of an Arabian Princess*, p 159 - 162

visit. The building's restoration was undertaken by the French state and President Mitterand personally inaugurated the building in 1992.
A visit to the **Bayt Al Zubair Museum**, a private institution, is worth making on account of its collection, which gives a good visual insight into the history and everyday culture of Oman. Bayt Al Zubair is located outside the Bab al Kabeer (the large gate) in Muscat, 200 meters towards Al Towyan. It has been rebuilt to reflect the style of the original house and traditional Omani architectural design. Among other things the collection contains a considerable assembly of historical curved daggers belonging to the Al-Zubair family, jewelry, robes, paintings, and historical photographs and documents. Within the grounds of Bayt Al Zubair can be found recreations of a traditional Omani mountain village, irrigation systems, buildings made from palm fronds and a variety of fishing boats used in Oman. There is an area for live exhibits which is used from time to time for activities such as traditional Omani dancing and handicraft demonstrations.
A neighboring building shows the ways of life in different parts of Oman. Due to the fact that large parts of the collections could not be displayed for lack of space, the museum is now being extended by one more building on the main road. *(open Saturday to Thursday 09:00-13:00 and 16:00-19:00)*
The largest of the old houses is the **Bayt Graiza** at the foot of the Mirani fort. The site was originally built upon in 1527 as a Portuguese trading post with a small church. Its name "Graiza" serves today as a reminder of this time, it being the Arab formulation of "egreja," the Portuguese word for church. From the 17th century the building served the Omanis as a warehouse and as residence of the ruling Imam. After the old Sultan's palace was built in 1800 the building lost its function and fell into disrepair. Bayt Graiza was built at the same time as the palace, and is now used by the government.

The Merchant's Beautiful Daughter

Muscat old town, the capital of Oman, extends along a bay between the imposing forts of Mirani and Jalali. When the Portuguese invaded the country in the 16th century they built Fort Mirani and considered it invincible. Imam Sultan bin Saif captured the fort from the Portuguese in 1649 through his outstanding leadership abilities coupled with the bravery and skill of his soldiers. According to legend however he had some extra help.

Narutem, an Indian merchant who supplied the fort with all provisions, had a very beautiful daughter. She had caught the eye of the Portuguese commander, Pereira, who wished to marry her. Narutem did not want his daughter, a Hindu, to marry Pereira, a Catholic. Alarmed, he refused permission.

Pereira was furious and he threatened to cancel the contracts Narutem had with the fort, which would mean Narutem's financial ruin. Narutem was worried and played for time. He pretended to change his mind and asked for a year to prepare for the Wedding. Once agreement was reached he proceeded to tell Pereira that the fort would never stand a long siege. He claimed that the water in the tanks was foul and must be replaced. He said that the old stocks of wheat should be changed and the gunpowder removed and pounded. Pereira told him to go ahead, but when Narutem removed the items he didn't replace them.

Narutem knew Imam Sultan bin Saif was waiting for the right moment to attack the fort, and when he saw an opportunity to get rid of Pereira he informed Imam Sultan bin Saif that the garrison was weakend. The Imam launched his attack against the Portuguese and successfully took the fort. And so it is said that an affair of the heart played a part in the final expulsion of the Portuguese from Muscat and Oman.

Hatim Al Taie and Joan Pickersgill, *Omani Folk Tales*, p 62 - 63
ISBN: 978-9948-03-654-8 / also available at www.oman-shop.com

A Hotel as National Showpiece

The Al Bustan Palace Hotel is the favored residence for state guests. To make way for the hotel the village of Al Bustan was moved to the western half of the bay.

As a rule modern international hotels are not, unfortunately, architectural masterpieces. They are often as alike as peas in a pod, whether in New York, Amsterdam, Frankfurt, London or wherever. But there are a few exceptions and the Al Bustan Palace Hotel, along with the new Grand Hyatt, belong to them. Run by the Omani state together with the Hotel Intercontinental group, the Al Bustan Palace Hotel is located a few kilometers west of Muscat. In specialist circles it is regarded as one of the world's most beautiful, interesting and best hotels. With its modern Arabic architecture it serves as a national showpiece for Oman. Bizarre, black-brown cliffs surround the hotel with an unreal fairytale-like aura. Even the drive from Ruwi with its grotesque contrasts has something fantastical about it. Natural and man-made landscapes compete for attention. The road leading to Al Bustan passes by the handicraft and service industry district and at the end of the Wadi Kabir ascends to a pass, a gate in the rocks, flanked by two columns topped by life-size, rearing horses. To the left of the road, strange, black-brown rocks rise upwards, and to the right soft ochre-colored sediment. The dark rocks are of volcanic origin from the oceanic plate. There are only a few places on earth where violent upheavals of the earth's crust have resulted in stone from the *Samail ophiolite* seeing the light of day, as here in the Hajar mountains. Normally this layer is covered by sediment such as you see on the opposite side of the road. This covering layer is to be seen most clearly in the formation of the left side of the rock gate.

Having passed the heights the road makes a wide curve down to the coast on the left and your eye is involuntarily caught by a steep road climbing the next mountain to the east, leading to Qantab. Only two kilometers outside of the capital the traveler gets an idea of what it means to drive a car in the mountains of Oman, and of what an achievement it has been to create these roads. To the right a waterfall suddenly appears, gushing from a wall of rock. The curtain of water conceals a spectacularly-colored mosaic. The waterfall is completely artificial and is only turned on in the evening and morning. Small patches of green, like bowling lawns with picturesque park benches in front of rugged cliff faces, add another surreal note to the picture.

The road runs into a roundabout which offers another very artificial looking attraction in its center: a traditional Arab dhow lies at anchor in a blue pool surrounded by fountains.

Unlike the horses and waterfall, however, the "Sohar" is real and is deserving of closer inspection. It was in this sailing boat that the Irishman Tim Severin made a journey in which he followed the age-old routes of the Omani traders from Sur to Canton in South China. He had a dhow specially built for him using ancient techniques in order to relive the adventures of Sindbad the Sailor. Leaving the roundabout in an easterly direction the road leads through an immense gate into the park of the **Al Bustan Palace Hotel**. Surrounded by coconut groves, green swards, black rocks and white beaches, the impressive nine-storey octagonal building, crowned by a shimmering gold dome, appears like a *fata morgana* among the surrounding mountain landscape. The soil of the park comes from the border region between Oman and Fujairah and most of the plants are native to India. The trees and shrubs are watered with used water from the hotel.

Designed by two Cypriot architects the Palace was intended to fulfill a dual role: on the one hand that of a world class international hotel and on the other as a guesthouse for the Omani government. The ninth floor is reserved for official state visitors. This accounts for the immense expenditure that went into the construction of the building. On April 25, 1983 work began and it needed to be completed by August 30, 1985.

Building the *Sohar*

The *Sohar* was to be a faithful reproduction of a dhow of the pre-Islamic period. The most distinctive characteristic of traditional Arab shipbuilding of this period was that absolutely no metal of any kind was used in the construction of the hull. The use of nails to hold together the 1500 fixed parts of such a boat only began later through the influence of the European colonial powers and as a result of the structural stresses put on the hold with the introduction of cannon. Until then a ship's planks were sewn together with cord made of coconut fiber, a technique which is almost unknown today. An accurate reconstruction of a dhow of the *boom* type was fraught with difficulties. The necessary skills can nowadays only be found among a few craftsmen from the Laccadive (or Lakshadweep) archipelago off the Indian Malabar coast and from the Indian town of Beypore. From time immemorial the Laccadives have been known as the "Coconut Islands." The ropes necessary for the boat-building were made and sold here, and constituted the islands' only export. Along with the craftsmen from Omani Sur and Indian Beypore the specialists from the Laccadives played a key role in the ship's building. To construct the hull, they calculated 640,000 meters of cord from some 50,000 coconut shells would be required to make the

This deadline gave the Intercontinental Group just three months to get the hotel services up and running. In December 1985 the government planned a grand opening to use it as the guesthouse for the first meeting of the Gulf Cooperation Council to be held on Omani soil.

The choice of location posed problems when putting the plans into effect. The old fishing village of Al Bustan lay behind a large freestanding rock in the bay, which divided the beach in two. The village had to be moved to the northern part of the bay, an amicable agreement being reached with the inhabitants. On the spot chosen for the hotel there was yet another rock, as immense as the planned hotel. This was blown up and the material from the exploded rock was used to lay a surface for the car parking area. The layer of rock is up to six meters thick. On August 16th 1983 the site was prepared and the actual construction work could begin. The modular assembly of individual building parts is typical for lavish modern Omani architecture. The building regulations allow a lot of latitude in the selection of materials and in a building's size, as well as in the design. The only significant restriction is the rule that stylistic elements of Arabic-oriental architecture should be used exclusively. This is similar to the attitude of some post-modern architects in the west.

arm-thick rope with which the seams were wadded on the boat's interior. The 140 tons of wood required were brought from the Indian Malabar coast just as they would have been in the past. Each tree was selected on site by Severin and a boat builder from Sur. The hull of the Sohar has a shell construction. First the sixteen meter long keel is laid out and each plank sewn into position. Using this method of construction, the ribs of the boat's interior are positioned right at the end so that the individual seams remain unbroken. Each plank has to be bent over steam in the required form so that they fit together with a millimeter-exact precision. The ribs consist of five pieces independent of one another, so that the hull retains its elasticity. The individual planks and the seams were sealed with quarter of a ton of resin from a cheaper kind of frankincense tree from India. The exterior coating consisted of a mixture of fish oil and sugar. In addition the parts of the hull below the waterline were coated with a protective layer of chalk and mutton fat, in the hope that this impregnation would serve to prevent damage from barnacles and algae. It took 165 day in all to build the Sohar. It was launched on November 18, 1980, Oman's 10th National Day. Seven months later the ship reached the port of Canton.

Free variations on old stylistic elements were made and realized using modern building materials. As with all new buildings in Oman, the basic material from which the Al Bustan Palace Hotel is made is poured concrete. Parts for windows, doors, domes and other irregular shapes were poured with the help of special forms. Altogether 70,000 cubic meters of concrete and 7,000 tons of steel reinforcement were used. The workers were almost exclusively from India, the Philippines, and Sri Lanka. During the busiest building phase over 3,500 foreign workers lived on the site, each being fed from various ethnic kitchens. Omani buildings are typically plastered, painted or clad with stone slabs and so it is in this case. Each of the 50,000 stone slabs, columns, decorative pieces and cornices were prepared by hand in Rajastan in India. Altogether 97 different types of stone have been used in the Al Bustan Palace, of which 800 tons were marble from Greece, France and Italy. The modular construction system consists of 4 different types of pillars, 12 types of arches and a further 504 standard parts.

Several times a day an artificial bow wave rolls over the „Sohar" on the roundabout in front of the Al Bustan Palace Hotel, its last resting place after the great China expedition in 1980.

The heart of the palace hotel is the atrium, with its 33 meter high central hall, a unique room, giving an almost sacred radiance. This impression is often reinforced by an Omani sitting at the entrance, burning large quantities of frankincense. Aromatic clouds curl up to the dome and increase the extraordinary atmosphere of the hall. The huge steel pillars, which give the atrium its octagonal form, were produced by three different companies in England. To check that everything would fit before shipping it out to Oman the metal construction was assembled on a sports ground in Liverpool. The "golden dome" is actually an optical illusion. The surface is coated with a layer of titanium, which most of the time gives it a golden shimmer. According to the weather it may sometimes also appear brown or green.

The total construction costs of the Al Bustan Palace came to 130 million Omani Rials, a fairytale price for a fairytale palace. The 250 rooms are fitted out partly in western style and partly in oriental style. In the years 2007 and 2008 the hotel was closed to the public. The rooms, lobby and even the garden were almost completely redesigned and the former garden rooms were given direct access to a pool landscape, now called "lagoon access rooms."

An overnight stay is certainly dearer than in any other prestige hotel in Oman. Here the mysterious, luxury world of the Gulf oil sheikhs raises its veil and bids everyone welcome to the fairytale.

Lonely Bays, Beaches and an Underwater Paradise

If all this is too much for you, the splendor and grandeur too artificial and you're more in the mood for a lonely, sandy beach with a dreamy backdrop of cliffs, you will not have far to look: Bander Al Jissah is only a few kilometers beyond the Al Bustan Palace.
The appearance of the coast east of the hotel is marked by high, bizarre, steep cliff formations along with offshore islands. This rugged stretch of coastline has the most picturesque sandy beaches including that of the small fishing village of Qantab, which can be reached by the spectacular Qantab Road. It is a drive winding through the mountains, at the side of which the whole spectrum of Oman's earthen colors puts on a breathtaking, ever-changing display. After about four kilometers the road descends once more to sealevel. If you turn left after Qantab and then take the first right fork, after a few kilometers you will come to a parking place alongside a ruined settlement: **Bander Al Jissah**. The bay is closed in by rounded cliffs reaching far into the sea. The water is crystal clear, always calm and is ideal for diving and snorkelling. Go along the rocks and, just one or two meters below the surface, you can see all sorts of corals and often huge shoals of rainbow-colored fish. On Thursday and Fridays the bay is a favorite destination for day-trippers, but during the rest of the week you will find yourself almost alone. Now and again fishermen wait with their boats in the bay. They offer a special service to the few tourists. For five to ten Omani Rials (depending on your bartering skills) they will land visitors at one of the small bays which are completely inaccessible from the land side. Agree when and you will be picked up at the appointed time, when you then pay for the service. The dream of a completely deserted beach easily becomes reality.
Little is known about the ruins of Bander Al Jissah. The foundation walls of five houses, a mosque and a fort still remain. The fort and the watchtower, set back on a rise in the wadi about 200 meters away, were built during the Portuguese occupation to guard against Turks landing near Muscat. When and why the place was destroyed is still unknown. The only tangible documentary evidence appeared in 1898, when Sultan Faisal ibn Turki signed a treaty with France to allow the construction of a coaling station for steamships in the bay. This agreement was shortly afterwards cancelled when Great Britain protested that it broke an earlier treaty of 1798, which guaranteed Britain exclusive European rights to use Omani ports.

Contrasting with the quiet idyll of Bander Al Jissah, **Qantab** is a bustling little fishing village. Additional to that on October 8, 2008 the first container of *Afzelia africana* planks from Ghana arrived at the beach at Qantab to allow work to begin at a unique shipyard that was laid out at the beach months before to rebuild a historic ship the ancient way.

The project is a historical and cultural initiative launched by the governments of Oman and Singapore. The ship's design is based on the archaeological findings of the Belitung Wreck, which was discovered in 1998 in Indonesia. As was done before in 1980 with the "Sohar," the ship will represent a major feat of maritime engineering. The hull is being sewn together with coconut fiber. Built without nails to seal the hull, each timber will have to fit perfectly. The wood will be protected by a layer of goat fat mixed with lime, and the sails will be square and made from palm leaves.

Once built the ship named **"Jewel of Muscat"** is expected to sail from Oman to Singapore, which is presumed to have been a key stopping point of the Belitung ship in its journey westwards before it was wrecked. It will travel along the same route as one of those described by Arab geographers, using the same knowledge as Arab seamen. The team on the ship will use 9th-century navigation techniques, plotting the course for the 18-meter ship with a "kamal" (a small block of wood connected to a piece of string that can calculate latitude), and the stars and the sun. Observation of the sky and sea color, marine and bird life, and wind direction will also be used as aids to navigation. Modern instruments will only be used to check the navigation techniques.

On the first of September 2009 the last plank was put in place in the "Jewel of Muscat." The journey is to begin in February 2010, with the ship reaching Singapore by June 2010. For more info about this thrilling project see *http://www.jewelofmuscat.tv*.

Drive along the main road further southeast and you will arrive at the complex of the new **Shangri-La Barr al Jissah Resort & Spa**, another highlight among the hotels of Oman. The complex, built on the edge of the cliffs, offers a fantastic view over the coastline, where the beaches are frequented, now as from time immemorial, by sea turtles during the egg-laying season. Its backer, Mohamed Al-Zubair, who is also responsible for the Bayt Al Zubair Museum in Muscat, has laid great emphasis on having the architecture and fittings in sympathy with Omani culture and environment.

The complex consists of three hotels, separated by the natural features of the terrain, with a total of 680 bedrooms and suites, a modern spa and health club, swimming pools and leisure facilities, all within 500,000 square meters of self-contained and attractively

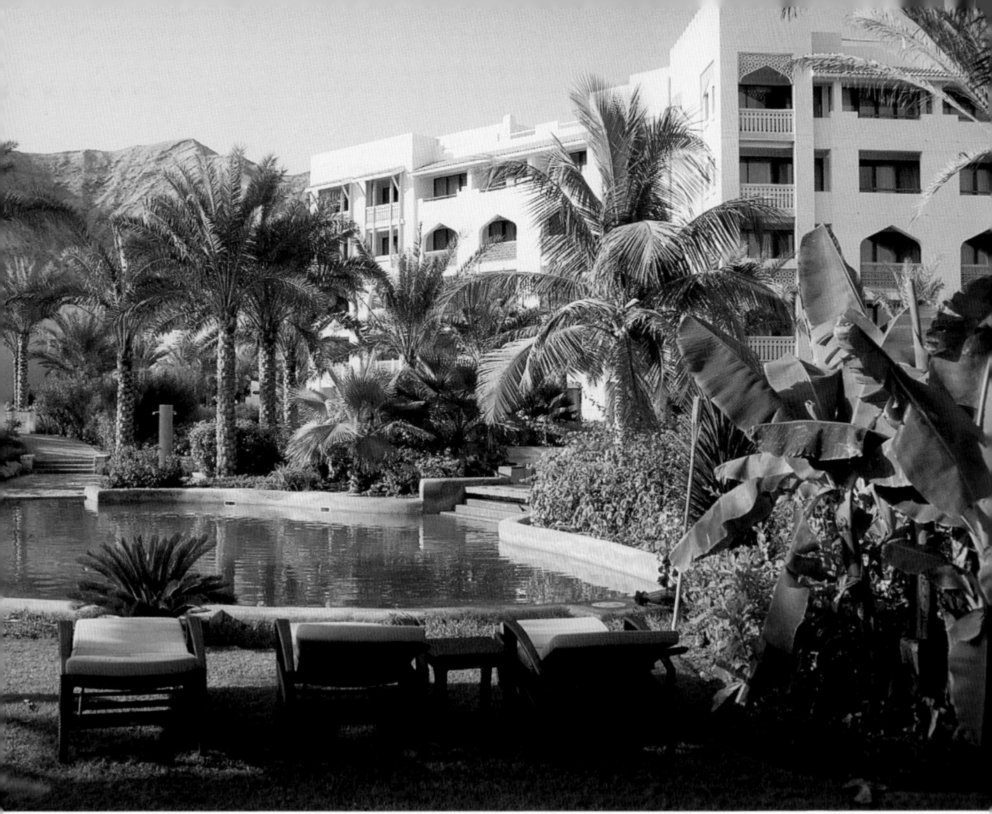

New but already surrounded by luxuriant vegetation: the Shangri-La Barr Al Jissah Resort & Spa

landscaped grounds. Right at the start of the construction 1500 palms were planted around the site. Also remarkable is that so many works of Omani artists are to be found here, more than anywhere else in the country. The hotel is in effect a museum of contemporary Omani art. A catalog can be found in the book "The Art of Barr Al Jissah", obtainable from the reception or in the Bayt al Zubair Museum in Muscat.

Given its secluded nature, the resort is almost entirely self-sufficient in essential services. Situated along the main beach area, the five-star deluxe Al Bander Hotel is the heart of the Resort as the embodiment of a seaside town built along traditional Omani architectural lines and embellished by a lush tropical landscape.

At the eastern edge of the resort separated from the Al Bander and Al Husn Hotels by a steep narrow mountain, the five-star Al Waha Hotel is enhanced by an atmosphere of fun and entertainment uniquely designed to cater for families and the younger generation. The six-star Al Husn Hotel (Castle Hotel) perched on an elevated plateau above the resort with commanding views of the ocean and surrounding landscape provides the ultimate beach resort experience, with butler service.

Cyclone Gonu and its Consequences

In early June 2007 large cloud formations over the Indian Ocean developed into an enormous cyclone. Named Gonu by the meteorologists, the whirlwind progressed slowly but steadily towards the coast of Oman. 285 kilometers from the island of Masirah, the whirlwind was already 200 kilometers across. Its wind-speed reached over 260 kilometers an hour with gusts of up to 315 kilometers an hour. It quickly became clear that this was the strongest cyclone ever seen in the Indian Ocean and posed a very serious threat to the Sultanate. On June 4th the precautionary evacuation of 20,000 inhabitants from the regions seen to be at greatest risk was begun; 7000 alone from the island of Masirah. It was assumed that the center of the storm would break here on the coast. All the authorities and institutions were geared up for the coming catastrophe, the populace was warned of the coming disaster and requested to lay in stores of water and provisions and to remain at home. At this time the fact that almost all Omanis were in possession of a mobile phone proved to be of inestimable advantage. All mobile phone owners were constantly informed by SMS of the development of the danger and the current path of the storm. The government declared a state of emergency and declared a five-day closure of all shops, companies and schools. The streets were to be kept empty for the emergency rescue services, which were all put on highest alert. On June 5th the storm turned northwest in the direction of Sur and Muscat. Muscat's ports and airport were closed, and the export of gas and oil was stopped. Shortly before hitting the coast the storm was checked by the land mass and slowed down to about 95 kilometers an hour. This tendency continued for the next hours. In Muscat the top wind speeds were "only" 100 kilometers an hour. Seven hours before the cyclone hit the coast heavy rains began, which amounted to a total of 610 millimeters per square meter. Consequently the damage caused by the water masses flooding through the valleys was far greater than that caused by the storm. In recent years the old Omani saying "the wadi takes his due" had increasingly been forgotten in the coastal area. Many houses had been built near wadis and some even within them. The elegant coastal roads in Sur and Muscat barred the passage of the waters to the sea as if they were dams.
The consequences were grave and beyond the imaginations of most Omanis. The old town of Sur already stood one and a half meters under water when the police decided to blow open the coast road in two places and so make an opening in the barrier.

In Muscat the entire shopping triangle surrounding the Sabco Center in Al Qurm disappeared in the floods; the Chedi hotel had already been evacuated as a precaution.
Electricity cables and water pipes were broken in many places and the seawater desalination plants had to be closed down for five days. The government distributed bottled water over a wide area but also neighborhood help organizations came to the fore. The whole country pulled together in order to overcome what had been the greatest natural disaster in the history of Oman. Offers of aid from abroad were self-confidently turned down. After a week the balance sheet for the catastrophe was 49 dead and 27 missing with damages totaling 4 billion US dollars.
The roads along the Eastern Hajar Mountains between Al Ashkarah, Ras Al Had, Sur, Qurayyat and Muscat were all severely damaged and in parts completely washed away. Since then they have been made once more passable, if only partly with the help of makeshift tracks and bridges. The complete reconstruction will last at least another year. Along this stretch of coast the locations will show the scars of this storm for a long time to come. The cyclone did not just destroy buildings and constructions, but also transformed complete landscapes. The wandering dunes in the hinterland of Al Ashkarah were simply swept away by the wind and south of Ras Al Had large lakes formed near the coast. The idyllic Wadi Shab was especially affected. The masses of water tumbling down the mountain swept the laboriously laid out fields of bananas, fodder grass and palm trees into the sea. Where once one had wandered along the valley, following a small watercourse through lush green scenery, the whole width of the valley is now a vast and desolate gravel bank.
In the western media the catastrophe was hardly reported. Anyone wanting to form their own picture of the events of June 5, 2007 should search for Gonu Oman in the Internet.
(http://www.youtube.com)

Driving in the region of the Eastern Hajars one should always keep an eye on the edge of the road, as it will take some time until before all the damage caused by the cyclone is made good again.

The lakes formed as a result of the storm on the edge of the Wihibah developed into biotopes with their own flora and fauna. Most of them meanwhile disappeared again.

Page 178:
Remains of fortifications can be found in even the most remote spots in the Hajar Mountains.

New Forts for Old

Apart from the most important forts, the clay architecture of Oman dispenses with reinforcing elements in the walls such as stones or bricks of mud. The building materials are extremely prone to damage from erosion through rainfall, which is infrequent but can be heavy. As long as the fortresses were in use such damage was regularly repaired. With the decline in power and the introduction of new military strategies and weapons in the 20th century, the fortresses lost importance and fell into disrepair. Holes in the walls and collapsed roofs exposed more and more areas to the elements and increasing amounts of clay would be washed away. Within a century the once proud forts and settlements had become ruins, often little more than large heaps of clay with a few beams or stumps of walls protruding. They had been built from earth and were returning to earth.

Restoring old buildings in the usual sense of the word is only very seldom possible, the substance of many of the estimated 500 fortresses in the Hajar and Al Batinah regions having been extensively washed away. Restoring these old buildings is expensive in terms of both time and money and has had to be restricted to the most historical or imposing sites in the country. The results of these efforts, especially with regard to the almost completely destroyed inner décor, should be seen more as replicas of the original fortresses - new buildings imitating the old style. The restoration of Barka Fort was completed in 1987, Nakhal Fort in 1990, Bayt An Naman in 1991 and Al Hazm Fort in 1997. In 1999 Ar Rustaq Fort was once more opened for visitors. For the reasons given these new old fortresses lack any historical charisma. Everything is smooth and new, with no crumbling plaster or peeling paint. Maybe in ten or more years they will look like what one imagines old forts to be.

Naturally only in very rare cases did some of the original décor survive in the caved-in rooms. The Ministry of Heritage and Culture has tried to give the buildings more atmosphere using various everyday objects, but these somewhat sparse exhibition pieces fail to make much impression in the sometimes very large rooms.

Happily there are exceptions: Bayt An Naman, Jabrin Fort, Al Hazm Fort and Qurayyat Fort in the north, as well as Taqah Fort in the south of the country. Only a few of the countless forts in north Oman come from the Portuguese period. The occupiers' focus was not directed at mastering the country's interior but solely on controlling maritime trade. As a result their fortresses are only found on the coast, at Muscat, Mutrah, Qurayyat, Sohar and Khasab. Most of the "Omani" forts, on the other hand, were built in the mountainous interior of the country. They arose in the first heyday of the Yaruba dynasty and were to protect the fertile coast and ports from attackers from the Arabian desert.

It is difficult to make a clear distinction between Arab and Portuguese fortress architecture. During the Middle Ages the Moors occupied parts of Europe, primarily in the Iberian peninsula, where there was a considerable cultural intermingling, which led to stylistic parallels.

What was decisive for the development of fortresses in Oman was not so much the architectural influence of the Portuguese, but rather their introduction of new weaponry. It was during the Italian Renaissance that a new European form of fortress architecture emerged, characterized by complex, star-shaped or polygonal outlines which never found their way to Oman.

The oldest and simplest form of fortified building in Oman consisted of a walled square, with several narrow watchtowers, at least one at each corner. If danger threatened, the surrounding tribespeople would take refuge in the fortress. The Al Batinah coast, without any natural shield against attack, was surrounded by some one hundred of these fortresses known as *surs*. At every settlement you can still find the remains of such fortifications or a new reconstructions of a *sur*.

The cannon introduced by the Portuguese could not be placed in buildings of this type. The towers and battlements were too narrow and cramped. The weapons revolutionized defensive warfare but they also had decided disadvantages. For one thing, the up to five meter long artillery pieces were enormously heavy and so had to be kept in a stationary position, and for another poison gases were often released after a cannon was touched off. Both of these had an influence on the design of fortresses. The cannon always had to be placed on a platform in the open air, so that the noxious vapors could be immediately dispelled. Also, the higher the cannon were placed above the surrounding area, the further their range.

Because of its exposed situation on a massive boulder, Nakhal Fort was one of the few old forts in the Al Batinah region which was suited to the new weapons technology. On several occasions in the course of its long history, it was completely rebuilt. The watchtowers were reinforced to become massive cannon towers. Enemies could be attacked before they approached close enough to use their own weapons, for the attackers could never drag comparable weapons along with them. With these new military developments in mind Saif Al Yaruba built the Al Hazm Fort in 1708. The whole region around could be watched over from its two round towers placed at diagonally opposite corners. This fort can be seen as a prototype for many other, similar buildings of a later period. To satisfy the new criteria for a defensive building, only one huge cannon tower surrounded by defensive walls was really required.

Nizwa Fort, with its central tower, over 30 meters high and having a diameter of 45 meters, satisfied this notion, as did the fort at Ar Rustaq. The lower parts of the walls in these forts are equipped with embrasures from which the defenders could fire on pressing attackers. As smaller, lighter, more mobile cannon were developed the outer walls had to be reinforced as happened, for example, at Bayt An Naman, originally built as a summer residence.

The country's volatile past with its countless tribal conflicts resulted in many Omani domestic dwellings incorporating aspects of defensive architecture. Many private houses have something of the character of a fortress about them.

The restored Fort at Nakhal.

The walls are thick, with towers and battlements, with the ground floor only lit by small light slits. Even in peaceful times this style of building has not changed much, only these details have mutated into decorative motifs. The residence of the *wali*, the leader of the local community, was traditionally always situated in the center of a village, and had the characteristics of a fort. The building's architectural style reflected his leading role in the community. As master of the oasis, the fertile area, he automatically controlled the destiny of the surrounding desert area. Interestingly, throughout Oman today, the new buildings belonging to the wali are always on the edges of an oasis. However if the settlements expand further, as planned, these residences will once more be in the center. They are easy to recognize: small, white-painted "forts" with towers, battlements and an Omani flag on the roof.

If you want to get an overview of fortress architecture in Oman but don't want to drive several thousand kilometers around the country then a visit to the *Sayyid Faisal Bin Ali Museum* in the grounds of the Ministry of Heritage and Culture is recommended. The most significant buildings and their various types of construction are documented on panels. Pictures of the buildings before and after restoration illustrate the problems involved in restoring clay buildings. The museum is open daily from Saturday to Wednesday from 08:00 to 14:00.

Through the Eastern Hajars to Qurayyat

At the Wadi Aday roundabout west of Ruwi the road branches off south to Qurayyat. Only a few hundred meters after the roundabout, on the right hand side of the road, you come across the small settlement of Wadi Aday, made up of mostly very simple, small one-storey buildings huddled together. It was here that, at the beginning of the 1970s, after Sultan Qaboos's accession to power, many of the returning émigrés from Zanzibar lived without electricity, air conditioning or plumbing. The thresholds of the doorways are raised, as in those days the wadi - unlike today - was not protected against floods. After the Zanzibari had established themselves in their new home country, they moved into new dwellings scattered all over the town.

The torrents of water thundering through the wadi as a result of Cyclone Gonu destroyed most of these buildings and several kilometers of the highway which winds its way through the narrow, meandering Wadi Aday bounded by steep cliff walls. As legend has it, while the route for the new road was being dynamited several ancient men were apparently freed from the rock where they had been imprisoned in the rock by an evil spirit.

Going through the valley you reach a plain with many small settlements. Here the road widens to four lanes. The further you drive, the more often you get the impression that the mountain summits are poking through the plain. Steep, pyramid-like cones of rock, only five to thirty meters high, are lined up next to one another on the plain, which is otherwise as flat as a billiard table. To the east of the road vast slabs of rock burst out of the earth reaching to ever-increasing heights, quickly reaching a level of over one 1000 meters.

About 25 kilometers from Muscat the road branches left to the small fishing villages of Yiti and Bander Al Kiran. Shortly after branching off, the road surface changes from asphalt to packed gravel, and the road leads through Wadi Al Mayh to picturesque bays with mangrove cover. The route's first kilometers run through a narrow gorge with impressive rock walls, in which the layers of rock are folded into bizarre forms, as though deliberately twisted by some giant. The way now almost exclusively follows the bed of the wadi and can be covered only slowly in a normal car - providing that it hasn't just rained. You just require patience and good shock absorbers.

If you want to press on to the coast, then it is best to hire a four-wheel drive vehicle and spend a whole day exploring the idyllic bays and simple villages at leisure. Since 1996 there is an alternative to the route through the wadi, an asphalt road which runs from Muscat to Bander Al Kiran and Yiti. Also an attractive route, you can join this road at the Hamriya roundabout in Ruwi. One more road is under construction along the coast from Bander Al Jissah to Yiti.

The road to Qurayyat climbs steadily. In the distance, to the southwest, is the 2000 meter high, relatively flat summit plateau of the **Jabal Al Aswad**, the "Black Mountain," with its steep slopes. These steep escarpments make this one of the most inaccessible mountains of Oman. Even the mountain nomads, the most undemanding of peoples, only manage to eke out the barest of subsistences here. Parts of the massif have been denominated as the **Wadi Sarrayn Nature Reserve**. The nature reserve offers protection to one of the least known and least researched, shyest mammals in the world, the **Arabian tahr**, *Hemitraqus jayakari*, a goat-like animal.

The *tahr*, a creature between a goat and an ibex, is a close relation of the musk ox and the chamois. A larger mutation of the tahr was earlier native to the oak forests of Europe, albeit between the last ice age, some 100,000 years ago, and one million years ago. The tahr is a relic of primordial fauna which has been able to survive in one of the most isolated corners of the earth. Similar ungulates can also be found in the mountains of the Himalayas and South India. The survival instinct of the tahr is such that the slightest sound is enough to put it to flight. With its immense agility it can vanish into the most inaccessible areas to escape the researcher's gaze. One of the few people who has ever encountered an Arabian tahr in the wild is the naturalist Paul Munton.

Gateway to Nowhere?

Along the main road to Qurayyat strange small constructions repeatedly catch your eye, which are hard to place at first: on open, unbuilt-up areas of gravel between the small mountain peaks next to the road, you come across accurately built pillars, the distance between them being the width of a gateway. Sometimes you'll see a gate hanging between the pillars, a splendid gateway to nowhere. No other signs of building work are to be seen.

This phenomenon can be seen throughout Oman. The function of these edifices is to mark out the plot of land as somebody's property. Omanis usually own a piece of land long before they have the money necessary to build on it. This is because every Omani, man or woman, receives a one time gift of a parcel of land from the state, (except if he is rich). When this happens is up to the individual. Everyone has a right to his land from his own tribal area. The individual plot is selected through drawing of lots.

Some Omanis use their plot of land as an investment, while some prefer to realize a profit immediately by selling it. Still others first secure the land and then begin to put aside the money to build a house over the succeeding years.

Admittedly the Oman Housing Bank offers very favorable loans, but those who do not wish to run up debts first expend a small sum in erecting the gateway to what will later be their home. Another way used to mark out one's territory is to build the corners of the walls which will later be completed to surround the property.

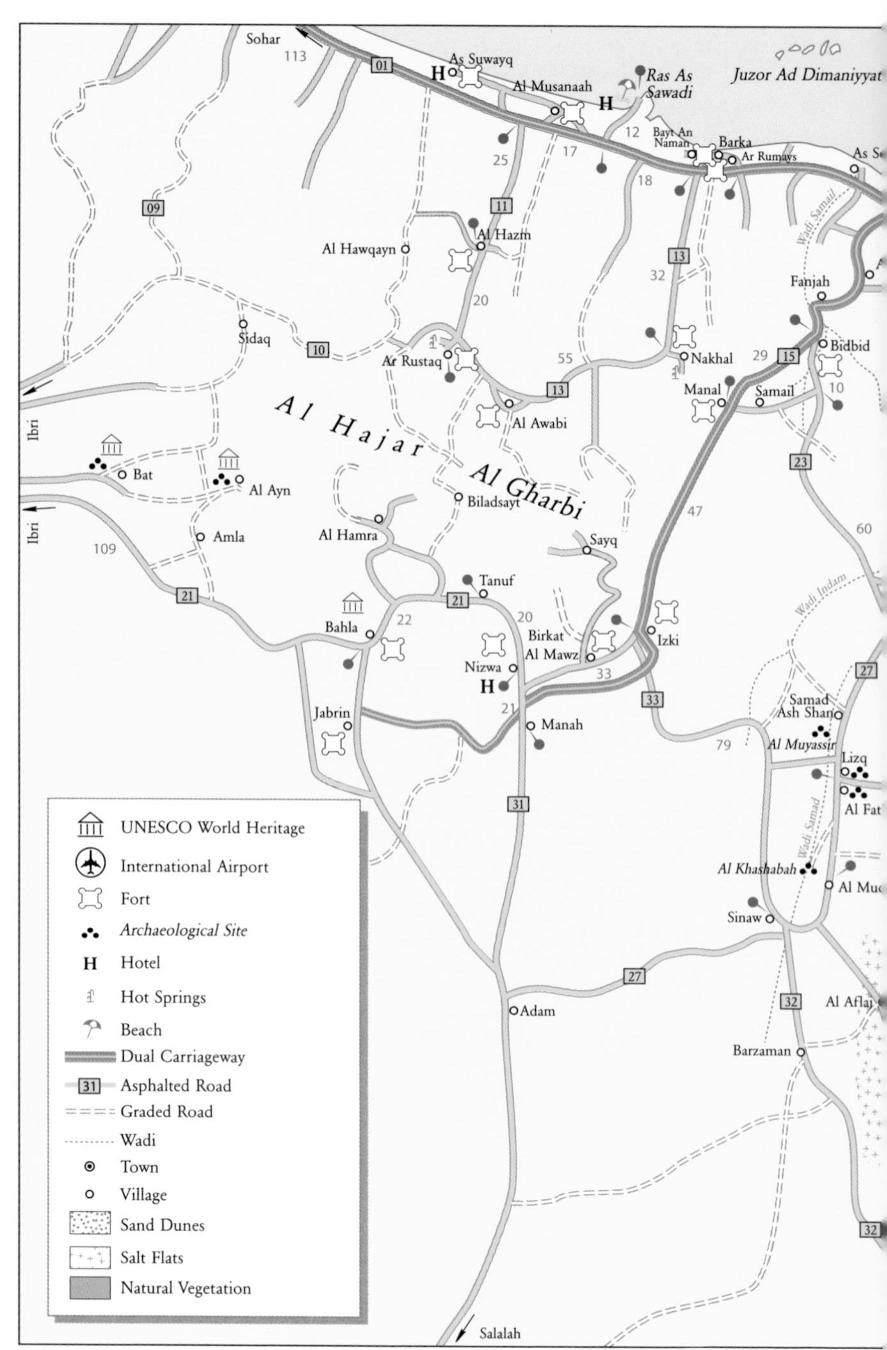
Sohar
As Suwayq
Al Musanaah
Ras As Sawadi
Juzor Ad Dimaniyyat
Bayt An Naman
Barka
Ar Rumays
Al Hawqayn
Al Hazm
Fanjah
Sidaq
Ar Rustaq
Nakhal
Bidbid
Manal
Samail
Al Awabi
Al Hajar Al Gharbi
Bat
Al Ayn
Ibri
Biladsayt
Amla
Al Hamra
Sayq
Tanuf
Bahla
Birkat Al Mawz
Izki
Nizwa
Jabrin
Manah
Samad Ash Shan
Al Muyassir
Lizq
Wadi Samail
Wadi Indam
Wadi Samad
Al Khashabah
Sinaw
Adam
Al Aflaj
Barzaman
Salalah
UNESCO World Heritage
International Airport
Fort
Archaeological Site
Hotel
Hot Springs
Beach
Dual Carriageway
Asphalted Road
Graded Road
Wadi
Town
Village
Sand Dunes
Salt Flats
Natural Vegetation

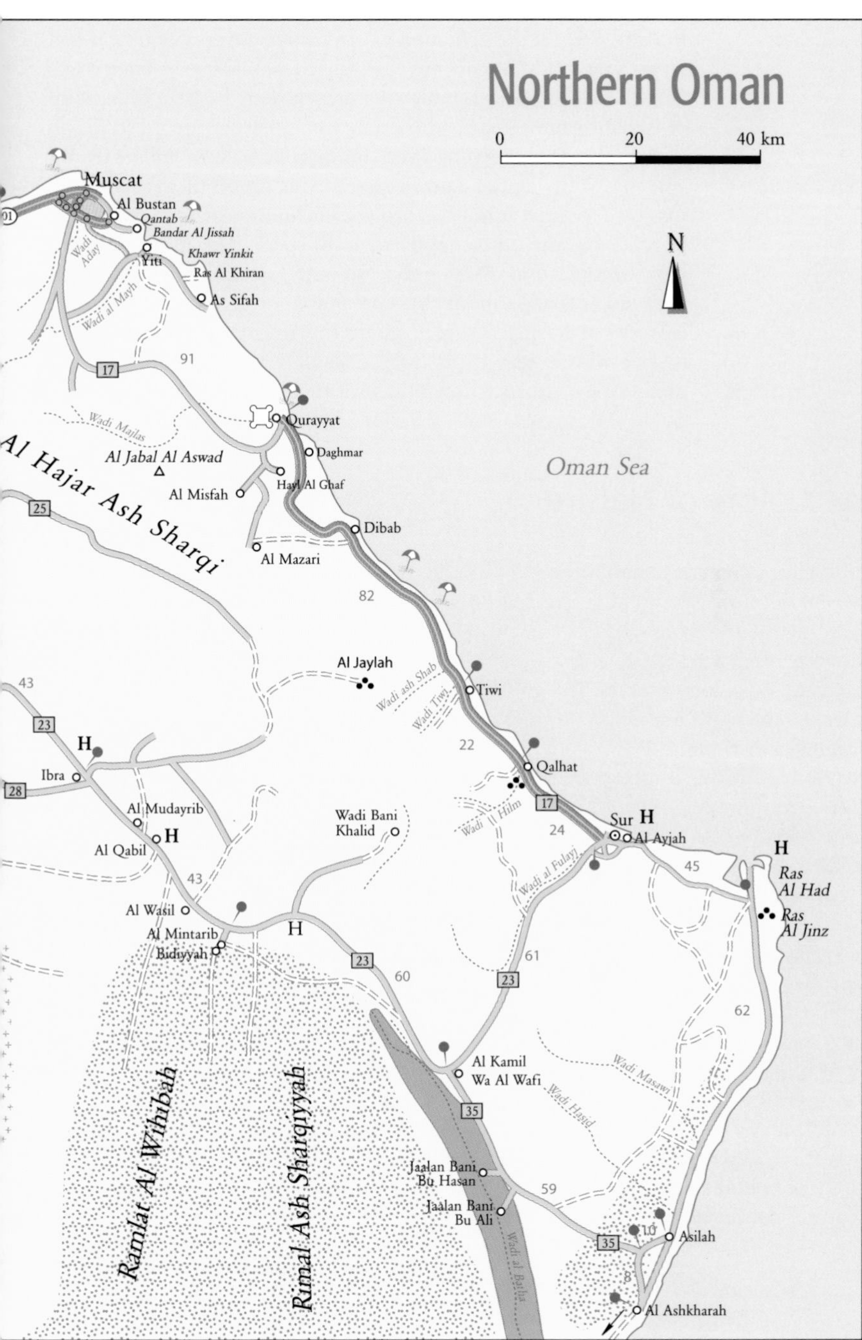
Northern Oman
0
20
40 km
N
Muscat
Al Bustan
Qantab
Bandar Al Jissah
Khawr Yinkit
Yiti
Ras Al Khiran
As Sifah
Wadi Aday
Wadi al Mayh
17
91
Wadi Majlas
Quriyyat
Daghmar
Al Jabal Al Aswad
Hayl Al Ghaf
Al Misfah
Al Hajar Ash Sharqi
25
Dibab
Al Mazari
Oman Sea
82
Al Jaylah
Wadi ash Shab
Wadi Tiwi
Tiwi
43
23
H
Ibra
28
22
Qalhat
17
Wadi Hilm
Al Mudayrib
Al Qabil
H
Wadi Bani Khalid
Sur H
Al Ayjah
24
Wadi al Fulayj
45
H
Ras Al Had
Ras Al Jinz
43
Al Wasil
Al Mintarib
Bidiyyah
H
23
60
61
23
62
Al Kamil Wa Al Wafi
Wadi Masawi
Wadi Hasad
35
Ramlat Al Wihibah
Rimal Ash Sharqiyyah
Jaalan Bani Bu Hasan
59
Jaalan Bani Bu Ali
Wadi al Batha
10
Asilah
35
8
Al Ashkharah

In April 1976, at the invitation of the Omani government, he began a two year study of this rare animal. He would never have come face to face with this nimble creature without the help of a group of Omani gamekeepers, whose job was to ensure the preservation of the tahr. These men had very intimate knowledge of the terrain and the habits of the animal. Indeed this group of conservationists was recruited from the former tahr hunters of the region. The poacher has turned gamekeeper, so to speak. The former hunters have become uniformed public servants proudly exercising their unique knowledge about this rare animal to protect the species.
In spite of having a superb guide the naturalist only came face to face with a tahr at his third attempt - and then only for five minutes; his efforts to keep up with the practiced hunters in high

The Colors of Nature

The geological wealth of Oman offers the viewer a unique aesthetic attraction: an unusual variety of natural shades of color. The last kilometers of the stretch between Muscat and Qurayyat, before the road winds its narrow, steep, serpentine path down to the Qurayyat coastal area, offer particularly striking earth colors. Oman's earth has an astonishingly broad palette of colors, from ochres and browns, greens and blues to red and violet. A great deal of the earth and rocks are ideally suited for obtaining pigments; they capture the bright, intense sunlit tones of the country. This natural source of color has hardly been exploited. In this respect the spirit of the age sweeps across Oman just as strongly as it does over Europe.
In our modern world natural pigments are often seen as "dirt." People have lost the knowledge of the cultural significance of this natural ingredient of art and design, although until well into the 19th century manufacturing paints out of natural ingredients was a considerable part of the process of painting! In this age of so-called progress, people look to the synthetic colors of the West, even in Oman where for ages plant pigments were traditionally used for dying textiles. There seems little chance for nonstandard methods of manufacture, as the decline of the indigo dyeworks in Oman bears witness.
Indigo is one of the oldest, most well-known and most valuable dyes in the world, a dark midnight blue which found its way to Europe by way of the maritime trade with India. Even in antiquity the indigo plant was extensively cultivated in India, the pigment being obtained from the petals. From the drying and fermentation processes a fluid is extracted which is then stirred so that air is mixed in. The oxidation results in the formation of insoluble, deep blue indigo from the equally insoluble indoxyl. The indigo must then be purified and concentrated. This characteristic means that the indigo does not penetrate the fibers. The blue easily runs and bleaches relatively quickly as jeans wearers the world over know from experience.

mountainous terrain caused too much noise. Mostly he could only follow and investigate the tracks and above all the burrows scraped out by the animals. His reconnaissance trips led Paul Munton over the whole range of the Hajar Mountains as far north as Musandam and the Strait of Hormuz. Only there was he able to sight a tahr. In his published study the naturalist comes to the conclusion that some 200 specimens of this rare species are spread over the whole mountain range. They prefer the steep northern slopes as habitat where it is relatively shaded and moisture is retained for longer. They have retreated to those regions which most resemble the more moderate climatic conditions of an earlier geological period. They would have no chances of survival in the deserts around the mountains of Oman.

As early as 1900 synthetic indigo was forcing out natural indigo, mainly because of the expense involved in its manufacture and its lack of durability.
During the long period when Oman was isolated from the rest of the world an indigo industry developed and flourished until 1970. The indigo plant thrives here in altitudes between 300 and 1000 meters. The centers of production were Bahla, Firq, Ibri and the coast of Dhofar. Indigo traditionally colored the blue black women's face masks and clothes, and was used to dye *dishdashas*, the men's robes, a light blue, using a smaller amount of dye. Dyed fabrics were much in demand as export goods from Oman. In 1985 Jenny Balfour-Paul investigated the indigo tradition in Oman. She found only two dye-works still in existence in the whole of Oman, in the suqs of Bahla and Ibri. Both of the master craftsmen were already old and neither had a successor. That the time-consuming and laborious manufacturing process may only bring a profit after a considerable length of time is not in keeping with the Zeitgeist, which is more fast-moving, so it is no wonder that neither of these businesses is in existence today.
Nonetheless it may be that this ancient craft can be rescued in the 21st century, a change of heart having taken place in western industrialized nations. Some synthetic dyes have been found to be damaging to health and have been withdrawn from use, while the demand for natural dyes has increased. In 2005 a kilo of good quality genuine indigo cost 230 Euro in specialty shops. As long as the manufacturing process has not been completely forgotten, these changes could bode well for indigo producers and dyers in Oman. The tradition has not completely disappeared and the knowledge is still on hand. This new attitude to natural products could be of interest to the export-oriented Omanis. Using colors obtained from minerals, of which the earth here clearly has an abundance, could also turn out to be commercially interesting to Oman.

Qurayyat and Environs

After a steep descent with a spectacular view you reach the coastal area of Qurayyat. Here a road forks off to the south leading to Hayl Al Ghaf and Al Misfah. **Hayl Al Ghaf** was famous for its extensive and impressive mango plantations, which were the largest and oldest in the whole of Oman. The huge trees formed a majestic avenue, a green tunnel leading to the village. This avenue, the beautiful gardens and many of the houses were sadly destroyed or extensively damaged by the cyclone. Picturesque Misfah, situated at the foot of the mountains, was also heavily affected by the violent storm. Misfah has an ancient, ingenious falaj system. As if by a miracle this survived the floods. Neither place is particularly inviting for walks at the moment. The inhabitants have their hands full getting their land and homes back into shape.

When on the road to Al Misfah, if you instead take the left fork in the direction of Al Mazari, after about 13 kilometers you'll reach **Wadi Dayqah**. Soon a big dam will be finished here to enhance the water supply of the Capital Area.

The variety and harmony of the colors of the Omani landscape can be seen in this palette of pigments obtained from ground stone.

The main road leads through the date gardens of **Qurayyat** direct to the old suq and the fort. Up until the mid-1990s the old suq was the most unspoiled in Oman and even worth a visit outside of business hours. Today most of the shops have been closed and the traders have resettled along the side of the road. More than in any other place in Oman Qurayyat symbolizes the change from a sleepy village to a small modern town. Diagonally across from the fort you come to an open fruit and vegetable suq as well as to a small restaurant, unnamed, that is to be recommended, the walls of which are covered in stainless steel. One of the buildings in Oman most worthy of a visit is the unimposing fort at Qurayyat. During the pauses between the few visits to the fort, the custodian passes the time in entertaining chit-chat with the traders of the vegetable suq. **Qurayyat Fort** was built by the Portuguese who, at the beginning of the 16th century were consolidating their position after the conquest of Oman. In the Middle Ages Qurayyat had been known as a port for exporting salt and the Arab horses which are bred in the surrounding area. After the arrival of the Portuguese and the accompanying destruction of the town, the port irrecoverably lost its importance. Qurayyat shared this fate with the more southerly ports of Tiwi and Qalhat. The Omani tribes united under Nasir ibn Murshid in 1624 to fight against the occupying power and bit by bit forced them out. By the middle of the century Qurayyat Fort was once more back in the hands of Omanis.

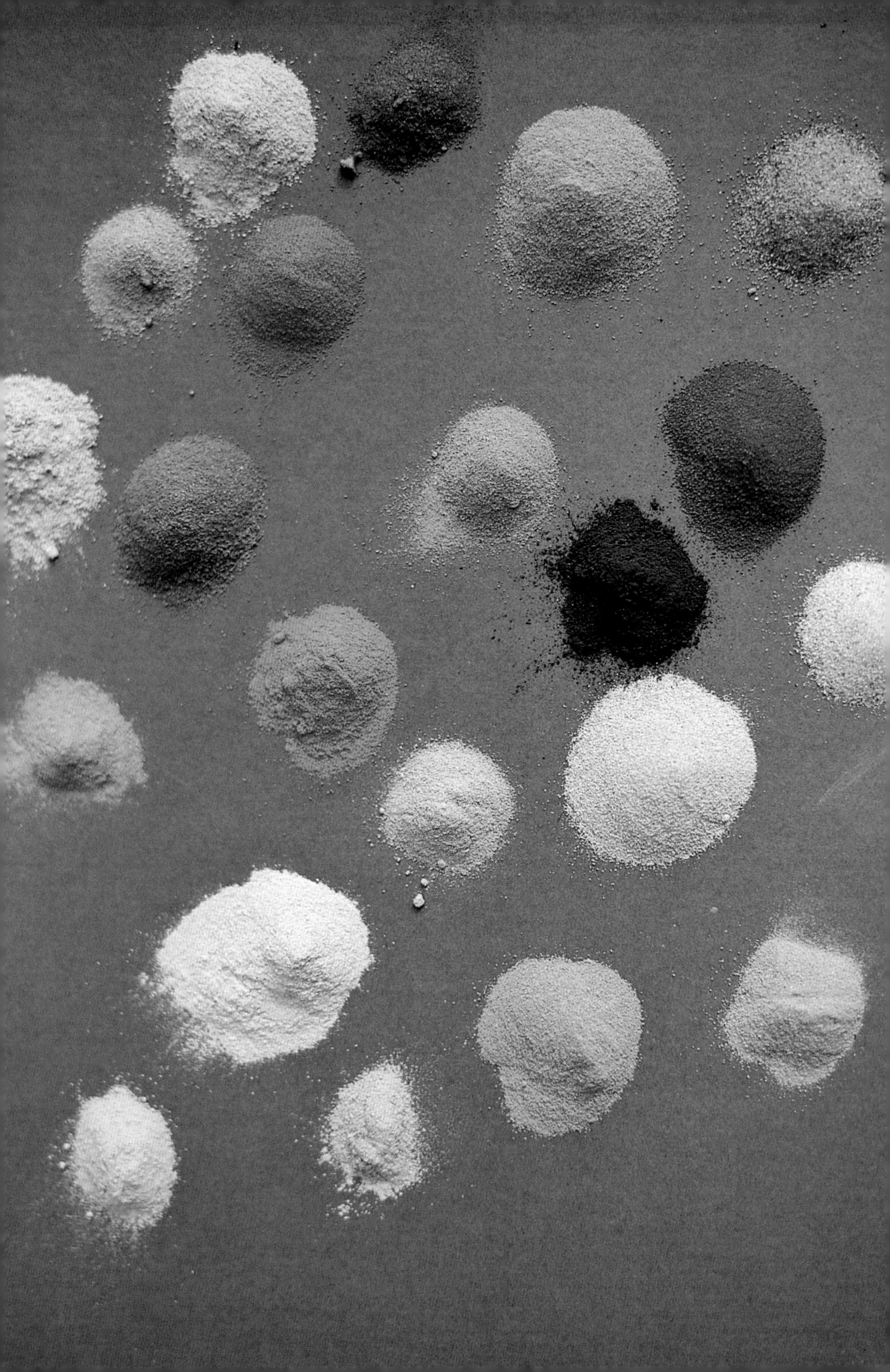

The relatively small fort has meanwhile been restored. In contrast to the mostly large fortresses in the north, the inside has a wealth of everyday objects on display, for example household goods, which give the visitor an impression of the life and atmosphere of earlier times.
The fort was traditionally the administrative residence of the wali of Qurayyat, who lived here with his entire family. It consists of a reception room, the *majlis*, his sleeping quarters, the women's room, a children's room, a kitchen and a mosque as well as a storeroom, as in every fort in Oman: an inclined floor would be piled high with sacks full of dates, emergency rations in case of siege. A channel ran along the bottom edge of the sloped floor, which ran into a hollow in the floor. Over time the juice dripping from the fruit flowed into a container placed in the hollow. The syrup obtained in this manner was spread like jam onto bread. Today you can find "date honey" in the markets, a nice souvenir and "taste of Oman". In a shady corner of the inner courtyard is a pole with several clay jugs hanging from it: an old Omani form of "refrigerator," which works on the same principle as a bottle cooler. They were filled with water and the coolness of the evaporating fluid as it slowly seeped through the porous clay ensured that the rest of the fluid in the jug remained pleasantly cool to drink.
The recessed entrance, with a slit-shaped opening above it accessible from the roof, is typical of Omani fortress architecture. If attacked the defenders could shoot through this slit, pour scalding hot oil or date syrup on the enemies already hampered by the narrow space, or, in case the door was set on fire, extinguish the flames by pouring water down from above. This type of entrance is known as a *kuwwa*.
You can get a good view of the whole oasis from the roof. To the east you can see a mangrove swamp and the sea, which provides the fishermen of Qurayyat with their living. In order to get to the sea you drive past the fort and curve to the right, passing a few small houses and gardens. After several hundred meters you reach the bay, the shores of which are thickly overgrown with mangroves. Follow the bank and you will reach the open sea. The area to the north of the road serves as a bathing beach. The beach to the south of the road is the preserve of the fishermen.
In the bay there is a small island with a round watchtower. Until 1995 the beach offered an idyllic picture: it was teeming with small, fiberglass boats. Goats jumped around between the boats and chewed at the nets. Old men, women and children would be sitting in the shade of the small fishermen's huts strung along the beach

Omani refrigerator: clay jugs for cooling water in Qurayyat fort

They were waiting for the fishermen returning with their catches, which would be auctioned directly on the beach. With the move to diversify Oman's economy at the beginning of the 1990s it was decided to develop modern ports at several places along the coast, including Qurayyat, which received investment sums to the tune of ten million Euros.

Today large natural stone jetties stretch far into the sea, providing mooring places for more than 300 boats, and a road leads along the coast to the new port. It is to be the economic motor for the area and will no doubt influence the appearance of the coastline over the coming years. Next to oil and gas, fishing is the country's most important source of income.

The fishermen of Oman

1700 kilometers of coastline and a protected zone that is 200 nautical miles wide secure Oman's rich stocks of fish. The coastal zones of Oman are among the cleanest and most abundant in fish species in the whole of the Indian Ocean. Up to now 150 different species of fish have been counted, of which 35 belong to the perch family, known as *hammur* to Omanis, as well as sardines, tuna and mackerel. The most highly valued fish in Oman is king mackerel, also known as the kingfish. The fisheries are still one of the most important branches of the country's economy.

The introduction of the "oil age" has not changed this although at the beginning of the 1970s it seemed as though it would. Many fishermen gave up their old jobs, which seemed outdated, to look for work in the newly emerging high-tech oil industry. Clever policy managed to rapidly put a stop to this new development. It was not that the fishermen wanted to quit the coast and work far off in the middle of the desert. Rather they wanted to escape their medieval way of life and become part of the age of progress. The government started an aid program which gave the fishermen the opportunity to purchase a modern fiberglass boat with an outboard motor on favorable terms, and to exchange their old nets for new ones. In addition their occupation was placed under

Tuna (above) are one of the most frequently caught fish off the coast of Oman. They are either sold at local markets or exported.

The sardines (left) which are caught in nets cast from the shore are dried in the sun and used as animal feed.

the protection of the law. Only Omani citizens could obtain a commercial fishing license. The new fiberglass boats matched the old wooden ones in form and size. In this way the fishermen's wealth of experience, which had been built up and handed down through centuries of dealing with the sea and its resources, could still be utilized. Most of the fishermen took up the government's offer and returned to their ancestral calling. In the last thirty years, far from declining, the number of fishermen has actually risen steadily. In 2005 32,400 fishermen were registered, 19,000 more than in 1984. In their standardized boats, now manufactured in Oman, they fish all of the country's coastal waters. The annual catch far exceeds the regional and national needs, fluctuating between 118,000 and 160,000 tons.

In 2004 the fish stocks in Oman were estimated at 47 million tons. The catch is mostly auctioned directly to dealers on the beach. Part disappears into large coolers which are lashed in the backs of pick-ups. These vehicles regularly make deliveries of fresh fish to remote spots and oases in the country's interior.

Another part finds its way into large cooling sheds which are scattered along the coast, and from there exported to the USA, Japan, Australia and Europe. In the coming years this share should grow to four percent of the total.
In the 1970s the large fleet of coastal fishermen were threatened by competition from a small number of sea trawlers. In 1977 a Korean company received a concession to fish in Omani territorial waters. They trained Omanis on their boats and 38% of their catch was given to the government by way of charges for the concession. The deep sea fishing fleet's share of the total catch is only some 30 percent. Until 1988 the catches climbed steadily and then came a slump. The stocks of the preferred species like king mackerel, tuna and perch had been overfished and closed seasons had to be declared and observed. Lobsters, crayfish and abalone shellfish were also affected. Curiously, until the country was opened up in 1970, lobster and crayfish had never appealed to the Omanis. However the fishermen were quick to note their commercial worth in light of the culinary interest shown in the crustaceans by Europeans. They exploited the new trend but as yet seldom eat crustaceans themselves - in this they are like the majority of Omanis. The fishing quotas are checked by government "beach guards." The landed catches are registered in detail and they also conduct the auctions.
In order to increase the chances of survival of young fish, and to protect the stocks, the minimum mesh size is set at fourteen centimeters.
Sardines are still caught with nets cast from the beach and they are immediately dried there. The dried fish are used as a high nutrient animal feed. This old tradition will probably soon be superseded thanks to the increased production of fodder grass in the Sultanate during the last few years. New ideas will still determine life on the coast. In recent years 200 million Omani rials have flowed into the fishing industry, 84 million of which were for the purchase of ships and fiberglass boats as well as the construction of installations near the coast and the necessary infrastructure. 13.5 million Omani rials were envisioned for the establishment of fish processing businesses, and 75 million for estimating stocks as well as the planning and building of plants. The construction of eight large and sixteen smaller harbors along the coast cost another 25 million. The ports of Sur and Qurayyat were extended so that deep sea trawlers could also dock. These measures should reduce the great pressure put on Mutrah's port, Mina As Sultan Qaboos. The future of the fishing economy in Oman now rests on so-called aquaculture, or fish farming. Studies for this have already begun at the Marine Science and Fisheries Center at Sidab. Sea aquaculture is planned on a grand scale, by which mussels, oysters, abalones and later also king mackerel and perch will be farmed. The methods developed at the research center should be taken over by the fishermen. One thing that is certain is that new harbors and fish farms will markedly change the image of the fishing communities of Qurayyat in future.

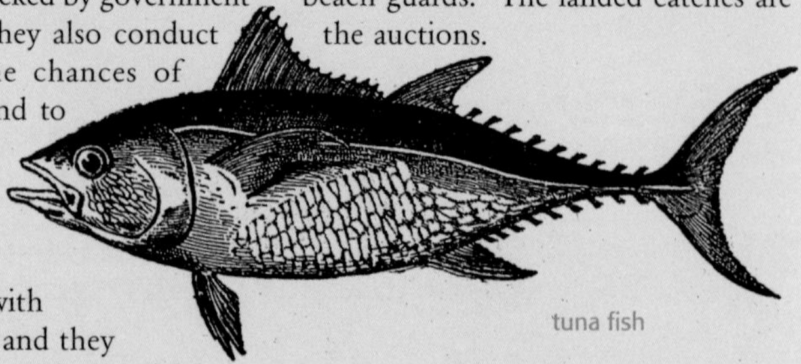

tuna fish

The Southern Al Batinah Coast

Dates, Fortresses and Hot Springs

If you had set off on this varied day trip over the southern Al Batinah Plain in the past, you would have had a good opportunity to collect experiences of Omani bureaucracy. The fortresses at Barka, Bayt An Naman, Nakhal, Ar Rustaq and Al Hazm could only be visited with official authorization. Currently however officials and tourists are spared the time-consuming procedure of applying for written authorization to visit each individual fortress. Nowadays it suffices just to enter your name in the visitors' book when you are there.

Simply leave Muscat by the main highway in the direction of Sohar. A few kilometers west of the Al Khod roundabout, on the right of the road, you pass **Nasim Park**, the largest park in the Muscat region with play areas, places to picnic and a miniature railway. There are two ways to get to Barka. Either following the highway until the roundabout near Barka, or you can leave the main road some ten kilometers before and take a small byroad sign-posted "Barka" running northwest. This winds through small villages and extensive date plantations and is certainly the more attractive of the two routes. Dates are the most frequently cultivated plants in the region around Barka, Ar Rustaq and Nakhal. They transform the bare earth into a swelling sea of green.

The small road leads directly to **Barka**. The large fortress with its three imposing towers rises up near the coast, surrounded by the remains of the old town wall. In front of the fortress gate there is a small suq which is worth a visit. On the beach the fishermen sell their catch. Because the Al Batinah coast is completely open to the sea it was always prone to attacks and invasions. Strongholds like the Barka Fort were important for the survival of the inhabitants all along the coast. According to Donald Hawley the fortress at Barka was built at the end of the 18th century by Imam Hamad ibn Said. The size of the fort corresponds to the importance given to the place; Barka is the second largest settlement in the region, after Sohar. The restored, or rather the partially newly built fort lacks any real trace of historical atmosphere, and as such is a typical example for the renovation of clay architecture in Oman.

The Fine Art of Harvesting Dates

From Musandam in the north to Sur in the east, Oman offers the ideal climatic conditions for the growth of date palms, but not however for a successful harvest of its fruit. Winged insects such as bees are rare in Oman due to its extreme dryness, so from an economic point of view natural pollination is completely unsatisfactory. If the date farmer, the *bidr*, wants a heavy crop then he has to undertake the pollination himself during the flowering season which, according to the type of date, falls between the end of February and the beginning of April. The yield also depends fundamentally on whether the palm has been grown from seed or cultivated from offshoots. Trees that have sprouted from seeds grow weakly and their fruit is meager and very sparse. As a result the generally preferred manner of propagation is to take offshoots from large, strong, yield-bearing trees, these qualities being passed on to the daughter plants. In its lifetime a date palm produces at most twenty offshoots, which can only be separated from the mother plant when they have themselves started to put out roots. The shoots are placed in deep pits, so that the roots are as near as possible to the ground-water level and so can be watered more easily. The price for such offshoots varies greatly according to their quality - between 5 and 100 Omani rials according to the type.

Date palms vary greatly, even if they do all look alike to the untutored eye. In Oman there are apparently 152 genetically distinguishable female sorts of date palm and five male. Only 20 sorts are of economic interest, even if at some oases such as Samail up to 60 different sorts are cultivated. All 157 varieties can be found on a state research farm at Wadi Qurayyat, a "genetic database" which should enable the cultivation of new types, with higher yields and better suited to the local climate. In order to pollinate all the female plants at an oasis, only one male plant is required. The pollen panicles are carefully gathered in their pods and during the flowering season they fetch high prices in the suqs. The *bidr* goes to the seed bank and purchases the pollen best suited to produce a good crop with his female plants. Using a wide belt made out of plaited palm branches as a support, he climbs up the tree with the bag of pollen and binds several of the spiky blossom panicles and one of the pollen panicles together. The success of this painstaking work can be destroyed by a single shower of rain and the whole procedure must be repeated.

The entire year's date harvest in Oman is estimated to be between 200,000 and 250,000 tons. The best time to harvest varies according to the type of date, from the end of May to December.

It also depends on the desired degree of ripeness. Four degrees of ripeness can be discerned by four different colorings. Dates that are still green are called *chimbari*, the yellow ones *busr*. The most widespread sort of palm in Oman, the *mefsli*, is harvested when yellow - the fruit is then boiled in large copper kettles and finally dried in the sun. The majority of these are exported. Red dates, *rutab*, taste best when they are round and juicy, especially *khalas*, the queen of Oman's date palms. A *khalas* palm produces fewer offshoots in its lifetime and so is rare and expensive. Its taste is so good that it

Bayt An Naman

Bayt An Naman is situated only a few kilometers from Barka. It is easy to find - simply keep to the small road by which you came, which ends about four kilometers further at a roundabout. Just before this a small asphalt road branches off inland to the left, leading you once more through date plantations direct to Bayt An Naman. You cannot miss it - its red brown towers rise up above the sea of palms.

The economic upturn which took place under the Yaruba imams found expression not only in the development of land with agricultural potential and the *falaj* system, but also in architecture. New towns were founded, for example Al Hamra and Birkat Al Mawz and the palaces of Jabrin, Al Hazm and also Bayt An Naman were built. As early as the first half of the 17th century the first Yaruba imam, Nasir ibn Murshid, had transferred his official residence from Nizwa to Ar Rustaq, presumably for strategic reasons. Here he was nearer the coast and the important harbors and could also control the routes leading to the Jabal Al Akhdar region. Bayt An Naman lay about half way between the seat of government and the

Set in a sea of palms: Bayt An Naman

rarely finds its way to the market or to export. Whoever has had the good fortune to harvest *khalas* dates shares the reward of his labors at most with members of his family. The juicy *rutab* were recommended by the Prophet Mohammed for breaking the fast during Ramadan. They are already as nutritious as the fully ripe brown dates, the *tamr*. They are brought to full ripeness by the strong, hot wind which blows across northern Oman in the summer.

While the world average for dates harvested per palm is 70 to 100 kilograms, in Oman it is often no more than 40 kilograms. The yield is heavily dependent on location and the attentiveness of the *bidr*. During the ripening process, dates need intensive care. The farmer protects the bunches of fruit against the possibility of rain, but also against too strong sunshine and must ensure that the tree is regularly watered. When harvesting, the palm bunches are bundled and slowly lowered to the ground on a rope. Here they are taken up by women and children who also gather the dates that fall to the ground. Because the labor-intensive running of date gardens, together with the low market prices for dates, no longer serve the aspirations to a more modern lifestyle, the interest shown in the plantations has diminished in recent years. On the Al Batinah coast, above all, usable land was left fallow or was used for building or as arable fields. You would see ever more abandoned plantations with dried-up, untended or even rotten trees. There were reasons for this other than the purely economic. The intensification of agriculture on the Al Batinah Plain during the last twenty years entailed an enormous increase in water

important seaport of Muscat. Today **Bayt An Naman** is one of the most sensitively restored and most atmospherically impressive of Oman's old buildings. Until 1990 it was one of the country's most interesting ruins. The building stood in the south west corner of a large unwalled courtyard, of which almost nothing more was recognisable. All of the ceilings had caved in and the splendidly decorated interior walls were exposed, but were still in relatively good condition.

This made the restoration easier and the archaeologist Paolo Costa was able to thoroughly investigate the building's construction and draw conclusions about the history of the building. The building was first mentioned in 1700 in connection with Imam Saif ibn Sultan planning a garden. From the beginning it was planned as a garden house rather than as a dwelling, hence the lack of inner courtyards. The rooms are all open, none of them having any doors; they were intended to be meeting rooms rather than living quarters. The ruins revealed highly interesting characteristics of construction. The outer walls are double. The inner part is 70 centimeters thick with an outer part which is even thicker. To everyone's surprise the outer surface of the inner wall showed every sign of having been an outer wall: stucco work and carefully finished plasterwork.

consumption, which was mostly covered by ground water. Every farmer bored his own wells at will and they were powered by diesel pumps. This widespread over-exploitation led to a sinking of the water table in the area directly by the coast and this in turn led to the increase of salt water. In some places near the coast, the seawater rose so high that salt crusts formed on the surface. Palms can tolerate a relatively high salt content in the water, but these quantities were too much even for them. The salty earth lost its agricultural worth.

The Omani government attempted to overcome these problems with several measures. On the one hand the work of the date farmers, similarly to that of the fishermen, should be relieved through modern technology and thus made more attractive. In Oman newly developed mechanical scaffolding with folding platforms and pollen sprays are the latest achievements in the field of innovation. Wells may only be bored under license from the authorities. The water table has been regenerated through feeding rainwater from a network of dams in the mountains. They prevent the uncontrolled flow of rainwater through the wadis into the sea and instead serve to raise the level of the water table. In addition many weak old date palms were replaced with high quality new seedlings from the genetic research laboratory. The laboratory went into service in 1992 and from the beginning was producing 15,000 seedlings per year. By 2004 this figure had risen to 30,000. Meanwhile the date plantations once more take up 46 percent of the available agricultural land in Oman. The date industry seems to have recaptured some of its attractiveness.

On closer inspection it was concluded that the garden house was originally nothing more than a rectangular block, which was later fitted out with the two towers and the extra wall, making it into a kind of fortress. According to Costa this transformation probably occurred around the middle of the 18th century. At this time the first ruler of the Al-Bu-Said dynasty, Ahmad ibn Said, decided to use Bayt An Naman for official gatherings and as a resting place on the way between Ar Rustaq and Muscat. When making these journeys he would always spend at least two days here and give audiences to the people of the surrounding coastal region. His sons actually lived occasionally in Bayt An Naman.

Bayt An Naman displays various characteristics of Omani architecture, such as the defensive slit above the entrance and the dim rooms on the ground floor which are only lit by the small, high window slits. You enter the building through a guardroom and an anteroom. The large rooms at the back are full of nooks and crannies but freely accessible; to the right are a kitchen and a bath, both of which are supplied with water from a *falaj* which runs along the west wall of the building. The *falaj* brings the water from the Nakhal area over twenty kilometers away. Near the entrance there are narrow steps up to the first floor. The rooms all have high niches and the edges of the walls have stucco cornices. The prayer room, situated above the entrance portal, has a beautifully designed *mihrab*. Its simple geometric ornamentation has clear parallels with the decorative strips above old Omani wooden doors.

Such simple forms can also be seen painted on the ceiling beams of the southeast tower. This, the only original wooden ceiling that remains, leads one to conclude that the others were similarly painted. On display are a camel bone with verses of the Quran written on it, Bedouin silverware and Chinese porcelain.

(open daily except Fridays until 14:00)

With a bit of luck you will be able to admire a real rarity a few hundred meters before the building: in 2009, at least, in an open area to the right of the road there was one of the old wells, a *zajara*. Before the age of the diesel pump these had been the norm in the Al Batinah coast. Even this example was not completely intact; the pulley for the rope was missing, as was the connection to the reservoir. The system, however, could clearly be made out: a triangular, wooden framework about five meter high was constructed over a well shaft. Beneath the framework the ground slopes downwards away from the shaft. This type of well was once widespread throughout the whole of the Arabian peninsula. It functions with the help of an ox, its harness attached to a rope from the framework. As the animal is led down the ramp, leather bags full of water are drawn up out of the depths. By means of a second rope the full bags are then emptied into the reservoir. Meanwhile, when the animal has reached the bottom of the ramp, it is given some fodder and then led back up. On the way back the person leading the animal lifts the harness so that it does not slip over the animal's head. The weight of the harness pulls the animal back up the slope. From the reservoir the water is fed into the *falaj* system. To limit the loss of water through evaporation as much as possible, the pool is covered with mats of palm branches.

Bulls used to be an important pillar of the agricultural economy along the Al Batinah coast. The animals not only brought water from the wells to the fields; they also drew simple wooden ploughs and were yoked to carts. Humped cattle from Pakistan were well suited to this work and were early on imported to Oman. Nowadays there is practically no work for these bulls, but they have certainly not become worthless, quite the contrary. Following an old tradition **bullfights** are held late on Friday afternoons in several places along the Al Batinah coast.

Settlement at the hot springs of Nakhal

In recent years this ancient custom has undergone something of a renaissance. The breeders are once more proud of their beasts and tend them carefully, taking them hundreds of kilometers to display at exhibition fights. Low-slung pickups, loaded with extremely heavy bulls, are not a rare sight on Fridays on the region's roads. The fights mostly take place on open land on the edge of the villages, although only insiders know the exact time and place. Barka is an exception to this, where there is a small concrete arena on an open area to the right of the road leading from Barka to Bayt An Naman. Trials of strength are held every two weeks, late in the afternoon. Bets are made on the outcome of these fights, but only for fun, never for money.

Bullfighting - Life in the Afternoon

In Madrid between May and June is the high season for the corrida: every day the elite of the matadors and six bulls are assembled before 25,000 spectators. At the beginning and at the end of the display, the arrival of the performers and their extravagant victory parade, or the humiliating exit following a shameful withdrawal, are ritualized. They quickly come to the point. The audience knows the rules, the course of events and the contestants. The next bull is simply announced on a board carried around the middle, with its weight written large. The bull arrives and bursts forth. Each new sequence of the six fights begins with a fanfare. If the bull has finally collapsed, after the *coup de grace* has been delivered a sling is attached to its horns. A troika drags the body to the exit. If in the short public culmination to its life, the animal defended itself strongly and tenaciously against the calm elegance of its superior opponent, then it receives posthumous applause. When at the end the youthful hero struts around the arena proud and victorious, a sea of white scarves wave in rhythm to the cries of "Torero."

The effect of the whole spectacle is both splendid and primitive, exciting and at the same time deeply confusing. While the slaughtering and processing of animals for food has been hidden from the public gaze behind factory walls, here one is presented with the ritual slaughter of cattle and drawn into a mass euphoria. Animal victims seem to be both celebrated as heroes for their vitality and treated with contempt as losers.

There are also bullfights in Oman but there are no similarities with this circus, in spite of Spain's Arabic history. In the late afternoon on almost every Friday Toyota pickup trucks descend on Barka from the whole of the Al Batinah region, cattle with camel-like humps in their truck beds. Apart from the occasional tourist there are no women to be seen here. There is also no *Torero*. Only the men leading the animals, dressed like the spectators in bright full-length *dishdashas*, stand out like the white-painted concrete ring from the yellow background. The entrance is open, the sand on the inside the same as that on the outside. It is at least ten degrees warmer than in Madrid. Only the red mountains and the occasional dry branches of trees rise above the scene. In front of a few bare rows of seats about twenty animals tied to one another stand around until a pair is let loose. There is no announcement of the breeders or the bulls, nothing at the start or finish. It simply begins and it is finished when the rounds are completed and the sun has gone down.

Apart from a subdued palaver and the occasional shout it is quiet. The breeders crouch on the ground in long rows in front of the audience, the patriarchal bamboo stick in hand or stuck upright into the ground. You too can step unhindered into the ring; no one will try to drive you away, apart from the fighting bulls if they come too close. At some point it may happen that one bull pushes another right across the ring. They may suddenly attack one another and vanish in a cloud of dust, dancing around the referee and the keepers with their ropes. The animals seldom hurt one another. It may happen that the two just stand there and don't want to fight. Or that one pushes headlong while the other always comes from the side. Or that one appears weak and only gets into a rage and shows his

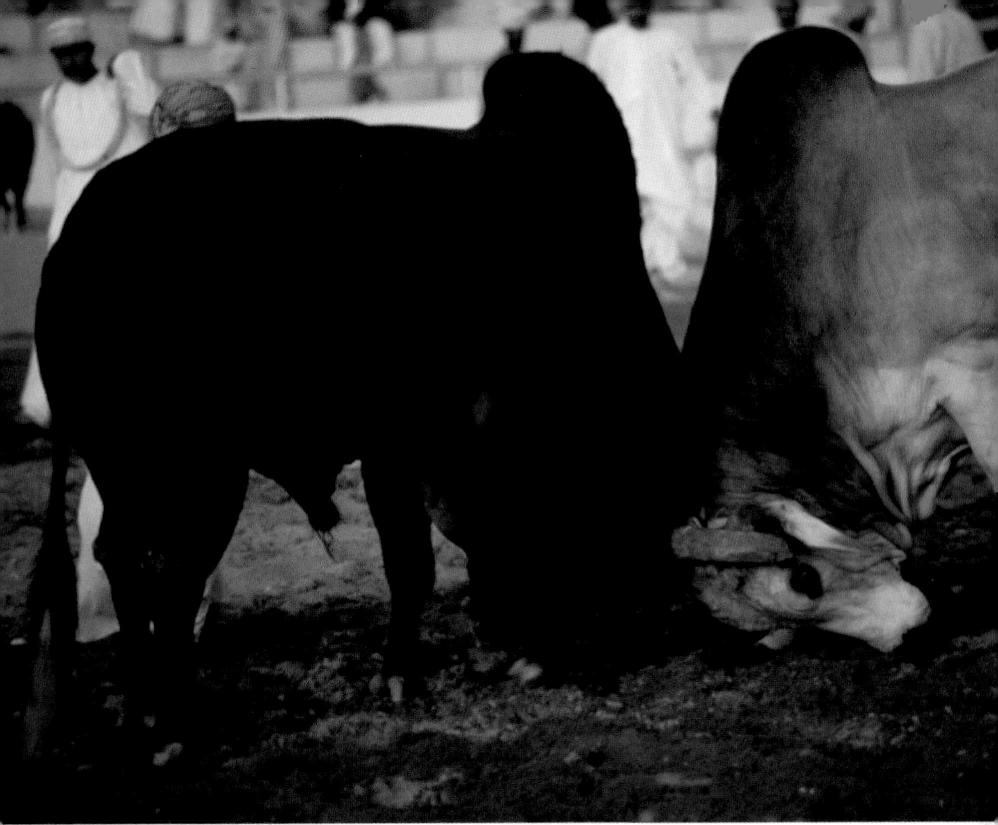

Fighting bulls, photographed in the "arena" at Barka, weighing a good ton.

strength after a few knocks. Or they brace their skulls against one another and neither gives way. Or one runs off straight away and disappears through one of the entrances to the ring and then has to be caught somewhere between the desert and the highway. As a result most people in the know park their cars as far as possible from the exits.
The referee declares a winner, although this mostly goes unnoticed by the uninitiated. Ropes are suddenly slung around the hindquarters of the bulls and the combatants are pulled apart and returned to the herd. There is no sign of public acclaim or condemnation. Instead of the adrenalin rush and fateful symbolism of the spectacle of dying in disgrace, or with applause, the animals are allowed to keep their lives and retain their dignity. Besides, the bulls are too valuable to sacrifice in slaughter, as there are many Fridays in a year.

Prof. Dr. Thomas Zacharias

Nakhal and its Hot Springs

A few kilometers beyond Bayt An Naman the small road opens onto the main road to Sohar. To get to Nakhal, drive back along the expressway to Barka and take the exit south from the roundabout. To the east of the road in the distance you can see **Nakhal fort** on a rocky outcrop. Shortly after the Omanoil petrol station a road branches off to Nakhal and its fort. The stronghold reigns majestically over the oasis. Its six towers command a view over the plain, enabling it to control it in the past. The site's excellent strategic position was recognized early on. The fort's beginnings stretch back to the time of the Sasanian occupation (from the 3rd century AD.) The first restoration happened at the end of the 6th century and a second in the 16th century. During the reign of Sultan Said ibn Sultan, in the middle of the 19th century, renovation work on parts of the fort was begun. The "complete overhaul" was declared finished in 1990 on Oman's 20th National Day. The defensive works cover an area of 3,400 square meters and because of its situation looking out over the oasis and the plain, it is the most impressive fort in the country.

Abandoned houses in the oasis of Nakhal.

If you follow the sign marked "Al Thowarah" from the fortress the road winds through the oasis behind the stronghold. Nakhal is the seat of the Yaruba tribe. As at many other oases there are several fortified living quarters scattered around the *aflaj*-irrigated fields. The road leads to the exit of the wadi and ends in a large car park. where on weekends there is intense activity due to the several thermal springs which come to the surface at this wadi. A constant stream of warm water transforms the narrow valley, hemmed in by rocks, into a luxuriant green oasis. Women scoop up water, children bathe and the picnic areas at the entrance to the valley throng with families. During the week a contemplative stillness pervades this garden of Eden. You can forget the car for once and wander a little into the valley along the bed of the wadi, and imagine how life was for Omanis before 1970. Or you can simply rest in the welcome shade of the trees ...

Ar Rustaq, the Ancient Capital

The oasis at Ar Rustaq is the largest in the whole region. Its extensive gardens are watered by five different *aflaj*. Ar Rustaq's inhabitants live in two distinct fortified areas. The suq - in front of the gates of the fortress, as we have already seen at Nakhal and Barka - retains the structure of the old market. A clay wall with several entrances surrounds the suq with three main alleys running through it. Ever more shops keep appearing alongside the road and have developed into a shopping center. Ar Rustaq's strategic importance as a trading place and as a stronghold was due to its favorable location between the coast and the most important entry points to the Jabal Al Akhdar region. It is not surprising that the fortress has its origins as early as the period of Sasanian rule.

The name of the **fort**, Qalat Kasra ibn Sharwan, probably goes back to the Persian military governor, Kisfa ibn Sharwan, who appears to have ruled Oman in the 7th century. The name Ar Rustaq is also Persian in origin and means "frontier district." The fortress was expanded and rebuilt several times. Two distinct bodies of the building can clearly be made out: a rectangular center with diametrically opposed round towers and joined on to this the outline of an oval, which recalls the cannon tower of Nizwa. This is the older part of the stronghold. The smaller towers were added later. Since the completion of restoration work in 1999, the rooms, which are richly decorated with stuccowork and painted wooden ceilings, are once more accessible. In the 17th century Ar Rustaq was a center of power and an important spiritual and religious center. In the following period the seat of government was often temporarily transferred to Nizwa, Jabrin or al Hazm, but in the 18th century it once more became the capital of Oman. The founder of the Al-Bu-Said dynasty, Ahmad ibn Said, is buried in the fortress. In 1779, for the first time in its history, Muscat became the seat of government. Ar Rustaq could no longer seriously contend with the port, although it was here, with the election of Azzan ibn Qais as Imam in 1868, that the Imam was declared regent in opposition to the British-backed ruler in Muscat. Ar Rustaq maintained its independence from Muscat until the 1950s. With the final defeat of the Imam in the Jabal Al Akhdar uprising, Ar Rustaq once more became subject to the Sultan's rule.

Back on the main road to Al Hazm, just a few kilometers beyond Ar Rustaq, a road branches off to "Ayn al Kafsha." The road leads to a newly-built mosque and several small houses. Here you will come across **thermal springs**, surrounded and protected by a fence.

The waters are considerably warmer than at Nakhal. Slightly apart from the water source, small, open bathing cabins are installed behind a wall. The half facing the waterhead is set aside for men and the other for women. The hot water is conducted through the cabins by a large *falaj*. The hot baths are said to be very effective against rheumatism. Before venturing into the water you should carefully test the water's temperature with your hand. If you suffer from high blood pressure or have circulation problems, you should refrain from bathing!

One of the two Portuguese cannon in Al Hazm's defensive tower

Al Hazm

This fortress juts like an oversized rock out of the small oasis, seventeen kilometers from Ar Rustaq. The stronghold was built as a residence in 1708 by Imam Sultan ibn Saif II, who also transferred his seat of government here. The small village had the same strategic advantages as Ar Rustaq, but was situated some distance from the tribal community and its conflicts.

Its construction apparently consumed all of his paternal inheritance, and was completed using generous loans from the mosque's assets. Several secret passages provided escape routes from the fortress, the interior of which rather merits the description palace.

The large main gates are covered with carved arabesques and the interior doors, too, are decorated with carvings. The rooms are adorned with the most varied of stuccowork, but until recently they had a somewhat sad appearance.

In 1998 a desperately needed restoration of this splendid and, for the architecture of Oman, pioneering building was completed. Al Hazm is certainly one of Oman's architectural highpoints. Particularly impressive is the still fully intact water supply system of the individual parts of the fortress. For example, on the first floor there is a large basin filled with water for tackling an outbreak of fire. Another interesting architectural feature is the separate passageway connecting the two defensive towers, which is indirectly lit by light-wells. Riders ascended from the stables to the first floor by way of a wide staircase.

Among the historic remains collected in the fort are the Portuguese cannon in the fort's towers which were brought here from Muscat in the 19th century by Azzan ibn Qais. Also, the remains of Imam Sultan ibn Saif are buried in the west tower of the fort. He died in 1718, after only ten years as regent.
Unfortunately the fort is currently being restored again and can only be viewed from the outside.
If at the moment you don't think you can face another fort, you should take a break at Wadi Al Hawqayn or at the beach at Ras as Sawadi. **Wadi Al Hawqayn**, which flows with water all year round, can be reached by the new asphalt road which leads up the mountains behind the fortress. At Al Hawqayn turn left at the T-junction. The road ends at the *wali's* house. From here a track leads down to the wadi. After a few hundred meters the view opens out onto a picturesque valley with terraced fields, a waterfall, huge rock formations in the bed of the wadi and a *falaj*, which winds along the rocks at the side of the wadi.
The way to Sawadi leads back to the main road to Muscat and from there on to a spit of land projecting out into the sea, in front of which are several small islands, the **Sawadi Islands**. The largest of the islands can be reached on foot at ebb tide and is a favorite destination for weekend excursions. In contrast, the **Dimaniyyat Islands** are a completely isolated Nature Reserve, being further out in the open sea. Uninhabited, they offer an important protected nesting place for various seabirds and also an underwater paradise. It is worth making a diving expedition to these islands from the nearby Sawadi Beach Hotel. The diving and snorkelling equipment, and even underwater cameras, can be rented there.
The wide beach, the proximity to Muscat and the good opportunities for outings led to the development of ambitious plans for tourist development under the name "Al-Madinat al-Zarqa". Whether this stretch of coast really is developed over the next few years into a bathing paradise with multiple hotel complexes, bungalow settlements and golf courses, remains to be seen. Up until now not enough investors have been found who could be persuaded of the profitability of a concept based on year-round tourism.

The Northern Al Batinah Coast

The wide arc of the Hajar Mountains west of the Al Batinah coast is known as the "backbone of the country," the Al Batinah coast protected within its curve is described as the "stomach" and Musandam is the "head." This has another meaning apart from the obvious pictorial representation. The mountains form a barrier to the air masses sweeping over the Arabian peninsula. Because of the rising ground, the air is raised above the level of condensation and clouds form, which results in precipitation falling on the mountains, running down through the wadis, being channeled into the irrigation system and replenishing the ground water of the Al Batinah coast. The fertile coastal strip is where the most food is produced, and as this is also the most densely populated region in the country, is also where the most food is consumed thus disappearing into the "stomach."

The appearance of the northern Al Batinah coast is less marked by date plantations and more by large agricultural operations. About half of the population is employed in agriculture and fisheries, the country's most important exports next to oil. The responsible ministry's target is to reach complete independence for foodstuffs. In 2003 this target was reached for bananas, dates, fish, fruit and vegetables, and the area under cultivation constitutes only two percent of the total area of Oman. The road to Sohar is lined with farms and plantations on both sides. For a distance of 200 kilometers these concerns are arranged side by side. Nearly all of the small towns on the coast have dilapidated fortress refuges or larger defensive strongholds such as those found at **Al Khaburah**, **Saham**, **Liwa** and **Shinas**. However it is not worth making an extra journey just to see these.

Along the coastal strip limes, melons, tomatoes, bananas, aubergines, grapes, cucumbers, onions, mangoes and papayas as well as potatoes, pepper, tobacco and fodder grass are cultivated. The Public Authority for Marketing Agricultural Produce (PAMAP) has supported farmers since 1981 in selling their produce both at home and abroad. In 2002 fruit, vegetables and fish with a value of 61 million Omani rials were exported. This is 26.5 percent of the value of the non-oil exports of the country. However the region's water problems already mentioned plus the immensely increased demand for water could endanger these ministerial targets. As early as the 8th century the land was being artificially irrigated. Archaeological finds

have revealed that in the hinterland of Sohar an area of 60 square kilometers was supplied with water by means of dams and channels. Even underground grain mills powered by water were discovered.

The fertile Al Batinah Coast supplies the country with all sorts of vegetables.

Sohar and Environs

In the early Islamic period Sohar was the most important port of Oman. Chroniclers of the time such as Al Istakhri and Al-Muqaddasi actually described it as the most important port in the whole Islamic world. Its origins stretch back to the 5th century BC and it is first mentioned in the 3rd century. In the first centuries after Christ, Oman was subject to the rule of the Sasanian dynasty of Persia, who gave the name "Mazun" to the place between the two arms of the Wadi Jizzi estuary. After Wadi Samail this valley is the second most important natural opening in the rock barrier of the Hajar Mountains. An important ancient trade route passed through it. "Mazun" already ranked as the regional economic center and overseas port; it was the seat of the Persian provincial governor and in the 5th century was the seat of a Nestorian bishop. Directly after Islamization the Persians were driven out of Oman and the flourishing town took the name of "Sohar."

In those days the sailors from Sohar brought home goods from the whole of the Far East. Their mastery of the art of navigation was admired throughout the world and found its way into many tales and legends. Sohar was given the nickname "Gateway to China" and counted as one of the richest towns in the world. It was surrounded by fertile arable land and consisted of 12,000 buildings which were made of clay bricks. Sohar accommodated numerous merchants, among them Jews and Persians. In Wadi Jizzi and the valleys leading off it, large quantities of copper were produced for export. Even in the town itself there were smelting furnaces for copper and iron, as well as a brickworks and a glassworks. The economic prosperity of Sohar provoked its competitors to want to destroy its dominance. In 965 the Persian Buwayhid landed with their troops at Ras al Khaimah and from there marched on Sohar. They conquered and occupied the town, destroying 79 ships in the harbor, and Sohar's maritime power was destroyed. After an uprising in 971 nearly the whole of the remaining population was killed by a Buwayhid punitive expedition.

In the following period, up to the 14th century, Qalhat developed into the new main port of Oman. Since the beginning of the 16th century, the Portuguese had also fought over Sohar, but were repeatedly driven back by the Persians. From 1616 the Portuguese were able to hold the town under their rule for 27 years and they used the time to once more build up Sohar into an important trading center. When the Portuguese took the port in 1616, the old fort was destroyed and they built a new stronghold on its foundations. In 1742 the Persians once more occupied Oman for a short period, and Sohar became a seedbed for resistance under Ahmad ibn Said, the legendary founder of the Al-Bu-Said dynasty, which still rules today. Now only the renovated fort bears witness to the former importance of Sohar. It contains an interesting exhibition about the great age of the port and of Omani seafaring. Modern Sohar has created a new image for itself, unique in Oman: it is a garden town flooded with light and having an almost Mediterranean flair and atmosphere. Today Sohar presents itself as the urbane center of an extensive agricultural region in the Arabian desert. At the end of the 1990s the harbor was once more built up into a large modern industrial port. But that in itself was not sufficient: with a capital investment of 3 billion US dollars an aluminum manufacturing plant is currently being built with an annual capacity of over 480,000 tons. In connection with this project a power station with a capacity of 1800 megawatts and a large seawater desalination plant are also being built. In addition a petrochemical complex will produce ethylene and polyethylene.

Sohar Fort has an interesting museum of maritime history.

Together all these plants will turn the place into the most important industrial location in Oman over the coming decades. A road leads from Sohar through Wadi Jizzi to the Al Buraymi oasis on the border with the United Arab Emirates. This wadi and its adjoining valleys was at the center of copper production in the early Islamic period.

Two of the fifteen large smelting plants in the hinterland of Sohar, Arja and Lasail, have been closely examined by archaeologists. To the North of **Arja** several walled fields were found, which were flooded with rainwater. Overflowing water was collected in a large cistern of about 30 meters diameter on the western edge of the site. The main settlement consisted of a collection of one-storey houses, grouped around an open area. Here cooking places, containers for provisions and grinding stones were found. South and east of the settlement were large slagheaps and to the north were the remains of the roasting shed where the ore was processed. The copper ore in Arja was mostly obtained through open-cast mining; the ore-holding seam in this region runs close to the earth's surface.

In **Lasail**, on the other hand, both open-cast and tunnelled mining were used to obtain the ore. The narrow tunnels, some 80 centimeters high, reached down to a depth of more than 60 meters.

Today there is only a freestanding rock gate in the landscape from where the ore was once obtained by open-cast mining from a seam that was up to 30 meters thick. Imposing bright red hollows and heaps made up of 150,000 tons of slag bear testimony that Lasail must have been one of the most efficient and impressive copper production sites in Oman.

Despite the one-time size of the site, the remains of the historic copper country are very hard to make out for people not familiar with the place.

The pillow lava bed is close to the mainroad from Sohar to Al Buraymi.

What you may find in Sohar's hinterland, with a bit of luck, are remains of slag at the side of the road: small grey-black lumps containing bits of green oxidized copper. Here in the north, the Hajar Mountains have a different character to the southeastern part. They are still rugged, but not so high, and the rocks are often red-brown, streaked with dark green bands. 31 kilometers after the turn-off to Al Buraymi from the coastal road and six kilometers after the new copper plant, the road follows a raised bed along the northern edge of the wadi. Directly on the southern side of the road is a bizarre **pillow lava bed** between two rocks. It looks like a giant heap of magma sausages. When the magma emerged the area was still below sea-level. The water immediately cooled the molten rock, forming these bizarre structures.

Follow the road further west and at the edge of the mountains you will reach a border control to the United Arab Emirates. Here your visa will be cancelled because you are officially leaving the country. If you want to return to Oman after a trip to Al Buraymi you will need to get a new visa on the way back. The **Al Buraymi** oasis was once made up of nine individual oases and today is split into two parts, one belongs to Oman and the larger part, Al Ain, which belongs to the United Arab Emirates. Nowhere is there such a clash of the Arab worlds of Oman and the neighboring Gulf States as in this divided oasis complex.

Al Ain is a modern, generously laid-out metropolis with multi-storey buildings, a university, parks and streets with greenery; in Al Buraymi the confrontation with the modern age is less spectacular.

Al Ain is like a western city where water is not a problem, everything is abundant, everything can be bought; Al Buraymi, in contrast, has kept the character of an oasis town. It is worth making a visit to the new market area with its masterly architecture. South of the oasis the massif of the **Jabal Hafit** rises up out of the desert in splendid isolation. Here archaeologists first discovered burial grounds from the 4th millennium BC, which are among the oldest in the land.
Academics named this early epoch of human settlement the Hafit Period, after the mountain. Al Buraymi experienced its first heyday in the Umm-an-Nar Period in the 3rd millennium BC, from which several settlements and graves were found in the Hili part of the oasis in today's Al Ain. The countless shards which have been unearthed here point to the oasis having been an important trading center in the time of "Magan." Al Buraymi was a junction for all of the region's important caravan routes. Other finds come from the 1st millennium BC, after which all traces vanish and for more than a thousand years it was very quiet around the oasis.
That first changed around 1800 when the Wahhabi made Al Buraymi their base, from which to conduct their missionary *dahwa* efforts. *Dahwa* means to "invite" (in Arabic literally "calling".) This era, marked by conflict and tribute payments, came to an end in 1867. In the 1950s new conflicts arose around Al Buraymi, this time with Oman's suspected oil reserves in the background. In 1974 Saudi Arabia finally accepted the border running south of Al Buraymi, relinquishing its claim to the oasis to the Emirate of Abu Dhabi.
You can explore **Al Ain**, the greater part of the oasis, without any further border controls. North of the center is the Hili Archaeological Park in which there is a reconstruction of a round tomb from the 2nd millennium BC. Near the Al Sharki fortress, south of the center, there is an interesting museum with archaeological finds from the region's tombs. Finally it is worth making a visit to the large camel market, which late in the afternoon is always loud with animal trading.

The ruins of old Fanja overlook a sea of palms and the new settlement below.

Through the Samail Gap to the Province of Ash Sharqiyyah

If you leave the Capital Area at the Burj al Sahwah roundabout in the direction of Nizwa and Salalah, right at the beginning of this multi-day tour, after seven kilometers you reach the industrial area of Rusayl and a few kilometers further on the first foothills of the Hajar Mountains. The steep flanks, up to 3000 meter high, tower up like a gigantic barrier to the country's interior, making any passage seemingly impossible. The mountain range today is crossed by asphalt roads in three places only. All routes follow the paths of large wadis, for thousands of years the most-used routes through this natural "wall." Wadi Jizzi connects Sohar in the north with the Al Buraymi oasis, Wadi Bani Ghafir connects Ar Rustaq with the Ibri oases, and Wadi Samail gives Muscat access to the eastern coastal province of Ash Sharqiyyah as well as to the old centers of Bahla and Nizwa on the southern side of the Hajar Mountains. The more important passage is undoubtedly the Samail Gap. It cuts through the whole breadth of the rock barrier and separates the Eastern from the Western Hajar Mountains and the two regions of Ash Sharqiyyah and Gharbiyah. The new highway to Nizwa runs through it. The strategic significance of the water-rich valley was recognized early on and consequently it is lined with a number of fortresses, watchtowers and oasis settlements. If you wish to see these, change to the old country road a few kilometers before Izki. Right at the beginning of the mountains, west of the highway, is the **Fanja** oasis on a low ridge of rock crouched in the shadow of a mighty wall. At its foot luxuriant palm groves and gardens spread around the deep channels of the wadi. The old road crosses the riverbed by a large bridge; just on the other side of the bridge a small track branches off to the right and leads past some new buildings to the old village. If you venture out on foot to the almost deserted old village you will be rewarded with a grandiose view over the wadi and the seemingly endless date plantations. The new Fanja suq has established itself in front of the bridge. Here you can find traditional ceramics and wickerwork alongside everyday articles.

Everywhere in the Hajar Mountains bizarre folds and faults testify to the powerful tectonic forces released by the movements of the continental plates when the mountains were formed.

The next town on the way south is **Bidbid** with its fort. Here the road forks off to Samail and Sur. The large fort has been very lovingly and individually restored by the villagers themselves, which gives it a uniquely authentic character. The **Samail** oasis is today still famed for the quality of its dates, which are exported all over the world. Currently 60 different varieties are cultivated here. A diet based on dates helped the oldest inhabitant of Samail, Salim ibn Said Al Hadhrami, to his legendary old age. He died of old age according to a press report in the Oman Daily Observer on January 22, 1994, having reached the incredible age of 147. Up to the very end he enjoyed the best of health. The settlement at Samail comprises two large, ten kilometer sites, which are occupied by members of different tribes. Villages like this are encountered throughout the Ash Sharqiyyah, for example Ibra. The lower part of the village has the additional name "Sufala" and the upper part "Alaya."

Some kilometers after the fork in the direction of Sur, the road winds in endless curves through the black-brown mountains. Numerous watercourses cross the road. Every hollow shows the aggressive and tremendous power of erosion that the infrequent but heavy rainfalls have. The road surface has to be renewed frequently. Kilometer after kilometer, curve follows curve, wadi crossing follows wadi crossing: just a single shower can turn the drive along this stretch into a whitewater adventure.

Between the Hajar Mountains and the desert of the Wihibah Sands, a large plateau spreads out, most of it as dark as the mountains. It stretches from Sinaw in the west to Al Kamil Wa Al Wafi in the southeast. Other centers of settlement are found at Al Mudaybi, Ibra, Al Mudayrib, Al Mintarib and Wadi Samad. For centuries the people of the Ash Sharqiyyah have wrestled with the desert, fighting against the earth becoming too salty or drying out, against destruction and damage done to the land's lifegiving water arteries, the *aflaj*. As though that were not enough of a struggle, in the past they fought bitterly against one another and covered the landscape with a thick network of defensive camps. The palaces of the Ash Sharqiyyah are structurally different to those of the Gharbiyah in the west. There are no great forts commanding the settlements; the houses and dwelling quarters are themselves built like forts, surrounded by walls with watchtowers.

During the great age of maritime trade, the geographical situation of the province at the southeast edge of the mountains contributed enormously to its wealth. A deciding factor was that the sheltered port of Sur could be reached more easily by the camel caravans from the country's interior through the Ash Sharqiyyah than could the harbors of the north through the few narrow passes and gorges

Geology of the Hajar Mountains

In the Hajar Mountains layers of rock which are normally deeply buried can be seen on the surface. A drive through this countryside gives you a fascinating insight into the geological history of the country. The Arabian plate on which Oman rests is more than 800 million years old. Movements of the different continental plates have at times pushed the Arabian plate beneath sea-level and sediments have been deposited. In the following millions of years the plate drifted several times between Antarctic and equatorial latitudes, was squeezed, thrown up, lifted and then once more lowered. It passed through several ice ages and was covered in great glaciers, the traces of which can still clearly be seen in some places today, especially in southern Oman. In stark contrast to these epochs it also experienced tropically wet periods with immense precipitation and rich vegetation. The changing conditions ensured that in Oman the most varied sorts of rock can be found: sediments deposited by the sea, limestone from primeval oceans and volcanic rock where liquid magma was able to press through the cracks of the earth's crust. Oil, the "black gold" of Arabia, arose from organic sea sedimentation.

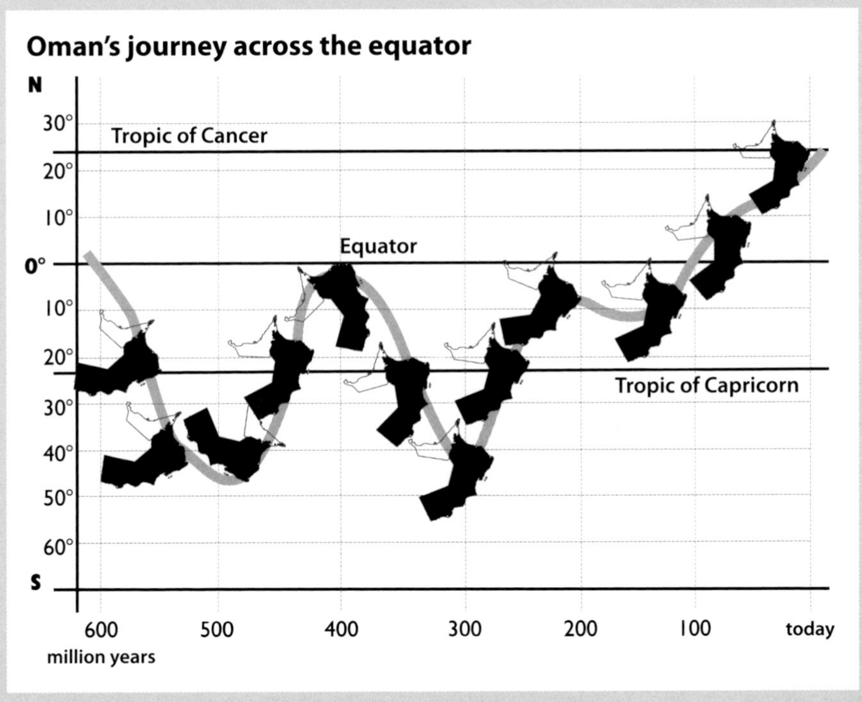

Today Oman is far enough away from the collision zones between the Eurasian, Arabian and Indian plates in the Red Sea and in Iran, that there is no constant threat of earthquakes. Far beyond the coast of Oman, the Indian and Arabian plates slowly slide past one another along the "Owen Fracture" without any great tectonic tensions. 30 to 40 million years ago, however, strong movements of the plates threw up the mighty massif of the Hajar Mountains, pressing the layers in some places almost vertically out of the earth. Although this was completed over 20 million years ago, its effects can still be seen across the whole mountain range. Soft sediments alternate irregularly with harder limestone or volcanic rocks and testify to the diverse upheavals of the earth's crust.
Exposed to the weather, the various layers eroded at different speeds. The originally deeper, hardest layers today form the highest mountains. Like mighty wedges, giant parts of the Arabian plate burst through the earth; large heaps of various colored, softer sediments turn the countryside into a sandpit of geological history. The massive layers of sediment have been extensively eroded. Together with the strength of the water of earlier, wetter times they have filled and smoothed over the valleys. Huge heaps of rubble were washed by the rain into the sea. Investigations off the Al Batinah coast revealed that a gigantic heap of eroded matter from the mountains was piled up there; a process which continues to this day. 150,000 cubic kilometers of slag has been swept into the sea and piled steeply up off the coastline 3000 meters deep.
The crystalline, very jagged, dark, volcanic Samail ophiolite layer stretches over an area of almost 20,000 square kilometers and appears everywhere on the eastern edges of the mountain range. It is one of the best preserved oceanic rock formations on the surface of the earth, material that is normally formed at the bottom of the sea bed. However the greatest geological feature is presented by the *Moho*, the boundary surface between the earth's crust and the earth's mantle, which is otherwise hidden 35 to 70 kilometers beneath the continents and can only be marvelled at on the surface here in Oman.

of the mountains. Moreover, many merchants from the Arabian Gulf preferred to send their goods on the safer route via Ibri, Bahla, Nizwa and Ibra rather than via the ports which were constantly being threatened by pirates.
The other safe port accessible from the Ash Sharqiyyah was Muscat, but that was not such a viable alternative as Sur was only four days' camel ride away and Muscat was seven. The tribes of the region did not just restrict themselves to business with the caravans passing through, but also took part on a grand scale in the lucrative maritime trade. Most of the profits from the trade with East Africa flowed into the building of towns and plantations at home.

The "roof of Oman," the summit plateau of Jabal Shams, corresponds to the same geological layer which is being drilled for oil throughout half of the Arabian peninsula.

Ibra and Al Mudayrib

According to oral tradition **Ibra** is the oldest town of the Ash Sharqiyyah, apparently founded before the Islamization of Oman. The layout of the town reflects the conflicts of days gone by. Ibra consists of two extensive, strongly fortified settlements: Ibra Alaya, the smaller part built on a piece of high ground, and Ibra Sufala, which is larger and lower down. Sufala was in the hands of the Al-Harithi tribe, which belonged to the Hinawiy federation. Alaya on the other hand was occupied by the Al-Miskery, a branch of the Ghafiriy. Both were enormously important in Oman's East African possessions. The capital of Somalia, Mogadishu, was said to have been founded by the Al-Harithi while the Al-Miskery held the governorship of Mombasa in Kenya. Zanzibar was a second home for members of both tribes.

The Harem – Fantasy World of Days Gone By

The possibility, anchored in the Quran, of a man marrying up to four women at once led in the west to the long-nurtured and still widespread picture of the Arab man as a pasha, surrounded by several beautiful women who can read every conceivable desire expressed in his eyes and long for nothing other than to fulfill those desires. Considering that the Sultanate had maintained its archaic social structure for longer than all other Arab countries, one might expect that there would be a large number of polygamous marriages. However, the first ever population census, in 1993, could not confirm this assumption.
What it did confirm is that 93.2 percent of all married men at that time lived monogamously, and only 6.8 percent had more than one wife. A glance at the age structure of this group reveals that the majority were older men. The figures demonstrate that polygamy in Oman is not the rule but rather the absolute exception, which is not surprising when you understand what duties a man has towards his wife in Islam.
The harem fantasies correspond at most – if at all – to social reality before the introduction of the Quran into daily life. Until that time wives had absolutely no rights and could be handled like any other property of a man. Having many wives was not a social issue at that time but a luxury, which one could do without. Moreover, in those times of military conflict and long, perilous sea journeys, polygamy provided the widows with the possibility of economic survival. In the Quran the status of women was defined for the first time, the breaking of which would be visited with divine punishment. According to these the husband is fully responsible for his wives' livelihood and welfare.

There is a story of an occurrence which is supposed to have happened during a crossing to Zanzibar. On board the ship there were numerous Al-Harithi and only one Al-Miskery. Out on the high seas the Al-Miskery went below deck and began to hack a hole in the stern of the boat with an axe. The other passengers heard the blows and overpowered the man. On being asked why he had done what he did, which would have resulted in him being drowned along with all the others, the Al-Miskery answered: "The life of one Al-Miskery for a hundred Al-Harithi!" The rivalry between the two tribes has a past as old as Oman's maritime history.

Both parts of Ibra nursed their vendetta for centuries, and so two autonomous settlements developed, each with its own *aflaj*: there were endless disputes over the water channels. The supply of life-giving water could only be ensured if the territory which the *falaj* crossed on its way to Ibra was in the hands of allied tribes.

If he has several wives he is bound to treat them all equally and look after them materially as well as spiritually. He must also spend the same amount of time with each. Even in Arabia the day has only 24 hours and however much money you have you cannot buy more time. From this it is clear that even a very rich man can only look after at most four women, treating them all equally. The wife does not have to provide for the husband but he has to provide for her. The Quran further provides a man the right to bring his parents and children by another wife to live in the matrimonial home, but denies this right to the woman. She can, though, stop her husband from bringing another wife to share the home. Marriage among relatives is also forbidden. This last has serious consequences for the old tradition of marrying within a tribe. The ban weakens the old clan structure and is more in keeping with a modern nation state and women's independence. Today women already make up 55 percent of the students at the university in Muscat. A large number of decrees have at the same time served to ensure free entrance to the professions and to guarantee equal pay with men for women who have equal qualifications.

The expense of life in modern Oman makes marriage to several women almost impossible. One of the few younger men with two wives works in Oman but comes from an oasis in the country's interior. He has one wife in the capital, living a modern city life. The second wife, on the other hand, leads a tranquil life in the old tradition at his oasis home. The husband is constantly commuting between the two villages, and also between two quite different worlds. His Omani colleagues feel only sympathy for him.

Both settlements ended up orienting themselves in opposite directions, Ibra Alaya to the west and Sufala to the southeast. They lay back to back, so to speak, facing away from each other. A 200 meter wide neutral zone, a strip of no man's land, separated them. A school was built here and also the residence of the wali, the head of the community. A tour of the place makes the effects of war on architecture clearly apparent. The residences have been built up into fortresses.

The immense prosperity of former days is still palpable, although today the old parts of the town are almost completely abandoned and dilapidated. After 1970 the new town of Ibra developed around the outside of the original settlements. The people have long since given up the separation into two zones and, at last, the old tribal enmity. Today the women from the whole region gather on Wednesday mornings in Ibra Sufala for the **women's market**.

In the first half of the 18th century some members of the large Al-Harithi tribe left Ibra. They founded Al Qabil, Ad Dariz and Al Ghallaja among other places, or moved to the settlement of **Al Mudayrib**, twenty kilometers to the south. As a result of the flourishing trade in those days, it developed into a rich albeit small town with many impressive buildings. In contrast to Ibra, which is today desolate and somewhat confusing, Al Mudayrib is still inhabited as it always was and has managed to keep its atmosphere and character, although here too new buildings are emerging around the old settlement.

The colors used in painting hands with henna are similar to the mineral colors used to paint the wooden ceilings.
While predominantly geometric forms are used for the latter, body painting mostly features organic forms.

The historical center is surrounded by small hills with watchtowers which are visible from afar. In the middle of the hollow the houses cluster around the only *falaj*. The oldest extant buildings in Al Mudayrib are from the 18th century. The comparatively good condition of the walls is thanks to the solid manner of construction – the stones were bound together with a mixture of clay and plaster. The large buildings equipped with defensive towers were used by the various clans as meeting points. In times of war they served as a defensive refuge for individual members of the tribe or for large families. This type of building, unique to the area, was known as a *sabla*.

Unlike other settlements of the Ash Sharqiyyah, Al Mudayrib never suffered from drought. The whole year round its underground *falaj* carried large quantities of water from Wadi Suwi, seven kilometers away. The inhabitants even allowed themselves the luxury of letting surplus water simply run into the desert beyond the fields, where it seeped away. Over time this wastefulness resulted in the formation of a swamp which was responsible for increasingly severe problems with malaria.

Embellishing Doors and Ceilings, Hands and Heads

Omanis are very careful not to show social status through dress - everyone from humblest fisherman to government minister wears the simple *dishdasha*. But when it comes to headwear or the door of a man's home, there is no such uniformity. Omani architecture is generally simple and unadorned without the dainty elaboration, ledges and wall reliefs found elsewhere. This plainness emphasizes the significance of doorways and the effect of decorative work on doors. The clear geometrical forms stem from the traditional repertoire of Islamic motifs: stylized lotus leaves and other simple floral patterns show the influence of India and Persia; sumptuous bands of carved flower motifs are typical of East African countries.

This unique cultural heritage is now seriously endangered: the old building materials of clay, stone and wood are being replaced by concrete, steel and cement. They are simply no longer fashionable. The building trade is nowadays dominated by Indians. These craftsmen have not mastered the traditional Omani method of building with clay; doors of steel are driving out those of wood. Although these replacements are often decorated with wrought iron and brightly painted, this development appears to be a step backward, a cultural loss, given that the steel doors are almost without exception decorated in Indian style. The dominance of Indian craftsmen in certain fields is very apparent and the new doors can be seen to represent the social order of modern Oman. If the ancient treasures are not at least photographed and documented, there is a real danger that a fascinating part of its culture will be forever lost to Oman.

A first step in the direction of bringing old Omani and Arabic decorative tradition into the digital age has been taken with the creation of a new font, "Sindbad," for graphic design computer applications. It can be imported and used in any application. Like the ornamental strips of the doors, the individual symbols of "Sindbad" can be strung together or woven into complete designs. This unique font was awarded 1st prize in the category Symbol Font in the 2nd International Type Design Contest. It is now published in the Linotype Library (www.linotype.com) and is available worldwide on the web. Who knows what will be produced with this new character set?

In addition to the doors, people liked to decorate the ceiling beams in the rooms of their homes. Alongside embellishments similar to those on the doors, you will often find calligraphy: verses from the Koran, details of the building's history, or stanzas of poetry. In contrast to the doorways these decorations are not carved, but painted. They range from the finely detailed, multi-colored ceilings of the palace of Jabrin, to the simple, rough, white markings on reddish-brown painted beams. You find these simple variants in many abandoned houses. The clear contrast of color draws a clear parallel with a completely different application of decorative motifs: the rust coloring of the ceilings is obtained from minerals, but bears a strong resemblance to the color of the henna designs with which

women decorate their hands. Hand-painting is an art in itself, a time consuming ritual, particularly practiced in Indian circles. The henna shrub is widespread throughout Oman. Its leaves are gathered, pulverized, mixed to a paste with water and lemon juice and then laid in the sun for several hours, the heat triggering fermentation. Finally the mixture is put into a kind of confectioner's piping bag made from a large leaf and then the desired pattern is carefully squirted onto the outstretched palm. The dark, greenish-brown paste slowly dries and dyes the skin beneath reddish-brown. The intensity of the color and the shading depend on the sort of henna and the preparation of the paste. Usually the coloring from the first application is not pronounced enough and the procedure is repeated.
Having done the palms, the women finally treat the fingertips and nails. For special ceremonies they will also decorate the feet. Before feast days, the female members of the family perform this beautification ritual together and paint one another with freely improvised filigree designs. This procedure entails hours of sitting still, but also allows them to forget the hectic rush preceding feast days; the communal waiting produces a mood of meditation, which spreads to the other members of the family.

This laborious traditional ritual is as popular as ever with women. One reason may be that using nail polish is forbidden on religious grounds: the ritual washing before prayer cannot clean the parts covered with lacquer. Henna, on the other hand, is absorbed into the nails and skin, is water-resistant and does not form an impermeable coating on the surface. After a couple of weeks the decoration disappears, the pigment being broken down by fresh skin-growth. The natural geometric form of the hand is complemented by the predominantly curving floral motifs.

Men living in towns have their own way of adorning themselves in everyday life. During the fasting month of Ramadan men may color their beards with henna - this symbolizes deep religious reflection. They wear cloth skull-caps richly embroidered with ornament. The diversity of designs is remarkable; one hardly ever sees two identical *kumma*, as these caps are called. Originally they were made by dock workers in their leisure time using the laborious technique of *broderie anglaise*. Now machine-made *kumma* can be had in the suqs relatively cheaply. On official occasions an Omani wears a similarly embroidered cashmere cloth worn like a turban, the *ammama*, together with his ceremonial dagger, or *khanjar*. The varied forms of decoration may have different applications but they have one thing in common: in Oman adornment is a sign of individuality and independence.

The whole of Al Mudayrib was once surrounded by a town wall, which had to give way to new roads and other buildings. Between the towers on the hills you can still recognize the remains of the fortification. From up there you get a magnificent view over the settlement, its individual buildings and their extensive gardens. There is also a terrific view in the other direction. On the other side of the heights a large gravel plain stretches to the dark, rugged mountains, and from the south the gently rolling yellow dunes of the Wihibah desert enter the panorama and partly bury the rocks beneath their sands. The traveler on his way south through the province Ash Sharqiyyah will often admire the fascinating scenery. Oman's history in the 18th and 19th centuries was formed by international trade and also found expression in the country's decorative ornamentation, especially in the form of doors.

Throughout the Ash Sharqiyyah you can find carved doors.

Doorframes and central beams decorated with carving are typical of the whole Arabian peninsula. In Oman motifs from Africa, India and Persia have been added to the decorative treasure chest. In Al Mudayrib, especially, there are many of these richly decorated doors, once common throughout Oman, to discover. Some of them, generally the largest and decorated with the most luxuriant floral ornamentation, were made by craftsmen in East Africa in the 19th century and then brought here by ship and camel! South of Al Mudayrib the road runs past **Al Qabil**, founded in 1795. Here was where the Al-Harithi sheikhs had their seat. It was the center of the whole region until, during a prolonged period of drought in the middle of the 19th century, the *falaj* gradually dried up and the oasis had to be abandoned. The inhabitants mostly migrated to East Africa. After the revolution in Zanzibar (1964) many of the Al-Harithi returned.

The **Al Mintarib** oasis forms the gateway to the desert of the Wihibah Sands. From here routes lead into the dune landscape. On Fridays Bedouin come here and to Sinaw in the west to do their shopping. Al Mintarib has been famous forever for its exquisite dates which are held to be the best in all Oman and used to be exported via the port of Sur. Beyond Al Mintarib the road follows the edge of the Wihibah. As soon as it reaches **Wadi Al Batha** the road is increasingly lined with trees, their green making an attractive contrast to the reddish sand dunes in the background. Wadi Al Batha, rich in water and having thick groves of trees, is an important reserve for fauna and flora and is known as the woodlands. About 60 kilometers before Al Kamil Wa Al Wafi the road branches to the right by the Oriental Nights Resthouse into **Wadi Bani Khalid**. Due to damage by heavy rainfalls the asphalt road is constantly being rebuilt. If you want to be sure of getting to the end of this valley then you should use an all-terrain vehicle. But even with a normal car it is worth driving through the colorful mountains with their mighty geological folds. If you like, you can park your car at the end of the road and wander along the remaining five kilometers of the valley. The path, which is lined with trees and bushes, leads through the wadi to a large natural water basin by the settlement Mogel. The wadi is luxuriantly green, and the water a shimmering turquoise green, inviting you to bathe. However this should be reserved for the inhabitants, for whom the water is the basis of life in this remote valley. The walk along the narrow valley beyond the pool with its bizarre rock formations and several small pools is also beautiful.

At Al Kamil Wa Al Wafi the road branches off to Al Ashkarah, leading you to an impressive interplay of landscapes: the foothills of the Hajar Mountains meeting with the dunes of the eastern Wihibah Sands. The rest of the way to Sur is not so varied.

Sur and Environs

The port of Sur was once Oman's most important East African port. Since 1992 the town seems to be exploding and parallels to Muscat in the 1980s spring involuntarily to mind. Suddenly there is not a single old building to be found, everything seems to be brand new. Sur has been developing with government support since the beginning of the 1990s, once more becoming one of the most significant regional centers of Oman. A large seawater desalination plant with adjoining power station is already in service and huge new jetties extend the natural lagoon as a sheltered harbor.

The main road leads past a small, but worthy of a visit, **Maritime Museum**, built on the grounds of the local football club, and continues east through the new town to a T-junction: to the left the road leads further to the coastline and harbor and to the right passes shops and banks winding up to a car park by the Sur Hotel. The hotel is easy to recognize by its entrance with blue-tiled pillars on top of which there is a large model of a dhow. On the opposite side of the road you can find the suqs and the almost hidden center of the old town: **Sur as Sahil**. There is little left to see of the historical buildings; Sur seems to have erased its past. But all is not lost. If you drive back to the T-junction and continue straight on you will reach the coast road. Keep going in a southerly direction and drive past almost the whole of Sur as Sahil, situated on a peninsula, and you will make a most astonishing journey into the past.

In the east the town is bounded by the deep inlet of the **Khawr al Batah** lagoon, on the outlet of which is the new Sur harbor. A few hundred meters further on, standing directly by the lagoon, is the old customs house, with a car park in front of it. It is a large plain building in which the former Sultan used to stay when visiting Sur. This tradition has not changed under the rule of Sultan Qaboos, who is keen on maintaining continuities with the past. A new bridge stretches over the lagoon to the opposite part of the town, al Al Ayjah. Early mornings the fisherman in their dhows landed their catches, mostly consisting of large quantities of tuna, on this part of the coast. Since the building of the new harbor, this morning fish market has been moved down the beach to the northern end of the coastal strip facing the open sea.

Nowhere else in Oman can you see so many dhows. Side by side they gently roll in the smooth waters of the bay and conjure up pictures of days gone by. Trade relations between Sur and East Africa go back to the 6th century (AD.) Sur could only step out from under the shadow of the port of Qalhat, situated further to the north, after its competitor was completely destroyed at the beginning of the 16th century as a result of an earthquake and Portuguese attacks. At the time its lesser importance rescued Sur from the destructive fury of the Portuguese and it was able to flourish after the Europeans were driven from the land. In the bay, which is today heavily silted up, the largest ships, with up to 400 man crews, were able to weigh anchor. Alongside Muscat, Sur developed into one of the most important ports for sailing to Africa, becoming a center of the slave trade. But since the middle of the 19th century it has seemed as though the whole world was conspiring against the town. First the British gradually enforced a ban on slave trading and then, in 1861, the country split into two Sultanates. In 1865 Sur was attacked by Wahhabi troops. In addition a storm took the large African fleet by surprise when returning from Zanzibar. The ships sought safety in a bay of the Al Hallaniyyat islands, but almost all fell victim to the full force of the storm. It smashed the whole fleet against the island's cliffs and many people lost their lives. This catastrophe seemed to be some kind of judgment from God; it sealed the end of Oman's great maritime age.

Today dhows in Sur are still made traditionally by hand.

Today the Suris' self-assurance is nourished by their great past, which in their eyes sets them apart from the rest of the country. The men's dress reflects this attitude: their *dishdashas* are the only ones in Oman with seams stitched in colored thread and with embroideries decorating the chest.

In spite of the port's great loss in importance, Sur was able to maintain its reputation as a shipbuilding metropolis until modern times.

Until recently the several **boatyards** around the bay used older methods of working. However, since 2004, the keels of only a few dhows to be built in Sur were laid. The timber came partly from Oman, and partly from India and Burma. Elastic cedar wood was used for the frame and teak hardwood for the planks and keel. The nails were forged in India. As in olden days the wood was prepared using hand drills, saws, planes and axes. Electrical tools were only used in a very limited way. There was no blueprint to follow and boats were built in different variations according to the client's wishes. Sadly the market for these ships has completely collapsed in recent years and most of the dhow makers have emigrated to the Emirates where this handicraft continues, not least as a tourist attraction.

The planks of dhows were secured using nails that were hand-made in India.

The road describes a wide arc along the lagoon. A large dhow, the **Yad al Karim**, stands on a platform on the inside bank of the lagoon, impossible to miss. The 300-ton, majestically curved ship was in service up until a few years ago flying the Yemeni flag. It was brought back by two businessmen from Sur and given a general overhaul and then placed here as a monument. This dhow of the *Ghanjah* type is one of the last ships of its kind to be built in Sur; it was launched in 1920. In Sur's heyday up to 400 such ships or even larger merchant ships lay at anchor in the large lagoon.

If you keep following the road along the bank of the lagoon you will come to **Al Ayjah**, situated on the bank opposite Sur as Sahil. It has not been as affected by the building boom as Sur as Sahil or Balad Sur right at the entrance to the town. Al Ayjah is occupied by the Bani Bu Ali tribe, whose other settlements are at Jaalan Bani Bu Ali, their maintribal home, and Al Ashkarah. The Bani Bu Ali, also known as the Alawi, form one of the main Sunni enclaves in Oman. This Sunni community owes its origins to the invasion of the region by the Wahhabites at the beginning of the 19th century. In 1895 they formed an alliance with the Sultan and supported him until 1923 against the Ibadhi Imamate. Then arose a dispute about the tax rights at the port of Sur. In the eyes of the Bani Bu Ali the town was no longer subject to the rule of the Sultan. In 1928 they pointedly raised the Saudi flag. The British countered these separatist tendencies with military action. The situation only relaxed again under the government of Sultan Qaboos.

A few kilometers beyond Al Ayjah the asphalt road leads through a landscape of gently rolling hills past the large **Khawr Garama** lagoon to the most easterly village of the Sultanate: **Al Had**. You can also reach here by following the tarmac road along the coast from Al Ashkarah.

Dhows laying in the lagoon of Sur.

The lively fishing village lies on a large sheltered bay and is famous for its sardines, dried on the beach, a favorite animal feed in Oman. The rocky coastline between Ras Al Had and **Ras Al Jinz**, occasionally broken by sandy beaches, was already settled in the 3rd and 2nd millennia BC as recent excavations have shown, .
Pottery that has been found bears witness to an exchange of goods with the cultures of the Indus basin in these early times.
The entire stretch of the coast between Ras Al Had and Ras al Khabba is a heavily protected nature sanctuary which can only be entered under strict supervision after obtaining official permission. It is one of the Indian Ocean's most important breeding grounds for **sea turtles** with an average of 30 thousand turtles nesting at Ras Al Jinz beach alone.
The Ras Al Jinz Sea Turtle and Nature Reserve was established in 1996, protecting a total area of 129 square kilometers with 45 kilometers of coastline. In 2008 the **Ras Al Jinz Scientific and Visitor Center** was opened on the site, housing a research library, interactive Sea Turtle and Archaeology Museums, restaurant and accommodation. The Center also arranges turtle watching in small groups daily. Bookings must be made in advance *(Tel: 96550606.)*

Along the Wihibah Sands

The Ash Sharqiyyah region is bordered on the southwest by the desert of the Wihibah Sands, which covers an area of 15,000 square kilometers, and in the east by the Indian Ocean. Here the sands and sea meet and create a breathtaking, almost surreal landscape. The fascination felt by Europeans for such a view is certainly comparable to what an Omani feels in the middle of a lush green meadow, with constantly flowing water and dense woodlands.
Today the days of tribal rivalry are over, there are asphalt roads and cars with air conditioning, but the extreme conditions outside

The Sea Turtles of Ras Al Jinz

Every year up to 100,000 sea turtles come ashore on the coast of Oman in order to lay their eggs. The rest of their life is spent swimming in the sea. Their natural life expectancy is on average 100 years and they first reach sexual maturity between 30 and 50 years. Fully grown specimens of the largest species occurring in Oman have a length of more than a meter. At differing times of year four different species of sea turtle use this stretch of beach for laying eggs. On account of its long life and the slow turnover of the generations this creature is particularly susceptible to ocean pollution, which threatens its continued survival. The leatherback turtle (*Dermochelys coriacea*), the largest living sea turtle, is still found in large numbers in Oman and feeds on a dangerous species of jellyfish. Off Thailand they have become almost extinct because they have confused plastic bags in the water for their main food and have died a wretched death trying to eat the inedible material. The consequence there, particularly dangerous for tourists, has been plagues of jellyfish.

To prevent the animals being disturbed by the improper behavior of tourists while eggs are being laid, the whole coastal area has been closed off and put under the control of the authorities for nature conservation. Even the slightest change in the silhouette of the coastline, through a standing person or even from a shimmer of light, is enough to excite the mistrust of the females ready to spawn. They then avoid laying the eggs and turn straight back to the water.

put almost insurmountable obstacles in the way of the scientists' thirst for knowledge and imperil their sensitive scientific equipment. Single research projects in deserts often pale into insignificance in the face of the endless expanses, yet incur immense logistical and financial expenditures nonetheless.
In spite of this, its surreal characteristics have made the Wihibah Desert into one of the most popular targets of desert researchers' investigations. In 1986 the Wihibah was declared a "model desert" for scientific purposes; it is representative of the other deserts of the world, which are less accessible and more difficult to investigate. Between January and April of that year an interdisciplinary

If you want to visit this stretch of beach and spend a night watching the sea turtles, you should contact the **Ras Al Jinz Scientific and Visitor Center** *(Tel: ++968 96550606, reservations@rasaljinz.org.)* The center divides all interested visitors into small groups for visits late in night or in the early morning. As the number of visitors per group is strictly limited it is required to register for a visit, at best several months in advance. The registration fee is 3 Omani rials per visitor to be paid on arrival on site. At the appointed time you will be led together to the beach by a guide.
As soon as a turtle has begun to dig a hole with its hind flippers to lay her eggs, she can be watched from nearby. It takes an hour or so for about a hundred eggs to be laid. After six to eight weeks the young turtles emerge from the eggs, dig their way to the surface of the beach at dawn and race as quickly as possible in the direction of the sea, although only a few actually reach it. It is a race between life and death; a few foxes and countless gulls await the mini turtles with their outsized flippers in the few meters between them and the sea. If they manage to reach the apparent safety of the water, large predatory fish are the next obstacle.
If you view the beach in the morning light it is hard to shake off the feeling that you are standing on a battlefield. Hundreds of funnel shaped craters cover the area, between them the torn and half-eaten cadavers of the young animals. From 10,000 eggs laid at most two turtles will reach sexual maturity. They will return to the beach where they were born to lay their own eggs only after almost half a century. You wonder how this species of reptile has managed to survive in this way on this planet, and appreciate the importance of the strict conservation measures taken in Oman.
It can happen though that you spend half the night on the beach waiting in vain for these creatures, because few of them come ashore in winter, the main traveling season for tourists: The best season for turtle watching is from June to September.

research team, unique at the time, was formed from 35 scientists under the aegis of the Royal Geographical Society and the government of the Sultanate. The Omani army provided the scientists with the necessary logistical support. In all 500 people took part in the project. The results justified the expenditure. Although the Wihibah is a small desert, nearly all known dune formations are found there; there are more than 20 variants. The researchers hoped to gain information about the emergence of deserts in the course of millennia.

The northern part of the Wihibah is characterized by mighty red dunes, up to 200 meters in height, piled up parallel to one another. In the southern part these are replaced by white, sickle-shaped dunes. Beneath the drifting sands that can be seen today is a giant sea of fossilized dunes which is several meters thick in some parts of the desert and on the coast at Ras ar-Ruways, where this bizarrely formed layer is exposed. It is the largest known geological formation of its type. The sand is blown about by the annual southwestern

Wilfred Thesiger's Expedition Across the Wihibah

Even today the great desert and ice wastes of the earth fend off, for the most part successfully, the march of modern civilization. Their exploration is mostly due to individualists and their personal drive. In 1949 the Briton Wilfred Thesiger was the first European to cross the Wihibah. His task was to investigate the possible breeding grounds of the dreaded desert locust. At this time Oman was a no-go area for foreigners - the Imam who ruled the interior of the country wished to protect his domains from undesirable influences. For geographers Oman in those days was just a blank area on the map. Thesiger could only undertake his expedition incognito, and with the support of Bedouin that he had befriended on earlier journeys across the central Arabian desert, the Rub al Khali (literally "Empty Quarter".) In his book *Arabian Sands* he describes the Wihibah for the first time and gives us an idea of the conditions under which research in Oman was carried out in 1949. In the Museum of the Frankincense Land at Salalah large-scale photographs of his journey across Oman are on display, which as well as having esthetic beauty have a documentary worth that is not to be underestimated.

"I explained to Ahmad that I wished to travel northwards to the Wadi Batha and then to return to Muwaiqih along the foot of the mountains. This route would take me across the Wihibah sands which I was particularly anxious to see, since they were separated from the sands of the Empty Quarter by more than a hundred and fifty miles of gravel plain. Ahmad said, 'I myself have never been in those sands; I am from the Yahahif and we live on the plains, but I can find a guide from the Al Hiya, the other branch of our tribe. They live in those sands.'

monsoon. It is made up of quartz, calcium carbonate and ophiolite, in other words from the products of the erosion of shells and the surrounding rock formations. The dunes wander with a speed of about ten meters per year towards the country's interior, where their progress is halted by the Indam and Halfayn wadis on the western edge of the desert. These are two of the largest wadis in the land and at regular intervals are filled with running water.

In the middle of the Wihibah researchers found areas that were free of sand, where there were trees and interesting fauna and flora. Above all, the dunes in the north and the eastern edge near the coast, known as the woodlands, are extraordinarily rich in vegetation. Altogether 130 different species of plants and over 200 animal species were identified, among them various species of gazelle, the white-tailed mungo, desert foxes, insects, and reptiles. The creatures obtain the water necessary for survival either from the large, primeval ground water reservoir beneath the desert in the northeast or also from the heavy daily morning dew, resulting

He went on: 'You are free to go wherever you wish in the country of the Wihibah. We are your friends, Umbarak; none of us would try to stop you. But the tribes under the mountains are different; they will certainly make trouble if they find out who you are, just as the Duru did. Anyway, they are all governed by the Imam and they will be afraid to let you pass without his permission.. It is different in the desert; there we could perhaps take you through the land of our enemies, traveling as raiders travel and avoiding the wells. But that is impossible in the mountains; the country is too narrow; we should have to use the paths, and they go through the villages; we could never keep out of sight. I will take you as far as I can, but just you and one of your companions. We will get hold of good camels and keep ahead of the news. [....]

I hired a fresh camel from Sultan; bin Kabina rode his own, and both Sultan and Ahmad were well mounted. We were riding four of the finest camels in Arabia and if necessary could travel both fast and far. At first we crossed a gravel plain, sprinkled with sand of a reddish tint, and broken up by small limestone tables among which we saw many gazelle, all very wild. Gradually, as went further, the sand increased until it entirely overlaid the limestone floor. On the second day we reached the well of Tawi Harian, which was about eighty feet deep. Several Wihibah were there with donkeys, but no camels. We left as soon as we had watered, for we wanted no awkward questions. We were now riding northward along valleys half a mile wide enclosed by dunes of a uniform height of about two hundred feet. A curious feature of these valleys was that they were blocked at intervals of about two miles by gradual rises of hard sand. The sand in the bottoms was rusty red, whereas the dunes on either side were honey-colored."

(Wilfred Thesiger, *Arabian Sands*, p. 306 - 307.)

The ancient camel routes are now crossed with car tracks.

from the proximity of the sea. The Wihibah Sands Project increased the interest in the desert of both the Europeans working in Oman and among tourists. To cater for this interest the first "Off-road in Oman" guide was published in 1992, propagating weekend excursions through the sea of sand. Within a few years "wadi bashing" and "dune bashing" began to impose a very real threat to a unique landscape. Weekend trippers careen over the dunes and there are many accidents resulting from drivers thinking that because they are in a four-wheel drive vehicle they are really masters of this very difficult terrain. With neither knowledge nor understanding, willfully abusing the desert as some sort of adventure playground destroys the naturally grown dune formations and much worse, destroys the fragile root structures of the plants. The wildlife flees and the damage that has been caused to some places is clearly visible. It has resulted in some Omanis wishing to put a stop to desert tourism and to declare the Wihibah Sands to be a nature reserve.

The Bedouin, who have lived for centuries in harmony with the extremes of this countryside, would once more have it to themselves. They themselves now drive four-wheel drive vehicles instead of riding camels but they respect their habitat and always keep to

In spite of the difficult living conditions in this extreme terrain, the majority of Bedouin still live in palm huts in the desert.

their old paths. 450 to 500 Bedouin families from the Al-Wihibah tribe occupy the barren landscape along with an estimated 15,000 goats and 1,500 camels. Nowhere in the whole world are there more camels than in the Sultanate of Oman; it has the highest camel density of the entire planet. But only the camels of the Al-Wihibah are famous throughout the whole Gulf region, not as beasts of burden, but as the fastest racing camels in Arabia. Accordingly they command high prices: the best of them may change hands for more than 20,000 Omani rials. They are the preferred buy of the princes of the neighboring United Arab Emirates.

In Oman camel racing takes place mostly on National Day and on the Eid festivals on a special racetrack at Nizwa. During the rest of the year racing is very rare and then, as a rule, in places very hard for visitors to get to, far away from the asphalt roads. In Oman camel racing is no tourist spectacle but a passion of the Bedouin - and also of the Sultan. He owns his own racing stables. Select grooms and the latest equipment ensure that his animals lack for nothing. Up until now the royal animals have always been left standing in races against the Bedouin's "ships of the desert," even at the "Sultan's Camel Race" in 1998. As a result of this the Sultan made a spectacular decision, which was much remarked upon in the international press. He ordered new genes for his racing stable, not from anywhere in the Arabian world, but from a completely unknown "Camel Insemination Institute" in Hanover. The Veterinary University there is world leader in certain fields. How good the world's best genes, "made in Germany," really are will be seen in races in the coming years when the supergene competes with the Al-Wihibah's supercamels, on the desert tracks of Oman.

If you drive along the new asphalt road from Al Kamil Wa Al Wafi to Al Ashkarah you will first pass **Jaalan Bani Bu Ali**, famous for its Friday market. Its renowned **Al Hamouda mosque** built in the Ommayed style, with 52 domes, may only be viewed by non-Muslims from the outside. After Jaalan Bani Bu Hasan you gradually press on into this impressive landscape. Large black cones of rock rise singly out of the gravel plain; ever more frequently small, sickle-shaped wandering dunes line the road, sometimes laying right across the pavement. Stately strolling camels cross in small caravans, sometimes directly blocking the road. Near the coast the expanses of sand tighten up, the bright yellow dunes become higher and cover the dark rocks. Again and again you see the simple palm huts of the Bedouin, apparently scattered at random over the land. The road meets the coast at **Al Ashkarah**. In recent years this place has been built up to become a secondary fishing center and it has its own dhow boatyard. You can also make a visit to the idyllic little fishing village of **Asaylah** a few kilometers to the north. The purpose of a journey in this area is not to see the villages but the fascinating landscape to left and right of your route. You can see just as impressive a landscape following the asphalt road along the coast, by which you will without difficulty reach the sea turtle reserve at Ras Al Jinz, the most easterly point of the Arabian peninsula.

There is a new asphalt road under construction along the coast of the Wihibah from Al Ashkarah to Muhut (Hejj) and further south which is planned to be finished in 2010. It will connect there with the asphalt road running from Muhut (Hejj) along the coast to Ras Madrakah and Sawqirah, leading from there into the interior to Thumrayt and on to Salalah (see also chapter "From Hell to Paradise".)

From Sur to Qurayyat

Coming from Al Kamil Wa Al Wafi just before the entrance to Balad Sur there is a turn on the left sign-posted **Qalhat**. The road leads to the northern flanks of the Jabal al Khadar and the Jabal Bani Jabir, which plummet abruptly down to the sea some twenty kilometers beyond Sur. In the last few years the stretch between Sur and Qurayyat has been reconstructed as a toll highway. Unfortunately, the delightful scenery of Wadi Shab, Wadi Tiwi and Qalhat has been adversely affected by the construction of bridges and by damage caused by the cyclone *Gonu*, such that this picturesque landscape has lost much of its original character and allure.

One of Oman's largest and most ambitious industrial projects was realized on the plain between Sur and the mountains: Qalhat's liquid natural gas plant. Liquefied gas has been shipped from here since 2000. In the same year Oman's first gas tanker was christened with the name "Sohar." Only nine years earlier large quantities of natural gas were discovered in Oman for the first time. Today the country's reserves of this important raw material are estimated to be 25 trillion cubic feet. In October 1996 a sale and purchase agreement (SPA) for two-thirds of the plant output (4.1 million tons per annum) was concluded with the Korea Gas Corporation (KOGAS) for a period of 25 years. The agreement runs from 2000 and is the largest-ever single gas contract between two companies. Other customers for the liquefied gas are Japan, Spain, France, the USA and Belgium. The plant's annual capacity is around 6.6 million tons of liquefied gas.

Having reached the massif, the road runs over a narrow, raised gravel terrace which is repeatedly crossed by wadis opening into the sea. The water channels have eaten deep into the mountains and also into the valley. At the estuary of Wadi Hilm the earth washed down by the waters has formed a natural platform. Here, more than half a millennium ago, arose the famed port of **Qalhat**. Qalhat first became famous after being incorporated into the kingdom of Hormuz in 1270. The uncertain origins of the settlement go back at least another 1000 years. Qalhat was always in the shadow of the most important trading city of northern Oman, Sohar, until the latter was destroyed, along with its fleet, in the 10th century. There was a lively exchange of goods from the country's interior through Wadi Hilmi and the port offered good connections to other towns on the Indian Ocean. Under Persian rule in the 13th century, trade flourished to such an extent that the port became the second most important transshipment port after Hormuz.

Qalhat came to be regarded as the "twin town" of Hormuz. At the end of the 13th century the Venetian world traveler Marco Polo visited Qalhat, which he called "Kalayati," and described it as follows: "Kalayati is a large town situated near a gulf which has the name of Kalatu, distant from Dulfar about fifty miles towards the south-east [Marco Polo's statements are not geographically accurate. (author)]. The people are followers of the law of Mahomet and are subject to the melik of Ormuz, who, when he is attacked and hard pressed by another power, has recourse to the protection afforded by this city, which is so strong in itself, and so advantageously situated, that it has never yet been taken by an enemy. The country around it not yielding any kind of grain, it is imported from other districts. Its harbor is good, and many trading ships arrive there from India, which sell their piece-goods and spiceries to great advantage, the demand being considerable for the supply of towns and castles lying at a distance from the coast. These likewise carry away freights of horses, which they sell advantageously in India."

Creeping Danger: Snakes and Scorpions

It will be of no surprise to anyone that numerous species of snakes are indigenous to Oman, with its heat and dryness. To get a more detailed description of them the small book *Snakes of the Arabian Gulf and Oman* by Michael Gallagher, the curator of the Natural History Museum in Muscat, which deals exclusively with this subject, is highly recommended. Up to now altogether 27 different species are known, of which 17 are poisonous. These extremely dangerous poisonous snakes have, however, mostly specialized in different ecosystems, so that they only occur in certain regions.

The exception to this rule, the carpet viper (or saw-scaled viper/*Viper echis carinatus*), is the most dangerous and most widespread poisonous snake in the Sultanate. The scale skin has the characteristic "sawtooth pattern," and the head a very distinctive shovel shape. Their habitat includes the Al Batinah coast, the area around Muscat and also - with one large mutation - the stony wadis of the Hajar Mountains. There is also a subspecies of the carpet viper to be found in Dhofar. It feels at home anywhere it can creep into holes or beneath objects. By rubbing its horny scales together the snake gives a hissing warning sound when it feels threatened. Like all vipers it is mainly active at night and moves forward relatively slowly. Omanis take great care not to allow these snakes any shelter within the area around their homes. Although vipers can also climb trees they apparently never enter houses.

The **horned viper** (*Cerastes cerastes*) is widespread in the interior of the country in northern Oman and hunts over the sand at night. The horn over the eye is not developed

"The fortress is so situated at the entrance of the gulf of Kalatu, that no vessel can come in or depart without its permission. [...] The inhabitants in general of this country subsist upon dates and upon fish, either fresh or salted, having constantly a large supply of both; but persons of rank, and those who can afford it, obtain corn for their use from other parts." (Marco Polo, *The Travels of Marco Polo*.)

The famous Arabian traveler Ibn Battuta completed the picture almost a hundred years later. He described a large mosque with painted tiles, countless merchants and several flourishing suqs. Today all that remains which bears witness to the size of the port are the ruins of the Bibi Mariyam mosque, built in the 14th century. The octagonal base of the collapsed dome, the outer walls of the cubic central structure and the wall niches with their stuccowork are still relatively well preserved. Otherwise the area is covered by a large field of rubble on the site which once made up the town. In a few other places the sparse remains of walls or fragments of gates can

in every specimen. The **false horned viper** (*Pseudocerastes persicus*), in contrast, always has a horn over the eye. As they prefer cooler ground, their habitat is restricted to the higher areas of the Hajar Mountains. The very fast and also tree-dwelling **cobra** (*Naja haje*) prefers the wooded hills of Dhofar. This area, rich in vegetation, is also the habitat of the strongly bright and dark contrasting patterned **puff adder** (*Bitis arietans*.) It lies in wait for its prey mostly at the edge of grassy tracks and strikes with lightning rapidity. The wearing of stout, protective footwear is therefore highly recommended. The **asp** or **mole viper** (*Atractaspis*) also inhabits Dhofar. However it only comes to the surface when there is rain. The danger with this snake lies in its unpredictability and its ability to project its long poison fangs from the sides of its closed mouth. They can thus attack in any direction. All nine of the species of **sea snakes** to be found in the waters of Oman belong to the family *hydrophiidae* and are poisonous. Eight species are hardly to be differentiated and prefer the shallow, and thus warm, coastal waters of northern Oman. Only the up to two meter long yellow sea snake sometimes strays into the cooler waters of southern Oman. Sea snakes are normally not aggressive and bite only when directly threatened.

In general you should keep your distance from snakes. To be on the safe side you should avoid thickly overgrown terrain, oasis gardens, and going on foot over terrain at night without a flashlight. The chance, or rather danger, of meeting a snake in the expanses of Oman and with the animals' retiring nature is in any case very small. Incidents with snakes are extremely few and far between. An example may illustrate this: the Omani geologist Salim Al-Maskiry worked for ten years as a field researcher in the most remote areas of Oman. During all these years he never encountered a snake. When he took part in a geological expedition to Spain in 1993, however he was bitten by a viper and was laid up in the hospital for two weeks. If someone does get bitten by a snake he should be brought be found. The ground is covered with shards and lumps of brain coral, which was the most-used building material. The outlines of the houses can only be properly made out from the air. What really lays buried under this enormous rubble heap remains hidden from us, and at best we can only guess at it. The site still awaits archaeological investigation. You should pay attention to the notices and not remove even the most worthless-looking fragment: it could turn out to be an important part of the archaeological puzzle.

The desolate state of Qalhat has two basic causes. Around the end of the 15th century the town experienced a heavy earthquake, which reduced parts of the port to rubble and destroyed countless houses. When the Portuguese general Albuquerque on his travels of exploration and conquest reached Qalhat in 1507, the town's beauty and wealth must have still been impressive in spite of the natural catastrophe. Qalhat surrendered to Albuquerque without a struggle and was initially spared further destruction.

directly to the nearest clinic or hospital and under no circumstances should drive himself! For the doctor treating the case it is very helpful to be able to describe the appearance of the reptile. If you find an apparently dead snake you should first make sure it is really dead using a long stick from a safe distance before approaching any closer. If it really is dead and you happen to have a suitable container on hand you can transfer the snake to it carefully with a stick and hand it in to the Natural History Museum in Muscat (Tel. 24605400) where it can be used for study.

The chance of meeting a **scorpion** is much greater, and must be reckoned with throughout Oman. There are twelve different species, their stings are all very painful and have to be medically treated. Scorpions hide themselves during the day in hollows, crevices and under stones. After spending a night out in the open you should always shake out your shoes and clothing thoroughly before putting them on. All ground snakes and scorpions can be seen as specimens in the Natural History Museum in Muscat/Al Khuwayr. A visit to this museum is very much to be recommended and will give you a much more realistic impression of the appearance and size of individual snakes than you can get from photographs or scientific drawings.

In the afternoon, Wadi Shab and Wadi Tiwi are exposed to a wonderful play of light and shadow.

The following year, however, Albuquerque changed his mind and returned and reduced the flourishing harbor metropolis to rubble and ashes.

Some twenty kilometers north of Qalhat, **Wadi Tiwi** and **Wadi Shab** flow into the sea. Situated between the estuaries of the two wadis is the small port of **Tiwi**, which played an important role in the Middle Ages. It offered ships the only anchorage and watering station along the coast between Qalhat and Qurayyat. In Wadi Shab the water has carved a spectacular canyon through the rock. A bank of gravel prevents the water from flowing directly into the sea and has allowed an idyllic lagoon to form. A narrow path over a small bridge once led into the idyllic valley. The path continued along small fields and houses to pools in the depths of the gorge. Unfortunately the lower part of the valley was heavily damaged by cyclone *Gonu* in 2007, covering the idyllic fields with a thick layer of gravel. But it is still worthwhile walking up the valley to the higher levels with its water pools. As this valley is inhabited, be sure to be properly dressed and refrain from turning your visit into a photo safari.

The Western Ash Sharqiyyah

At Ibra, on the extreme western edge of the Ash Sharqiyyah, the road branches off towards Sinaw. Along with Al Mudaybi, Al Mintarib, Adam and Jaalan Bani Bu Ali, **Sinaw** is one of the most southerly oases in Oman. The modern settlement has formed around the large, newly-built suq. To the east the old, almost deserted quarter slumbers on and to the west, as before, stand the palm branch homes of the Bedouin from the Al-Wihibah tribe. These huts are used during the date harvest and for the Friday markets. But even during the week, mornings in Sinaw bustle with activity. The settlement is one of the most important market places for the Bedouin of Oman, a place where all kinds of wares are exchanged, information and rumors included. The suq, which is enclosed by a wall with four gates, is directly at the end of the asphalt road leading into the town. In front of the walls trucks are parked and double as market stalls. Besides fresh fish, camels are sometimes on offer in the market. Bedouin women, heads held proudly erect, cleave their way through the throng and purchase exquisite cloths and finely worked jewelry, dates, paprika and sun-dried lemons.

A widespread network of underground qanat aflaj supplies all the towns south of the mountains as far as Adam with water from the mountain range.

South of the market the new asphalt road begins, and runs along the western edge of the Wihibah Sands to the coast and then along to the northern edge of the Dhofar mountains at Wadi Shuwaymiyah. **Al Mudaybi** has had to cede its importance as a market place to Sinaw and the old suq has fallen into disrepair. However, it is thanks to its minor economic importance that it has been able to maintain so much of the character of an oasis town. The clay houses huddle together and a wall of clay bricks shelters the settlement on the outside. The fields are dug deep in the earth; they are at the same level as the underground channels which bring the precious water here from afar. East of the asphalt road, not far from Al Mudaybi, the shafts of the *qanat-aflaj*, an underground water channel, give the appearance of kilometers of outsized molehills laid out in a straight line. You will rarely get so good a picture of what an incredible human achievement the construction of these channels is. For centuries the *aflaj* have delivered the precious elixir of life to the edge of the desert. Most of the channels have been renovated. In order to do this the shafts were opened, the channels cleaned, and concrete poured over the bed. This should prevent the loss of sometimes large amounts of water through seepage. Newly built access shafts have ensured that in the future maintenance will be easier. This age-old system of channels has not been disturbed by this modernization, and the desert's highly sensitive primeval

water table has not been encroached upon. These water reserves stem from the epoch when Oman was tropically moist and could never be regenerated by today's meager rainfall.

The settlements in the northern interior of Oman are supplied with water by means of a dense network of around 4000 *aflaj*. Over the centuries the subterranean channels were hacked out of the rock with the most primitive of implements. The longest channels run underground for up to twelve kilometers without a break, sometimes reaching depths of 50 meters. Oman's *falaj* system may well be regarded as one of the most magnificent and impressive achievements in the history of human settlement.

One of the most significant prehistoric settlement areas in Oman lies to the north of Al Mudaybi, in the region between Samad Ash Ahan, Al Fath and Lizq. In the area round **Al Fath** you can still find beehive tombs from the Hafit Period, some in very good condition. Like all burial structures of this period they are on higher

The Awamir – Oman's Water Experts

The Awamir tribe lives in the Ash Sharqiyyah and its most important settlements are Adam, Al Ayun, Al Mudaybi and Qalaat al Awamr. Smaller tribal groups also live in the vicinity of As Seeb on the Al Batinah coast and in Abu Dhabi in the United Arab Emirates. The Awamir in Oman applied successfully for the monopoly of the maintenance of the existing water distribution system, the *aflaj* and for the tapping of new springs. Now as then they are considered to be the most competent water experts in the country, an estimation which was confirmed in 1975 by a study carried out by the University of Durham. At that time there were some 250 Awamir men in the whole of northern Oman occupied with such specialized work. Many of them only return to their home villages during Ramadan and during the fasting month the hard physical work on the water channels is put to one side.

The water distribution system in northern Oman is in parts up to 2000 years old. Its vitally important function can only be kept going by constant maintenance and adaptation to conditions which are constantly changing due to the movements of the level of the water table and droughts. The excavation of the well shafts and the underground water tunnels, called *qanat*, is a most labor-intensive, highly dangerous handiwork which requires a great measure of expertise and specialized knowledge of geomorphology. Richer villages would as a rule commission the water experts of the Awamir, the so-called *basr* and specialist workers from the tribe to extend and maintain their systems. The inhabitants of poorer places carried out the work themselves having first been advised by the *basr*.

The tunnel was fundamentally laid against the flow direction of the water, its dimensions depending on the hardness of the rock. The diameter, length and amount of work required also formed the basis for calculating the costs. Each project would be completed in various stages, each piece being paid for on completion. Such systems have special units of measurement which at first glance seem very imprecise. The deep vertical shafts are measured in *kama*; a *kama* is ground and not directly at the side of a path. Some of the tombs can be seen from the road and you can approach them in a car to within a half hour's walk. If you turn off the asphalt road at the sign for "Al Fath," to the left you will see a long hill rising out of the plain and behind it another one. On the crest of the second hill you will be able to make out the irregular, jagged silhouette of a row of beehive tombs. Between the main road and the oasis a track leads up to the hill, though for the last few meters the gravel is extremely rough. It is best to get out here and proceed on foot. Tombs of this type first emerged in Oman between 3500 BC and the middle of the following millennium.

The construction of the tombs at Al Fath matches those of the Hafit Period. Around the generally oval burial chamber dry stone walls rise up in a cone shapes. The usually triangular entrance, at ground level, would have been sealed with stones after the burial. This characteristic shape with the relatively small entrance lends

the average height of a man. The horizontal unit of measure is a *baa*, which is the distance from fingertip to fingertip of a man with his arms outstretched. The *dhraa* is a subunit and is the distance from the elbow to the outstretched fingertip and is a quarter of a *kama* when measuring vertically. These apparently willful units of measure, which can be very differently interpreted, would be defined on a special measuring rod which was used for reckoning how much work had been done and was accessible to all. Everyone could thus check the work of the Awamir. The technical plan for the system was also based on this system of measurement. 1 *kama* is the equivalent of 100 *baa*. In 1975 a tunnel one *dhraa* wide and two *dhraa* high cost between 40 and 130 Omani rial per *baa*, depending on the hardness of the rock.

On the Al Batinah coast the knowledge of the Awamir was not needed as the water table is so close to the surface here that it can easily be directly tapped without any great specialized knowledge. In the other regions of northern Oman at the beginning of the 1990s the lively demand for this specialist knowledge had not diminished, quite the contrary. The technical and social progress of the country has brought with it an enormous increase in the demand for water. The Awamir, with their limited capacity, could hardly keep up with the demand and accordingly their prices rose dramatically. This had the result that many of the small and poorer settlements could no longer afford the very expensive maintenance service and urgent repairs and extensions of the water network were not carried out - to such an extent that the old water distribution system was in serious danger of collapse.

In this situation the government stepped in and a special authority for *aflaj* was founded within the Ministry for Water Resources, which now coordinates and finances the expensive restoration and maintenance of the extensive network of water channels. It is small wonder that many of its employees are members of the Awamir tribe. In the period between 1991 and 1995 this authority was responsible for restoring 1144 *aflaj*. The total costs came to over 25 million Euro and repair works on a further 1000 *aflaj* have been carried out since then.

itself to comparison with a beehive. The tombs in Al Fath have a diameter of between four and six meters. In other places some have been as large as nine meters across. If you look to the north from the hill, your eye will be caught by a dead-straight, wide track, which begins at the foot of the hill and seems to lose itself into nothingness in the distance - this is Al Fath's **camel racetrack**. The Bedouin tribes of the region use it mostly during the Eid festivals and also on National Day.

Only a few kilometers to the north, at **Lizq**, you can view the remains of a monumental Iron Age fort. The site can only be reached on foot and is located on a hill on the other side of the wadi to the east of the oasis. The thick wall and the remains of the buildings as well as the remains of a huge set of steps make it the largest in Oman from this period. From the top of the hill, facing northwest you look out over Wadi Samad, which was one of the most important historical deposits of copper ore in Oman. The fort at Lizq was probably built to protect the copper production. The actual center of copper production was four kilometers southwest of Samad in the neighboring wadi at **Al Moyassar**, and can only be located with the help of a knowledgeable guide in a vehicle suited to the terrain. From the 3rd millennium BC to the Early Islamic period copper was mined here. Today the slagheaps bear witness to copper production on a grand scale. Researchers from the German Bergbaumuseum (Museum of Mining) in Bochum succeeded in uncovering a settlement from the Umm-an-Nar Period.

The finds, among them copper ingots, anvil stones, furnaces, carved soapstone, and seals, bear witness to a community with copper production, ceramic workshops, soapstone operations, dam building, fields and a residential district separate from the working areas. The ore came from the open-cast mine on the slopes of the wadi, and the extracted copper was exported from here to Mesopotamia and to the Indus valley. Like the settlement itself, the numerous tombs of the attached necropolis have been greatly damaged by erosion and people stealing the stones. There is a fortress from the Umm-an-Nar Period (ca. 2700-2000 BC) which is still relatively clear to make out.

The old entry points to the underground channels' maintenance shafts (upper right) are being renovated today (upper left) and are still in use.
Within the oasis the water is led though open channels (bottom left) to the individual fields. Supplying water from traditional wells (bottom right) has meanwhile been replaced almost everywhere by diesel pumps.

The western Hajar Mountains

At the Foot of the Jabal Al Akhdar

The Samail Gap runs along the southeast flank of the Jabal Al Akhdar, or "Green Mountain." It not only connects the newer capital of Muscat with the old seats of government, Nizwa and Bahla, but is also the most important passage between the interior of the country and the Al Batinah coast. The towns which line the pass in the shadow of the highest mountains were always the spiritual center of Ibadhism. It was from here that the country was indirectly, and even sometimes directly, governed by the Imam. Here was always the seedbed for resistance against any foreign rule. You reach this region from Muscat via the Burj Al Sahwah roundabout. Up until the Bidbid oasis the route is identical to the tour to the provinces of Ash Sharqiyyah. If you want to visit this town on the edge of the mountains leave the new highway before Izki and take the old country road. Fortresses and watchtowers will accompany you the entire length of this important trade route.

Some twenty kilometers beyond Bidbid the otherwise relatively wide passage through the mountains becomes narrower. To the west of the road is the small village of **Manal**. Several narrow watchtowers are perched on a large freestanding rock overlooking the ruins of the old village. Directly behind them the southeast flank of the Jabal Al Akhdar rises like a gigantic steep ramp to a height of over 2000 meters, dwarfing the watchtowers which seem to shrink to the size of chessmen in comparison.

The road continues along the Samail Gap. Parallel to it runs a yellow and black painted steel railing which marks the main pipelines for oil. As well as quantities of traffic, all the fossil fuels of Oman pass through the Samail Gap. The town of **Izki** lies at the turn-off to Sinaw. Like Ibra in the Ash Sharqiyyah, Izki was inhabited by two feuding tribes who built their own residential areas apart from one another. The large five-cornered fort, built in the 19th century, is situated in the neutral zone between the two fortified sections of the town. This used to be occupied by the wali, who had not only to maintain peace in the town but also controlled the entry to Nizwa and Bahla. Izki is supposedly the oldest place in Oman

and its origins go back to the 7th century BC. Today Izki is less characterized by its history, but is more an extensive area of new buildings arranged around a junction for traffic from all over.
A must to see is the imposing, completely intact *falaj* **siphon** some four kilometers before Izki, not far from the old main road. You reach it by the small road running parallel to the south. You get onto this road by turning off at the bank and following it as far as the wadi crossing. Only a few meters away from the street on both sides of the crossing you will see the high walls of the *falaj*, which abruptly stop at the bed of the wadi.
The *falaj* water swirls into the pipes, crosses beneath the wadi and gushes up again in a stream at the other side. The *falaj Al Malki* at Izki is one of the oldest, most abundant water channels in the whole country.
In July 2006 UNESCO added *falaj Al Malki* at Izki, plus four additional *aflaj* (the plural of *falaj*) to its list of World Heritage sites: *falaj Daris* at Nizwa, *falaj Al Muyassar* at Rostaq, *falaj Al Jeelah* in the eastern Hajar Mountains, and *falaj Al Khatmeen* at Birkat Al Mawz. The *falaj Al Malki* is reckoned to be 1500 years old. It has over 300 branches and delivers its water as far as the Adam oasis over 80 kilometers away.
In spite of all innovations **Birkat Al Mawz** has managed to retain the atmosphere of an oasis town. The oasis itself is a little further off to the north of the old main road. The extensive forests of date palm are cultivated and watered in the traditional manner. The *falaj* system is still largely intact and wandering around the oasis you will get a good feel for the importance of its social function.

The falaj siphon at Izki is the most imposing in Oman.

The vital significance of the network of channels in this region is reflected by its central role in people's lives. Everybody needs water and everybody consumes water. Using the *aflaj* requires a highly developed sense of collective responsibility and is never just a private matter. The word "*falaj*" is derived from the Arabic word for "share," clearly indicating the social aspect of the ancient water distribution system. A strictly followed sequence in using the *falaj* ensures that its purity is maintained. First women fetch drinking water from the village well, where they meet daily at fixed times and exchange news and gossip and discuss problems.

The well is at the center of everyday life in the community. In the vicinity of the mosque there is a place fed by the *falaj* and used for ritual cleansing. Then come the bathing and washing areas and - right at the end of the village - the place where the bodies of the dead are prepared for their final journey.

Beyond the village the *falaj* branches and the water here is used exclusively for watering the fields. The complicated usage rights are regulated on a principle of rotation, which ensures the fair distribution of water to the individual plots of cultivated land. In Samail, for example, seven watering periods each of four hours duration used to be auctioned. Because the day only has 24 hours in it the last share would always be on the following day and so all the other cycles would be pushed back by four hours. In this way over a week everybody got their allocations and nobody had advantages or disadvantages. After a week the shares would be newly allocated. The money raised from the auction flowed into the community fund, from which the *waqil*, responsible for the *falaj*, is paid. He ensures that the water is fed to the various fields at the specified times and he is also responsible for the upkeep of the channels. During the day the correct intervals for distributing the water are controlled by the *waqil* using a solar clock, and at night by the position of certain constellations over a marker in the ground. The appearance of certain constellations in the sky was also used to determine sowing times. Nowadays looking up at the firmament has largely been replaced by a glance at a wristwatch.

The government has taken trouble to see that this 2000 year old method of using the raw material of water in harmony with nature is not called into question. The lavish renovation works and investments in new channels and natural sources should safeguard the future of this proven system of water distribution.

At the southern edge of the oasis there is the newly restored large fortress of **Bayt Ar Ridaydah** with its imposing towers and painted wooden ceilings.

The building is not so much of architectural as of strategic and historical importance. It controlled the entry to Wadi Muaydin, the most important passage to the high plateau of the Jabal Al Akhdar: the fort served as residence for Suleiman ibn Himyar, the sheikh of the large and mighty Bani Riyam tribe of the Ghafiri federation. In the 1950s he fought alongside Imam Ghalib ibn Ali in the Jabal Al Akhdar uprising against the Sultan and the British. Until 1959 the rebels were increasingly forced back into the mountain region of the Jabal Al Akhdar and when the revolt eventually collapsed after the destruction of Tanuf and Bayt Ar Ridaydah, they had to flee to the plateau.

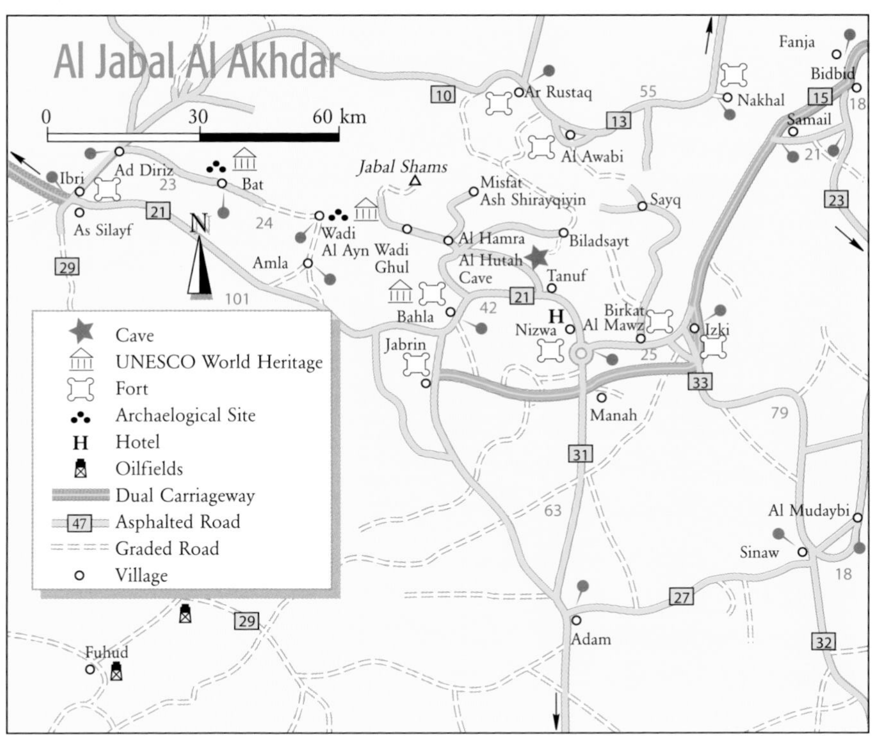

Looking up at the steep, barren rock walls it is hard to imagine that the summit plateau of the **Jabal Al Akhdar** was one of the most feared, as well as being the most remote, regions in the country. At over 2000 meters on the Sayq Plateau, the extensive terraced fields and small villages create their own world, an island of green set in a sea of rock, hence its name "Green Mountain."

A visit to this region, completely closed off until recently, can now be done effortlessly, best in combination with booking at one of the two hotels on the Jabal Al Akhdar. There is the old Jabal Akhdar Hotel and the new Sahab Resort which is expected to be opened at the end of March 2010 on the edge of the cliff with a spectacular view of the mountain massif and the steep-terraced fields.

On the Sayq Plateau of the Jabal Al Akhdar

Up until a few years ago entry to the Jabal Al Akhdar, the "Green Mountain," was forbidden to foreigners and to Omanis who did not live there. But since the establishment of social conformity in the living conditions and an infrastructure for the villages of the Sayq Plateau, situated more than 2000 meters above sealevel, the region has been increasingly opened up to visitors.

You can approach the mountain from Birkat al Mawz, passing left of the Bayt Ar Ridaydah Fort into the wadi. After four kilometers the road branches off to the left into Wadi Muaydin. Straight ahead you come to the checkpoint. Although the road to the top has been paved a four-wheel drive vehicle is required. Having managed the ascent, the Jabal Al Akhdar Hotel awaits you right at the start of the plateau, providing a perfect base for excursions and walks on the plateau. If you visit in winter you should take warm clothing with you, while in the furnace of the Omani summer, it has a pleasant Mediterranean climate here. Grapes, peaches, pomegranates – fruits which otherwise cannot be found in the country – flourish in the temperate climate. The region is above all famous for its roses, from the petals of which rosewater is distilled in late April and May.

The plateau is surrounded by numerous deep gorges. Many of the relatively short paths and tracks lead to spots with breathtaking views. One of the most beautiful is certainly *Diana's Point*, only a few kilometers distant from the hotel. Here Princess Diana and Prince Charles are supposed to have taken a picnic. A great deal of Arabic graffiti scratched in the rock by admirers bears witness to the famous visit.

But more impressive is the view over the rock slopes opposite. Countless terraced fields cling to the steep slope beneath Al Ain. The luxuriant green of the roses and other plants stands in stark contrast to the grey of the deep gorge.

A walk through the terraced fields along the narrow walls of the *aflaj* which serves Al Ain, Al Sharijah and Sayq is certainly an experience never to be forgotten. A fantastic view over the surrounding mountains opens up before you, giving you an instructive insight into the life of the people in this remote region. These walks should best be taken with a guide who knows the area. He will know not only the people but also the paths along the steep slopes, with their often deep abysses. As elsewhere it is expected of foreigners that they dress properly and return greetings that are offered them.

The road in the direction of Sayq ends in a parking place next to a large rock from which steep steps run down on the left into the Wadi Habib. The old settlement is today deserted, but its clay architecture is still worth admiring. The lush gardens are still cultivated as before.

The Sayq Plateau invites you to make a number of personal discoveries. If you're good on your feet you should reckon on spending more than just one night in one of the hotels.

Here, on a ledge overlooking the yawning canyon and the green terraces of the villages below, is a treasure trove of fossils, just meters from the road. And it is right here that you will find the second hotel in Jabal Al Akhdar, its opening promised for 2010, the fantastically situated *Sahab Resort;* a unique hotel with a unique story.

In the summer one finds pomegranates, grapes and wild olives, among other things, flourishing on Jabal Al Akhdar.

After almost 18 years in the Omani navy, Nabhan al Nabhani returned to the Jabal Al Akhdar with an idea for a boutique hotel which would do justice to the culture of the mountain he calls home, and to introduce new concepts for tourism, with emphasis on respecting the local habitat. Nabhan and his brother Ibrahim started working on their 6000 square meter land grant years ago. Rather than lay the foundations over the fossil-filled bedrock, the hotel has been built around them, making them the primary attraction, alongside a breathtaking view. The fossil-bejewelled rocks also surround an infinity swimming pool which, filled to the brim, seems to spill out over the cliff into the canyon. The outer walls of the hotel are covered with local stone which blends perfectly with the surrounding landscape, making the building nearly invisible from a distance. The stones are handcut and were collected in the mountain area by ten men over the last four years. The ceilings and verandas are decorated with wooden beams imported from Zanzibar. There are also gardens in which the endemic plants are as much an attraction as the fossils. The hotel offers 38 rooms. Accommodation ranges from VIP suites to regular rooms, the premium ones with private terrace and garden, separate bedrooms and sitting room, plus a walk-in closet. (For contact info see Green Pages: Hotels)

Nizwa, the Center of Inner Oman

Nizwa was always the religious center of Oman and remains so to this day. It is here that Mohammed's envoy is said to have delivered his letter to the Julanda kings and here that the new teachings of Islam immediately fell on fertile soil. Julanda ibn Masud was elected as the first Ibadhi Imam and the town was declared the capital of the country. In the 12th century Nizwa had to yield its leading status as the seat of government to Bahla, although the town remained the spiritual and religious center for the Ibadhis. Consequently Nizwa remained the preferred place for the election of the Imam and later once more became the capital. Finally, from 1913 until the defeat of the Jabal Al Akhdar uprising in 1959, it served as the capital of the Imamate.

Steep steps lead to the walkway of Nizwa fort's defensive tower.

The oasis at Nizwa contains territories pertaining to various tribes. At the center of the town is the large fort with the suq in front of its gates. The suq and the fortress were completely renovated between 1992 and early 1994. **Nizwa fort** is a unique monument, an architectural witness to the economic and military success of the early Yaruba dynasty. It was built around 1660 under Imam Sultan ibn Saif and was twelve years in construction. Its main feature is a gigantic cannon tower, about 23 meters high and 40 meters across. To keep it stable it was filled with scree and earth to a height of 14 meters. Only a narrow, meandering staircase, with defensive shafts above the doors through which hot oil could be poured on attackers, leads to the main defensive platform which is surrounded by a nine meter high wall with a walkway for the defenders. The gunners were supplied with water from their own well, and a small mosque catered for their spiritual well-being. The round tower forms the eastern flank of the otherwise rectangular fortification. The tower was also made safer against attackers by a veritable maze of staircases, platforms, storerooms and walls, laid out over different levels. There is a small building between the outer defensive wall and the fort itself which carefully documents the restoration work of both the fort and the suq.

South of the fort the **suq** glows in its new splendor. It not only looks like new, but other than a small part, it actually is brand new. If you go straight down the slope from the fort, you pass on your left the new silver suq and after about 200 meters, you come to a large wooden gate. On the other side of this gate are the modest

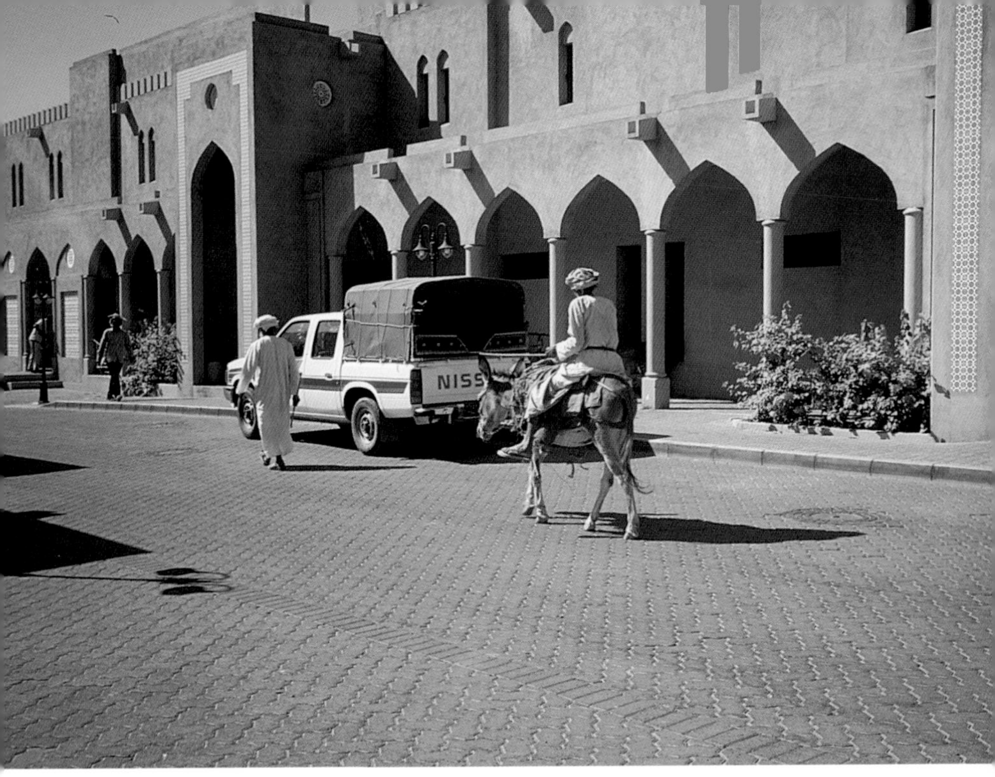

Now and then the mountain farmers of the Jabal Al Akhdar ride their donkeys down the steep and narrow paths to the new suq at Nizwa.

remains of the old Nizwa suq, famed throughout the land on account of its atmosphere. Here an old piece of the Orient currently runs counter to the town planners' ideas of how things should look as embodied in the policy of "beautification." But the outcome of the battle is already decided, as a stroll around the neighboring new suq makes clear. The old suq has the effect of a flashback into the past, whereas the new suq looks like a modern production on an oriental film set. While the streets and the shops in the area around the new suq were alive with a cheery, colorful bustle, you would hardly meet anyone in the new shopping center, which had looked so fine on the drawing board. In the course of the last few years this has gradually changed. At first there was only activity on Friday mornings, when the Bedouin come from all over the region to the large **goat market**. They clearly had the fewest problems with fitting into the new environment, for the traditional place for the goat market at the south end of the suq had also been plastered over and subjected to "beauty treatment." The buyers sit around in a large circle in the middle and the goats and sheep on offer are led around within the ring on a line and their qualities extolled until the highest possible price is reached. At the edge of this "arena" cattle are tied to posts, and grass feed is everywhere on sale.

Omani Silver Jewelry

Oman's ancient tradition as a seafaring people was constantly introducing new ideas from all over the world to the Sultanate. Over the centuries they have managed to take design ideas and handicraft techniques in silverwork from the most varied of cultures and melt them together to make their own new developments on a very high artistic level with world-class craftsmanship. Influences from India, Persia, East Africa and China are recognizable. The stars, leaves and petal forms of the Omani repertoire of motifs come from India and Persia. From Africa they took colored glass beads, from Europe fine beadwork processes, from China rattling bracelets and bells. The emergence of Islam also extended the formal repertoire and thus the palette of jewelry pieces on offer: the crescent moon, the full moon and simple geometrical forms appear on objects. Among them the rectangular, richly decorated, small silver containers known as *hirz*. They contain verses of the Quran and are worn around the neck as a kind of talisman.

The carrying of amulets is, especially for children, an old custom which is still practiced. All possible objects were set in silver and then worked into an amulet: colorful semi-precious stones, pieces of glass, corals, coins, teeth and much more. For an amulet to have an effect attributed to it, color plays a decisive role. Blue fends off the "evil eye," green is the color of fertility and red protects against illness. The brighter the color shines, the correspondingly stronger is the magical power. It was on account of this that the bicycle, introduced during the period of modernization and not being particularly suited to the country's climate or topography, aroused such an interest in the Omani silversmith - at least a small part of it: the multi-facetted rear reflector. Today you will often find parts of these red reflective discs worked into silver jewelry or rings: an unmistakable sign of creative vitality and originality.

In earlier times jewelry was usually made out of silver because it was cheaper and easier to get than gold. The precious metal came to Oman mostly in the form of Maria Theresa thalers from the Austro-Hungarian Empire or in ingots from India.

The Maria Theresa thaler was first minted in Austria in 1753, weighed 28 grams, and the silver had a fineness of 833. This type of coin continued to be minted in Vienna after the death of the monarch (1780) almost always as a commemoration of the year of the death of the empress. Because of its standardized material worth the thaler quickly developed into the favorite method of payment in the bartering of the Orient, thereby receiving the moniker "Levant thaler." In Oman the Maria Theresa thaler was first effectively replaced by the rial in 1968. The silversmiths either melted down the coins to rework the silver or they integrated them directly into their jewelry, above all in heavy necklaces. These sumptuously decorated pieces, together with the large matching ear pendants reached a substantial weight, which was partially offset by the equally decorated headcloth, as the jewelry around the neck and ears was suspended with cords from the headpiece. This ancient jewelry tradition is as lively now as it always was among the Bedouin of the country's interior.

"Life insurance" around the neck: Omani jewelry

Valuable jewelry always played an important role in traditional Arab society. The husband gave jewelry to his wife in order to provide some financial security in case of an accident or death in war. Because women were regarded as untouchable during military conflicts, they became a sort of "portable treasury." The silver carried by the woman served as her family's life insurance. This attitude to jewelry is still widespread in Oman. As people have meanwhile become significantly more prosperous, silver has gone increasingly out of fashion; today gold is the material to satisfy people's ideas of quality. Most of the silversmiths of the country have meanwhile become goldsmiths. They imitate the old silver pieces with the more precious material, which unfortunately has led to a cultural impoverishment. The old forms and patterns gained their effect from the material used. Silver oxidizes quickly and blackens. Even after cleaning black remains in the crannies, adding to the attraction of the ornament through the effect of the contrast of polished and black silver. Even the finest patterns achieve a strong optical effect of exceptional appeal. Gold, on the other hand, does not oxidize. The language of form developed over the centuries often appears muted and hard to accept, even though it has been worked in exactly the same way as silver. Gold requires its own formal ideas and techniques, which have not yet been developed by the craftsmen. In the interior of the country these changes can also be felt and silver is no longer the dominant material. It is best to first admire the attractive products of traditional Omani silverwork in all their stylistic variety that are still to be found in Nizwa and Bahla - and then buy.

The Bedouin women remain inconspicuously in the background but it is mostly they who finally decide on the purchase and who look after the money. Men, like walking market stalls heavily laden with curved daggers and rifles, mix among the lively crowds which are intently discussing and comparing. The weapons are still treasured as status symbols. Bedouin prefer rifles, while town-dwellers prefer the curved dagger, the *khanjar*.

Nizwa has been the most important center for silverwork in Oman for generations. The small shops in the new **silver suq** offer a high standard of the craft as practiced in the country's interior.

A few kilometers north of Nizwa, you can freely visit the main water supply for the town, the ***falaj Daris***, named after the small neighboring town. The channel runs through a small, beautiful park and is an ideal resting place after the exertions of a long sightseeing tour around the town.

The defensive tower of Manah.

From Nizwa to Manah, Adam and the endless Gravel Desert

Six kilometers south of Nizwa at the Salalah roundabout, begins the more than 800 kilometer long road over Oman's vast central gravel desert to Salalah, the capital of the province of Dhofar. As flat as a billiard table as far as the horizon, the desolateness is occasionally broken by large, freestanding blocks of stone. A few kilometers after the roundabout a road branches off to the east which leads to several small oases, all lying close to one another. The largest of them, **Manah**, is about nine kilometers from the main road and was once an important trading center. This town and the oasis at Adam formed the southernmost outposts of the settled mountain region of northern Oman. Here the caravans from the frankincense land in the south would rest and market their wares after the desert crossing: Manah boomed, becoming large and prosperous. But the age of the caravans is over and now the old town lies completely abandoned at the edge of the new road. Next to it the inhabitants built a modern and comfortable settlement.

With its semi-derelict town center, which nonetheless gives the impression of being complete, Manah offers one of the most impressive townscapes in Oman. The tall, mostly two-storey, clay houses press closely together. In their cooling shadows, the narrow, crooked lanes of this large ghost town create an atmosphere of mystery. Many of the old wooden doors are decorated with carved wooden strips, the single decoration in these typically Omani

Looking at Adam, you would never know that the ruling Al-Bu-Said dynasty originated here.

buildings, which are plain but make a powerful impression. The imposing wooden town gates and a narrow, tall, rectangular-shaped tower provided the town with protection. Today the whole city is closed off and surrounded by a fence due to the restoration work which will occur here in the coming years.

In the neighboring oasis of **Al Fiqayn** there is an interesting **defensive tower** with a unique form. Visible from afar, the newly-restored building rises high above the date plantations. Steep, narrow steps lead to the upper platforms which provide a grandiose view over the region and over the decayed old town center. After another 50 kilometers' drive along the main road over the gravel plain you reach the **Adam** oasis. The easiest way to find the settlement is to turn left at the Shell petrol station and follow the winding road as far as the mosque with its green dome and then keep to the right. The central area of the oasis can only be viewed on foot. Many people still live here and new buildings are still going up beyond the town walls. In contrast to Manah, Adam is not made up of a single large settlement, but of several groups of buildings scattered around the oasis. Each of these complexes forms a unit, closed to the outside like a fortress. The sites are inhabited by various clans and tribes. Adam is the tribal home of the Al-Bu-Said; Ahmad ibn Said, the founder of the dynasty which still rules today, was born here and built the fortress north of Adam. The entire oasis is divided into parcels which, lower than the surrounding ground, are on the same level as the *falaj*. It supplies the oasis from the Izki region, a distance of over 80 kilometers, with life-giving water. The paths through the gardens, planted densely with dates, bananas and vegetables, run along dikes between the plantations, repeatedly passing the inhabited area. It is easy to imagine that Adam must have seemed like paradise on earth to the caravans arriving from Dhofar. The astounding variety of green hues, the dense, shadow-giving date palms, the protective wall surrounding the town, all of this splendor is in stark contrast to the endless, cheerless gravel desert south of the oasis. An old social agreement ensured the keeping of the peace within Adam and for the security of those traveling through. Whoever came to the oasis from the desert with peaceful intentions could enjoy a week's unlimited hospitality: food, drink and a place to sleep with no questions asked. During this time no one would inquire after the name of the stranger's tribe. In an emergency, even members of an enemy tribe could in this way enjoy a period of immunity and count on the help of a potential enemy to survive. If the stranger stayed more than a week he was bound to reveal his identity. The desert wrote its own laws to deal with life-threatening situations and all people are equal before these laws. The Bedouin code of law, developed over centuries on the basis of these extreme living conditions and completely in keeping with them, is generally respected by the Omani state. Many Omani laws do not apply to the Bedouin. There are a few exceptions: the country's hunting laws apply to them as to everyone and when visiting towns they have to lay their weapons aside. On the other hand the Bedouin are not subjected to the strict test to obtain a driving licence, so long as they limit their driving to the desert and surrounding area. The ability to drive a vehicle through the desert is handed down through the family in the same way as the knowledge of how to deal with camels. The demands that this environment makes on the driver are significantly more wide-ranging and more complex than the regulations for road traffic.

The arcade architecture of the residential area of the Adam oasis is unique in the country.

West of Nizwa – ruins, pottery and the palace of Jabrin

Nizwa's main road makes a wide arc through the northern parts of the town and then continues west along the Jabal Al Akhdar massif. After twenty kilometers a track signposted "Wadi Tanuf Dam" branches off to the right and leads to the dam at the end of the Wadi Tanuf. After a few kilometers the road forks. The left fork ends at Tanuf, newly built with a mineral water plant of the same name. The right fork brings you to the old settlement and to the new dam.

Historic **Tanuf** is situated right at the end of the wadi that bears its name. Next to Wadi Muaydin at Birkat Al Mawz, this forms another important entry-point to the high plateau of the Jabal Al Akhdar. Superficially viewed, Tanuf today resembles many other abandoned and consequently dilapidated towns in Oman. But the peaceful, romantic idyll which the ruins present is deceptive. Tanuf was not voluntarily abandoned by its inhabitants. It was a center of the Jabal Al Akhdar uprising and in 1959 paid the price when attacked by the Sultan's troops and the British. It was the tribal seat of the Bani Riyam, and the inhabitants fled to take refuge in hidden caves. Tanuf was destroyed by military helicopters and the rebellion was quashed.

Only the large cubic central part of the mosque remains standing within its outer walls. All the other houses were more severely damaged. The buildings stretched from the floor of the valley up to the overhanging rock which barred the entrance to the wadi, the rear side of which falls away steeply to the mountains. If you climb up to the edge of this rock, to one side you will enjoy an impressive view over the landscape of ruins and to the other you have a good view over Wadi Tanuf.

In contrast to Tanuf, **Al Hamra**, "the red," is one of the best preserved clay house settlements in Oman. Many houses, some of them two-storey, are still inhabited and village life continues much as it always has. At **Bayt Al Safa** you will see how Omanis used to live in a traditional Omani house. Visitors have the opportunity to enjoy lunch with an Omani family and they can also observe how Omani *kahawa* (coffee) and Omani bread are made.

Before reaching Al Hamra, a road branches off to **Ghul**, and leads to the highest mountain of Oman, **Jabal Shams**, and to the **Grand Canyon of Oman**, the Wadi Nakhr gorge. From here you get a spectacular view into the thousand meter deep gorge and the summit of the Jabal Shams with its radar station on the other side.

The Weavers of Jabal Shams

Whether you drive cross-country through the desert, simply use the asphalt roads or clamber through the almost impassable wadis and mountains of northern Oman in a four-wheel drive vehicle, everywhere you will see nomads with their herds of goats. The long hair of Omani goats was once an important raw material, which would be spun into wool. Up until the middle of the 20th century cotton was also cultivated in Oman to meet the needs of a small, local textile industry. Cheap imports of cotton and textiles from the Far East had already reduced the importance of cotton weaving well before 1970. Work at the weaver's stool became confined to the domestic arena. Today if you drive a four-wheel drive vehicle on a weekend over the road through the abandoned settlement of Ghul on the heights of the Jabal Shams, at about 3000 meters you will experience a surprise. Seemingly far away from any human settlement in the middle of this gigantic, treeless sea of rock, a wooden frame stands at the side of the road. Small woven carpets with simple geometric patterns hang next to larger ones, finely worked in black, dark red and orange. They are being offered for sale in the remoteness of this mountain landscape. Next to this improvised stand sits an ancient Omani with his brother and quietly spins wool with a simple hand spindle. A picture from days of old were it not for the few small travel groups, who are attracted here on weekends to dare to look down at the 1000 meter deep, vertically falling, spectacular canyon landscape at the summit of Jabal Shams.

The interest of the visitors in Omani handicrafts motivates the weavers of the Jabal Al Akhdar massif to demonstrate their skills. Increasing numbers of tourists could also lead to an increased demand in other areas of the country and so lead to a higher rate of production of materials woven in the old style, for instance in the traditional textile centers of Samail and Khaburah on the Al Batinah coast. Among the mountain nomads of northern Oman the wool is spun equally by men and women, but here the weaving itself, in contrast to the Al Batinah coast, is purely an affair for the men. The looms are extremely simple in their construction, actually only two large branches on which the warp is stretched, a weaver's comb and a sort of shuttle. They are thus simple to assemble and disassemble, important for herders who are always on the move. The traditional colors are white, black, red and orange. The white and black yarn is natural, while the reds and oranges were originally colored by a laborious process using plant dyes. The set of colors has not changed in its use but today the dyes come from chemical factories in India and are bought in the suq. The repertoire of patterns ranges from stripes and simple geometric shapes to extraordinarily attractive, variously patterned, decorative bands which are joined together, requiring a clever "pick-up" technique and great skill on the part of the weaver. An excursion with a four-wheel drive vehicle to the Jabal Shams is certainly one of the most highly recommended off-road excursions that can be undertaken in Oman. Naturally you can buy woven wares at the best price directly from the weavers in the mountains. Your bargaining skills may come in handy.

With less effort you can also buy them alongside other products of Omani handicrafts in the shop of the Ministry of National Heritage and Culture (in the SABCO shopping center in Al Qurm) and also favorably in the Omani Heritage Gallery (in the Jawharat al Shatti complex in Shatti al Al Qurm, Tel: 24696974.) The latter one is a gallery for Omani handicrafts which is operated on a non-profit basis, the proceeds going directly to the craftsmen.

In Wadi Bani Awf

The road running from Al Hamra towards Bilad Sait/Hat and further on through **Wadi Bani Awf** in the direction of Ar Rustaq can only be managed with a four wheel drive vehicle and offers beautiful landscapes. This crossing of the Hajar Mountains, with its often very steep sections, should only be undertaken by skilled drivers of four-wheel drive vehicles. Another nice excursion is from Al Hamra to the picturesque mountain village of **Misfat Ash Shirayqiyin** (Misfat Al Abriyyin) which is easily accessible by an asphalt road. A marked footpath from the small parking place before the village leads you through the narrow lanes of the village down to the terraced gardens on the cliff slopes and through these to the wadi. If you followed this path right to the end, after about seven hours you would reach Bilad Sait in the Wadi Bani Awf.

Finally you are directed to the new road leading from Al Hamra to the **Al Hutha Cave**, a 4.5 kilometer long system of caves developed as a tourist attraction. As the number of visitors is limited due to environmental protection of the cave it is suggested to make reservations in advance *(reserve@alhoothacave.com, Tel: 24490060.)*

Bahla – a Town of Clay

In the region around the Bahla oasis there are large deposits of clay. It is striking that this important raw material has always been superabundant here. In contrast to the other oasis towns of Oman, in Bahla not only the settlement itself is protected by high clay walls, but also the whole area of the oasis in the wadi. A fortified wall, up to five meters high and over ten kilometers in length, with numerous watchtowers built in, surrounds the extensive date gardens and fields, and winds through the mountains at the edge of the wadi and the depths of the river bed. Your thoughts turn to the Great Wall of China, or to the Sumerian town of Uruk in the Gilgamesh epic. Even today the wall with its two gates is almost completely intact along its whole length. Only the new road cuts through this imposing construction.
At the eastern end of the oasis the ruins of the **Hisn Tamah fort**, another masterpiece of clay architecture, rise above a hill. It is named after the presumed architect of the gigantic fortification, a tribal chief of the Nabhani tribe in the 17th century. But the origins of Bahla stretch much further back into history. The first fort was probably built on the heights in the pre-Islamic era. When exactly it was founded by the Bahila tribe is not known. In 1406 Bahla was ruled by Imam Makhzum ibn Al Fallah and was the capital of Oman and the seat of the ruling Nabhani dynasty.
Today the impressive ruins bear witness to the former importance of the town. They resemble a vast, rugged landscape, immense rocks piled up by human hand and bizarrely eaten away by the forces of nature. Fragments of wall and tower soar over the steep cliffs of the outer walls, the foundations of which were reinforced with blocks of rock. Niches in the walls placed at dizzying heights give you an idea of the dimensions of the fortress. You first get a real impression of the mammoth complex from some distance. Follow the way along the west wall, past the remains of the old mosque, now restored, and you will reach a hill and the large mosque, also restored. From here you can get a clear impression of the richly artistic architecture of this clay fortress and its site commanding the wadi. This fortress is certainly not only the largest example of the art of building in clay in Oman, but in its own way one of the most impressive. Bahla Fort has been inscribed in UNESCO's World Heritage List since 1987. Only a year later it was added to the List of World Heritage in Danger. Following rains further sections of the walls had collapsed and the ceiling of the old mosque at the foot of the fort had collapsed. Unfortunately the conservation

measures then taken were not always in keeping with maintaining the building's authenticity. After another visit in 1996 a commission of experts charged the Omani authorities with keeping to the appropriate international standards. As long as the work continues, the inside of the ruins will not be open to visitors. The already completed work on the mosques in front of the citadel and the restored parts of the fortress complex document a positive difference to the usual methods of restoring forts in Oman.

On the other side of the road, opposite the fort, is Bahla's new suq, and, to the east of it, the old **suq**. A narrow track starts here, leading into the oasis and to the country's famous potters. To avoid any problems with vehicles coming in the opposite direction it is best to leave the car at the suq and go on foot. Two large ceramic workshops are directly at the side of the path and can be easily found. After about ten minutes walk you will reach Said Saif Omar Al Shaqsi's workshop. In a courtyard on the right hand side of the road he sells frankincense burners, water jugs and small pottery objects. A few meters further on, on the left hand side, you enter through a wooden door and come to his workshops with their old kilns. If you are seriously interested in the art of **pottery** then a visit to Abdullah ibn Hamdan Al Adawi and his sons is recommended. A few hundred meters further on, on the right hand side of the road, they practice their craft in a workshop in a palm garden.

A defensive wall several kilometers long surrounds the Bahla oasis.

From the path you can clearly see his old traditional kilns. The unfired pots are stacked up to the ceiling in the three dome-shaped clay kilns, which are a good two meters high. The duration of the firing varies between one and six days. In the palm garden you can see the potter's clay pits, where the clay is worked until it has reached the consistency necessary for the potter's wheel. Numerous earthenware pots are piled up around the kilns. They are sold as multipurpose containers for dates, water, grain and such things.

Abdullah Al Adawi is an experienced old potter, with a good understanding how one can combine traditional and modern technology to marvellous effect. He produces some pieces using the foot-driven old potter's wheel, but most are made using electrically driven wheels, cutting down on the physical effort required. He also possesses a highly modern electric kiln as well as a gas-fired kiln. With their exact temperature regulation and uncomplicated firing mechanism they give more possibilities for making test firings and experimenting with glazes. The outcome of these experiments are then put into mass production using the large, labor-intensive clay

This picture of the ruins of Bahla fort before renovation demonstrates the problems of renovating clay buildings. Large areas of the site had been completely eroded.

kilns. The master potter prefers for the future to continue firing in the old kilns. Because of their huge capacity they are much more economical than the modern kilns. Nowadays Abdullah no longer kneads the large quantities of clay required by hand - a self-made electrical mixer takes away most of the effort. In his workshop he has the latest catalogues from European ceramic dealers on hand; he is well-informed about the state of international pottery. The symbiosis of the most modern ceramic techniques and the age-old handicraft tradition, as exemplified here in Bahla, is one of the quiet, inconspicuous, and so all the more remarkable, discoveries in modern Oman.

Jabrin – the Palace of Imam Bilarub ibn Sultan Al-Yaruba

Pottery from Bahla can be found in every household in the country.

Only five kilometers west of Bahla the road to Jabrin branches off to the left. Up until recently Jabrin was a small oasis, surrounded by date plantations. Half of the area was taken up by a huge ruined fortress which rose high above the treetops of the palms. Low clay-built houses bowed before the gates of the fort, emphasizing its majesty. This picture has now changed.

Today if you journey to Jabrin, your attention will first be taken by a large estate of new buildings. The modern estate, built under the aegis of the government-sponsored Low-cost Housing Program, is made up of inexpensive terraced housing given an Arabian touch - each has a tower and battlements! - and replaces the old town, taking away the effect that the palace once had. Imam Bilarub's 17th century residence has been completely restored and is now one of the country's most popular tourist attractions. So it is no wonder that here you come across a phenomenon that is completely atypical for Oman: groups of tourists in large buses.

Investigations carried out by an Italian archaeologist led to the conclusion that the rectangular fort, with its diagonally opposite corner towers, begun in 1675, is probably made up of separate wings. You can understand this theory better if you look at the fort from the outside. At first the two blocks of differing heights were built close together but completely separate. Some time later the two were connected by a high tower completing the frontage. The entrance to the palace is at its base. To reach it you first go through a courtyard which was originally the open ground between the two buildings. Opposite the tower, making the fourth side of the courtyard, is another section which, along with the two round

cannon towers at each end, were later additions. The fortress-l exterior character of the complex is misleading: the design of t interiors clearly shows the building to have been intended a palace. The high rooms are fitted with narrow niches which rea from the floor to just under the ceilings. They are topped w Moorish arches richly decorated with stuccowork, and which a serve as the rooms' main windows. On the outside the windows screened by decoratively carved stone latticework, whi protects against too much sun and lends the room pleasing, subdued light. The design of the latticew shows Persian influence, as does the harmonious spa arrangement.

Interesting quotidian utensils and vessels are on display in an interior court of the palace.

Rectangular windows, with folding wooden shutt are set in the bottom parts of the niches. The ceili of nearly all the rooms are painted, and are conside to be the most exquisite examples of such work in t country, a claim which, when you are faced with t splendor, seems not to be exaggerated. An astonishin rich repertoire of various floral forms unfolds across t wooden ceilings: chains of flowers follow chains of flc ers, leafage winds around Arabic verses celebrating Al and the builder of the palace. Other rooms have f ceilings or are vaulted. The design of the ceilings abc the stairs leading to the formal rooms is also impr sive: the segments of the vaulted ceiling with poin arches are completely covered in geometric stuccowo A band with Arabic calligraphy in stucco runs arou the base of the vaults. The numerous precisely and lovingly work details make Jabrin a jewel in the crown of Omani architectu Imam Bilarub, an intellectual art lover, gathered around him in palace astrologers, physicians, lawyers and poets, and financed t academics and their pupils. But this haven of joy and knowlec was later to become his prison and, in 1692, his final resting pla His brother Saif wanted power for himself and was able to gath some tribes to back him and, still during Bilarub's lifetime, he w elected as the new Imam. He laid siege to the fortress of Jabrin wi a large army until his brother finally died there. Saif did not both himself with the magnificent building. His concerns lay elsewhe He drove the Portuguese out of their East African possessions a established Oman as a maritime power in the Indian Ocean. Af a brief heyday and a further period as capital at the beginning the 18th century, Jabrin fell into a long period of quietude.

Beehive tombs close to the village of Bat.

The Province of Adh Dhahirah

Between the southern foothills of the Hajar Mountains and the sea of sand that is the Rub al Khali, lies the desert province of Adh Dhahirah, to the west of Jabrin. From the flat roof of the Bilarub palace, you have an uninterrupted view far into this region. As far as the eye can see there is nothing but the immense plain. Almost 100 kilometers away to the west is the large Ibri oasis, the old center of the region. Just before Ibri, south of the road, you come to the **As Silayf** oasis, on the edge of Wadi Al Ain. The settlement is surrounded by mighty walls with a large gate tower, and for centuries successfully repelled the attacks of the Wahhabi. What military attacks couldn't achieve, the changing spirit of the age managed. Slowly but steadily the population moved to neighboring Ibri and left the old village, which stretched along a rising cliff ledge, to fall into decay.

At one time **Ibri** was one of the most dangerous places in Oman. The pirates of the southern Gulf coast offloaded their goods here and helped to give the place its bad reputation. People only ventured here if they were armed to the teeth or were already destitute. These times are now finally past and Ibri has remained an important trading center, particularly for the many Bedouin living in the Adh Dhahirah. In the future its location on the main route between Oman and the Emirates should help ensure its increasing significance.

The northeastern hinterland of Ibri is rich in prehistoric sites. The majority date from the 3rd millennium BC and belong to the Hafit and Umm-an-Nar civilizations. In the 1970s a team of Danish archaeologists discovered, north of Bat, a settlement with a necropolis, a highly important find. It turned out to be the largest known site from the Umm-an-Nar Period in Oman and, together with Al Ain's beehive tombs, it has been added to UNESCO's World Heritage List (see Archaeology Chapter.)

As well as the numerous tombs you will also come across a large tower with a diameter of up to 15 meters. In places the walls still remain up to a height of five meters. Interestingly, its ground-plan resembles that of the tower at Nizwa fort. Just as at Nizwa, the base of the tower is filled with earth and on the platform there are rooms and also a well shaft. It is assumed that the towers, which were originally up to ten meters high, served the function of a fortified refuge. The site of the settlement is a type of oasis that is still common in Oman.

The thousands of **beehive tombs** scattered over the mountain are further important witnesses to this period. They form the largest known necropolis from this time. The most impressive collection of relatively well-preserved beehive tombs are in the neighborhood of Al Ain some 23 kilometers beyond Bat. Twenty one of these tomb constructions are strung like pearls over the mountain range before the impressive backdrop of the Jabal Al Misht.

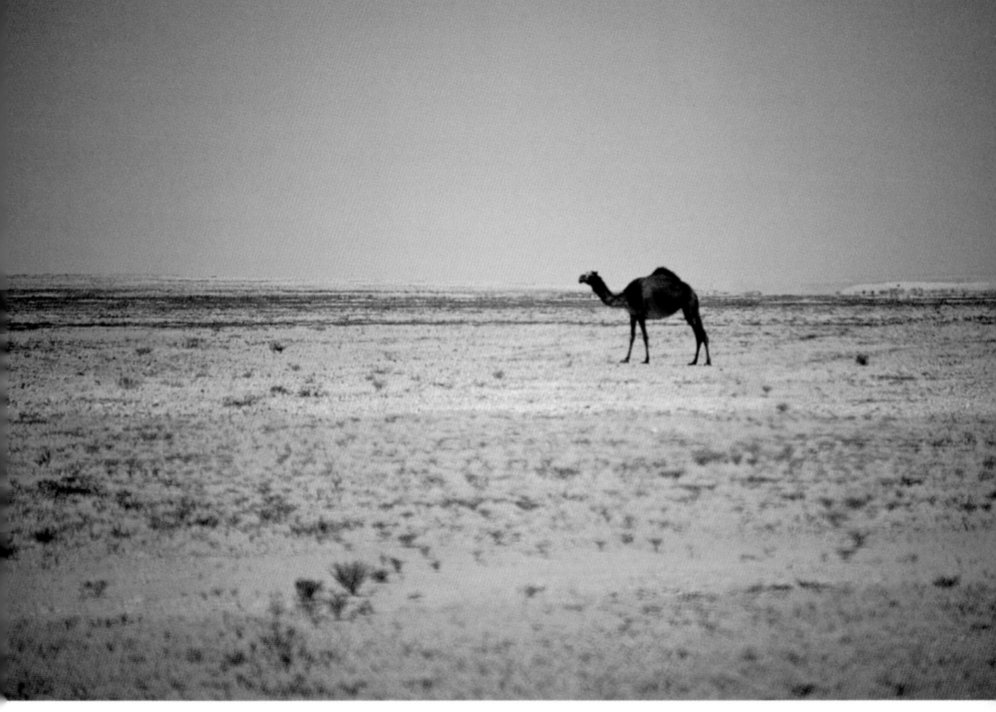

The infinite gravel plains of central Oman, between Adam and Thumrayt.

Jiddat al Harasis – the Gravel Desert as Habitat

South of Adam the road to Salalah crosses a vast desert, the province of Wusta. The character of this countryside is fundamentally different from that of the central Arabian sand desert, the Rub al Khali. The landscape is not defined by graceful dunes, but by complete emptiness, 700 kilometers of absolute nothing stretching beyond the horizon. Only now and then is the emptiness broken by a lone acacia tree.

The heart of the Wusta province is the 40,000 square kilometer Jiddat al Harasis. The Harasis are a nomad people who have survived for centuries in this hostile region. Up until the 1980s almost nothing was known about this tribe, who lived in almost complete isolation. In order to carefully integrate these people into the newly-emerging nation state and to give them useful assistance in the fields of health care and education, in 1981 the Omani government commissioned the anthropologist Dawn Chatty to carry out a study of the Harasis. Since then she has carefully observed the habits of the tribe, above all their reactions to the rapidly advancing modernization of the country.

The Harasis' reaction to new living conditions hardly differs from that of other desert nomads such as the Wihibah or the Janaba. As the researcher found out, up until very recently the life of the Harasis had hardly changed over centuries. They lived off that which the land naturally provided them. In winter they wandered with their herds from pasture to pasture over the Jiddat al Harasis. In summer, when the temperatures in the gravel desert became unbearable, they would move with their animals to the coast in the al Huqf region, where they found new pastures. A household was normally made up of a married couple, their children and other family members. A family group needed to be large enough to manage to support itself alone as a unit, among the Harasis this was at most ten to twelve people.

A last Chance for the Unicorn?

The Orient has always been an unbeatable source of fairy tales and legends. One of the most impressive creatures of fable in these tales is the unicorn. This brilliant white cross between a horse and an antelope with its long, spiral-twisted horn was held in the West to be the embodiment of nobility, wisdom, beauty, purity and chastity as well as the impetuous instinct for freedom. At the beginning of the 1980s the cartoon film "The Last Unicorn" conquered European cinemas in the period before christmas. This sentimental piece of cinema naturally had the obligatory happy end: the last unicorn gains his freedom and the world remains intact. Purity and goodness conquer over evil; not a compelling conclusion when you take a look at reality and the animal which may well have stood godfather to the creation of the fabulous creature.

Next to the narwhal which, with its long, twisted tusk, may well have delivered the idea for the horn, there is another possible model which up until a few years ago lived in the deserts of the Arabian peninsula: the white oryx (Oryx leucoryx.) During the course of evolution this large species of antelope has suited itself to its habitat as perfectly as the dromedary to its. Its hide is white in summer, even the black markings on its head and legs bleach to a pale brown so that in the gleaming sunlight and the shimmering heat it is almost invisible. The animals can cover their needs for water with a few dry clumps of grass and acacia leaves; looking for fresh pastures it travels up to 80 kilometers by night. During the summer the antelopes remain almost motionless in the shadows of acacias and only become active after dark. The oryx avoids quick and unnecessary movements. Its normal tempo is walking pace; fights between rivals are very short.

At the time of Aristotle (4th century BC) it was customary in Egypt to bind the horns together of young oryx antelopes which had been caught: These would then grow together into a single horn – the source of many legends. Later the animals increasingly fell victim to culinary popularity. In Bedouin society the killing of the large antelope with its needle-sharp horns also brought increased kudos. Where the animals had once inhabited the entire interior of the Arabian peninsula, already at the beginning of the 20th century they had been pushed back to

The herds of goats, about 100 strong, belonged exclusively to the women, who had to ensure their survival alone. Each family had an average of 25 camels and these, on the other hand, were the preserve of the men. In summer, during longer periods spent in one place, the women often found time to busy themselves with handicrafts. They would weave mats and baskets or blankets. The finished products were then gathered together and at set times brought by the men to the markets of Adam, Sinaw, Manah or even Salalah. They would then exchange their goods and animals for things which the desert did not offer: rice, tea, sugar, wheat, weapons and munitions. In the 1980s the Omani government began to build up an infrastructure for the nomadic tribe in **Hayma**, 318 kilometers south of Adam.

the area of the great Nafud desert, the Rub al Khali, and the areas bordering it in southern Oman and in Yemen. By the mid Sixties there was still one last remaining population in the wild in the Jiddat al Harasis in central Oman. Motorized hunting parties, mostly Arabs from outside Oman, finally reduced the surviving animals to between 100 and 200 specimens, and took no measures to preserve the remainder. On October 18th 1972 the last six white oryx antelopes living in the wild were tracked down in the interior of Oman. Three of them were caught and sold and three ended up in the cooking pot!

Two years later Sultan Qaboos proposed returning the Arabian Oryx to the wild, where it had last existed. Several antelope herds had survived in captivity. The only ones biogenetically suitable for the project were a group of animals descended from white Oryx antelopes captured in 1962.

In cooperation with the World Wildlife Trust, a safari club as well as zoological societies from Arizona and London, a "world oryx herd" was successfully raised. In 1980 the first 18 oryx were released into an enclosure in Jaaluni in the Jiddat al Harasis. After an acclimatization phase they were released into the wild and new small herds followed in 1984, 1988, 1989, 1992 and 1995. A troop of gamekeepers with the latest equipment from the Harasis tribe watched over the movements of the shy animals and looked after their well-being. By the middle of the Nineties the number of Arabian oryx in inner Oman had grown to a population large enough to survive: some 350 animals. The general ban on hunting in the country is certainly a prerequisite for the long-term success of the action. The Arabian gazelles in Oman, whose population was also severely reduced, has been able to recover by itself thanks to this law and they once more put life back in great numbers into the otherwise sterile seeming scree deserts.

Since 1998 there has been the possibility for tourists to visit the strictly enclosed reserve on a guided tour organized by local travel agents.

Hayma belonged neither to the main territory of the Harasis or of the neighboring Janaba, and had two decisive advantages. Firstly it lay directly on the new road to Salalah, and secondly it had water. Drilling teams for the PDO had already laid a well there in the 1950s. Within a few years there were a hospital, schools and several shops. No innovations have had such a great influence on the life of the Bedouin as the introduction of the four-wheel drive vehicle. The dark red Toyota pickup quickly became the favorite means of transport in the desert. In 1976 the first members of the tribe possessed such vehicles: young people who, as is customary, had traveled in order to try their luck, with the result that they had worked hard and earned money. By 1982 16 of 17 households among the Harasis possessed a car. Their upkeep required even more money. Petrol and spare parts could not be obtained by the normal bartering. If the nomads wanted to maintain their new standard of living at least a few members of each family would have to complete some formal education. By so doing they could improve their chances of getting work and strive for a settled job in the town. For these Hararis it meant giving up the life of the nomad.

The anthropologist asked herself how the old tribal structures would adapt to the new, completely changed way of life. To her astonishment the Harasis adapted very quickly to the new situation. The families made up for the reduced workforce resulting from the relatives living in the town by themselves employing outside workers for wages. The rhythm of life remained much the same and the value of an education for future prosperity was fully accepted. In order to let their daughters take part, some clans are prepared to separate temporarily. While one part of the family travels around as usual with the animals, others remain in the neighborhood of Hayma and look after the schoolgirls.

Even without schooling women have traditionally had a very strong social position among the Bedouin. Running the household is their responsibility, and they also administer the finances. Whether at the Friday markets at Nizwa, Sinaw or Al Mintarib, you can observe the same scenes everywhere. The men negotiate volubly over the purchase price of the goats but before the deal is closed they turn to the women standing in the background in order to obtain their agreement and to get the necessary money. Bedouin women radiate great self-confidence, travel alone, without any male accompaniment, to the next town to do their shopping with the pick-up. Since plastic products have appeared in the desert the market for their traditional products has collapsed. However this did not cause them to give up their handiwork. They have extended their range of products to include modern accessories such as belts and key-holders, popular

The wild coast at Ras Madrakah during summer monsoon.

souvenirs for tourists. The self-assured behavior of the women is reinforced by their typical traditional dress: boldly colored dresses and trousers, "investments" in the form of gold or silver jewelry, a diaphanous black cape and a mask protecting the face from the sun and dust. The *burka* emphasizes the kohl-decorated eyes and lends the women an unapproachable, indomitable, mystical aura. The women dominate the character of the nomadic tribes, both psychologically as well as physically. Among the Harasis, this is also demonstrated in the handing down of names. Unlike the generally known Arabic tradition, whereby the children always take the name of the father, it is not at all unusual among the Harasis that the men proudly take the names of their mothers.

Bizarre landscapes characterize Wadi Shuwaymiyah.

From Purgatory to Paradise

To make a journey from Muscat to Salalah in high summer is to experience nature at its most extreme. This tour, lasting between four and five days, should only be undertaken by those in good physical health, equipped with sufficient provisions and water, traveling in two four-wheel drive vehicles complete with camping equipment. In summer the sun burns directly overhead onto the dark cliffs of Muscat, turning it into an oven, burning day and night, and ensuring that even in the depths of darkness the temperatures never sink below 40 degrees centigrade. The high humidity gives another reason for the visitor from a more temperate zone to doubt the wisdom of his decision to journey to Oman. What of the many Omanis who are constantly congratulating one on having arrived at exactly the right season, when Salalah has the best weather? It is cool and is raining.

Somewhat sceptically you set off, drive through the Samail Gap to Sinaw and from there along the western edge of the Wihibah and Wadi Halfayn in the direction of Muhut (Hejj). The heat shimmers above the tarmac surface, the wind blows flurries of sand across the road, drying the roof of your mouth.

In **Muhut (Hejj)** there is a simple hotel, the last accommodation on the coast road to the south. From here on, you need to seek out resting places by the many bays and capes along the coast, which you can reach via tracks leading from the road. The further you press south, the mistier the atmosphere becomes and the more bearable the temperatures.

Whereas outside of the monsoon period fishermen are to be found all along the coast, going about their work, in summer you'll hardly meet anyone. The small habitations are mostly deserted, the doors and windows sometimes nailed shut. A brief detour to the sea and all is quickly explained. During the *khareef*, as the monsoon is known in Oman, the sea swells are so strong that no one dares venture out in a boat on the open sea. The strength of the sea is especially impressive at **Ras Madrakah**. The cape is well suited as a place to stay overnight.

The picturesque Three Palm Lagoon and the coastal lagoons of **Khawr Ghawi** and Al Kahil stand in stark contrast to the heaving waves offshore. Many migratory birds rest by their tranquil waters, including flamingos. The **Pink Lagoons** are not far from Khawr Ghawi. Cut off from the sea, its waters are colored bright pink by algae.

The road continues after **Sawqrah** to **Jinawt**, the most southerly point on this stretch of coast that can be reached. Just before this you can turn off and visit **Wadi Shuwaymiyyah**, with its picturesque canyon, from the walls of which hang huge stalactite formations from which water drips into pools where reeds and palms grow.

In order to get to Salalah, you need to cross inland to Thumrayt via **Shalim** and **Marmul**. This means leaving the temperate coastal climate and once more submerging yourself in broiling heat, which is made visually stronger by the burning torches of the oilfields at the edge of the track.

From Thumrayt you climb imperceptibly the slopes of the Dhofar mountains and suddenly run into a layer of cloud at ground level. Within a few hundred meters you are enveloped in mist and drizzle; green mountains loom spectrally and now and then you can make out the silhouette of a camel or a cow.

Slowly and with utmost care, with blinking warning lights and flashing headlights you cross through the mountain pass and descend to the plain of Salalah. Here you will see countless tourists from all around the Gulf region sitting on blankets in the drizzle and barbecuing, beaming with delight - they are having a holiday in paradise.

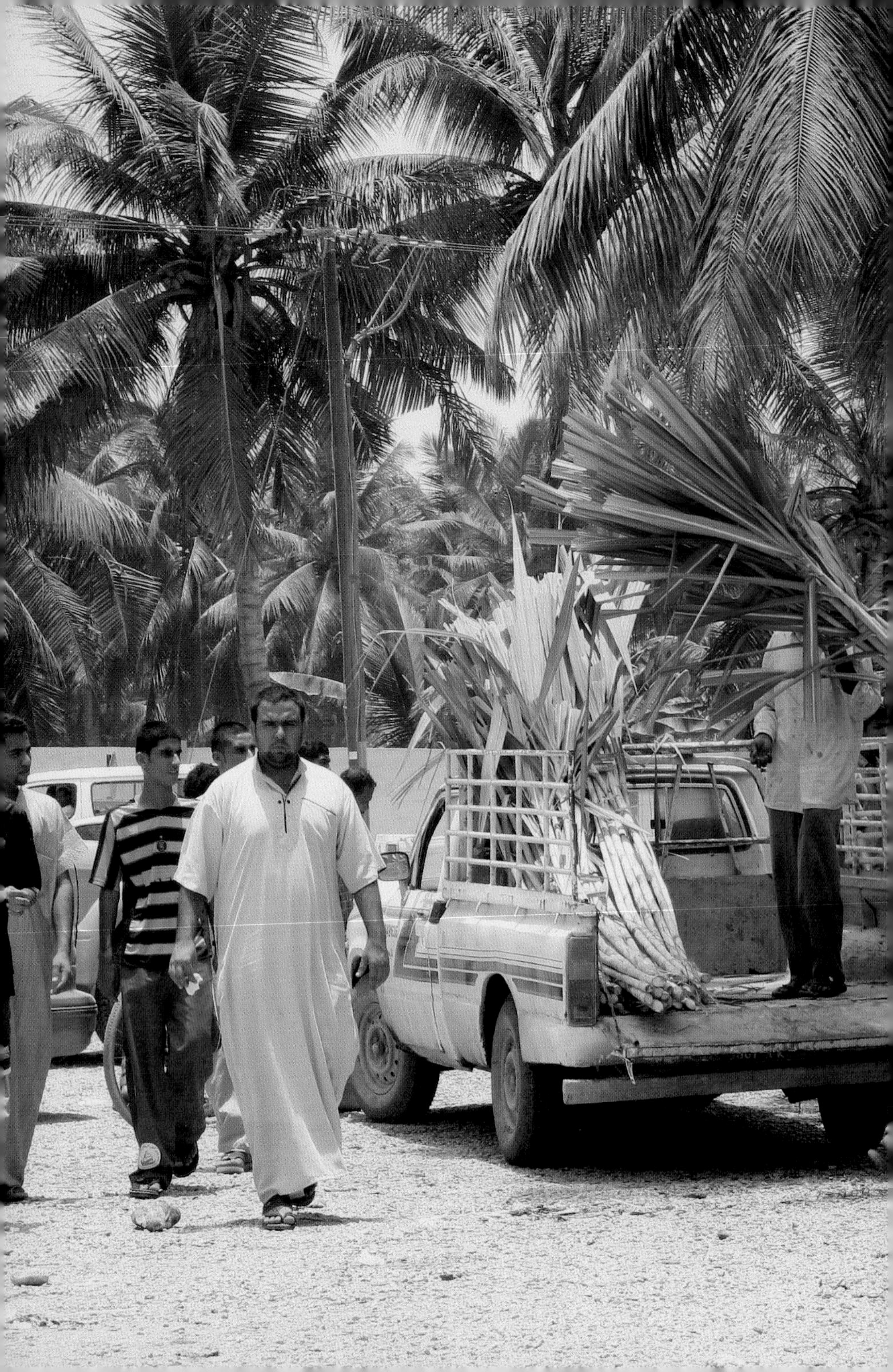

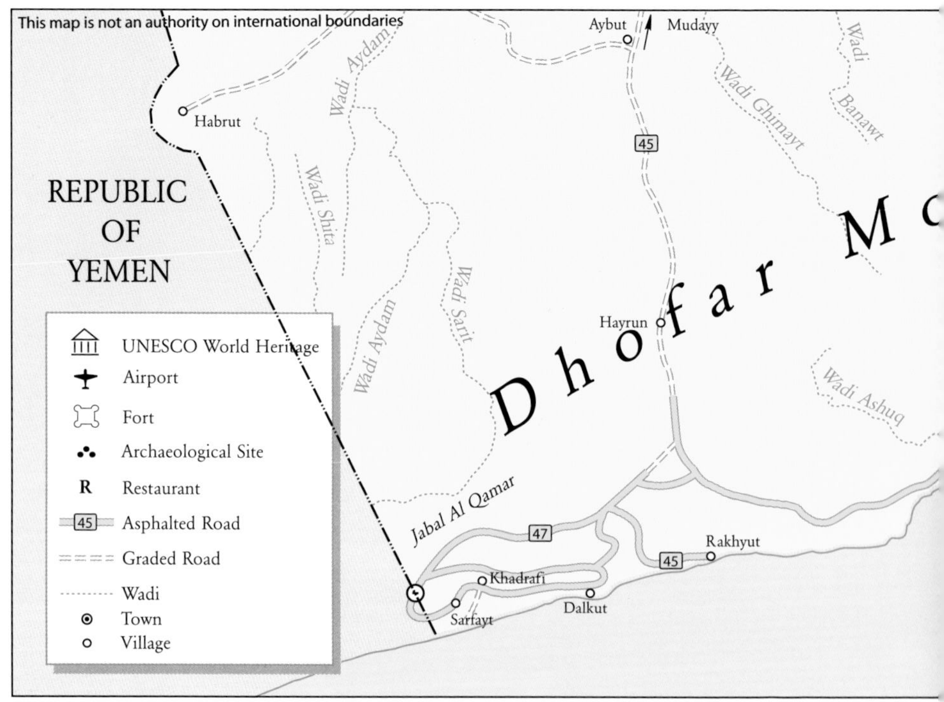

Dhofar - an Oriental Wonderland

It is impossible to make a spur of the moment visit to the province of Dhofar. Seen from Muscat, the south of Oman seems every bit as unapproachable as the northern exclave of Musandam. Where forbidding mountains bar the visitor's access to Musandam, in Dhofar it is the endless gravel plains which merge in the west into the largest sand desert in the world, the Rub al Khali, or Empty Quarter. Faced with this vast, barren region, it is hard to believe that somewhere beyond the horizon there is a fertile swath of land, which in the summer, when the rest of the country has become a furnace, is shrouded in mist, accompanied by a cooling drizzle. It is a region where gently rolling hills have a lush greenness that brings to mind the alpine meadows of Europe. The sight of cows and camels grazing side by side and waterfalls tumbling over rocky

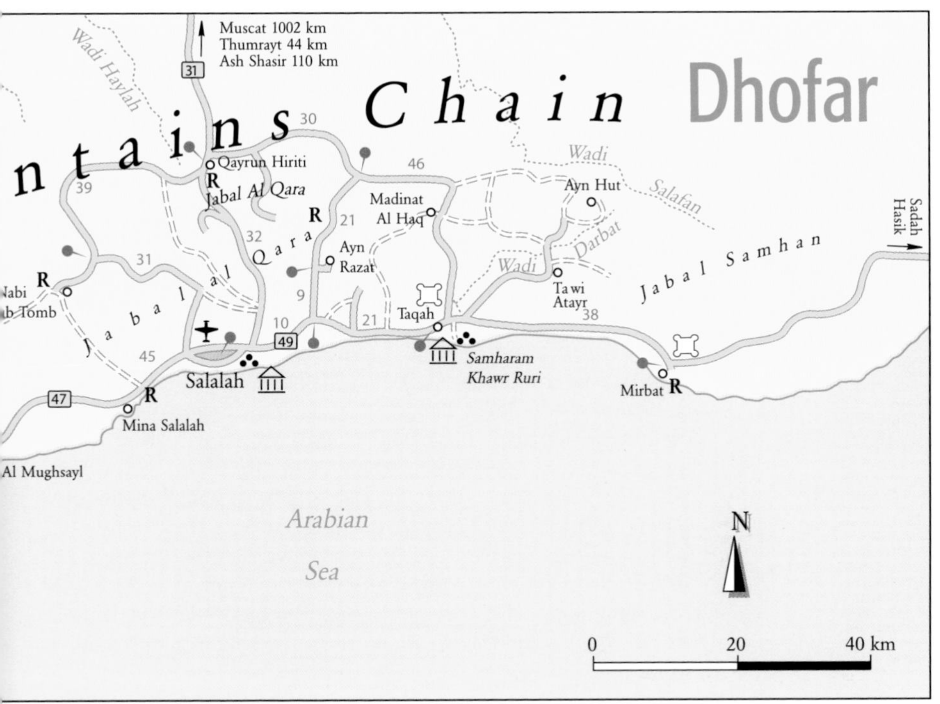

precipices heightens the air of unreality. As if this were not enough this wonderland boasts trees, from the bark of which constantly drips gold - gold in the form of a precious resin. This must be the fabled *Arabia Felix*, happy Arabia!

The rationalist European would be rash to banish this label to the land of myth and fairy tale. Had not the classical world prized the fragrant frankincense resin for millennia and did it not come from this legendary part of the Orient? In contrast to the metal whose preciousness lies in its immutability, the resin's value is fleeting - it can only be enjoyed through its irreversible destruction, by burning it on glowing coals. Rather than being a capital investment, it is an extraordinary luxury item, as mysterious as its place of origin.

If you have enough time you can make your way from Muscat to the wonderland of Dhofar by bus, a day's journey along the Hajar Mountains, across the desert and then through the mountains of Dhofar to Salalah. However it is far quicker by plane. Several times a day medium-sized jets head south. Unlike the flights to Musandam, it is no problem to book flights to Salalah on relatively short notice.

Most Salalah hotels offer transfers from and to the airport. The high season in Dhofar is from the middle of June to the middle of September, during the *khareef*, the monsoon in Salalah and the surrounding area. During this period guests come from all over the Gulf region in order to enjoy the greatest of luxuries - strolls and picnics in drizzle and mist, surrounded by lush dripping greenery. Even as you await your flight to Salalah at As Seeb airport your image of Oman appears to change. It is often here that foreign travelers to Oman for the first time see women completely veiled in black from head to foot. However they are not as they are in cliché - shadowy or reserved. Using determined gestures they shoo foreign workers, youths, men or tourists from their seats in the airport. It is not only the black veil which differentiates them from the women of north Oman, but also the rest of their appearance. Their clothing is not made out of light, brightly colored cotton fabric but often out of heavy velvet in dark colors, decorated with glitter, glass beads and a majestic train. They appear to be the mysterious queens of the Orient. Later, on board the aircraft, the stewardesses are scrupulously careful to sit these women where they wish to be seated. The religious proximity of Dhofar to Yemen can be felt at the beginning of the journey; the majority of Dhofaris are Sunni. As the flight route follows much the same course as the road, a window seat away from the wings furnishes a good overview of both the route and the country. From the air, the Sumail Gap and the structure of the Hajar mountains can be clearly made out. You get an insight into remote wadis and mountain landscapes. From this distance the roads and tracks, the pride of modern Oman, seem like mere scratches on the earth's hide. As the sloping cliff faces of the mountains give way to the endless plateau, you become ever more aware of man's insignificance. The network of rivulets feeds the mountain rains into the Umm As Samim (known locally as the 'Mother of Poisons' or the 'Mother of Worries'), one of the largest salt flats in the west, on the border with Saudi Arabia. Occasionally the dust trail of Bedouin traveling across the desert can be seen. Half way along the route small sand dunes mark the eastern approaches of the Rub al Khali. Imperceptibly the plain inclines higher and higher. A few kilometers from the coastal plain, wadis, now meandering from the south, etch their path into the earth. On the high grounds circular patches can be seen scattered around, the plantations of the mountain farmers of Dhofar, the Jabali. In a steep decline the mountain runs directly down to the sea. The narrow strip of the coastal plain of Salalah bids the visitor welcome.

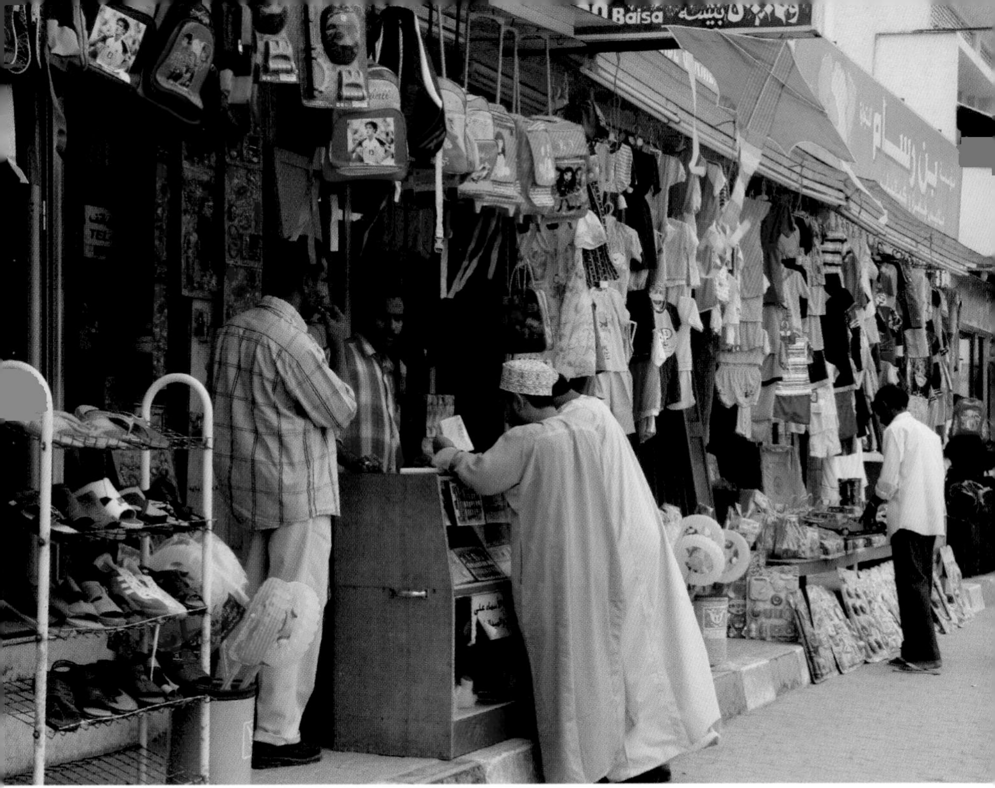

Numerous small shops edge the main streets of Salalah and make the city one of the most lively in Oman.

Salalah

The capital of Dhofar has much in common with Muscat. Salalah, too, stretches like a belt of modern buildings along the coast, and presents a variety of faces, not all of which may be noticed by an outsider at first. It is the seat of administration for the south and the economic center of Dhofar. An airport, hotels, and, to the west, the container port of Mina Raysut, are all to be found here. The extensive development of the town's infrastructure and economy serves to demonstrate that the period of Muscat's neglect for Oman's most southerly province is finally a thing of the past. Numerous plantations are stretched out between the town and the coast. Coconut palms thrust heavenwards and in their shadows banana and papayas cluster together. Small, narrow roads wind their way through these miniature tropics. Small huts arrayed alongside the road offer freshly harvested fruit and coconuts. This verdant landscape is especially impressive during the winter months, which can be considered Dhofar's 'summer.' During the dry months in Salalah's hinterland, the leaves on the bushes, the grass and the trees all wither and the lush mountain slopes appear to have been

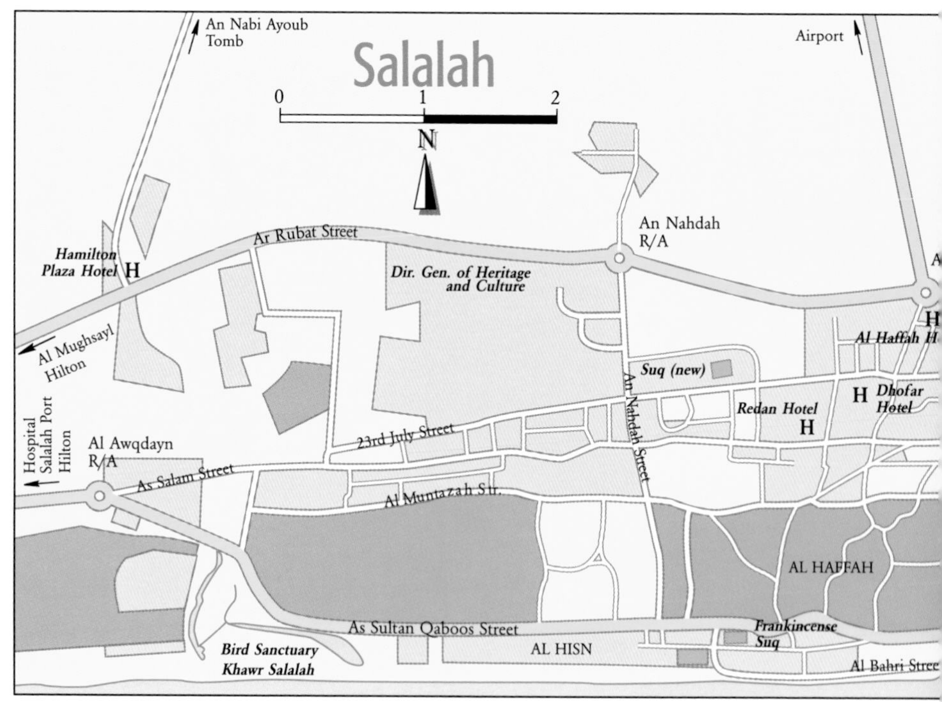

draped with thick brown felt. The grass is an orange-brown and sandstorms sweep through the town. A characteristic autumnal mood takes possession of the town and the artificially irrigated evergreen islands of the plantations.

The earliest documented port of this region was in the 1st century and was called 'Moscha' in the ancient mariner's handbook *Periplus Maris Erythraei*. In the Middle Ages what is modern-day Salalah outstripped ancient 'Moscha.' The chroniclers now spoke of a trading center called 'Dhofar,' the center for the export of frankincense and magnificent Arabian horses. In the middle of the 13th century, while still at its height, 'Dhofar' was attacked and plundered by a naval force from Hormuz. This was followed by conflicts with tribes from Yemen. Because the town offered maritime traffic the last Arabian port before the long passage to the south, it was able to profit from the trade with East Africa. A stop was put to this by the Portuguese, who imposed a blockade. After the Portuguese intermezzo Muscat and Aden developed into the most important

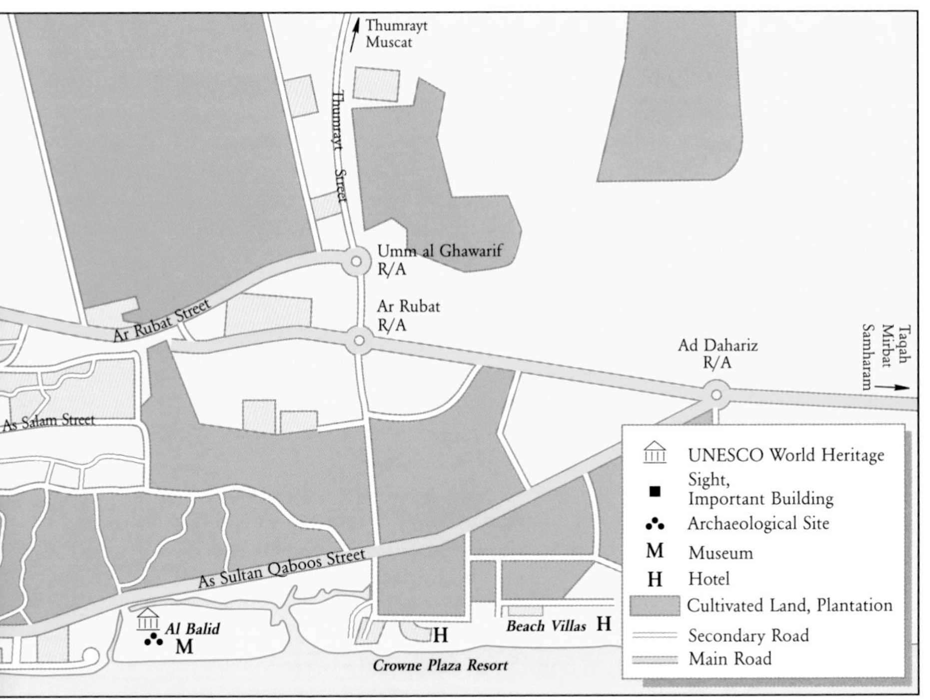

seaports of the Arabian Peninsula. There was no more chance of putting a stop to the slow, centuries-long decline of Dhofar. In the last 150 years the new town of Salalah has grown out of the stones of ancient Dhofar.

Remains of the ancient Middle Age settlement, which once reached as far as today's plantations, can now be found at Al Balid (from al Balad, meaning 'town'), a spit of land in the lagoon at the eastern end of the beach at Salalah. This UNESCO World Heritage site is now an archaeological park. You enter through a gate from the main street, after paying a small entrance fee. For an additional 2 Omani rials, one of the security personnel will drive you around the extensive park in an electric cart. It is a good idea to visit the park in the late afternoon, after the heat has abated somewhat. In the buildings to the left of the entrance are two museums, which are included in the entrance fee. One documents the development of Oman as a seafaring nations in a fascinating and vivid way, and the other offers an outline of the evolution of the land from the Stone Age till the present day.

In excavations during the past 5 years, the ruins of various phases of the historic port and town have been uncovered. The former center of Dhofar, as the port was called, was surrounded by a trench and a defensive wall with gates in the western, southern and eastern sides. At the western end of the site you can clearly make out the remains of the large court mosque. Originally there were 148 pillars, which were arranged in rows of four, surrounding an inner courtyard. Only a few stumps remain of these originals. The missing pillars were replaced with new stone pillars of half the height, the idea being to give the visitors a better impression of the original spatial effects of the architecture. On the northeastern corner of the building one comes across the foundations of a minaret and on the eastern side the areas for ritual cleansing, or purification, one of the essential duties of Muslims. A peculiarity of this sacred building is that its entrances were situated on the west side, in the Qibla wall with its mihrab facing Mecca.
Parts of the old city walls, the remains of a construction for extracting fish oil, and another smaller mosque with its attendant washhouse, have been uncovered. The archaeologists' greatest pride is the discovery of the old fortress under the largest of the mounds of rubble. Experts had examined this mound many times and each time declared that it really was nothing more than a pile of building rubble. Small parts of the several meter high outer wall and a round tower are now visible - the work of an entire season's excavation. Uncovering the entire building will certainly be the work of many years to come. The fortress is filled with earth and rubble which can only be cleared away laboriously by hand, bucketful by bucketful. The earth then has to be shaken through a sieve by the archaeologists and even the most insignificant looking finds have to be drawn, photographed and documented in writing. The excavation works have been carried out by a German archaeological team which also developed the educational concept of the archaeological park. The site is extensive; you are exposed to the full power of the sun's rays and it is recommended that you visit in the early morning or late afternoon.
Many Omanis see the Corniche, the newly-built coastal road running westwards alongside the beach from Al Balid, as one of the greatest blots on the landscape of southern Oman. Salalah's picturesque white beach, with its imposing coconut palms, is brutally split in two by this featureless, concrete strip. At the end of this promenade a road leads through a guarded gate to the new palace of Sultan Qaboos, which lies hidden behind a high wall. This palace is built on the same spot as that in which the Sultan's father lived from 1958 when he was Sultan until his replacement by Qaboos in

The lush green belt of plantations along the coastline of Salalah.

1970. The Corniche leads to the oldest parts of Salalah, al Husn and al Hafah, whose suq has been completely rebuilt and remains a lively trading post for fruit, handicrafts produced in southern Oman, and for perfumes. The women of Salalah mainly offer incense and their own famous mixtures of incense, known as *bokhur*, often sold in old nondescript cosmetic tins and jars, together with clay incense burners. These mixtures of scented woods, flower oils and resins are made up according to secret recipes, their aromas beguiling as soon as the container is opened, not just when they are burnt. Incense burners have distinctive forms according to whether they are from northern or from southern Oman.

The relatively coarse clay of the south is not suited to the potter's wheel and the ceramics are made using slab and press-forming techniques, which limit the formal possibilities of the artifacts. The fine clay of northern Oman is a bright ochre, whereas the coarser southern clay is a distinctive red-brown. Complex, perfectly rounded forms, often of imposing size, are typical of artifacts thrown on the wheel. Smaller, rectangular forms, made up from layers, or irregular round vessels are characteristic of pottery built up by hand. The most usual type of incense burner in the south is a rectangular vessel which narrows towards the bottom with a flat handle, the corners of which are decorated with stylized crenellations. The incense burner's edges and simple scratched ornamentation are often highlighted through the use of red, orange-yellow and bright blue gloss paint. The passage of time has not spared the houses of this residential part of Salalah, but at least the few remaining traditionally built dwellings are now listed for preservation. Their form is quite different from the architecture of northern Oman. The large two to three storey houses are built out of limestone in the style of South Yemen. The roofs are crowned with stylized stepped embrasures. On the house facades wide whitewashed stripes separate the individual storeys. The windows are faced with skillfully carved wooden latticework - an outward sign of the cultural closeness of neighboring Yemen.

Qaboos Street leads westwards alongside the fenced-off bird reserve of **Khawr Salalah**. With a bit of luck and some patience it is possible in winter to see through the fence and watch migratory birds resting, among them storks, ibises, ducks, flamingos and pelicans.

No sun, at last! Dhofar's coast is a popular destination in the summer, due to the fog and drizzle. Especially popular are the blow-holes at Mughsayl.

At the next roundabout, As Salam Street branches off to the east. This brings one back to the modern, future-orientated town. The street, the economic hub of Salalah, is crowded with innumerable small shops, as well as the entrance to the new suq.

A visit to **Job's Tomb**, An Nabi Ayoub, is a worthwhile half-day expedition from Salalah. In order to reach this holy Muslim site continue along Robat Street westwards until you come to the Hamilton Plaza Hotel. From there a large road branches off to the right in the direction of the mountains. After about 30 kilometers, a road off to the left is signposted An Nabi Ayoub. This shrine is much-visited by pilgrims and should be approached with discretion and respect. Shoes should be removed and women in particular should cover their hair. Alongside a mosque, the shrine accommodates a sarcophagus, covered by a green cloth. Pilgrims lay flowers and pages of the Quran upon it and set themselves down to pray at the graveside.

Frankincense - God's Gift

Frankincense trees are considered a gift from God. They cannot be cultivated or transplanted, and they only grow in certain places with the correct soil consistency and humidity. The area of distribution is therefore naturally very limited; in Hadramaut in Yemen they are already rarer than hitherto, although some trees are still to be found in Somalia. In Dhofar, where they are mostly to be found, they grow in a belt along the northern flank of the coastal mountains, where they are not directly affected by the monsoon rains. An exception to this rule is the area around Salalah's port, Raysut, where the climatic conditions resemble those of the classic frankincense regions.

The trees belong to individual families, rather than all belonging to a common stock. The quality of the frankincense resin is dependent on the humidity of the location. The best quality comes from trees in dry regions away from the coastal areas. Its resin is yellowish white, having a clear consistency and is named after *Nejd*, an area north of the Dhofar mountains. The resin from trees further south, nearer the monsoon's watershed, is darker in color, less pure, and is called *shazri*. The lowest quality, *shaabi*, comes from the wetter coast. There is also a noticeable East-West divide in the quality of the produce, known in the trade as *olibanum* - the best quality comes from the east of the distribution area.

Harvesting the resin is an art in itself. Using a special knife, known as a *mingaf*, shallow incisions are made in several places in the tree's bark. The incision should be just enough to induce the manufacture of resin, but must not seriously damage the tree in any way. Initially, only small, white drops of a sticky, milky fluid are exuded - this resin is worthless and after some three weeks is simply scraped away. Only now does the actual olibanum make its appearance. The 'pearls,' or 'tears,' are harvested at intervals of three weeks, mainly during the hot spring months. After harvesting over a maximum of three years, the trees are left undisturbed for several years in order to recover. The laborious toil of gathering in the resin was, and still is, carried out not only by Omanis, but also by experienced seasonal workers from Somalia. Production was drastically reduced during the Dhofar war when, in the 1960s and 1970s, many of the trees were considered worthless and were used as firewood.

The increasing interest in frankincense today is not just due to the prize-winning luxury perfume, Amouage, which contains olibanum. Western medicine has begun to discover the precious resin. In 1988 the University of Heidelberg began a study to investigate whether frankincense is as effective as standard medicines for chronic inflammatory illnesses. The study examined patients suffering from Crohn's disease, an inflammatory bowel disease resulting in acute complaints with diarrhea and stomach pains. The curative effect of the frankincense had already been demonstrated by pharmacologists from Tübingen. Were the study to confirm an equal effect, then a frankincense-based medicament could provide a viable alternative to classic treatments such as cortisone. Subsequent clinical trials in Tübingen, using medicinal compounds based on boswellic acids, have shown promising results in patients with rheumatoid arthritis, chronic colitis, ulcerative colitis and bronchial asthma, as well as Crohn's disease.

West of Salalah – Frankincense and Natural Grandeur

Before setting out on expeditions from Dhofar's capital, make sure that the petrol tank is full. Petrol stations are few and far between outside of Salalah, especially to the west. To the west of the town, having passed Mina Raysut, one of the world's largest container ports, the road leaves the coastline and presses on into the country's interior. The region is less marked by the monsoon and more by the steep, southern flanks of the Jabal Al Qara to the north of Salalah and the Jabal Al Qamar further to the west. There is markedly less vegetation here. The few small, rather bush-like trees that grow singly on the bone-dry slopes or in the wadis have only a few rather thick, strangely-formed branches and seem like the disconsolate skeletons of formerly magnificent trees which have been starved of water in the desert. However first appearances are deceptive. Here and there a small clump of leaves can be seen at the tip of a branch, the only sign of life in the otherwise puny-looking plants. You stand bewildered before such ruins of trees and can hardly conceive that these are the famed **frankincense trees**, so desperately sought-after in ancient times. The bare rocky landscape near the coast bursts abruptly upon us. The lunar backdrop is suddenly transformed into a dream setting: the bay of **Al Mughsayl**. Glittering turquoise-blue water, five kilometers of unbroken, dazzlingly white sands, a large, green lagoon and inviting, shady pavillions at the sea's edge. To the west the picturesque bay is cut off by high, black rocks, at the foot of which is a small parking area. A narrow footpath leads under an overhanging bluff to the neighboring rocky bay. Here the sea has washed away the lower, softer layers of stone creating a rocky terrace projecting out over the water. Heavy seas, mainly during the monsoon season, make the mighty waves wash under the terrace and gush out of naturally created **blowholes**, creating fountains of water as high as a house. Even when the sea is calm, now and again clouds of spray spurt up, and a deep roar can be heard from the depths.

The water fountains of the blowholes are only active in winter when the seas swell.

After Al Mughsayl the road once more leaves the coast and rises up from sea-level, climbing the heights of the **Jabal Al Qamar** and running near to the Yemen border. With many a dramatic hairpin bend it winds its steep, serpentine way through rocky fissures and within a short space of time you are at 1000 meters above sea level. Large chunks of the mountain were simply dynamited to make way for the road. The core of the soft rock is white to ochre, whereas the outer surface has oxidized and ranges from dark grey to black. Each explosion, every little landslide, has clearly left its mark on the mountain. The monsoon eats away at the stone, reshaping it to create an exhibition of weird rock sculptures along the road. From the ridge of the mountain you can see how the precipitous coast spreads its magnificent panorama before a backdrop of endless ocean. If you follow the road as far as the Yemen border (which is also open to tourists providing they have the requisite visa), deep below you can see the fishing villages of **Dhalkut** and **Rakhyut** – the last outposts of Oman on the southwestern coast.

If you follow the Yemen border to the north, just beyond Fasad you come to the foothills of the **Rub al Khali**. The sand dunes at the edge of the Empty Quarter rise up like mountains from the plain. The deeper you penetrate into this fascinating landscape, the further you will find yourself from everyday life with its hubbub and noise. Here you plunge into absolute stillness, surrounded by an endless sea of swelling sand dunes. An expedition into the desert should only be undertaken in the company of a local guide.

While in summer the sands of the Rub al Khali become an oven, the coastal mountain region around Salalah is transformed into a paradise for Omanis and Gulf Arabs.
The gentle rains and mists of the monsoon cover the hills with a lush green, and the temperature remains a steady 30 degrees centigrade.

The East Coast, Samharam and the World of the Jabalis

The coastal plain stretches from Salalah far to the east. Springs, known as ains in Arabic, can be found at the foot of the mountains bounding the plain to the north. The porous rock soaks up the annual monsoon precipitation, mostly mist and drizzle, like a sponge. For the rest of the year the mountains release the stored water through bubbling springs. This enables the cultivation of areas of the plain such as the garden of the Mamura Palace with the Royal Farm of Sultan Qaboos, a few kilometers outside of Salalah, the water for which is supplied from **Ayn Razat**. A number of small springs well up into this natural pool to the north of the palace. A small wood and a park round off this idyllic natural spectacle at the foot of the mountains. 150 liters of water per second flow out of the pools, enticing not only day-trippers from Salalah but many exotic species of birds.

At Taqah the fissured mountains approach the sea. Although **Taqah** is comparatively small, it is still the third largest town in Dhofar. In winter, at the start of the fishing season, large quantities of sardines are sun dried on the beach and then used mostly as animal feed and fertilizer. Taking a stroll through old Taqah, you will discover quite a few old buildings with beautifully carved wooden latticework. The restored **Taqah fort** stands in the center of the village. This is a must if visiting the town. In contrast to the castles of northern Oman, it appears small and cosy from the outside. The walls and ceilings are crooked, the few rooms are low-ceilinged, spread with carpets and filled with precious objects. Apart from numerous objects of daily use, such as chests, drinking vessels, Chinese porcelain bowls and braided dishes and carafes made in Dhofar, one is astonished by walls hung with mirrors, vibrantly colored Indian glass paintings of peacocks, bright flowers, and also a wonderful old portrait of the Sultan. Nothing appears to have been polished or given an artificial showroom luster. Everything seems to belong in its place, where it has spent the last century. The space and the interior décor blend together in complete harmony. The various cultures which have influenced Oman in the past can be felt in the atmosphere. Here you can breathe in the spirit of the ancient maritime nation. No other historical collection in Oman brings history back to life in such a convincing manner as this collection. A young Omani takes care of the collection and provides accompanying explanations.

The ancient frankincense storehouse in Samharam.

Taqah and Mirbat and Sadah to the east were formerly centers of the frankincense trade. Only a few large old merchants' houses in these towns bear witness to this earlier heyday, as do the ruins of Samharam, on the banks of the **Khawr Ruri** lagoon. Four kilometers to the east of Taqah a road branches off to the left leading to **Tawi Atayr** and to **Wadi Darbat**. After heavy rains, wide hundred meter high waterfalls cascade down. The floodwaters of Wadi Darbat have created the lagoon of Khawr Ruri, the largest in Dhofar, on the coast. Shortly after this two tracks branching off on the right are signposted "Khawr Ruri," but only the first of them leads to the ruins of the ancient frankincense port of **Samharam**.

This path forks after the guardposts, where you get your entrance ticket and an informative brochure about the enclosed site. If you choose the righthand pathway you will wind up on the promontory. Together with Al Balid, Ash Shasir and the Wadi Dawqah region, with its ancient frankincense trees, Samharam has recently been added to UNESCO's list of World Heritage Sites.

Up until the 1st century AD the transport of frankincense had been the domain of the camel caravans. As a result of improved navigation techniques, the trade routes became increasingly maritime, via the Red Sea. At that time Dhofar was part of the Yemeni kingdom of Hadramaut. The King recognized the importance of having a safe storage place and a port for the export of frankincense in the vicinity of where the frankincense was harvested, and in the 2nd century AD he ordered the building of Samharam. The ruined city was first uncovered by a research group of the American Foundation for the Study of Man, under the leadership of Wendell Philips, in three excavation campaigns between 1952 and 1962. At the beginning of the 1970s Andrew Williamson, an American archaeologist, renewed the investigations. He made latex casts of the wall inscriptions, which were later decoded by the archaeologist Jacqueline Pirenne in Paris. Among other things the texts provided information about the origins of the town. According to a six-line inscription decoded from a 49 by 27 centimeter stone tablet which had been broken in two, Samharam was founded by King Asadum Talan from Shabwa in Yemen. The inscription gave the name of the site as "SMRM"

The Lagoons of Dhofar

The heavy monsoon rains flowing through wadis on the southern flank of the Dhofar mountains have resulted in the formation of a number of lagoons on the south coast. The largest of these is Khawr Ruri. Some two kilometers long, it covers an area of 54 hectares. Each of Dhofar's lagoons has a differing salinity. Lagoons like Khawr Ruri, which are sealed off from the sea by sandbanks and with an inflow of fresh water, have very little salt; lagoons that are more affected by the sea have rather more. The heavy seas during the monsoon storms in summer lead to an increase in salt as the waters between sea and lagoon are exchanged. Every *khawr* is a unique habitat, a biotope for a variety of plants and animals, adapted uniquely to its ecosystem. Mangroves, for example, thrive best in very salty waters. The warm waters, high in nutrients, offer a habitat to 30 species of fish, and are a preferred spawning ground.

The abundance of food on offer in the middle of a large desert region brings innumerable flying visitors, especially in winter. Many species of migratory birds take a break around the *khawrs* in southern Dhofar in order to feed before continuing their journeys. At Khawr Ruri alone, 180 different species of bird have been noted since the mid-1970s – a birdwatcher's paradise. The lagoons serve the local inhabitants as fishing grounds and around them are pastures for their animals. The growing threat which urbanization poses to these unique biotopes, so vital for the survival of many animal species, should in the future be countered by their declaration as nature reserves – as has already happened with some of the lagoons, such as Khawr Salalah and Khawr Ruri.

which had been equated by the first American researchers with the Sabaean dialect "Samharam," meaning "his name is exalted." Now it was interpreted as deriving not from Sabaean, but from the Hadramaut dialect "Samaram," meaning "the site is impressive."
Two low, rocky promontories cut off Khawr Ruri from the sea, making the lagoon a perfect natural harbor. The narrow opening to the sea, today blocked by a sandbank, is directly opposite the town. Two and a half meter thick fortified walls, made from carefully cut blocks of stone, surrounded the town, the only way in being a gate to the north. The houses, mostly two-storey, were densely packed within this protective ring. The meticulously-built wall still stands at a height of a good two meters. Storehouses for the resin were in the southeastern part of the site with a row of rectangular pillars in the middle, and in the southwest there was a large, deep well. In the north, to the west of the immense entrance gate a temple, up to five meters high, abutted the outer wall. According to the inscriptions in the stone tablets embedded in the wall, the temple was dedicated to the lunar god Sin. The inscriptions are easy to find; simply climb the steps at the town entrance and at the top follow the path to the left. We have the anonymous author of the mariner's handbook *Periplus Maris Erythraei* to thank for a closer description of the port, known to the Greeks as "Moscha." The town served to enable the king of Hadramaut to have exclusive control over the quantities of frankincense harvested and traded in the most important frankincense area of south Arabia. Dhofar's entire resin production was gathered and taxed in Samharam. Just how far-reaching Samharam's flourishing trade contacts were is evidenced by finds of Roman pottery as well as an Indian figurine. The site is currently being developed and a resthouse constructed for the use of visitors and scholars.

The two onion domes of the mausoleum of the holy Sheikh Mohammed bin Ali Al Alawi near Mirbat show the architectural unity between South Oman and Yemen.
Until the 7th Century, Dhofar was ruled by Yemeni tribes.

Two kilometers before Mirbat, on the right, Bin Ali Street leads to a parking place at the **shrine of the holy Sheikh Mohammed bin Ali Al Alawi** and a large, adjoining cemetery. You should not approach too close to this Muslim shrine, but keep a respectful distance. At the edge of the burial ground there is a whitewashed mausoleum with two onion domes and a small, adjoining pump-room for water used for ritual cleaning. The architecture and layout of the cemetery are typical of south Yemeni culture. The descendant of the Prophet Mohammed came from Hadramaut and died in Mirbat in 1161. The genealogical table listed within the mausoleum goes back as far as Mohammed's son-in-law, Ali.

After the decline of the port of Dhofar and the withdrawal of the Portuguese the small port of **Mirbat**, near Sadah farther to the east, was able to establish itself as the center of the frankincense trade on the coast of south Oman. The houses in the center once belonged among the most impressive and well-known buildings of the coastal region. Most have now, unfortunately, fallen into a state of dilapidation. Nevertheless there are a few interesting historical buildings, or at least remains thereof, to be found. The remaining architectural treasures of the town are houses with typical South Yemen gypsum plasterwork and large murals showing merchant ships, a selection of richly-ornamented window lattices, as well as the restored fortress, although the latter's collection cannot compare to that of Taqah.

Follow the road eastwards; after 68 kilometers you reach **Sadah**, the other renowned erstwhile frankincense trading port. A small village, built on a rocky bay, Sadah is a perfect natural harbor. Take a walk here and you can still see, unlike in Mirbat, imposing, completely intact merchant houses from the age of the frankincense trade. It is also recommended to visit the lovingly-restored fortress.

The road runs along the **Jabal Samhan** range and 60 kilometers beyond Sadah comes to the small fishing village of Hadbin, known for its abalone divers. It then runs on for 45 kilometers to **Hasik**, where it ends. The road provides dazzling views over white beaches with azure waters, and impressive geological rock formations. All of the wadis that run from the road into the Jabal Samhan area are barred to cars and can only be explored on foot. They are part of the vast Nature Reserve of Jabal Samhan. Just before Hasik a road branches off to the left, leading to the **mausoleum** of the regional prophet Hud, who has always been honored by the people of Dhofar.

Returning from an excursion to the east of Salalah, it is recommended to take a small detour by way of Madinat Al Haq ("the place of hope") and Qayrun Hayrati. The road to the mountains branches away from the coast at Taqah. After just a few kilometers the road ascends to the heights of the coastal mountains. This is the realm of the **Jabalis**, the 40,000-odd mountain nomads of Dhofar. For centuries their livelihood has been based on keeping goats and camels. In recent years the Jabalis have largely given up their nomadic existence in favor of a settled farmer's life. In doing so, their traditional stone-layered round dwellings with a covering of branches, where snakes were often unbidden guests, have been exchanged for simple houses. However, for reasons of personal prestige, they have not reduced the numbers of goats and camels.

Fodder for the winter months is grown in the damp summer in a large area, walled off to protect the crop from the animals. Later the mown grass is dried and the hay stored.

Nowadays, though, this is not enough to feed the large herds. The whole family may have to work in order to buy fodder for the animals. In recent years the large herds, no longer wandering from feeding place to feeding place, have caused extensive damage through overgrazing and gnawing at trees and bushes. Where thirty years ago there were once trees, today there is only grass.

To counteract this a culling program was started in 2003 to control the camel population. The animals were first counted and registered - there were 70,000! This relatively small area had the highest population density of camels in the world. The state began by buying the camels from the families and breeders and then sold them as fresh meat to neighboring countries. In this way the camel population was reduced by 20,000 after only one year. An initial success, which may perhaps have given the unique vegetation of the mountains of Dhofar the chance to flourish in the future. The aim is to reduce the total camel population by 90 percent.

The huge camel population did severe damage to the natural vegetation of the mountains of Dhofar in the past.

Musandam - a Journey into Seclusion

The northeastern tip of the Arabian peninsula is made up of a mighty limestone mountain range which soars up to a height of 2087 meters. Its sides tower steeply out of the turquoise-blue water, and then abruptly down to the deep valleys of the wadis. They form a bizarre tangle of fjords, which make you think of Norway. The most striking difference with northern Europe is the complete lack of trees. Water, and consequently vegetation, is rare on the peninsula. The cliffs look like the gigantic walls of a fortress designed to keep people from entering the area - and yet Musandam has been inhabited for thousands of years. Currently about 35,000 people live in this rocky fortress. More than 18,000 of them live in Khasab, the coastal oasis, the peninsula's largest and greenest place. In addition there is a small military airport that is served commercially by Oman Air with a propeller plane.

Since 2009 Khasab is also connected to Muscat by a highspeed ferry some days a week. The ferry needs about six hours one way. If you come by car from the Emirates, you have to take the asphalt road along the west coast of Dubai to Khasab, as all other tracks are closed to tourists for the time being. The required visas can be obtained at the frontier.

Once a week a tanker from Khasab delivers spring water to the remote villages in the fjords. The water is stored in tanks at the beachside

For non-Arab foreigners Oman is a land mostly unknown. Musandam, however, owing to its geographically isolated position is *terra incognita* for many Omanis. Even 30 years after the founding of the modern state of Oman, the region has retained much of its austere, unspoilt nature. The capital, Muscat, seems infinitely distant. Tourism is less part of the normal vocabulary than in the rest of Oman. Apart from the new asphalt road running along the coast from Khasab, by way of Bukha to the Emirates, Musandam's remaining sparse network of roads consists of tracks, some of which are extremely difficult to drive along. Bigger expeditions from Khasab into the countryside or around the fjord landscapes are best made using a local tour operator. Large regions of the strategically important peninsula are a closed-off military zone, or only accessible by sea.

Traveling by the very impressive mountain road, which leads over the highest peak in Musandam, the Jabal Harim, requires experience in driving a 4WD in high alpine terrain, together with exact knowledge of the current weather situation and the state of the roads. A single stormlike shower and the road can be impassable

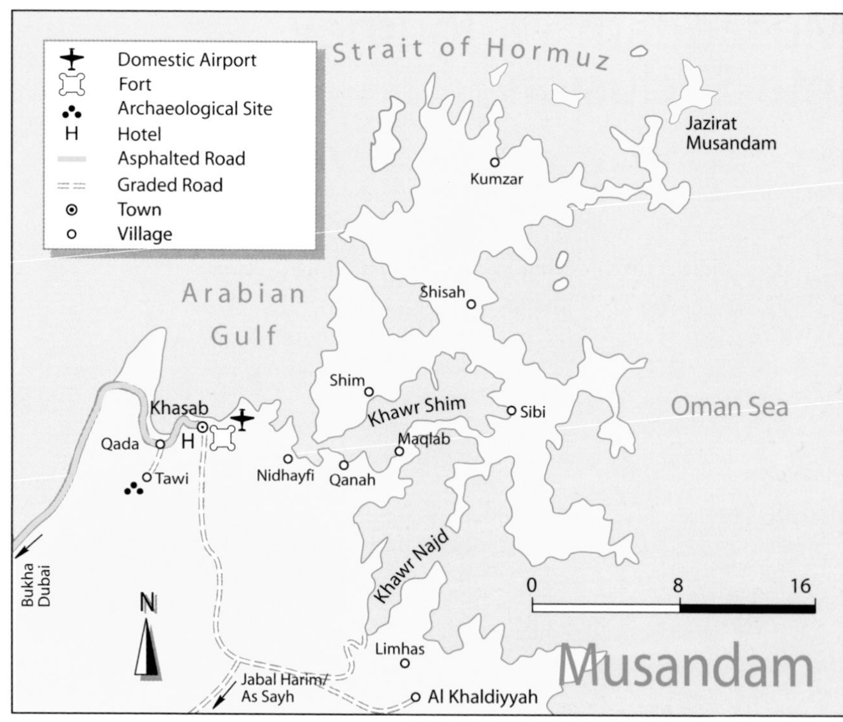

for days and you can easily become trapped. You can comfortably wander by yourself around and through the oasis Khasab in three or four hours. It is especially worthwhile to visit the museum in the old fortress. There are two hotels in Khasab: the Khasab Hotel, near the airport, and the Golden Tulip Khasab, which is situated somewhat outside town on a plateau overlooking the sea. The latter has been named best 4-star hotel in the Middle East & Africa numerous times since it opened a few years ago.

The Omani town of **Daba** belongs geographically to Musandam, but the two hotels there, Six Senses Hideaway Zighy Bay and Golden Tulip Daba, can only be reached by road via the Emirates.

A Walk through Khasab

The Khasab Hotel is situated about 2.5 kilometers from the harbor on the southern edge of the town. Musandam's new administrative center spreads out between this hotel and the old palm groves. The new buildings on the right hand side of the road accommodate almost exclusively local authority and ministry offices. Their presence greatly eases the bureaucratic life of the inhabitants of Musandam, while at the same time making manifest Oman's claim to power over the peninsula.

The inhabitants have more or less recognized the supreme authority of the Omani sultans since the 18th century, but the rulers showed very little interest in the barren area. Their chief object of interest was directed to the north at Hormuz and the so-called pirate coast west of Musandam.

Musandam first achieved strategic importance when the British laid a telegraph cable from London to Bombay which ran north of Khasab through Musandam. The necessary telegraph station was built on a small island in the Shim fjord, now known as Telegraph Island. Taking the cable "round the bend" of the Gulf gave rise to the expression, as living on Telegraph Island in the summer reputedly drove men crazy. In order to guarantee its functioning undisturbed, the British insisted that Sultan Tuwainy ibn Said make his claim over the region clear.

Since then the post of the *wali* of Khasab has always been occupied, and Khasab has been the political center of the province. Oman's possession of the territory was first recognized under international law in 1970 as part of the border treaty between the Sultanate and the United Arab Emirates.

The palm groves directly adjoin the new quarter. Their economic importance can be immediately recognized by their well-tended appearance. Alfalfa, feed grass, onions and even bananas are cultivated among the palms. Low mud dikes divide the gardens into small parcels, which are briefly flooded as a means of watering. The old wells have meanwhile been taken out of service and today the groundwater is directly tapped using diesel pumps. Until now this practice has not resulted in any damage such as increased soil salinity due to a decreased level of the groundwater. Fortunately, the groundwater reserves in Khasab are very large in comparison with the number of inhabitants and the amount of land under cultivation. Unlike in the other mountain regions of Oman there is no *falaj* system to be found in the whole of Musandam, although supplying water to the region outside of Khasab is a real problem.

The water from the springs which seeps out of the predominantly ophiolite stone of Musandam is not suited for drinking due to the amount and number of substances dissolved in it.
On average the climate of Musandam is even drier than in the rest of the Sultanate. Clouds build up over the mountains but then rain over the sea. In some years, 1981 for example, with a total of 36 millimeters, there is as good as no rainfall. If the thunderstorms do come inland, then the short but very heavy showers turn the mountainsides into torrents. They flood the narrow wadis, destroying everything in their path.
The older inhabitants of Khasab remember August 1975 with horror. A heavy thunderstorm turned Wadi Khasab into a raging stream from cliff wall to cliff wall. The inhabitants fled to the mountains. Most of their houses were torn up by the meter deep floodwave and swept out to sea. Houses which remained standing were severely damaged. Many inhabitants quit the area.

Khasab, a Place on the Sidelines of History

The flourishing maritime trade between Sumer, Magan and Meluhha in the second half of the 3rd millennium BC mostly bypassed the coast of Musandam, although the peninsula was a part of the Magan empire. Its steep cliff walls hid many dangers for ships, offered hardly any places to land and barred the way into the hinterland. The Persian coast opposite and the Al Batinah plain offered far better preconditions for economic development. The large campaigns of conquest were never directed against Musandam. In the 4th and 3rd centuries BC, Hormuz developed into the main port for the region. There is no evidence of trade connections between Persia and Musandam but given their geographical proximity such connections very probably did exist. Historians such as the Italian Germana Graziosi Costa see in the language of the Kumazarah possible evidence for these contacts. The fishing village of Kumzar on the Strait of Hormuz forms a language island, where a unique dialect, strongly influenced by Persian, is spoken.
At the beginning of the Christian period the immigration of the Yemenite tribes around Malik ibn Faham began. They also migrated to Musandam and to the south of Iran. The Shihuh population in Musandam view themselves as the descendants of these immigrants. Finds of shards and remains of buildings on the coast of Jazirat Al Ghanam and at Khasab point to the peninsula coming under the influence of the Persian Sasanians, just as the remaining coast of Oman did from the 4th to the 6th century. Porcelain from China and ceramics from Hormuz demonstrate the integration of Musandam in the trading network between Iran and China in the 15th century. In 1515 the maritime power of Hormuz was

The government could only halt the exodus by delivering an immediate aid program to motivate people to make a new start. Three dams were built in the upper courses of Wadi Khasab to protect the town from the masses of water. Work on the area's infrastructure was driven forward. Sultan Qaboos's government thereby not only demonstrated Omani authority over Musandam, but also that it took responsibility for the region. Naturally the new Khasab should have a standard of living in keeping with modern times. The inhabitants, who up until then had lived under difficult conditions, insisted on that. Today Khasab presents itself as a modern oasis town and the trading center of the region.

If, during your walk through the palm groves, you continue eastwards you'll come across an area predominantly inhabited by Persians. They have lived here for many generations and, since 1970, have had the opportunity to acquire Omani citizenship. Their settlement extends down to the bay which is skirted by the coast road.

destroyed by the Portuguese. In order to secure their position, the Europeans immediately began to erect 23 fortified sites at strategically important positions from East Africa to Hormuz. The fort at Khasab was only built in 1600, when Portugal's star had already begun to wane in the Indian Ocean. In 1622 the colonial powers once more lost Hormuz to the Persians. The Yaruba Imam Nasir ibn Murshid successfully campaigned against the Portuguese from inner Oman. In 1644 he took Khasab Fort. The Portuguese attempt at reconquest in 1650 failed and in the same year they were even forced to quit Muscat. Khasab played no role in Oman's maritime policy which was directed at distant shores. Only in the 19th century, when the tribes of the Arabian Gulf coast (generally described by the British as Qawasim) drew attention to themselves by their unashamed acts of piracy – plundering Omani and British ships, even bringing the coastal parts of Musandam under their control – did the peninsula become interesting to the world of power politics. At the beginning of the 19th century the Sultan of Oman, with support from the British East India Company, led several punitive expeditions against the pirate coast and its center Ras al Khaimah. In 1820 the hostile conflicts came to an end in a peace treaty, the observance of which was enforced by the British navy.

Only in the age of telegraphy did Khasab and Musandam come into the focus of Western strategic considerations in the Arabian Gulf. In the year 1864 the British wanted to secure a telegraph cable between India and England. Since the oil crisis of the 1970s the tanker traffic in the Gulf Region can be monitored from Musandam.

The road leads west to the harbor, the most northerly point of Khasab, and from there continues to Dubai in the United Arab Emirates. In the middle of the wide arc of the bay, directly on the coastline, the restored fort of Khasab rises up.
The **fort** was probably erected by the Portuguese at the beginning of the 17th century, after they had been driven out of Hormuz. Khasab's great merit, then as now, was the large reserves of groundwater, unusual for the region. Of the fortress's various wells, today only the main well in the central round tower remains. Khasab fort embodies the simplest basic form of Omani fortress architecture, as found throughout the entire country. The outer walls form a square, the corners of which are fortified with projecting towers. The large inner courtyard contains the main tower and the most important well, offering the final bastion of retreat. As in Nizwa it is a simple round tower, although the whole area of the Khasab fort would fit within the main tower at Nizwa. The new and well-designed museum in the fortress is extremely informative. It provides a detailed look into life, artisanry, and the music traditions in the region. In the inner courtyard various traditional fishing boats are on display, as are replicas of the summer homes used by the fishermen of Kumzar.

The round tower in the center of the Khasab fortress houses an exhibition, which is well worth seeing, about the life and traditions of the peoples of the Musandam region.

Harbor Scenes at Khasab

Today the free port of Dubai can be reached in a three hour drive from Khasab along the coast road. The completion of this road in 1981 and its extension at the end of the 1990s gave new earning opportunities to the inhabitants of Khasab. Without any problem they could now fetch cheaply-purchased electrical goods, cigarettes and other luxury goods in large quantities with a pick-up and bring them to Musandam. Due to the steadily rising volume of business, the bay has been filled in to a great extent, to create space for the customs offices along with a commercial zone. Huge jetties seal off the harbor from the open sea.
Khasab itself has nowhere near enough inhabitants to make such an import business profitable on a large scale. But if you walk in the morning inside the harbor through the small gate at the harbor police and take the time to quietly watch the daily comings and goings in the small harbor of Khasab, you will quickly realize the destination of these "exported" goods.
In sheer numbers the dhows dominate the wharves on the eastern side of the bay. These old-fashioned wooden ships bob up and down as in ages past, but ply the waters today primarily carrying tourists on tours of the fjords. On the southwestern side of the bay

quite a different, and modern, spectacle is on display. A number of small fiberglass speedboats are disturbing the calm. Every day up to a hundred of them buzz over the Strait of Hormuz between Bander Abbas in Iran and Khasab. The twin-engine motorboats need just 45 minutes to cover the roughly 50 kilometer long stretch and a single-engine requires one and a half hours. On arrival at the cordoned off port the Iranians are taken in by the port police, searched for weapons and - when there is nothing to hold against them - issued with a purchasing permit. The visitors then go to the suq which is not far from the harbor. Here as many goods as the boat can carry are purchased. Duty having been paid according to the regulations, Oman pick-ups and truck-taxis transport the goods which are wrapped in waterproof packing down to the harbor. Box after box is loaded into the boats, which have all superfluous ballast removed. In the evening a flotilla of about 20 boats leaves the harbor in the direction of home, from where the goods are distributed throughout Persia - naturally without any duties having been paid. The Iranian coast guard clearly tolerate this flourishing smuggling in one of the most closely watched stretches of water in the world. However if they do choose to take action the pack simply disperses in all directions and makes pursuit impossible.
The big boom in this commerce is apparently over. A couple of years ago as many as 500 boats and 5000 sheep landed here daily. This number dropped in 2007 to approximately 200 boats and 1000 sheep, a deep cut for such a recently expanded port.

The form of the rock and wall etchings in Oman give little clue as to when they were made.
The depictions on the palace wall of Jabrin (above) can only be a few hundred years old, whereas those at Tawi (below) were perhaps etched more than 2000 years ago.

"Rock Art" at Tawi

If you follow the coast road beyond Khasab harbor to the north you will reach a small, sheltered bathing bay and then **Qada**. The small fishing village of Qada is located where the Wadi Qada opens into the sea. Follow the wadi back towards the mountains and after about three kilometers you reach **Tawi**. Here the water has eroded a deep channel into the valley floor on the right hand side of the wadi. The cliff walls rise vertically, stretching heavenward. Next to two trees on the left hand side of the wadi, mighty blocks of stone rise as high as a house, rubble from an earlier cavern which was created by weathering and, as the stone eroded further, had tumbled down from the cliff wall. The caves were decorated with numerous drawings which had been engraved with stones in the rock face and are typical for the whole region of the Hajar Mountains. They stand out brightly against the weathered dark background. Look more closely at the stones, which lie next to the track and you will make out camels, riders and magic symbols. The closer and longer you look the more pictures you can make out on the boulders. They are apparently 2000 years old. The good state of preservation is thanks to the fact that the cave only collapsed in the last century and, on the other hand, that these small works of art are mostly in the shadow during the day. Those drawings which are subjected to direct sunlight are already extremely weathered, have darkened, and are almost indistinguishable from their background. No other archaeological finds are currently known in Musandam: up until now no extensive archaeological investigations have taken place apart from in the small towns and villages.

"Graffiti" in Oman

Depictions on walls, graffiti, are visible signs in Western countries of the existence of a youth subculture, which contradicts the often only superficially maintained appearance of order, beauty and a secure existence. Whether treated as art or condemned as a mess, they are still in their way expressions of the spirit of the age and also of the ancient, primeval human urge to leave some trace in history. This connects modern signs and pictures sprayed on walls with the cave paintings, the oldest cultural traces of humankind. On account of their unspoilt nature and their reduction to essentials they belong to the most fascinating documents which the people of previous millennia have left us. Western-style graffiti, in the form of sprayed signs and slogans are almost nowhere to be seen in Oman. There are neither loyalist, nor critical, nor simply trivial graffiti - also not in the form of fresh whitewash. This is certainly not due to a lack of suitable surfaces in the towns and villages. The conclusion that in Oman today there is no youth subculture seems to be correct. The enthusiasm for the many new things in the country, and the progress which they have brought, is too big. However the conclusion that there is absolutely no graffiti would be presumptuous and wrong. The ancient tradition of painting on walls and surfaces still finds expression in its most original form, simple scratched drawings on rocks and walls or made by children in the sand on the beach. The tools used are not the spray can and the marker but finger, stone and blade.

Above all, countless drawings from various epochs are to be found in the limestone of the narrow valleys of the Jabal Al Akhdar. During research made in the mountain range in 1975, 47 places were discovered, some even piled up with depictions of thousands of people, animals and objects. The drawings could be clearly made out in the already weathered dark surfaces of the limestone, where the scratches and carvings exposed the white color of the stone. An exact dating was not possible and probably never will be. The

Continuing in the direction of the Emirates, the road winds in steep, narrow curves over the mountains and, a few kilometers from the frontier post, reaches **Bukha** with its restored fortress, which, legend has it, was built in a day, by human and not supernatural means. Nearby you will find the newly renovated old **mosque**. Until recently this building was a ruin dense with atmosphere. The building is supported by pillars, the capitals of which are covered with geometrically patterned stuccowork.
Today Bukha lives from fishing. It is one of a number of places on the coast, whose harbor has been modernized and extended in recent years.

Following 2 pages: Along the shore near the villages in Shimm Fjord you can still find *battils*, a skiff traditional to this area.

drawings were almost all made in natural stone, isolated from remains of other cultural artifacts of the period such as campsites or the remains of settlements. Their unprotected situation meant that many of the oldest pictures were severely weathered, and often they were covered in newer drawings.
The depictions illustrate contemporary happenings, fights against warriors with shields, swords and bows, with riders and camels, but also with meanwhile extinct animals such as the Arabian ostrich. Apart from the degree of weathering, the depicted subjects themselves give the only other vague indication of the age of the drawings and at the same time demonstrate the unbroken continuity of this tradition. Various Arabic and European types of ships were immortalized in rock. The depictions of people numerically outweigh all other motifs. They range from the simplest, barely differentiated stick figures, no more than a few centimeters high, to the life-sized naturalistic half reliefs of the so-called Coleman's Rock. (see chapter Archaeology)
The scratched drawings are spread along the historic routes through the mountains, far away from today's roads and tracks. As a result they are mostly impossible to find without a guide with local knowledge, apart from the drawings at Tawi in Musandam. Interesting scratched drawings can also be admired in the Fort at Nizwa and in the palace at Jabrin. True, they do not belong to the oldest, but cover the spectrum of the last three hundred years. Stylistically they hardly differ from the other drawings, at least a thousand years older, which makes you realize the problem to be had in dating them. In Nizwa groups of warriors riding camels are depicted and can be seen just after the main gate on the left wall. In Jabrin the scratches can be found in the first inner courtyard as well as in the vicinity of the entrance.
Numerous caves of the Dhofar mountains are also covered with drawings. Most of them were carefully documented by the Omani Ali Al Shahri in an opulent volume published in Arabic.

By Dhow into Khawr Shim and to Kumzar

With its 16 kilometers the Khawr Shim is the longest fjord in Musandam. Its imposing 1000 meter high cliff walls, the small islands and peninsulas, coral reefs and villages can only be explored by boat. Not a single track leads to this fjord, as is the case with most of the others. The only exception, **Khawr Najd**, is near to Al Khaldiyyah, which in winter offers a parklike landscape with its lush meadows and trees. The trip with the dhow along the banks, past fishing villages and islands, takes an entire day.

If it is bad weather and not suited to bathing and snorkeling, you can make the tour in half a day with a speedboat and afterwards make an excursion to Kumzar, the northernmost point of Oman. You should certainly visit this bay which, first seen from the sea, impresses you not only with the way of life of the people of this region, with all of its problems and laboriousness, but also with the beauty and stillness of the cliff landscape. The seemingly impenetrable cliff walls east of Khasab suddenly open up to admit entrance through a narrow opening to **Khawr Shim**. The water is as smooth as glass in the fjord, completely sheltered from wind, its shining dark turquoise giving an idea of its great depths. The cliffs enclosing the fjord soar up above the depths, their tectonic layers pointing like arrows to the heavens, reminding you of the primeval forces of the earth.

Dhows are still used for the transport of goods and people between Khasab and Kumzar.

The few human settlements seem helpless in the face of this awesome nature, clinging on in tiny bays, shut in between deep sea and steep cliffs, without electricity or water. In the past the inhabitants of the five villages here collected the rainwater in cisterns; today aluminum or steel tanks are used for storage. Once a week a blue tanker from Khasab delivers springwater. Bottled gas provides a modern energy supply.

Life has thus become easier, but nonetheless in recent years many people have left and settled in Khasab. The government encourages this by making new housing available, but forced resettlement is out of the question in Oman. Above all the older inhabitants of **Qanah** would not abandon their accustomed homeland for anything in the world: For them Khasab is the byword for a loud, hectic and smelly city. Their few houses have now at least been renovated at the state's expense.

The steep cliff walls rise majestically over the always calm waters of the Shim fjord.

At the end of 1993 only forty people still lived in this comparatively large village with its houses walled with lumps of rough rock; when these have died then the place will be given up. Qanah was once an important local trading center for pottery from Lima. **Lima** is still a remote but vital place on the eastern coast, only accessible by boat. Also **Nadhayfi** und **Sibi** are today still lively fishing settlements with several hundred inhabitants.

The small village of **Shim** on the other hand is practically deserted. The fishermen there are considered the shrewdest in the region. They use the new coast road primarily to export fish to the United Arab Emirates and get prices there that are several times higher than the normal prices for fresh fish in Oman. They invested their profits in pick-ups and built up their trade in Khasab. Unlike the other places, the small village of **Maqlab**, now only inhabited by eight families, is not directly at the water's edge but built on high ground. After the old village had been several times exposed to attacks by the Persians, the inhabitants moved to the more secure heights of the 80 meter high and 250 meter wide land bridge separating the Persians from the rest of Oman.

In the middle of Khawr Shim, just offshore from Maqlab, a small, flat island rises out of the water on which you can see the remains of walls, all that's left of the British telegraph station. Only 5 years after going into service in 1864 it was abandoned. The main reason was the dreadful living conditions. In summer, in a period before air conditioning, the hellish heat and the high humidity were unbearable for Europeans. On top of that the local population were hostile both to the British and to the new technology.

From the foundations of the formerly two-storey building you can look deep into the crystal clear waters. You can easily discern the coral reef which surrounds the island, can make out the different species of fish and with a bit of luck you may also see small sharks or dolphins. Today the island is a popular destination for excursions. You can snorkel here, have a picnic, or simply enjoy the quiet and let your glance wander over the fantastic landscape. Ruus al Jibal, "the heads of the mountains," is the local name for Musandam, perfectly suited to this natural scenery. Strictly speaking "Musandam" is the name of the small island **Jazirat Musandam**, lying in the Strait of Hormuz off the extreme northeast of the peninsula, even if today it is used to designate the entire region.

If you sail further along the coast to the north, past this island and a large naval base, you come to **Kumzar**. This is the most remote place in Oman, but is nonetheless the second largest settlement in Musandam. The 1,500 inhabitants are a discrete society in themselves, with their own language and strong self-confidence. A gas-fuelled power station combined with a seawater desalination plant allows a modern life to be led in this remotest of locations. Several old *battil*, the wooden boats which were earlier characteristic of Musandam, lie on the beach. They differ from normal fishing boats in the strong curvature of the keel and the wide, raised stern fins. The inner edge of the bow and stern deck is often decorated with simple ornamental carving. The most striking characteristic of the boats of Kumzar is the bow which is covered with furs and decorated with chains of shells. This décor was supposed to bring luck to the boat's crew. Nowadays the boats are no longer generally used as a means of transport; low-maintenance fiberglass boats now predominate here as they do in the whole of Oman.

Jabal Harim by Four-wheel-drive

Birkat Al Khaldiyyah: a natural acacia park

You can gain a different insight into Musandam's mountain world by driving to the top of the highest peak in the region, Jabal Harim. The route leads over the Omani Mountain Road, which starts a few kilometers south of Khasab, marked by a large sign. It urges the traveler to pay attention to safety measures and brings all possible dangers to your attention. Directly after the sign, you see that the warnings were justified, as the road steeply climbs the mountain. In the background the 2087 meter high Jabal Harim rises impressively, seemingly unconquerable and certainly not to be driven over. But the road continues to the radar station on the summit. Strange, deep gorges hollowed out of the rock walls by rainwater, and simple houses built out of lumps of rock and hidden in crevices and under overhangs, line the dangerous road. The wild, almost untouched mountain world of Musandam is home to the **Shihuh**, a Bedouin people. They make up 85 percent of the population of Musandam and also inhabit the coastal oases. Their own Arabic dialect has many elements of Persian. As a tribal insignia they carry a ten to fifteen centimeter large axe on a long handle, the *jerz*. It serves both as status symbol and a weapon.

During the periods of possible rain, in winter, the Shihuh live scattered throughout the mountains in their small stone houses, raising small farm animals and cultivating their fields where they manage to grow a little barley, wheat and alfalfa. In summer they wander down from the mountains to the oases for the date palms. Flying to Khasab your eye is caught by the small, cultivated plots of green, apparently scattered at random over the mountains. However their location is well thought-out: they are always placed, gently terraced, on the lower slopes of the rocks. Using a system of low walls, which act as dams, they catch the water which pours down the slopes in torrents during thunderstorms. The water cascades from the highest terrace to the one below and so on. Each field is flooded in turn. In order to better dam the precious water each of the fields is surrounded by a wall, about chest-high, often with the top edge secured with brambles to protect the precious plants from the depredations of the ever-present, always hungry goats. This ancient system of "flood irrigation" has not changed. As in the remote fishing villages, drinking water is kept in large tanks which are placed along the road at villages and hamlets.

Strings of cowrie shells hang from the prows of *battils* to ward off evil spirits.

Halfway to the summit you are taken by surprise by a large, flat valley which, after rain, is covered in a gigantic green carpet. This is the settlement of **As Sayh** with its extensive fields. Even small date palms grow here and there. In the future it is planned to cultivate them here on a larger scale. Today the old stone houses, called *bayt al qufl*, mostly stand empty and are gradually falling apart. In the most remote corners of Musandam, huts made of concrete blocks are a sign of modern times. *Bayt al qufl* means "House of the Lock." The mighty, technically complicated door lock is a major part of this type of house, unique in Arabia. It serves to secure the clay storage jars and grain in the Bedouin's buildings from thieves during their absence in the summer months.

At the end of the valley the road climbs steeply once more until you reach a plateau just below the summit. Here the rugged rock landscape mellows with gently rolling hills covered in low, bush-like perennials. On the summit of Jabal Harim the radar station, the center of Oman's defense strategy, reigns over all, the sentinel of the Gulf. The summit region itself is a sealed military zone and may not be entered. Below it the road winds around the mountain and disappears on the other side, following its steep, serpentine path in the direction of the United Arab Emirates. The first turn on the way down to the depths is actually the point of the journey: here the spectacular view of the ridges of the Musandam mountains, a landscape cleft by narrow, deep valleys, is one of the most impressive natural panoramas to be seen throughout Oman.

The Archaeology of the Sultanate of Oman

by Paul Yule

From the archaeological point of view, the Sultanate of Oman belongs to the least known countries of the Arab world. In the Early Islamic Period, when the "time of darkness" was still fresh in the memory, even the term "historian" was considered offensive. Only in the middle ages did writers of history begin to interest themselves in the "dark age," i.e. the period before Islam. Our knowledge about it is therefore limited and patchy. We know from clay tablets from Persepolis that during the Achaimenian Empire (6th - 4th centuries BC), "Gedrosien" (southern Iran) and "Maka" (southern Iran and central Oman) were united in a satrapy (province within the Persian empire) with its capital in Purush (near Bampur in south-eastern Iran.) Also when the classical author Herodotus mentions the inhabitants as being "Maciya" his picture of the geography of the empire is vague. The famous ancient historian W.W. Tarn writes that the entire peninsula of Oman, i.e. the extreme east of the Arabian peninsula, was unknown to the classical Greek world. Alexander the Great dispatched his admiral Nearchos of Crete to explore the Arabian Gulf (internationally more frequently called the "Persian Gulf"), but only limited information has been handed down. In his *Natural History* the Roman Pliny (23-79 AD) mentions towns on the "Arabian Gulf" including "Ommana." An anonymous travel description from the 1st century AD, the *Periplus Maris Erythraei*, describes a maritime route from the Red Sea to the Arabian Gulf. The text is marred by being handed down over generations and says little of the "fisheaters" who lived on the Omani coast.

The Greek scholar Ptolemy, who lived in the 2nd century AD, wrote a geography of the world with maps that had a great influence on cartographers of the middle ages. In his work he mentions the tribe of "Masonitae" living in this area. The same name, "Mazun" also appears in the *Res gestae* (the Acts), conceived by the Persian Sasanian ruler Shapur I (241-272 BC), which he had engraved on the tower-like Kaba-i Zardusht in Naqsh-i Rustam near Persepolis. The medieval Arab geographers and historians also regarded Oman as the eastern frontier of their world - Arabic and Islamic but at the same time close to India. Did Oman not belong to the Sasanian (224-651 AD) "Land of India," the "Ard al Hind"? Because of its proximity to, or rather its connections with, East Africa, Arabia and South Asia a unique cultural mix arose in Oman, which - also in regard to archaeology - gives this exotic country its attraction. Archaeological research on a scale worthy of the name first began in 1970 with the opening up of Oman. The modern frontiers in the east of the Arabian peninsula resulted from European colonial politics and only roughly correspond to the earlier territories and spheres of influence of the individual tribes and peoples. How the borders of Oman developed over the centuries is known in broad terms. The area to be described here includes both geographically and historically the United Arab Emirates as well as today's Sultanate, and so covers an area larger than Poland, for example, or the state of New Mexico in the USA.

Archaeology differentiates between northwest, central and south Oman. The first includes the United Arab Emirates, the second, the central and northern parts of the Sultanate and the last, the southern province of Dhofar. Archaeological investigations in the Sultanate were spurred on by Geoffrey Bibby, with his exciting book, *Looking for Dilmun*. "Dilmun" is known to us from being handed down through Sumerian and Akkadian cuneiform writings as a kind of land of milk and honey. The clay tablets and statues found in Iraq from the time between 2500 and 1800 BC confirm that the country between the Euphrates and the Tigris obtained a large part of its copper from a country called "Magan."

Merchants and priest-kings organized what was for those times an astonishing foreign trade. Freight-carrying ships from "Dilmun," "Magan" and "Meluhha" moored at the quay of the capital Akkad during the reign of King Sargon (late 3rd millennium BC) and were unloaded or prepared for foreign journeys lasting several months. In the flourishing city states of Mesopotamia, which was poor in natural resources, there was a great demand both for expensive luxury goods and for the urgently needed raw materials for everyday life. But the Sumerians knew nothing more precise about the distant land called "Magan," other than it was from where the dark stone for the king's statues, copper and certain goods came.

The locating of "Dilmun" on the island of Bahrain and its Arabian hinterland on the coast has been confirmed by historical reconstructions as well as texts which were excavated on the island. "Magan" appears to have been situated on both sides of the Gulf of Oman - probably in today's Sultanate and in Iranian Makran. The last of the four trading partners, "Meluhha," is the least known. It corresponds with the Harappa civilization of south Pakistan and the northwest coast of India. In comparison to the later Roman ships, which could carry 1000 tons or even more, those from "Magan," with their twenty ton capacity were tiny, considerably smaller than the dhows which sailed between the Gulf and East Africa up to the 1950s. In contrast, the "Meluhha" ships, which, among other things, were laden with foodstuffs, teak wood, pearls, gemstones and precious metals, were larger. The archaeology of the Sultanate has favored the theme of foreign trade of historic "Magan" (called "Makkan" in the 2nd millennium BC.)

The **Hafit artifact period** (ca. 3000-2700 BC) was the oldest metal-using civilization of Oman and took its name from the sites of finds on the Jabal Hafit (United Arab Emirates, near Al Buraymi), where for the first time Mesopotamian import ceramics were excavated. Some experts even think that at the beginning of the third millennium BC there were Mesopotamian colonies in the lower area of the Arabian Gulf. It could be proven that there was copper production in central Oman at this time. Tombs are the most outstanding type of monument in Oman in this and in later periods. Apart from the typical beehive tombs, hardly any other constructions remain from the population at that time. Tombs - always severely plundered - can be found everywhere on the mountain crests and summits. Although one can see the sites from a distance, the buildings are frequently only recognisable from close up, as they are the same color as the surrounding rock. It is amazing how numerous these architectural records are as only a few burial constructions from other periods have survived the passage of time.

The succeeding **Umm-an-Nar artifact period** (Arabic: "mother of fire," ca. 2700-2000 BC) was named after the island on the coast of Abu Dhabi (United Arab Emirates), where large collective tombs, typical of this civilization, were first investigated. The period roughly coincides with the heyday of "Magan." On account of the carefully worked cladding of these charnel houses they are the most beautiful constructions of the whole of Oman's prehistory. In contrast to the beehive tombs they could hold well over a hundred bodies. Investigations of the skeletons revealed similarities among the people buried together, that is to say they were actually relatives. In addition numerous small stone bowls with circular drilled ornamentation and attractive wheel-turned ceramics were found. Unfortunately only very few metal artifacts, which belonged to the original grave goods, remain. The custom of collective burial lasted until the middle of the succeeding **Wadi-Suq artifact period** (ca. 2000-1200 BC) in the north of the Sultanate. At this time single graves are found in central Oman. Not only are ceramic and stone vessels from this period known to us, but also a number of swords and other weapons. About 1700 BC trade between "Sumer," "Dilmun," "Magan," and "Meluhha" was interrupted by political circumstances. The beginning of the **Lizq/Rumaylah artifact period** (13th century BC) marks the end of the Bronze Age and the beginning of the Iron Age in Oman. From 1200 BC there must have been new conceptions of the next world, as we know from the "hut tombs" which now appear and other finds typical of this time. We have just a few chance remains from which to determine and characterize this epoch. The most important evidence can be seen in fortifications such as those in Lizq, a local fortified refuge, to which the populace could retreat for a certain time during attacks. Shortly before the birth of Christ the Azd tribes from Yemen came to Oman, led by their legendary chief Malik ibn Fahim Al-Azd. In the country's traditional history they are considered to have been "Omanis." These tribes, however, did not leave Yemen at a specific point in time; rather, there was a migration of peoples lasting some centuries. The Azd are known to us through their graves and grave goods, especially at Samad Ash Shan.

The work of the German Archaeological Expedition to the Sultanate of Oman uncovered the **Samad artifact period** (ca. 3rd century BC - 5th century AD) at the place of the same name. This civilization was confirmed by the finds of iron objects and hand made pottery in the graves.

As a result of the excavations carried out during the 1980s more is known about this pre-Islamic period than about all others. We know, for example, that luxury articles such as silk, precious metal, pearls and iron weapons were imported to central Oman perhaps from South Asia (even Ceylon.) The population consisted of farmers who lived from cultivating dates and keeping small animals. There was no standing army. Tribesmen often were equipped with a short and a long dagger as well as a bow and arrow. Boys were given first a single arrow with which to play. There was also a social hierarchy and one can establish proof of a scale of wealth and, accordingly, status. The religion of these people was probably based on holy stones, spirits such as the Jinn, as well as ancestor cults.

In the wadis rows of three stones leaning against each other, so-called triliths, stem from this period. However, the largest and best preserved stone rows in Oman are to be found in the southern province of Dhofar. They sometimes reach 20 meters in length and could occur even longer.

The names of some pre-Islamic gods have been handed down: Yaghut, Naghr and Jurnan. Worshipping the stars was widespread and right up until today black magic has remained a "lesser religion" in parallel to the official religion. Circumcision of girls and boys was universally practiced in late pre-Islamic times. Although we know these details our knowledge about the religion of this era is limited. At the end of the 4th century Oman had its first bishop and numerous Christians lived here prior to the Islamization of the country. At every oasis on the peninsula of Oman there are watchtowers of stone and clay, which are on occasions up to 8 meters high. Their entrances can only be reached with a ladder. In recent years buildings of this ancient type have been built or rather renewed. The population then consisted mostly of settled farmers who had very uneasy economic relations with the nomadic Bedouin herdsmen. The towers served the local farmers as "early warning systems" against mounted Bedouin making raids, who could attack quickly with their camels or horses.

The Arabic term for these buildings is *burj* (singular, plural *abraj*), which recalls the Greco-Roman word *burgus* (defensive tower.) These towers possibly superseded the fortresses of the early Iron Age Lizq period. The explanation of why fortresses should be replaced by watchtowers lies in the growth of the population. The number of settled farmers increased, which made an effective defence possible. Instead of retreating to the fortresses, the meanwhile numerically superior farmers with improved weaponry could simply shoot masses of arrows at invaders.

Constructions that are especially typical in the Omani countryside are the underground water channels which, similar to Roman aquaducts, exploit a gradient to lead water from a spring to a distant settlement or oasis. In Arabic this is called a *falaj* or a *qanat*. Because over the centuries the water table sank, the bed of the *falaj* had to be laid ever deeper. The water could still flow along the channel to the settlement and its gardens but then either the water had to be raised or the settlement and gardens moved to a lower place if the water was to once more emerge by force of gravity. An instance of this is the site of the historic settlements Maysar-42 and Maysar-43 as well as today's village of al Moyassar. They are connected in a north-south direction by the same underwater channel. The current *falaj* results from laying the prehistoric canals deeper. So in the course of time the settlements moved from north to south to the current location of Al Moyassar. The water extraction system, without which Al Moyassar-42 could not have existed, is as old as the settlement itself. It goes back to the first millennium BC.

How old are the *aflaj* and what are their origins? Mentions of them in new Assyrian cuneiform texts testify to the early origins of the *aflaj* in Anatolia and Assyria at the beginning of the first millennium BC. When the Parthians conquered Persia (from 250 BC) the underground water channels there were possibly already widespread.

A reconstruction of the arrangement of columns in the Grand Mosque, in the archaeological park Al Balid, in Salalah.

In comparison to Oman they are of markedly larger dimensions and attain lengths of up to 20 kilometers and depths of up to 300 meters. Persia was probably a promoter of this technology but not its inventor. The historical roots of the technical development lie hidden in the darkness of mythological traditions. In Oman a large *falaj* is also called a *daudi* (David's channel) after the biblical Suleiman ibn Daud (Solomon, son of David), its mythical creator. Suleiman plays an outstanding role in Arabic legend. If the figure of the story is combined with the historical King Solomon of Israel, then theoretically the 10th century BC would be the beginning of this tradition of construction. The fairytale origin of the 10,000 *aflaj* built by Suleiman ibn Daud in the national chronicle (the Kashf al-Gumma) is in any case not credible. Many canals were supposed to have been destroyed by the Persian governor after losing a battle against the Omanis. When David of Israel died Suleiman/Solomon was chosen as successor from among the various sons, according to the legend. He was equipped with wonderful talents and God had lent him secret knowledge. The traditional story lays particular stress on his supernatural abilities in magic and his prophetic sayings. Legions of demons (shaytan) were at his service, ready to fulfill all his wishes, for example to dive for pearls. The *jinn* were forced to bow to his will, for if they refused obedience they were threatened with the tortures of hell. They made shrines, statues and costly vessels for Suleiman and heaped untold wealth upon him. They helped him build palaces, forts, baths and irrigation systems. The ruler ended up having 1000 glass-ceilinged houses with 300 rest camps and 700 wives. Even if the Suleiman tales actually take the historical King Solomon of Israel as their example, this does not mean that there is a historic kernel to the numerous tales about him. As regards the creation of the *aflaj*, it can be assumed with high probability that in the course of their development projects the Persians extended them throughout the Near East.

Such plans included, for example, the re-opening of the canal between the Nile and the Red Sea in the 6th century BC under Darius the Great. The revenues of the Persian empire were to be increased by the development of an efficient infrastructure. According to the results of the excavations the *aflaj* in Oman were first laid on a large scale under the Sasanians. Until the early 7th century Oman was under Persian rule.

Although the Persians called the country "Mazun," it was probably called "Oman" among the Arabic speakers. The term "Ommana" was first minted relatively late in the history of the region - shortly after the birth of Christ. The first mention of the name of "Oman" is known to us in an alleged letter from the Prophet Mohammed to the Sasanian governor of Oman, when the description had already existed for some hundreds of years. The Prophet posed the question to the Persians whether they wished to convert to Islam. He made the following conditions: they could keep their property with the exception of the treasure of the fire temple (the Persians were followers of the Zoroastrian fire cult), and they must pay a poll tax. The independence struggles of the Arab tribes of Oman, the new power of Islam and the attack on the Persian empire by the Byzantines eventually sealed the end of Sasanian rule in Oman. That in 631, the Prophet's envoy, Abu Zaid al Ansari ibn Al-Asi al Sahmi, came to Sohar Fort of all places, was not chance. The town was the seat of the Persian governor in Oman. But this event does not yet end the history of pre-Islamic central Oman, for even afterwards large numbers of inhabitants remained true to their old beliefs. They were Christians and Jews, Zoroastrians (followers of the Persian prophet Zarathustra and his fire cult) or other "heathens." After the death of Mohammed many of the "converted" reverted from Islam, the cause of several wars against the central Islamic power in Mesopotamia. Only in the course of the 9th and 10th centuries did Islam become established as the religion of Oman's towns.

The remains of thousands of beehive tombs can be found scattered around the entire Hajar Mountain range.

Important Archaeological Sites in Oman

Whoever proceeds with a rented car into remote regions should consider that the desert with all its unpredictability begins directly at the road's side. This (and special clauses in the rental contract, see Information section Cars) should make you think before you continue on the tracks away from the asphalt road. The conditions of the tracks and long-distance routes are constantly being changed by mudslides, new development, or simply the increased usage of certain routes. The tracks drawn on common maps often feign a clarity which cannot always be understood on the ground. The most up to date maps possible and a compass make orientation easier. Whoever rents a four-wheel drive vehicle should ensure that the four-wheel drive actually functions and that there are spare tires and the correct rim is fitted. A day with trips in the Capital Area will show whether (especially with older cars) the vehicle is reliable enough for demanding off-road trips. Filled spare cans, stores of drinking water and a strong rope, or rather a winch, should ensure additional safety, especially on wadi expeditions. Most of the expeditions presented here can safely be made with a four wheel drive vehicle.

Bat: Prehistoric Megalithic Ruins and Coleman's Rock

How to get there:
If one leaves the Capital Area early under normal weather conditions one can drive to Bat and back in a day. From Ruwi the route follows the highway west to As Seeb where one follows the signs to Nizwa from the underpass. Past Rusayl and Bidbid the road leads to Bahla with its fort (208 kilometers from the capital.) Turn right at the sign for "Amlah." After Amlah (90 kilometers from Bahla) turn left at the road sign for "Bat" (a further 36 kilometers from the main road.)
To get to Coleman's Rock (145 kilometers from the capital) from Nizwa you take the exit from the main road to the North - turn right at the road sign "al Hamra." Drive about 12 kilometers to the sign "Bilad al Seid" (still before Al Hamra.) 50 meters after the sign, to the right a track leads into a wadi. 1200 meters from the road there is an 8 meter high rock with the relief drawings.

The Coleman's Rock.

Description of the sites:

Perhaps the most interesting archaeological site in the Sultanate, Bat is on UNESCO's World Heritage List. In Bat Danish and German archaeologists investigated settlement remains and tombs. Bat is in the northern hinterland not far from Ibri. The most important sights here are the beehive tombs from the Hafit period and the collective tombs of the Umm-an-Nar Period in the 3rd millennium BC. In most cases the beautiful exterior stone cladding of these large structures have been removed as a building material.

Near the tombs the massive remains of several defensive towers are still to be seen, which are made of stones measuring up to a cubic meter. There was probably a further construction made of clay bricks built on this stone base, as one knows from the centuries-later, similarly built, fortified towers of Ar Rustaq (5th-18th century) and Nizwa (17th century.) In the 3rd millennium BC Bat was a settlement center as there was good arable land here and adequate water, and because of its proximity to the road to the coast. During the course of centuries copper was mined and smelted. In the 2nd millennium BC the inhabitants abandoned their settlement in Bat for reasons unknown.

On your way to Bat from the Capital Area, you can detour to **Coleman's Rock** at al Hamra, with Oman's most outstanding rock relief, named after its western discoverer. A life-size adult man and to his left a woman and to his right a child are depicted there. Left of this group a second man can be recognized. The dating of the relief drawings is uncertain, as there is nothing with which to compare. The figures probably did not appear at a single point in time but within a probably prehistoric period.

Samad Ash Shan/Al Moyassar, Lizq and Al Khashbah

How to get there: Being close to one another these two fascinating sites can be visited from the capital within a day. From Ruwi the route follows the highway west to As Seeb where one follows the signs to Nizwa from the underpass. One kilometer after Bidbid turn left on the road to Sur and Ibra. After altogether 127 kilometers, at a Shell petrol station follow the fork to the right which is signposted "Samad al Shan." Drive past the turnoff to "Shariah" to the next village (Al Mamurah) which is not signposted. Directly at Al Mamurah turn right. Drive through the small village westwards in the direction of Al Moyassar. 800 meters after leaving the expressway, on the left hand side of the track you can see numerous heaps of rubble from the excavation work. Here were the most substantial tombs of the people of the Samad period. You drive a further two kilometers westwards through the village of Al Moyassar and a few kilometers south of the new village you reach Mayar-1, a copper producing village of the Umm-an-Nar Period. Because there are several tracks which change their courses from year to year it is not possible to give a more exact description of how to get there. There are more sites one kilometer north of today's Al Moyassar. Afterwards return to the asphalt expressway. At the same point where you turned off here, turn right (south) in order to get to the large **Iron Age fort of Lizq**. After 8.3 kilometers turn left at the road sign "Lizq" and head east. You drive along a track through the village. Two kilometers southeast (i.e. to the right) you pass gardens. The fort is recognizable by a monumental set of stone steps that lead up the slope. You can climb up them if you have a good head for heights. Afterwards return to the expressway.

Al Khashbah (also known locally as "Lakshebah") is situated further to the south. Drive back to the expressway and then go left until you reach the sign "Khashebah," which is some six kilometers from the exit signposted "Lizq." Follow the track to the right. When, after about twelve kilometers, you come to the village, bear gently right. 400 meters further on you reach the remains of a ruined tower, 30 meters in diameter, of the Umm-an-Nar Period. In the area there are more monumental constructions of this period.

Description of the sites: Extensive burial grounds of an early necropolis are located at **Samad Ash Shan** to the east and south of the oasis area. They indicate several phases of civilization from the 2nd and 1st millennia BC as well as the first millennium after Christ. No Muslim graves can be found in the largest burial area. They are easily recognizable by their long shape and vertical stones: two for a man and three for a woman. The largest graves are probably from an ethnic group who came to central Oman around 300 BC at the earliest. Their civilization developed conservatively over hundreds of years, that is to say very slowly and without any great radical changes. Burial grounds of the same type are also known on the coast. The people of the Samad civilization are the immediate predecessors of today's Omanis. In the late 5th century the Samad tribes disappear from view. In the year 893 AD an Abassid governor in Bahrain undertook a campaign against the rebellious Omani tribes. Mohammed ibn Nur stormed through central Oman and destroyed – as part of his military tactic – the irrigation systems, among other things. The campaign ended at Samad Ash Shan in a catastrophic defeat for the local tribes. A few hundred meters west of the Samad oasis the dead of this devastating battle are apparently buried in an Islamic cemetery. Even now Omanis speak of the destructive fury of "al Bur." This name is pronounced harshly, and is a play on "al Nur," the name of the governor and means in a metaphorical sense "Unland," "land that can no longer be used." The prehistoric copper-producing **Maysar-1**, about one kilometer south of today's al Moyassar, is the only extensively excavated settlement of the Umm-an-Nar civilization in the Sultanate. These ruins have been dated to the period about 2000 years BC when Oman carried out a lively trade in copper. Several buildings which were connected to copper extraction and working have been investigated. In the immediate vicinity, adjoining to the east, there is an abandoned copper mine. In the course of his excavation work, Professor Gerd Weisgerber emptied and reinforced the well, which still functions and fills with water each year. Parts of broken smelting furnaces and copper slag are scattered around. It is difficult to imagine how the copper ingots could have been transported the 150 kilometers to the coast. Donkeys were probably used as pack animals. The copper extracted from the ore was purified of unwanted residues by roasting and then exported to Mesopotamia. As we know from cuneiform writings, ships transported the copper first to "Dilmun" and then further into Mesopotamia. There the metal was traded for wool and foodstuffs. 1100 meters southwest of Maysar-1 you can see a fortified tower (**Maysar-25**) on the edge of a rock, which also comes from the Umm-an-Nar Period. A few years ago the bottom layer of stones was still intact. Within the tower there was a well and the remains of two beehive tombs from the previous Hafit period. Less than a hundred meters northeast of the site a prehistoric dam, now severely eroded, can be recognized. 300 meters northwest of this little fort are the ruins of two charnel houses of the Um an-Nar Period (Maysar-4.) Now drive back to the northern end of the modern settlement. From here you follow the track one kilometer to the north to the *falaj* funnels at the foot of a great mountain. On the slopes there are **remains of tombs and a settlement** which have partially been uncovered by the Archaeological Expedition to Oman: Maysar-42 is a village of the Lizq period by Oman's oldest known *falaj* (latest 1st millennium BC, dated by physical methods.) By the *falaj* there are some small mounds, house tells of the Samad period (Maysar-43.) West of the *falaj*, at the foot of the slope, the remains of several tombs were discovered (Maysar-8 and -27.) Back on the expressway you soon reach **Lizq Fort**, undoubtedly one of the most impressive monuments in Oman. Similar early Iron Age sites are known but none are in such good condition as this one. It stands 80 meters above the surrounding savannah. A lower and upper defensive work as well as a fixed staircase have partly survived through the ages. 79 steps were restored by the German Archaeological Expedition to Oman. They are made of stone and simply set in clay. There are indications that the fort, built between 1200 and 300 BC, was besieged and that the defenders had barred the staircase to the well.

The last part of this tour is to the structural remains of at least four monumental buildings of the Umm-an-Nar Period near the settlement of **Al Khashbah**. Two of them have suffered so much from stone theft that their original appearance remains unclear. Best preserved is the third building, which describes a rectangle with a maximum side length of 28 meters. The body of the building was probably made of transient, perishable material such as clay bricks. The building's function is unknown. Perhaps it is a cult building. Its age (about 2700-2000 BC) could be determined with the help of the vessel shards found lying inside and the megalithic way of building.

The beehive tombs near the oasis Al Ayn, en route vom Amlah to Bat, are among the best-preserved of Oman.

Ras Al Jinz: Trading Post and Nature Reserve

How to get there:
The burial grounds are situated on the site of a nature reserve for sea turtles. To gain entrance you best book in advance with an overnight at the Ras Al Jinz Scientific and Research Center in combination with a guided visit to the turtle site. From Muscat follow the route to Al Jaylah and then continue along the road via Ibra, Al Kamil Wa Al Wafi, Jaalan Bani Bu Hasan and Asilah to the coast, and from there take the new asphalt road north until Ras Al Jinz.

Description of the sites:
At the end of the 3rd and beginning of the 2nd millennium BC, Ras Al Jinz (Ras al Junayz) was a trading station between the eastern region of Oman and "Meluhha," modern-day Pakistan, Gujarat and northeast Maharashtra. Here the "black ships" arrived from south Asia, the sterns of which were sealed with bitumen.
An Italian-French excavation team was active in Ras Al Jinz in recent years and a British team in nearby Ras Al Had. Finds from the 3rd millennium up until the Islamic era have been uncovered here. Because of weathering, the clay architecture is not well preserved and has partly been reburied with earth by the excavators.

Al Jaylah: Tower Tombs of the Umm-an-Nar Period

How to get there:

The drive to Shir to the tower tombs is long and only possible with a four-wheel drive vehicle. Only if you leave the capital early in the morning can you visit this magnificent site in a day. Spending a night in the mountains is exciting, but at a height of 1800 meters it can be extremely chilly.

First follow the description of how to get to Samad Ash Shan. Drive past the sign "Samad Ash Shan" and continue in the direction of Ibra. Before you proceed into the desert fill up with petrol at the al Nasirfa Shell station. Turn left one kilometer further on at the sign "Esmaiyah 64 km" (170 kilometers out from Muscat.) Traveling from Al Kamil Wa Al Wafi, the turn-off is marked "Naam."

Follow the paved road 61 km until you see a small hospital on the right, in the village of Mantiqat al Bedu, shortly before Esmaiyah. Directly in front of this building a dirt road to the right leads into the wadi. The road in the wadi is poor: if it is raining do NOT drive into the wadi; you should hasten to turn around and go back! The road forks 13 km into the wadi; keep to the left. At 15 km from the paved road you will come to a sign "Al Gailah 3 km." Turn right. 2 km further on you will pass a sign in Arabic and then after another 3 km you will reach the first plateau, with a small blue mosque, two small concrete houses and a watertank. Take the steep dirt road to left, going up the mountain to the high plateau. Attention: attempt this only in a 4-wheel drive vehicle using the first gear! After another six kilometers you reach the first towers. (From Ibra to the towers a Nissan Patrol, for example, uses about a third of a tank with careful driving. From the village of Mantiqat al Bedu in the wadi it takes more than one and a half hours for the 26 kilometer climb. The return journey to the village takes more than an hour.)

At 1800 meters, the tower tombs of Al Jaylah in the Eastern Hajar Mountains are very remote.

These tower tombs have only survived the millennia on account of their isolated situation. Please do not climb around on them!

Description of the sites:

About 60 stone towers stand on a mountain crest some 1800 meters up. The largest are up to 8 meters high. The upper stones are missing from all of the buildings. They were probably removed by Muslim believers who saw the towers as monuments of a heathen religion and so partially demolished them. These towers combine the characteristics of the rustic beehive tombs of the Hafit period

with the charnel houses of the Umm-an-Nar Period, which were clad with smooth stonework. These probably arose in the first quarter of the 3rd millennium BC. They have neither steps nor embrasures and are isolated and far from all sources of water. They are without doubt tombs.

Among the first group of tomb buildings (6 kilometers from the edge of the plateau), two almost completely preserved towers rise up on either side of the track. The one on the right hand side as you are driving was partially restored by the German Archaeological Expedition to Oman. To the right of it is a ruined older tower. Five meters from the two of them a fifty centimeter high platform can be made out. It is made up of stones which the archaeologists took from inside the immediately adjoining tomb and its surrounding area. It enables you to draw conclusions about the original height of the tower tomb. The platform is also intended as somewhere to sit.

Local inhabitants tell legends of the origin of the tower tombs: there was once a goatherd in the mountains looking for his animals. In a distant valley he spotted a waterfall and a small pond. He took a drink and fell asleep. When he awoke again a beautiful genie (jinn) was swimming in the water. Surprised while bathing, she was at first angry but because she believed in God and the goatherd reminded her of her son, she did not kill him which she would otherwise have done. Instead she let him in on a secret which should be of help to him: the way to the towers.

In one of them lived a demon (*shaytan*) called Kebir beb. If his eyes were open then he was asleep, if they were closed then he was awake. His long knife was a thunderbolt, sharp enough to cut stones for all the towers. The knife hung in the tower where he slept. Our hero crept in and made sure that the fiend's eyes were open. He secretly took the knife but as he was leaving the room he accidentally awoke the demon. Fortunately the demon was unable to cross water and so did not pursue the man over a stream. So the spirit lost the secret of his weapon. Later the goatherd returned and killed the demon with the knife. The tomb of Kebir keb is said to have been alone and isolated in a tower not far from Ibra. Others say that Kebir keb was a *jahil* (heathen), who killed people.

The not very spectacular remains of the walls of Ash Shasir, which was recently celebrated as the site of Ubar.

Ash Shasir: Oasis from the 1001 Nights?

How to get there:
Inexpensive flights are available from the capital to Salalah. It is usual to approach Ash Shasir from there (about 140 km.) The way is signposted. Take the expressway 31 from Salalah to the north in the direction of Thumrayt. About 12 kilometers after Thumrayt there is branch to the left. After another 22 kilometers you now turn right in the direction of Ash Shasir.

Description of the sites:
The lonely little settlement at the well of Ash Shasir in the Rub al Khali, the "Empty Quarter," has been described by various travelers in the early 20th century. In recent years filmmakers have run an advertising campaign and claimed that Ash Shasir is the legendary town of Iram from the Koran, or rather Ubar from the Thousand and One Nights. According to this Allah destroyed a rich fortified metropolis which was inhabited by wicked people. Up until now no serious publication about the excavation has been published. The equating of Iram/Ubar with this small watering place is in any case pure wishful thinking.

Khawr Ruri/Samharam: Hadramaut Frankincense Trading Place

How to get there:
Drive from Salalah to the east in the direction of Taqah (about 30 km.) Some 3.5 kilometers after Taqah a road branches off to the right to the ruined town. Since the enclosed site was entered into UNESCO's World Heritage List, there is a small custodian's hut at the entrance were you can buy a ticket and get a map of the site.

Description of the sites:
The well-known, fortified settlement of Khawr Ruri near Salalah was known to its builders in the 1st and 2nd centuries AD as "Samhar" and to the Greeks as "Sachalitis," or rather "Moscha." It was first partly uncovered by an American expedition in 1950. From an inscription found there we know that King Ilad Yalut of Hadramaut appeared to be the founder. This isolated colony was an important collection point for frankincense and myrrh, which was sent on to Yemen and then on to the north over the Red Sea. Today a sandbank bars the entrance to the harbor which was fortified on both sides. The remains of these sites on the rocks are clearly visible. In classical times the harbor offered protection for merchant ships, which sailed along the coast of the "erythraean sea" (Red Sea.) Throughout the land the site is held to have been the palace of the king of Saba (Sheba), although there is no connection with this famous ruler of Yemen, who lived a good 1000 years earlier. In the area around the fortified settlement there are also numerous Islamic graves of fishermen.

Al Balid: A Medieval Arabic Jewel on the Coast of the Southern Province Dhofar.

How to get there:
The ruins of the fortified city Al Balid (lit. "the hamlet") is located along Salalah's coastline, 3 km west of the Crowne Plaza Resort.

Description of the historical sites:
Since the middle of the 19th century this exotic trading center has fascinated researchers. In 1997 preparations began for tourism to these ruins stretched along more than 2 km of coastline. The city was continuously inhabited from the 7th and 8th centuries until 1600. Its wealth was based on the trading of luxury goods between East Africa, the Red Sea, India and China. Since there was no proper

harbor, ships were loaded and unloaded using small boats. The city was known as Zafar, which lent its name to present-day Dhofar. The area is criss-crossed with paved roads, which were illuminated at night. Remnants of houses and mosques are easily discernible, with the grand mosque and the palace making the greatest impressions. The site was thoroughly studied by American, German, Italian and Omani colleagues. Presently a joint American-Omani excavation team is at work in Al Balid.
The archaeological park and the integrated Museum of the Frankincense Land are open to public Saturday to Thursday from 08:00 to 14:00 and 16:00 to 20:00, on Friday 16:00 to 20:00 only.
Electric carts with driver are available on request for a small additional fee.

Dr Paul Yule earned his doctorate at the Institute of Fine Arts, New York University, and in 1990 he became professor at the University of Heidelberg's Faculty for Oriental Studies and Antiquities. He led excavations in the Sultanate of Oman at Amlah, Al Balid, al Bustan, Samad Ash Shan and Al Jaylah, and currently is working in the ancient city of Zafar/Yemen, and in Orissa/India. His professional specialties include the following topics: metallurgy; Iron Age and Early Arabia; Bronze Age tower tombs; and the care and preservation of ancient monuments. His "Gazetteer of Archaeological Sites" is a primary source of information for sites of discovery in the Sultanate of Oman, and is being expanded to comprise the entire Persian/Arabian Gulf.
He is a special correspondent and member of the German Archaeological Institute. Yule holds a professorship at the University of Heidelberg, Seminar for Languages and Culture of the Middle East. Email: paul.yule@t-online.de

P. Yule/G. Weisgerber, The Tower Tombs at Shir, Eastern Hajar, Sultanate of Oman, *Beiträge zur allgemeinen und vergleichenden Archäologie (BAVA)* 18, 1998, 183-241, ISBN 3-8053-2518-5 (Digital version: http://archiv.ub.uni-heidelberg.de/propylaeumdok/volltext/2009/291/)

P. Yule, *Die Gräberfelder in Samad Ash Shan (Sultanat Oman) Materialien zu einer Kulturgeschichte*, Deutsches Archäologisches Institut, Orient-Abteilung, Orient-Archäologie vol. 4 (Rahden 2001), ISBN 3-89646-634-8

P. Yule/G. Weisgerber, *The Metal Hoard from Ibri/Selme*, Sultanate of Oman. Präh. Bronzefunde XX.7 (Stuttgart 2001), ISBN 3-515-07153-9

P. Yule, *Himyar - Die Spätantike im Jemen/Late Antique Yemen*. (Aichwald 2007) ISBN 978-3-929290-35-6

Ancient south-Arabian inscription from the settlement Khawr Ruri, also known as Samharam.

The Green Pages

Travel Information from A to Z

Oman is a country with many different cultural influences. This is reflected in the various ways in which Arabic names are transcribed. Sometimes even members of the same family write their names differently, according to the country in which they have studied or whichever system is most familiar to them. When taken to task by a proof reader for inconsistencies of spelling of names of both places and people in his manuscript for *Revolt In The Desert*, T. E. Lawrence refused to make any changes, replying: "Arabic names won't go into English, exactly, for their consonants are not the same as ours, and their vowels, like ours, vary from district to district." This book aims to maintain consistency. Most place names in Oman have anglicized transcriptions assigned by the National Survey Authority of the Sultanate of Oman but much travel literature in English does not follow these conventions. For instance, most Anglophones will be more familiar with the "Wahibah Sands" than with the "Wihibah Sands."

Addresses

See also **Telephone**
A problem for strangers that should not be underestimated is how to locate an address. Apart from the largest thoroughfares almost none of the roads shown on the town maps carry names. Street names and numbers are only of meaning for the administration and the surveyor's office. Postal addresses are almost always written without a street name, consisting of just a name, P.O. Box, postal code and town. However the P.O. Boxes of most Omanis (and companies) are not located where they live or work but at the most convenient post office on their way to work.
The easiest way to locate an unknown address is to ring in advance and have the way described to you. To get a general orientation the various roundabouts can be used. These are either named after the local topography (e.g. Ruwi roundabout) or after the direction of the turnoff (e.g. University roundabout.) More precise bearings can be gotten using reference points such as prominent buildings, hotels, mosques, or with the aid of advertising billboards.

Accommodation

As there are only a few hotels in the country's interior, they are used as bases for business people and tour groups and it is necessary to make reservations in advance. Hotel bookings for unmarried couples do not present a problem. In Oman breakfast is not normally included in the hotel price. Please note that an **additional tax of 17 percent** will be added to the quoted price. The quoted prices are a guideline and will vary according to season and the standard of the room. The following list is simply a selection of what is on offer. Detailed **information** about traveling to Oman can be found on the website of this book's author: **www.oman-tours.com**.

Hotels in North Oman

Musandam

Golden Tulip Resort Khasab ****
P.O.Box 434 Khasab P.C. 811
Tel. 26730777, Fax 26730888;
Single: 80 *OMR*, Double: 90 *OMR*
sales@goldentulipkhasab.com
Luxury hotel, beautifully situated on a bay near Khasab.

Khasab Hotel ***
P.O.Box 111 Khasab P.C. 811
Tel. 26730267, Fax 26730989;
Single: 21 *OMR*, Double: 34 *OMR*
khoman@dolphintourism.net
For the most part a newly built hotel, with swimming pool, near the airport.

Golden Tulip Resort Dibba ****
P.O. Box 272 Daba P.C. 800
Tel. 26836654, Fax 26836653
Single: 60 *OMR*, Double: 70 *OMR*
info@goldentulipdibba.com
A superior category hotel, well-situated on the sand beach of Daba.

Six Senses Hideaway Zighy Bay ******
P.O. Box 112499 Al Karama, Dubai
Tel. 26735555, Fax 26735556;
Poolvilla from 260 *OMR*
reservations-zighy@sixsenses.com
This top luxury hotel, located on a private bay near Daba, consists of individual villas built of stone, each with a pool and at least 247 m² of floorspace.

Al Buraymi

Buraymi Hotel ***
P.O.Box 330 Al Buraymi P.C. 512
Tel. 25652010, Fax 25652011;
buraimi@alburaimi.com
Single: 38 *OMR*, Double: 47 *OMR*
The hotel situated on the road to Sohar is a popular stopover for Omanis on their way to the Emirates.

Sohar

Sohar Beach Hotel ****
P.O.Box 122 Al Tareef P.C. 321
Tel. 26843701, Fax 26843766,
Single: 42 *OMR*, Double: 55 *OMR*
soharhtl@omantel.net.om
Situated right by the sea, this is a miniature version of Sohar Fort in the north of the town with large rooms and its own swimming pool.

Al Wadi Hotel***
P.O.Box 459 Sohar P.C. 311
Tel. 26840058, Fax 26841997;
reservationsalwadi@omanhotels.com
Single: 23 *OMR*, Double: 31 *OMR*
Built along the road to Dubai at the Sallan roundabout this hotel has its own swimming pool.

Barka

Al Sawadi Beach Resort ****
P.O. Box 747, Barka P.C. 320
Tel. 26795545, Fax: 26795535
Single/Double from 80 *OMR*
Supplement for sea view 4 *OMR*
sales@alsawadibeach.com
Ideal base for exploring the region. Excellent opportunities for water sports. Snorkel and diving tours to the Dayminat islands are especially to be recommended.

Al Nahda Resort & Spa*****
P.O. Box 502 Barka P.C. 320
Tel. 26883710, Fax 26883175
Single/Double from 90 *OMR*
stay@alnahdaresort.com
This lovely spa hotel complex has bungalows and duplexes placed throughout the extensive mango plantation, on the road to Nakhl, not far from Barka. The rooms are spacious and tastefully decorated with natural materials.

Muscat Capital Area

The most reasonably priced recommended overnight accommodations in the capital region can be found in the Mina hotel, the Corniche hotel and the Naseem hotel, all along the Corniche in Mutrah. The rooms all have TV, refrigerator, telephone, air-conditioning and at least a shower and WC.

Muscat / Mutrah

Corniche Hotel
P.O. Box 1800, Mutrah P.C. 114
Tel. 24714707, Fax: 24714770
Single: 9 *OMR*, Double: 14 *OMR*
Clean simple hotel directly by the bus station and the fish market.

Mina Hotel
P.O. Box 504, Ruwi P.C. 112
Tel. 24711828, Fax: 24714981
Single: 12 *OMR*, Double 15 *OMR*
Simple hotel, also directly by the bus station and fish market.

Naseem Hotel
P.O. Box 360, Jabroo P.C. 114
Tel. 24712418, Fax: 24712419
Single: 11 *OMR*, Double: 15 *OMR*
Relatively newly renovated rooms and baths. On the Corniche near the suq.

Muscat / Al Bustan

Al Bustan Palace Hotel *****
P.O.Box 1998 Matrah P.C. 114
Tel. 24799666, Fax 24799600;
Single/Double from 140 *OMR*
albustan@interconti.com
This fairytale luxury hotel, built in a lonely bay cut off by dark cliffs, is known in trade circles as one of the most beautiful in the world. It was completely redesigned in 2007/2008.

Muscat / Barr al Jissah

Shangri-La's Barr al Jissah Resort & Spa
This relativly new complex of three luxurious hotels stretches along a marvellous coast some 10 kilometers south of Al Bustan. They can be booked centrally.
Tel. 24776666, Fax 24776677
slmu@shangri-la.com

Al Husn Hotel ******
An exclusive retreat perched on an elevated plateau above the Resort with its own private beach and commanding views of the ocean and surrounding landscape.
Single/Double: from 190 *OMR*

Al Bander Hotel *****
Situated along the main 450 meter beach, the five-star deluxe Al Bander Hotel is the heart of the Resort, with 9 of the 19 food and beverage outlets located here as well as the Grand Ballroom.
Double: from 130 *OMR*

Al Waha Hotel *****
At the eastern edge of the resort separated from the Al Bander and Al Husn Hotels by a steep narrow mountain, Al Waha Hotel is enhanced by an atmosphere of fun and entertainment uniquely designed to cater for families and the younger generation.
Double: from 80 *OMR*

Muscat / Al Khuwayr

Radisson SAS *****
P.O. Box 939 Al Khuwair P.C. 113
Tel. 24487777, Fax 24487778
Single: 110 OMR, Double: 120 OMR
muscat.sales@radissonsas.com
The hotel is alongside the highway and has a shuttle bus to its own beautiful beach club in Al Qurm.

Ibis Hotel
P.O. Box 1512 Al Khuwair P.C. 130
Tel. 24489890. Fax 24487970
Single: 32 OMR, Double 32 OMR
www.ibishotel.com
This newly opened (Oct 2009) hotel of

the renowned Ibis chain has standardized rooms (twin or double bed) throughout its system. With its low prices and adjoining rooms quite comfortable for families. Breakfast not included.

Muscat Holiday Hotel ****
P.O.Box 185 As Seeb P.C. 111
Tel. 24687123, Fax 24680986,
Single: 49 *OMR*, Double: 69 *OMR*
mcthinn@omantel.net.om
The hotel is situated in the middle of the ministerial and administrative quarter of al Khuwayr. The rooms are very spacious. Recommendable for families.

Muscat / Al Ghubbrah

The Chedi Muscat *****
P.O.Box 964 Al Khuwayr P.C. 113
Tel. 24524400, Fax 24504486
Single/Double from 160 *OMR*
chedimuscat@ghmhotels.com
This bungalow style hotel with its meditative asiatic character is situated on the beach at Al Ghubbrah and has two beautiful pools.

Midan Hotel Suites ****
P.O. Box 1359 Muscat P.C. 130
Tel. 24499565, Fax 24499575
Studio: 80 *OMR*
Suite with 1 bedroom: 90 *OMR*
Suite with 2 bedrooms: 130 *OMR*
enquiries@midanoman.com
This hotel, not far from The Chedi, offers very spacious rooms and suites, with kitchen, and is ideal for families. The colorful interior appointments were designed by a Brazilian artist.

Muscat / Al Qurm

Grand Hyatt *****
P.O. Box 951 Al Khuwayr P.C. 113
Tel. 24641234, Fax: 24605282
hyattmct@omantel.net.om
Single: 128 *OMR*, Double: 138 *OMR*
This hotel is a dream out of the Thousand and One Nights come true. You should at least pay a visit to this luxury hotel with its spacious rooms on the beach at Al Qurm, and try out its excellent Italian restaurant.

Muscat Intercontinental *****
P.O.Box 398 Mutrah P.C. 114
Tel. 24600500, Fax 24600012;
muscat@interconti.com
Single/Double from 128 *OMR*;
Centrally situated hotel with garden, large pool complex and access to Al Qurm beach.

Crowne Plaza Hotel ****
P.O.Box 1455 Ruwi P.C. 112
Tel. 24560100, Fax 24560650;
Single/Double from 85 *OMR*
sales@cpmuscat.com
Situated on a rock ledge at the Eastern end of Al Qurm Beach, a comfortable hotel with its own beach and beautiful view over the town and the bay.

Beach Hotel ***
P.O. Box 86, Muscat P.C. 134
Tel. 24696601, Fax 24699933
Single: 25 *OMR*, Double: 27 *OMR*
beachhtl@omantel.net.om
300 meters from the beach. The architecturally unusual arrangement of entrances to the rooms by way of several staircases gives it a private atmosphere, which in summer is prized by guests from the neighboring Gulf states.

Muscat / Ruwi

Oman Sheraton *****
P.O.Box 3260 Ruwi P.C. 112
Tel. 24799899, Fax 24795791;
Single/Double from 90 *OMR*
sheraton@omantel.net.om
Situated directly in the new Business District, still closed for renovation. The hotel is expected to be reopened in summer 2010.

Al-Falaj Hotel ****
P.O.Box 2031 Ruwi P.C. 112
Tel. 24702311, Fax 24795853;
Single: 45 *OMR*, Double: 55 *OMR*
Old but comfortable, middle-sized hotel on the edge of Ruwi, still central but quietly situated.

Muscat / As Seeb

Golden Tulip Seeb ****
P.O.Box 69 As Seeb Int.l Airport P.C. 111
Tel. 24510300, Fax 24510055;
Single: 55 *OMR*, Double: 70 *OMR*
sales@goldentulipseeb.com
The only hotel near the airport. Offers free airport shuttle on request.

Muscat / Bed & Breakfast

Villa Shems
P.O. Box 536 Mina al Fahl P.C. 116
Tel. 24561197, Fax. 24563697
Single: 27 *OMR*, Double: 37 *OMR*
villashams@hotmail.com
Situated in the exclusive quarter of Al Qurm Heights. The house is run by a German lady and has its own pool. About three kilometers from the sea.

Villa Luluat
Tel. 92469917
Single: 38 *OMR*, Double: 55 *OMR*
asp23@sunrise.ch
www.villaluluat.com
The villa is run by a Swiss lady and is situated in the small fisher village of Qantab south of Al Bustan not far from the sea. Few but spacious rooms in a familiar atmosphere.

Bayt al Ahlan
P.O.Box 735, Al Athaiba P.C. 130
Tel. 24494877 or 99075356
Single: 42 *OMR*, Double: 58 *OMR*
sultanatoman1@gmail.com
This private mansion, with few but spacious rooms, is 50 meters from the Beach Road, very close to The Chedi.

Central Oman and the interior

Ibra

Al Sharquiyah Sands Hotel ***
P.O. Box 585, Ibra P.C. 413
Tel. 25587099, Fax 25587088
Single: 18 *OMR*, Double: 22 *OMR*
operations@sharqiyasands.com
A small hotel with a pool. Located on the main road at the end of the town in the direction of Sur.

Ibra Motel *
P.O. Box 132, Ibra P.C. 400
Tel. 25571666, Fax 25571777
Single: 12 *OMR*, Double: 18 *OMR*
ibramtl@omantel.net.om
Simple hotel, coming from Muscat turn right by the petrol station on entering the town.

Nahar Tourism Oasis
Tel. 99387654, Fax: 99207012
Single: 17 *OMR*, Double: 22 *OMR*
emptyqtr@omantel.net.om
Signposted from the main road, an extensive camp north of Ibra with bungalows, a small pool and animal enclosure. Breakfast and evening meal are included in the price.

Wihibah Sands

Various camps have been set up by local operators with Bedouin style *barasti* huts for accommodation. An overnight stay always includes evening meal and breakfast. Price per person: between 15 and 25 *OMR*

The only camp run by a real Bedouin family is the **Nomadic Desert Camp**. It has a pleasant family atmosphere and is beautifully situated on the edge of the dunes. You will be picked up from the petrol station on the asphalt road at Al Wasil. If requested with prior notice, camel rides in the desert can be made.

Nomadic Desert Camp
P.O.Box 153 Bidiyyah P.C. 421
Tel. 99336273, Fax 25586241;

info@nomadicdesertcamp.com
Price per person 26 *OMR*

The new **Desert Nights Camp** is a one-of-a-kind blend of luxury hotel and Bedouin camp. The masonry cabins, all with air-conditioning and private bath, are sumptuously decorated in Bedouin style.

Desert Nights Camp
P.O. Box 889 Muscat P.C. 100
Tel. 24702311, Fax 24795853
reservations@desertnightscamp.com
Price per person 60 *OMR*

What a tourist might imagine as a typical desert camp corresponds to the **1000 Nights Camp**. The Bedouin tents were imported from Tunisia, however, and are not ideally suited for the Omani climate. The camp is in the desert 40 km away from Al Mintarib.

1000 Nights Camp
P.O. Box 9 Medinat Qaboos P.C. 115
Tel. 99387654, Fax 25570112
emptyqtr@omantel.net.om
Price per person 23 *OMR*

Al Qabil

Al Qabil Rest House**
P.O.Box 654 Muscat P.C. 113
Tel. 25481243, Fax 25481119;
Single: 18 *OMR*, Double: 28 *OMR*
Well placed for desert tours.

Ras Al Had / Ras Al Jinz

Ras Al Had Beach Hotel ***
P.O. Box 400 Sur P.C. 411
Tel. 99376989, Fax 99314002
Single: 27 *OMR*, Double 38 *OMR*
surbhtl@omantel.net.om
Clean hotel with large rooms and beautiful view at the end of the road between lagoon and sea.

Turtle Beach Resort
P.O. Box 303 Sur P.C. 411
Tel. 25540068, Fax 25543900
Single: 21 *OMR*, Double: 29 *OMR*
surtour@omantel.net.om
Bedouin style barasti huts situated idyllically on the sandy shores of the lagoon of Ras Al Had.

Ras Al Jinz Scientific ans Visitor Center
P.O. Box 296 Sur P.C. 411
Tel. 96550606 or 96550707
reservations@rasaljinz.org
Single: 55 *OMR*, Double: 65 *OMR*
Situated on the nature reserve for sea turtles at Ras Al Jinz. Also hosting the interactive Sea Turtle & Archaeology Museum and a restaurant. Turtle watching only possible with advance booking.

Al Ashkarah

Areen Al Ashkarah Youth Hotel ***
P.O. Box 3087 As Seeb Airport P.C. 111
Tel. 25566266, Fax 25566179
Single: 28 *OMR*, Double: 35 *OMR*
admin@ashkhara-youthhostel.com
Very attractive and spacious rooms and apartments, and not only for "youth"! This accommodation is managed by the Golden Tulip Group, and is found along the coast just a few kilometers outside of Al Ashkara, in the direction of the Wihibah desert.

Jabal Al Akhdar / Jabal Shams

Sahab Resort ****
P.O. Box: 72, Jabal Akhdar P.C. 621
Owner: Nabhan al Nabhani, personal telephone +968 92888842
Hotel telephone and prices not available on date of publication. Inquiries to info@oman-tours.com
This unique hotel is situated on the edge of a canyon with spectacular view. Ideal for trekking tours in the region.

Jabal Akhdar Hotel ***
P.O. Box: 26 Jabal Al Akhdar P.C. 621
Tel. 25429009, Fax: 25429119
Single: 32 *OMR*, Double: 44 *OMR*

jakhotel@omantel.net.om
Right on the main road at the beginning of the Sayq plateau. Mid-range hotel.

Jabal Shams Resort
P.O. Box: 1897 CPO P.C. 111
Tel. 99382639
www.jabalshams.com
Single: 60 *OMR*, Double: 60 *OMR*
The Sunset rooms offer a private sitting area with a sofa bed for an extra person. Satellite TV, dining table and separate bathroom with shower and toilet. All rooms are equipped with individually controllable air conditioner, with a heater for the winter months. Arabic tents are also available on request.

Center of Traveling & Camping in Jabal Shams, Tel. 99839898
rahb75@hotmail.com
Double: 45 *OMR* with half board
The small bungalows are situated close to the Jabal Shams canyon. Self-catering if you so wish, sharing the main kitchen or, if you give notice you can have your meals prepared for you. Ideal for trekking tours in the region.

Ibri

Ibri Oasis Hotel ***
P.O. Box 387, Ibri P.C. 516
Tel. 25691626, Fax 25692442
Single: 22 *OMR*, Double: 30 *OMR*
On the main road to Al Buraymi, some 10 kilometers from Ibri.

Jabrin

Jibreen Hotel ***
P.O. Box 733, Bahla P.C. 612
Tel. 25363340, Fax 25363128
Single: 21 *OMR*, Double: 29 *OMR*
www.jibriinhotel.com
New mid-range hotel situated between Jabrin fort and Bahla.

Nizwa

Al Diyar Hotel **
P.O. Box 1166 Nizwa P.C. 611
Tel. 25412402, Fax 25412405
Single: 25 *OMR*, Double 30 *OMR*
aldiyarhotel@hotmail.com
Simple but clean hotel on the left hand side of the road from Muscat.

Falaj Daris Hotel ****
P.O.Box 312 Nizwa P.C. 611
Tel. 25410500, Fax 25410537;
Single: 45 *OMR*, Double: 50 *OMR*
fdhnizwa@omantel.net.om
Some three kilometers south of the town center situated on the main road. Small, intimate hotel with very good restaurant and 2 pools.

Golden Tulip Nizwa Hotel ****
P.O.Box 1000 Nizwa P.C. 611
Tel. 25431616, Fax 25431619;
Single: 42 *OMR*, Double: 58 *OMR*
info@goldentulipnizwa.com
Some 20 kilometers before Nizwa near the new stadium. Luxuriously equipped hotel with swimming pool.

Sur

Sur Plaza Hotel ****
P.O. Box 908, Sur, P.C. 411
Tel. 25543777, Fax 25542626
Single: 38 *OMR*, Double: 43 *OMR*
This hotel with 108 rooms relieved the shortage of accommodation in this region, but is unfavorably situated at the beginning of the town.

Sur Beach Hotel ***
P.O. Box 400 Sur P.C. 411
Tel. 25542031/2/3, Fax 25542228
Single: 35 *OMR*, Double: 45 *OMR*
Renovated and recently expanded hotel situated at the extreme western edge of the town, right by the sea.

Sur Hotel *
P.O.Box 299 Sur P.C. 411
Tel. 25540090, Fax 25543798;

ww.surplazahotel.com
Single: 14 *OMR*, Double: 27 *OMR*
Very simple and relatively clean hotel. It is easy to recognize by its entrance: blue tiled columns supporting a huge wooden model of a dhow.

On the 800 kilometer long road from Nizwa to Salalah there are rest houses which are connected to the Arab Oryx Hotels and the Al Qabil hotel. At each resthouse there is also a petrol station, a garage and a snack shop. **Al Ghaba Rest House****, 340 kilometers from Muscat, (Tel/Fax: 25951385), **Al Ghaftain Rest House****, 640 kilometers from Muscat (Tel/Fax 25956872), **Quitbit Rest House****, 767 kilometers from Muscat and 280 kilometers from Salalah (Tel/Fax: 25951386.)

They can all be booked centrally:
P.O. Box 654, Muscat P.C.113
Tel. 99485881, Fax 24590012;
Single: 15 *OMR*, Double: 20 *OMR*

In South Oman

Salalah

Crowne Plaza Resort *****
P.O.Box 870 Salalah P.C. 211
Tel. 23235333, Fax 23235137;
Single: 38 *OMR*, Double: 45 *OMR*
reservations@cpsalalah.com
Near the center situated directly on the beach, surrounded by Salalah's plantation belt.

Hilton Salalah *****
P.O.Box 699 Salalah P.C. 211
Tel. 23211234, Fax 23210084;
Single: 40 *OMR*, Double: 48 *OMR*
sllbc@omantel.net.om
Luxury hotel situated on the beach some 10 kilometers outside the town near the container port.

Hamilton Plaza Hotel ****
P.O.Box 2498 Salalah P.C. 211
Tel. 23211025, Fax 23211187;
Single: 28 *OMR*, Double: 35 *OMR/*
Town hotel with very spacious rooms, a new pool area and a variety of sport and fitness offers, at no extra charge to hotel guests.

Arabian Sea Villas
P.O. Box 2403, Salalah P.C. 211
Tel. 23235833, 99495175
Fax 23235830
seavllas@omantel.net.om
Single: 33 *OMR*, Double: 38 *OMR*
These beachfront villas, once belonging to the adjacent Beach Villas, have been lovingly renovated and decorated. The casual atmosphere is highly recommended for everyone who prefers peace and quiet to the hustle and bustle of the big chain hotels. Local excursions in the surrounding areas can be organized on request. Price include breakfast, airport transfer, local calls and access to WLAN.

Salalah Beach Villas
P.O. Box 2772, Salalah P.C. 211
Tel/Fax 23235999
beachspa@omantel.net.om
Single: 33 *OMR*, Double: 38 *OMR*
This hotel and its duplex accommodations, with swimming pool, are located directly on the beach just a few hundred meters from the Crown Plaza Resort.

Areen Salalah Youth Hotel ***
P.O. Box 3087 As Seeb Airport P.C. 111
Tel. 23234810 Fax 23234855
Single: 28 *OMR*, Double: 35 *OMR*
admin@salalah-youthhostel.com
Very attractive and spacious rooms and apartments, and not only for "youth"! These accommodations are managed by the Golden Tulip Group. Situated on the mountain side of the city, 10 minutes drive from salalah airport and the city center.

Airports

See Entry & Exit Regulations, Getting There
Oman's international airport is at As Seeb, some 55 kilometers west of historic Muscat The approximately thirty minute taxi ride from the airport to Muscat costs between 6-20 Omani rial (OMR) according to the distance.

Airport information:
- International flights: Tel. 24519223
- Domestic flights: Tel. 24519230
- Lost luggage service: Tel. 24519504
- Visa issues: Tel. 24519289

There is an airport in the south of Oman, the Dhofar region, in **Salalah** (Tel. 23291016). Oman Air flies here from Muscat several times a day and from Dubai two to three times a week. A return flight from Muscat to Salalah costs 90 OMR. The airport at **Khasab** (Tel. 26831592) in Musandam has flights from Muscat once a day at present. (When there are problematic wind and weather conditions in Musandam it may happen that the plane is not able to land at Khasab or even take off from As Seeb.) The return flight to Musandam costs 50 OMR. Flights to Salalah and Khasab can be booked over the phone with the office of Oman Aviation in Muscat (Tel. 24519302.) The current flight schedule for Oman Air can be found in the Internet under **www.omanair.aero**

Airport tax

Airport tax is included in the price of the ticket.

Confirming your return flight

You should always telephone the airline to confirm your return flight booking at latest 72 hours before departure:
- Air France, Tel. 24704318
- British Airways, Tel. 24568777
- Emirates Air, Tel. 24786700
- Etihad Airways, Tel. 24823555
- Gulf Air, Tel. 24703544
- KLM, Tel. 24566737
- Kuwait Airlines, Tel. 24798861
- Lufthansa, Tel. 24796692
- **Oman Air Tel. 24531111**
  - Muscat airport: 24519591, 24519347
  - Salalah airport: 23290293
  - Khasab airport: 26731592
- Qatar Airways, Tel. 24783388
- Royal Jordanian, Tel. 24796680
- Singapore Airways, Tel. 24791233
- Swiss, Tel. 24791710
- Turkish Airlines, Tel. 2476 5000

Banks

see also Money, Opening Times
Branches of the national banks can often be found in the larger shopping centers. In the Mutrah suq there are money changers who will exchange foreign currencies at fair rates. Markaz Mutrah at Tigari Street in Ruwi has developed into a proper banking district and all the major banks have their head offices here.

- Bank Muscat, Tel. 24768888
- HSBC, Tel. 24799920
- Central Bank of Oman, Tel. 24702222
- Citibank, Tel. 24780845
- Habib Bank AG, Tel. 24817142
- Oman International Bank, Tel. 24682500
- National Bank of Oman, Tel. 24778000

Beaches

see Sport

Bookshops

In the Capital Area there are only a few shops with English language literature. As a rule these are branches of the Family Bookshop or the Al Oloum chain; they stock interesting specialist literature about Oman which can only be obtained in Oman, as well as

international newspapers and magazines and the most up to date maps. Branches of the Family Bookshop can be found in the Muscat Intercontinental Hotel, opposite the SABCO shopping center in Al Qurm's large shopping complex at the Al Qurm roundabout and in the Sultan Building in Suroor Street in Ruwi, as well as in Nizwa and Salalah. The Al Oloum Bookshop has branches in the Al Harthy complex in Al Qurm and in the Al Bustan Palace. Small bookshops can be found in the lobbies of almost all of the large hotels and there is a new "Turtle's" bookshop at As Seeb airport with an extensive range of English books and periodicals.
Currently the largest bookstore is Borders, which is located in the Muscat City Center, near As Seeb.

Capital Area

The capital of the Sultanate is ***Muscat***. This term is used not only for the small historical city center but also for the whole Capital Area which stretches over 50 kilometers to *As Seeb*. *Greater Muscat* is divided into various town districts. The most important are: *Musca*t - the historic town with the Sultan's palace and the palace offices; *Mutrah* - also a historic town, the traditional trading center with suq, fish market and harbor; *Greater Mutrah* - the new business and residential center with the central bus station; *Mina al Fahl* - the oil port with its adjoining oil refinery; *Al Qurm* - a smart residential area and new diplomatic quarter; *Al Khuwayr* - seat of most of the ministries. Other town quarters are *Ruwi, Al Ghubbrah, Al Udhaybah, Madinat As Sultan Qaboos, Al Khawd* and *Bawshar.*

Car rental

see Driving

Churches

see also Mosques, Religion
As long as no one develops missionary zeal, anyone is free to exercise his belief - a tolerance which is not usual in other Gulf states. In Ruwi you can find a Hindu temple, a catholic church (St. Peter and St. Paul) and a protestant church (Oman Protestant Church).

Climate and when to travel

Muscat lies on the Tropic of Cancer. Since ancient times it has been known as one of the hottest towns of the world. In the 14th century the Arab geographer Abdul Razak described the climate as follows: "The heat in Muscat was so great that it burns the marrow, the sword melted in the sheath and the precious stones in the handle burnt to coal." In summer (May - September) the temperature rises to 50°C and the humidity to 95 percent. Strong, hot winds blow over the country from the interior of the Arabian peninsula, ripening the dates on the palm trees. The dark brown mountains surrounding Muscat store the heat and even at night the temperatures barely sink below 40°C. In the summer life becomes bearable only with air-conditioning in homes and vehicles. From October to April the temperatures and humidity are more bearable; the climate is comparable to a European summer. The best time to travel through the country is between November and February. The temperatures are between 20 and 30°C, the air is dry and clear, with only rare rainfall. The average annual precipitation in the mountain region is about 100mm. South Oman, on the other hand, is a favorite destination for tourists from the neighboring Gulf states from mid-May to September. During these months the monsoon brings cooler, moister air masses with it, which are blocked by the mountains of Dhofar. Mist shrouds the country and the temperatures reach no higher than 35°C, there is a steady light drizzle, and the countryside along the coast of Salalah is decked in a green carpet. During this season many Omanis from the extremely hot north retreat here. Western tourists generally visit Dhofar in the warm, dry winter months when the air is clear, the seas are calm and even northern Oman has moderate temperatures. The average annual precipitation in southern Oman is 400 mm.

Clothing

Light summer clothing is adequate in Oman the whole year round. To have suitable "winter dress" in Oman, it is enough to have a pullover. Rainwear is normally not needed. Clothing should, however, not offend the countrywide Muslim sensibilities. That is to say shoulders, upper arms and knees should be covered and clothing should not be figure-hugging. Light, bright, long summer trousers and wide cotton shirts are ideal, also serving as protection against the sun.
The correct bathing dress for men is bermuda shorts, and for women single-piece swimsuits. Bikinis are only allowed at private hotel swimming pools. Unless you are on a beach designated for swimming you should remain completely dressed. Please show respect for the country's customs by sticking to this rule.
Every Omani, whether man or woman, carries a head covering when outside of the home. This is not just a matter of fashion but in this climate you would be wise to follow suit. The intense sunshine in Oman is easy to underestimate. Protection against the sun, sunglasses and sun cream should be an essential part of your packing. The usual footwear is open sandals. When making trips into the countryside you should wear ankle-high trekking shoes or boots.

Crime

Crime and petty theft are practically unknown. Oman is nowhere near as rich as Saudi Arabia or Kuwait, but it is also not a poor country. Any foreign workers convicted of a crime are immediately deported. Thefts and other crimes are extremely rare but you should not lead anyone into temptation by a too showy display of wealth.

Customs

see Entry and Exit Regulations

Disabled, facilities for

People with disabilities in Oman have organized themselves well in recent years and have achieved many improvements in their everyday life. All large department stores and ministries have designated parking places for the disabled and all public buildings have to have wheelchair access and toilets for the disabled. The staff at As Seeb airport are prepared for the arrival of people with disabilities, as are all the larger hotels. However only the Al Bustan Palace Hotel offers rooms designated and equipped for the disabled. Disabled Omanis are very active in the field of sport and also very successful. Ever keen on making new contacts they are always happy to advise disabled travelers on holiday planning and welcome visitors to join in their activities. More information can be obtained directly from the Association for the Welfare of the Handicapped Children, Al Qurm Heights, P.O.Box 2056 CPO, Tel. 24561008.

Doctors

see Medical Care

Driving

see also Off-Road

Traffic regulations

It is impossible to explore Oman without a car. Visitors to Oman will spend a good deal of time driving. Driving is on the right hand side. Road signs along the main roads are in Arabic and English, and the traffic signs and regulations are the same as those in Europe. Women behind the wheel are normal in Oman, something which would be quite unthinkable in Saudi Arabia. Since 1996 seat belts must be worn in the rear as well as the front seats. In the capital it is forbidden to drive very dirty vehicles. If you do you may be faced with an instant fine from the police.

Speed limits

The speed limit is generally 120 kilometers per hour. This also holds for the four-lane divided highways. Within built-up areas and wadi areas the limit is 40 kilometers per hour throughout. The Omani police have the latest radar equipment, which is continually in use. Breaking the speed limit can be very expensive. As all vehicles are equipped with a warning system which sounds immediately whenever the speed limit is exceeded, no one can claim that they were not aware of exceeding the limit. In fact, many trucks have equipment which cuts off the delivery of the fuel for half an hour if the speed limit is exceeded.

Rental cars

On presentation of an international driving license and a valid credit card a car can be rented without any difficulty. The daily rate (with 200 free kilometers) is generally between 14 and 16 Omani rials. It may turn out to be cheaper to rent a car or especially a 4WD if rented in advance through one of the larger car rental companies. The four-wheel drive vehicles cost between 30 and 40 Omani rials per day, also including 200 free kilometers.

Booking a car from abroad

The following international car hire firms are represented in Oman:

Avis	www.avis.com
Europcar	www.europcar.com
Hertz	www.hertz.com
Sixt	www.e-sixt.com

All of these companies have representatives at As Seeb airport and in various large hotels.

Booking a car within Oman:

Avis	24601224
Europcar	24700190
Hertz	24566208
Sixt	24794721

Of course there are now a number of smaller car hire firms, although they may not always have the best vehicles. However even with the cars from the large companies you should check the cars thoroughly before starting out; especially the tire pressure in the spare tire and that there are suitable tools for changing tires. The Omani company **Mark Rent-a-Car** is known for the immaculate condition of all its vehicles (Tel. 24782727, Fax 24786885.) They also have a 24 hour counter at the airport in Muscat (Tel. 24510033) and a counter at the airport in Salalah too. The company's four-wheel drive vehicles are constantly maintained and are also equipped with special fittings particularly suited to Oman's difficult terrain. The car ordered will be handed over to you either at the airport or at your hotel. Credit cards accepted.

Note: Make sure you check the oil and water every day – this is part of the Omani rental contract! If there should be damage caused by lack of water or oil the renter of the vehicle will have to pay the equivalent of some 1000 Omani rials for gross negligence, even if the vehicle was insured.

Roads

The few kilometers of asphalt roads which existed in 1970 have since been extended into a network of over 20,000 kilometers. Today the roads connect all the larger communities of the country, and are of a technical standard as high as in Europe and are very well signposted. It often happens that an asphalt road has to traverse a river bed at a wadi crossing. Because rainfall is so scarce, no expensive bridges have been built. Instead a special system of roadside markings has been established. It consists of several round steel poles, about one meter high, set in the ground a few meters apart. The upper part of the post is painted red and the lower part is painted white. If water is flowing across the road and the white paint is still visible, then you can safely drive slowly across here. If the water level is up to the red marking then it is extremely dangerous to continue, and the current can often be strong enough to sweep away cars. This danger is often underestimated even by Omanis and each year several people lose their cars – or their lives! – in this fashion.

Not to be compared with the asphalt roads are some 30,000 kilometers of tracks which have also been laid. They form a network which covers all inhabited corners of the country; these tracks mostly vanish in the wadi beds. You are strongly advised not to take these tracks without having a 4WD and experience in handling it, and without having made proper preparations. You cannot expect to find sufficient signposts in the open country and still less can you expect to find English-speaking Omanis whom you can ask the way. In addition Bedouin crisscross these tracks when driving their vehicles. They make so many turn-offs that it makes it almost impossible to follow the original routes without having precise local knowledge. Up until today there exists no good general map of the country with correctly marked tracks. Field geologists working in the country's interior get their bearings using high resolution satellite pictures or the GPS satellite system.

A further problem can be presented by the surprisingly sudden rainfalls in the Hajar Mountains. The over 3000 meter high massif of the Jabal Al Akhdar forms an excellent rain trap. The heavy regional rains flow rapidly through the narrow mountain wadis in a dangerous flood wave. Natives of Oman point out that there are more deaths caused by water than by drought. When a flood wave passes through a valley it fills all hollows in the ground with water and it becomes impassable even for a 4WD and can remain so for several days. If you are making excursions into the country where the terrain is difficult it is highly recommended to take advantage of the offers of experienced local travel agents. Off-road excursions with a guide are adventurous enough. Motor vehicles can be driven on beaches only by fishermen and fishmongers.

Driving Safety Tips

In general you should always check the oil and water before making any trip; it is easy to underestimate how much gets used in a climate like Oman's. Petrol stations are distributed relatively evenly around the country but nevertheless it is easy to run out of petrol if you don't check often whether you have enough petrol. You should also carry a petrol canister in reserve. Several liters of drinking water and provisions will enable you to better endure unexpected waits and long delays due to flooding or a car breakdown. In case of a breakdown it is best to remain near the vehicle, especially in remote regions. Local Bedouin would certainly find you more quickly than you would find their settlements. Camels at the side of the roads present a potential danger, as they ignore cars and can run on to the road at any moment. You should also take into consideration that when such an event occurs the vehicle in front of you may brake sharply or even stop!

These precautions should also be followed with wild donkeys, sheep and goats at the roadside.

Accidents

ALL accidents must be reported to the police, even if the damage is very slight. IMPORTANT: The vehicle may then only be moved on instructions from the police, regardless of how much traffic chaos it is causing. Driving damaged cars is illegal; the police will stop damaged cars and check if the mandatory official damage report is on hand, without which no workshop will carry out repairs. If there is an accident with a pedestrian the motorist has to take complete responsibility: as the stronger party he is supposed to take more care. Driving into a tree is punishable in the same way as running over a person.

Eating and Drinking

see Restaurants

Electricity

The electricity grid is fed with alternating current of 220/240 Volts, 50 Hz. The sockets are three pin as in Great Britain. You should pack the proper plug adapters.

Embassies and Consulates

Embassies of the Sultanate of Oman

Australia
Oman Consulate General
Level 4 Suite 2
493 St Kilda Road
PO Box 7174, VIC 3004
Melbourne
Tel. +61/3/98204096
Fax +61/3/98204076
c.general@oman.org.au

Canada
Oman Consulate
1115 Sherbrooke O
Montreal, QC H3A 1H3
Tel. +1/514/2888644
Fax +1/514/2888175
omanconsul@bellnet.ca

China (The People's Republic of)
6 Liang Ma He Nan Lu
Chao Yang District
Beijing 100600
Tel: +86/10/65323692
Fax: +86/10/65325030
omnbeijing@chnmail.com

France
50 Avenue D'Iena
75116 Paris
Tel. +331/47230163
Fax +331/47237710
ambassade.sultan.doman@wanadoo.fr

Germany
Clayallee 82
14195 Berlin / Zehlendorf
Tel. +49/30/8100500
Fax +49/30/81005199
info@botschaft-oman.de

India
16, Olao Palme Marg
Vasant Vihar
New Delhi 110057
Tel: +91/11/6140215
Fax: +91/11/2688 5621
omandelhi@vsnl.com

Italy
Via Della Camilluccia 625
P. C. 135,
Rome
Tel: +39/06/36300517
Fax: +39/06/3206802

Japan
2-28-11 Sendagaya
Shibuya-Ku
Tokyo 151
Tel. +83/1/34020877

Fax +83/1/34041334
omanemb@gol.com

Korea (Republic of)
309-3 Dongbinggo-dong Yongsan-ku
Seoul
Tel. +82/2/7902431
Fax +82/2/7902430
omanembs@ppp.kornet.nm.kr

Malaysia
6 Jalan Langgak Golf
Off JalanTu Razak
55000 Kuala Lumpur
Tel: +60/3/2452827
Fax: +60/3/2452826
omanemb@jaring.my

Netherlands
Konginnegracht 27
2514 AB the Hague
Tel: +31/70/3615800
Fax: +31/70/3605364

United Kingdom
167 Queen's Gate
London SW7 5HE
Tel. +44/20/72250001
Fax +44/20/75892505
theembassy@omanembassy.org.uk

United States of America
2535 Belmont Road N.W.
Washington DC 20008
Tel. +1/1202/3871980
Fax +1/1202/7454933
emboman@erols.com

Thailand
82 Swng Thong Thani Tower, 32 Floor
North Sathorn Rd.
Bangkok 10500
Tel: +66/2/6399380
Fax: +66/2/6399390
muscat@wnet.net.th

Foreign Embassies in Oman

The country code for Oman is +968.

Austria	24793135
Bahrain	24605075
Canada	24791738
China	24696698
Denmark	24703289
France	24681800
Germany	24832482
India	24810536
Iran	24696944
Italy	24695223
Japan	24601028
Jordan	24692760
S. Korea	24691490
Kuwait	24699627
Lebanon	24695844
Malaysia	24698329
Netherlands	24603719
New Zealand	24794932
Norway	24703289
Pakistan	24603439
Qatar	24691152
Russia	24602894
Saudi Arabia	24601744
South Africa	24694793
Spain	24713253
Sri Lanka	24697841
Sweden	24708693
Switzerland	24658202
UAE	24600988
UK	24609000
USA	24698989

Emergency and Important Telephone Numbers

Police/Fire emergency	**9999**
Airport Police Station	24510099
Khasab Police Station	26830199
Nizwa Police station	25425099
Ruwi Police station	24701099
Salalah Police station	23290099
Seeb Police station	24420099
Sohar Police station	26840099
Sur Police station	25540099
Directory Information	1327
International Operator	1305

Passports & Immigration	24569606
Medical Services	603988
Medical Emergencies	563625
Talking pages	24600100
Flight information	24519223
Lost Luggage	24519504
Weather Forecast	24519113
Foreign Exchange Rates	1106
AAA	24697800

Arabian Automobile Alliance (24 hours roadside assistance 365 days a year)

English-language Media

English language daily newspapers are *The Omani Daily Observer*, close to the government; *The Times of Oman*, considered by Omanis to be liberal; and the United Arab Emirates daily for the whole region, *The Khaleej Times*. These three papers also report daily on events in Europe.
An English language radio channel broadcasts daily from 07:00-22:00 in the Capital Area on UKW (FM) 90.4 and in Salalah on 94.3. BBC and CNN can be received via satellite in all of the large hotels and in many private households.

Entry and exit regulations

see **Airport**

Tourist visa

If you travel to Oman you require either a tourist visa or a Non Objection Certificate (NOC) sponsored by someone in Oman.
Visas can be obtained from the Omani Embassy or much more simply directly on entry into the country by paying 6 OMR at the border. The actual list of nationalities that may obtain the visa on arrival is published in the Internet at www.rop.gov.om.
A tourist visa entitles you to stay for 4 weeks and for another 6 OMR can be extended for a further 4 weeks. It is much more expensive to apply for a visa from an Omani diplomatic mission abroad. You must request the necessary forms from the responsible embassy, supplying a stamped self-addressed envelope. You make the written application by sending your passport and the S.A.E. with the forms typed out in English together with a check or money order and you can reckon on automatically receiving a visa, providing the passport is not Israeli and there are no Israeli visa stamps issued in the preceding six months. The application takes two to three weeks to process. Individuals can also have their visas arranged by large hotels or by their travel agents.

Non Objection Certificates

If you have friends or business partners in Oman they can get a Non Objection Certificate (NOC) for you. Along with your sponsor's details you need to give the following: Name; place and date of birth; nationality; passport number, issue date, issuing office and expiry date; address, occupation; reason for visit and four passport photos. Instead of requesting a tourist visa on arrival, you then hand in the NOC when entering the country at the airport. An NOC allows you to stay in Oman for up to three months. The current visa regulations can be found in the site of the Royal Omani Police (www.rop.gov.om.)

Import and export restrictions

The import of weapons, pornography, alcohol, Israeli currency and fresh food is forbidden. Bringing in plants or flowers with roots or bulbs requires a special license. Videocassettes or DVDs may be retained by customs for censorship.
Domestic pets must go into quarantine.
The export of antiques and historic cultural assets, such as old curved daggers (*khanjars*) and archaeological finds, as well as fossils or

corals, is strictly forbidden. The current legal restrictions designed to protect national cultural assets are detailed in a list of forbidden objects which can be obtained at As Seeb airport - please stick to these regulations and be prepared for stringent checks on leaving the country. The customs at As Seeb airport has the most up to date screening devices which will not damage film.

Events

see also Markets

Exhibitions of native artists, as well as guest exhibitions, take place regularly in the exhibition rooms of the Omani Society for Fine Arts in Shatti al Al Qurm, next door to the Ramada Hotel. Concerts of the Omani Symphony Orchestra are put on at irregular intervals in the Al Bustan Palace Hotel. Exact times and places are announced on posters in hotels.

At then end of each week the **Friday Bazaar** is held in the large covered fruit market halls on the edge of Wadi Kabir. Here you will find everything from used cars to plastic vases and chocolate box paintings. You drive along the road from the incense-burner roundabout in the direction of Al Bustan, turn right at the petrol station and keep to the small parallel road running in the direction of Al Bustan. If you miss this exit you can turn off in the direction of Ruwi just before the horses mounted on pillars, and drive back along the parallel road. **Friday markets** are common to all of the larger towns of central Oman and take place in the morning. Bedouin then come to town to do their shopping. Everything is on offer, but mainly domestic livestock. The markets of Nizwa, Bahla, Sinaw and Barka are famous.

Camel racing and **horse racing** are held in many places on National Day and sometimes on other feast days, especially in As Seeb. If you are lucky you will hear about them by asking insiders and sometimes they are announced in newspapers. The best thing is just to keep your eyes open!

You can marvel at **bullfights** (see related article) of a special kind which take place on Fridays late in the afternoon and in the evening at Barka in a special simple arena. In these bloodless encounters two bulls try to push one another from the spot. The first one to take a step backwards has lost. The concrete arena is on the right on the way to Bayt An Naman, 3.6 kilometers from the turn-off for Barka in the direction of the roundabout (on the country road to Sohar) on the link road.

Cinemas with English language films are in a round building in the Business District (Stars Cinema, Tel: 24791641) and in Shatti al Al Qurm (Al Shati Plaza, Tel: 24692656) close to the Ramada Hotel.

At the foot of the clock tower next to the Ministry for Commerce and Industry in the Mutrah Business District television programs are sometimes screened on a giant monitor.

Omani Night – with camels, traditional dancing, dining and music – takes place every Wednesday evening at the Al Bustan Palace Hotel (Tel. 24799666) and is organized together with the inhabitants of the neighboring al Bustan village.

All of the large hotels in Muscat have daily changing **theme evenings**, dedicated to the culinary pleasures of various countries. The events have such illustrious titles as *The Best of British*, *Fiesta Italiana*, *Neptune´s Kingdom* or *Mexican Night*.

Night owls will have to make do with the few **night clubs** on offer in the capital. These are: *Al Hamra* in the Al Bustan Palace (open daily except Saturday 20:00-24:00), *La Boite* in the As Seeb Novotel (open daily 19:00–24:00), *Saba Nightclub* in the Oman Sheraton (open Sunday, Tuesday and Thursday 22:00–01:00) and the *Sur Nightclub* in

the Muscat Intercontinental (open Sunday to Wednesday 18:00–02:00.) The Grand Hyatt brightens up the nightlife with the *John Barry Bar*, the Brasilian club *Cocacabana* and the *Jungle Bar.*
The listings magazine ***Oman Today*** has restaurant tips and all sorts of useful information. It is published once a month by Apex Press and Publishing and can be bought in bookshops for 500 baisa.

Festivals and Holidays

see Ramadan, Opening Times
The Arab weekend falls on Thursday and Friday. The Arab equivalent of Sunday is Friday. The only non-religious festival is National Day which is always celebrated on the 18th and 19th of November. The occasion commemorates the assumption of the throne by Sultan Qaboos, replacing his father, on July 21st 1970. Because it would be too hot to have a festival on this date, the remembrance day was deferred until November 18th, Sultan Qaboos's birthday. Ceremonials and fairs then take place throughout the whole country and the 55 kilometer length of the main road from As Seeb to Muscat is completely decked out with flags, chains of lights and portraits of the Sultan.
All other festivals and holidays are religious and are determined by the Islamic calendar which is lunar and made up of 354/355 days. Each year the Islamic calendar is 11 days "ahead" of the Western calendar. A lunar month has only 29 or 30 days. The Islamic calendar started with the emigration (hejira) of the Prophet Mohammed from Mecca to Yatrib Medina on the 15th/16th July in 622 AD. To convert from hejira years to Christian Gregorian years follow this formula: take the Islamic year and subtract 1/34th and then add 622 (beginning of the Islamic calendar.)

New Year, a festival on the 1. Muharram (Dec 07, 2010/Nov 26, 2011/Nov 15, 2012)

Prophet's Birthday, a festival on the Rabi al-awal (Feb 26, 2010/Feb 15, 2011/Feb 04, 2012)

Eid al Fitr, four day festival beginning on the 1. Shewal, the end of Ramadan, starting Sep 10, 2010 / Aug 30, 2011 / Aug 19, 2012.

Eid al Adha, five day festival beginning on the 9. Dhu-l-Hiddia, traditional time of reflection and the Pilgrimage to Mecca (*hajj*) in the last month of the islamic calendar year, starting Nov 17, 2010/Nov 8, 2011/ Oct 28, 2012.

Ramadan (Aug 11, 2010 - Sep 10, 2010/Aug 01, 2011 - Aug 30, 2011/Jul 20, 2012 - Aug 19, 2012)

During the Islamic fasting month of Ramadan it is forbidden to eat, drink or smoke in public between the hours of sunrise and sunset. This does not apply to people who are ill or traveling, or children under the age of twelve. During this period the whole country becomes an alcohol free zone, including the hotels and the mini bars in the hotel rooms. The restaurants will not serve alcohol but are still open during the day for hungry non-Muslims, as are many of the grocery shops. Opening times begin later in the morning.
The exact beginning of the fasting month and the holidays are subject to local observations of the moon and are only definitively announced shortly in advance.

Geography

The Sultanate covers the southeastern part of the Arabian peninsula; it is situated between 16 and 18 degrees northern latitude and 51 and 59 degrees eastern longitude. With a complete surface area of 309,500 square kilometers it is the Arabian peninsula's third largest country after Saudi Arabia and Yemen. Oman borders Yemen in the southwest, Saudi Arabia in the west and the United Arab Emirates in the northwest. It is divided into

8 administrative districts: the government district of Muscat (along the coast of the Capital Area as far as Qurayyat), the Al Batinah Region (coastal strip between Sohar and Muscat), the Dakhiliyah Region (from Muscat into the interior Hajar Mountains), the Adh Dhahirah Region (semi-desert from the southern flanks of the Western Hajar Mountains to the "Empty Quarter," the Rub al Khali, Wusta (a desert plain between Dhofar and Adh Dhahirah), Ash Sharqiyyah (sandy plains and valleys from south of the Eastern Hajar Mountains to the Wihibah desert and the coast), the government district of Dhofar (south Oman) and the government district Musandam (peninsula on the Strait of Hormuz.) The district of Musandam is separated from the main area of Oman through a 50 kilometer wide strip of land which belongs to the United Arab Emirates. Between is another exclave, the Madha oasis. Oman has a coastline of over 1700 kilometers; the highest mountain is the Jabal Shams (3019 meters) in the Jabal Al Akhdar massif in northern Oman.

Getting there

see Airport, Entry & Exit Regulations
The most practical way of traveling to Oman is by air to Muscat. Flight prices vary from airline to airline. There are nonstop flights from Europe with Oman Air from London Heathrow (also British Airways), Paris, Frankfurt and Munich. Other airlines flying to Oman, generally with a stop and change of planes at their main hubs, are Emirates (via Dubai), Etihad (via Abu Dhabi), Gulf Air (Bahrain), Lufthansa (Frankfurt and Dubai), Qatar (Doha), Swiss (Zurich and Dubai), and Turkish Airlines (via Istanbul and Dubai). Principle cities throughout the Gulf region, and countries around the Indian Ocean are served by Oman Air and the national carriers of each country. Nonstop flights to Bangkok are offered by Oman Air and Thai Airlines. There are currently no nonstop flights between Oman and North America.
You can also drive from the United Arab Emirates to Oman. The required visa can be bought at the frontier for 6 Omani rials. It is not possible to cross from Saudi Arabia but you can enter Oman from Yemen at the Sarfayt and Maziounah border crossing. There are no regular ferries to neighboring countries. Now and again a cruise ship puts in at Mutrah or Salalah. If you want to take up quarters in the area of Muscat and surroundings, all the hotels can be reached by taxi from the airport for at most 20 Omani rials. To get to hotels in Nizwa, Sur and Sohar it is best to rent a car, as there is no regular public transport to these places from the airport. The distances are generally too great for taxis, but if you do manage to find a willing driver, the fare will be correspondingly high. The car rental companies at the airport are open around the clock.

Health

see also Medical Care
The extreme heat causes increased perspiration which leads to large losses of fluids and to subsequent salt and mineral deficits. It is important to stay hydrated, and it is reckoned that each person should drink at least three liters of fluid every day whenever in such heat. Omanis often sprinkle a little salt in their drink, regardless of whether it is water, cola or fruit juice. You can also take mineral concentrates from a health shop with you; however it is both simpler and cheaper to take to the time-honored custom of the Omanis and eat 20 dates every day.
The sunshine in Oman can lead to bad burning. In cases of bad sunburn you should

cover the affected areas of skin with wet cloths. Preventive protection against the sun is the best option; the local custom is to have a break in the middle of the day and avoid the midday sun. Sunglasses not only provide protection against the sun but also from fine particles of sand which can all too easily scratch the cornea. This can result in the most unpleasant eye infections. Before the trip it is a good idea to obtain an antibiotic eye cream from an eye specialist.

Travellers often catch cold; this is usually as a result of sudden exposure to extreme changes of air temperature, usually involving air conditioning in restaurants and hotels being set at very low. If you experience discomfort, either avoid a long stay, open a window, or ask the staff to adjust the thermostat setting.

In the coastal waters of Oman poisonous jellyfish appear now and again. The chest area coming into contact with the stinging cells is dangerous and can be avoided by wearing a T-shirt when swimming. If you do come into contact with stinging tentacles do not rub the area as you may be working invisible cells further into your skin, making matters even worse! Wash the area thoroughly with white vinegar and seawater (do not use fresh water!). Allergic reactions should be treated with antihistamines and if in doubt please visit a hospital.

There are no vaccinations that you are required to have before a trip to Oman but for world travelers generally it is recommended to be vaccinated against hepatitis A, typhus, diphtheria, tetanus and poliomyelitis; for the last three a booster shot is normally sufficient.

Malaria has been successfully campaigned against over years but can still be found in the regions of Ash Sharqiyyah, Dhofar, Adh Dhahirah and in wet areas. These have been designated "moderate" risk by the Institute of Tropical Medicine in Tübingen, Germany. In other parts of the country the risk is minimal. Simple preventive measures directed against mosquitoes, especially the anopheles which is active at night, will significantly reduce the risk of malaria. These are: wear long trousers and long-sleeved shirts; use insect repellent creams and sprays and fumigating sticks (mosquito coils or – as is the custom in Oman – burn frankincense); use mosquito nets and make sure the windows and doors are secured against mosquitoes.

To prevent an infection you can take a chemoprophylaxis which must be started a week before or at the latest as soon as entering a malaria area. If the need arises there is the so-called standby therapy: in cases of suspected malaria where no doctor is on hand a therapy can be self-administered: 3 tablets of Mefloquin (Lariam), 6 hours later 2 tablets, and after another 6 hours 1 tablet. This "self treatment" should only be carried out if there is no chance of getting to a doctor! It is very important that the symptoms should be correctly interpreted – not every fever is a sign of malaria! It is recommended that before making a journey you visit a doctor for any vaccinations necessary. The Hospital for Tropical Diseases in London provides information and travel tips on the Internet: (www.thehtd.org), as do the World Health Organization (http://www.who.int/ith/links/national_links/en/index.html) and the Centers for Disease Control in Atlanta (http://wwwnc.cdc.gov/travel/destinations/list.aspx).

Hotels

see Accommodation

Information

Information in English about Oman and traveling there can be obtained from:

Directorate General of Tourism
P.O. Box 550
Muscat, Postal Code 113
Sultanate of Oman
Telephone: +968 771-7085
Fax: +968 771-4213
Email: dgt@mocioman.gov.om

Oman Tourist Office
11 Blades Court
121 Deodar Road
London
SW15 2NU
Tel. +44 (0)208 877 4524
Fax. +44 (0)208 874 4219

Embassy of the Sultanate of Oman
64 Ennismore Gardens
London SW7 1NH
Tel. +44 (0)20 7225 0001
Fax. +44 (0)20 7589 2505

In the Internet:
Detailed **travel information** about hotels, travel organizers, the country and its people can be found at the domain of this book's author under **www.oman-tours.com**.

Internet

Exchanging information first hand is still highly valued in Omani society. It is not surprising that since its introduction in 1997 the Internet has proved to be so popular. **Internet cafes** can be found in all the larger towns in Oman. If you want to get an overview of what the worldwide web has to offer on the theme of Oman, you should visit **www.oman.org** maintained by the Oman Studies Center. Arranged in categories this site provides nearly all the addresses relating to Oman. Among the interesting links you will find the Omani news agency ONA (**www.omannews.com**), the cultural periodical Nizwa Magazine (**www.nizwa.com**) and the Oman Daily Observer (**www.omanobserver.com**), which is the English language newspaper. Official governmental information can be found on the site belonging to the Ministry of Information (**www.omanet.om**.) The current visa regulations can be found in the site of the Royal Omani Police (**www.rop.gov.om**.)
Detailed **travel information** about hotels, travel organizers, the country and its people can be found on the website of this book's author under **www.oman-tours.com**.

Languages

see Useful Phrases *in reference section*
The official language of the government is Arabic. In the Capital Area, larger towns and on the Al Batinah coast almost everything, from items on the menu to road signs is written in English. Many Omanis in these areas speak good English. The majority of guest workers from India and the Philippines are employed in the service industries and trade, and so here English is used more than Arabic. Other languages frequently encountered - as a result of ancient trading ties and the course of history - are Urdu, Hindi and sometimes also Swahili.

Libraries

British Council Library, Madinat As Sultan Qaboos, Tel. 24600548
University Libraray, Muscat
Tel. 24622635
Islamic Library, Salalah,
Tel. 23292934
Library for Science and Technology, PDO
Mina Al Fahl, Tel. 24673111

Maps

A fairly correct map of Oman to a scale of 1:1,300,000 was published by the National Survey Authority in June 2003. The same authority has published a very detailed overview of greater Muscat to a scale of 1:20,000 on four sheets and a town plan of Salalah. You can obtain these maps in Omani bookshops. There you can also obtain detailed but not very easily understood street maps of Muscat and Salalah. GeoPro publishes a map of Oman, including street maps of Muscat, Mutrah, Ruwi, Al Qurm and Salalah. This can be ordered on the Internet (www.themapcenter.com.)

Markets

see also Events, Shopping
Every historic town has its market (*suq*). The suqs which are most interesting on account of their unspoiled nature are those at Bahla, As Seeb, Ibri, Barka and Sinaw. The suq is where you can most easily find gifts for friends and relations: frankincense, spices, jewelry or textiles. The largest and historically most significant are those at Nizwa in the country's interior and Mutrah in the Capital Area. In the winding lanes of the Mutrah suq traditional oriental wares are on offer side by side with plastic products from India and the Far East. It is also worth seeing the fish market on the northern edge of the harbor at Mutrah (open daily from 06:00-12:00)
The most modern shopping centers can be found in the Shopping Area at the Al Qurm roundabout, the Capital Commercial Center (C.C.C.), SABCO and opposite, on the other side of Qaboos Road, the Al Harthy Complex and the Sultan Center. Among other things the C.C.C. offers the whole European range of groceries (excluding alcohol.) Hypermarkets have recently been opened at the Al Udhaybah roundabout. The main shopping street for guest workers is the High Street in Ruwi.
The biggest shopping mall, the Muscat City Center, can be found on the highway to Barka some kilometers beyond the airport.

Medical Care

An optimal healthcare system is now operated throughout the land, which is particularly good in the vicinity of the larger towns. Alongside the many private clinics spread around the whole of Muscat, there are also seven state-run hospitals and some health centers in the capital. If in need it is best to go to these. At the moment there are still quite a few European doctors working in the clinics; the doctors all speak English. A visit to the doctor is free for Omani citizens, but tourists have to pay. It is recommended that you take out medical insurance before traveling. The most modern **clinics** in the Capital Area, equipped with the most up to date technology, and their emergency numbers are listed here:

Royal Hospital at Bawshar.
Tel. 24590491
Khoula Hospital in Wutayyah
Tel. 24563625
University Hospital in Al Khawd
Tel. 24513355

Other larger clinics in Muscat:

Al Nahdah Hospital in Ruwi
Tel. 24837800
Ibn Sina Hospital in Wadi Hattat
Tel. 24877361

The Al Shatti Hospital (Tel. 24604263) is a small, private clinic fitted out with the latest equipment: It is located on the beach of Shati Al Qurm and offers its own ambulance service. European doctors are among the international team of doctors at the clinic. Credit cards can be used to pay for treatment.

The most important hospitals outside of the Capital Area and their telephone numbers:

Adam	25434055
Al Buraymi	25652319
Al Nahda	24837800
Armed Forces	24331997
Hayma	25436013
Ibra	25571709
Ibri	25691990
Izki	25340033
Jaalan Bani Bu Ali	25553011
Khasab	26830187
Masirah	25504018
Nizwa	25449361
Qurayyat	24845004
Rustaq	26877186
Saham	26855148
Salalah	23211151
Samail	25352236
Sinaw	25524377
Sohar	26840399
Sur	25561373

A large number of **Pharmacists** are scattered around the Capital Area and can also be found in most of the larger towns, mostly in the suq; they stock the common medicines. There are pharmacies with an emergency night service in Muscat, Nizwa, Sur, Ibri, Salalah, Saham ad Al Buraymi. A selection of pharmacists in the Capital Area:

Al Hashar Pharmacy, Mutrah taxistand, Tel. 24602737

Mazoon Pharmacy, Mutrah suq, Tel. 2471714563

Al Khuwayr Pharmacy, near the Zawawi Mosque in Al Khuwayr, Tel. 24600052

Muscat Pharmacy, Ruwi High Street, Tel. 24703345

Every evening on Omani television after the 8 o'clock news the pharmacists which are available for emergencies are announced. You will find an overview of all pharmacists and hospitals in the country, ordered by region, in the first pages of the official telephone book.

Money

The country's currency is the Omani rial (OMR) which is divided into 1000 baisa. The currency is convertible with the exchange rate tied to the US dollar and is thus affected by the same fluctuations. The exchange rates given here are to be viewed only as an approximation:
1 *OMR.* = 2,60 US Dollars; 1 *OMR.* = 2,00 EUR; 1 *OMR..* = 1,57 GBP.
There are **bank notes** with the value of 200 *OMR.*, 100 *OMR.*, 50 *OMR.*, 20 *OMR.*, 10 *OMR.*, 5 *OMR.*, 1 *OMR.*, ½ *OMR.*, ¼ *OMR.*, 200 Baisa, and 100 Baisa. **Coins** are seldom used. There are coins for 50 Baisa, 25 Baisa, 10 Baisa und 5 Baisa.
There is no limit on the **import and export of currency**. Principle currencies can be exchanged at current rates at exchange offices at the airport or also with the currency dealers in Mutrah. Banks will generally take US dollars of small denomination notes.
US **Traveler's cheques** can be used but can be very time consuming as their authenticity has to be checked.
Nowadays almost every town in Oman has **ATMs** which will accept most bank debit cards as credit cards, such as **Visa** or **Mastercard**. The use of credit cards is widespread throughout the country and they are generally accepted by shops, restaurants and hotels. Other credit cards that are usually accepted are American Express and Diners Club. If you have a cash card, such as the ec-card or belonging to the Maestro and Cirrus systems, you can withdraw money from ATMs using your normal PIN number.

Mosques

see Churches, Religion

Islam allows believers of other monotheistic religions to visit a mosque for purposes of prayer. However, as tourists are generally more motivated by voyeurism than spirituality, their presence is not welcomed in Islamic houses of God. Spectators disturb the prayer services of believers and can even, under unhappy circumstances, render the prayers invalid; most mosques make this clear with a sign saying "for Muslims only." The single exception is the Sultan Qaboos Grand Mosque in Muscat which can be visited by non-Muslims on Islamic workdays (i.e., daily apart from Fridays) from 08:00 to 11:00. If, on religious grounds, you wish to visit a place of worship, you may go to the churches in Muscat. You will be able to pray undisturbed by curious Omanis. The interiors of Ibadhi mosques are not decorated and not especially worth seeing. The attitude of Ibadhis to places of worship is similar to that of low church protestants: the less distraction, the better for prayer.

Museums

Museums in Muscat

Bayt Al Zubair, Muscat, situated outside the city wall, in front of the Bab al Kabir gate to the South.

Tel. 24736688; open from Saturday to Thursday 09:00 -13:00 and 16:00-19:00. Easily the most professional museum in the country. This outstanding private collection of the ancient Zubair merchant family includes historical photographs, documents, jewelry, everyday objects and a valuable collection of old *khanjars*.

Alongside this you can see traditional handicrafts and gain an insight into the earlier way of life of people in the country.

Bayt Al Baranda, Mutrah, coming from Ruwi the museum is on the right immediately before reaching the roundabout on the Corniche. Tel. 24714262; Open Saturday to Wednesday 09:00-13:00 and 16:00-18:00. Thursday only 09:00 - 13:00. This excellent museum is in a beautifully renovated historical townhouse. Shown are the historical and geological evolution of the capital region from prehistoric times to today, plus descriptions of Muscat by travelers and cartographers over the last few centuries.

Children's Museum (Science Museum), Al Sarooj, Tel. 24605368, located in two white low-domed buildings directly next to the Sultan Qaboos Road. Open Saturday to Thursday 09:00-13:00, October 1-March 31, also 16:00-18:00. Approaching from the direction of Ruwi or Mutrah, pass the exit for the "Muscat Intercontinental," and then right. A modern educational museum in which children are brought closer to modern technology through experiments in a hands-on manner.

Muscat Gate Museum, Muscat, in the first floor of the new city gate over the coastal road from Mutrah to Muscat.

Open Saturday to Thursday 09.30-12:30 and 16:30-19:00. The history of the town of Muscat, as well as the geology of the region, depicted on very informative display boards and through a 20-minute film presentation.

Museum of Omani Heritage, im Madinat al-Alam, Tel. 24600946; open Saturday to Wednesday, 08.30-13:30, and from October 1 to March 31 also from 16:00 to 18:00. Also known as "the Oman Museum," it is located three kilometers southwest of Al-Qurm roundabout in the Al Alam Street on a hill behind the Ministry of Information. Downstairs, the developments of the traditional ways of life of fishermen, farmers, artisans and ranchers are outlined. Numerous exhibits, archaeological finds, photos and graphics, combined with concise English texts summarize, without missing a point, the stunning picture of life in Oman over the past 5000 years.

The rooms on the first floor depict normal daily private life. As you wander through the lifecycle of the peoples of this land, from birth to old age, you learn about the rituals and traditions along the path of life and become familiar with the associated signs and artifacts. Though seemingly familiar, many of the different and unusual things a stranger to this land will encounter throughout his travels is on display and and explained in this museum.

National Museum, in Ruwi, in Al Noor Street, Tel. 24701289; open Saturday to Wednesday from 08:00–14:00. Seen from the bus station, Al Noor Street leads to the left past the Abdul Ridah Mosque (blue dome). The museum contains a somewhat sparse collection of objects and furnishings from the old Sultan's palace, silver jewelry, models of dhows and national costume.

Natural History Museum, al Khuwayr, in the building of the Ministery of National Heritage and Culture, Tel. 24641510; open Saturday to Wednesday 08:00–13:30, Thursday 09:00–19:00. Closed on public holidays. At the Al Khuwayr roundabout go in the direction "Shatti Al Al Qurm" and follow the sign "Ministries." Overview of the geology, animal and plant worlds as well as the landscapes of Oman; many specimens, partly in dioramas; interesting new section on whales and dolphins.

Oil and Gas Exhibition Center, to the right of the main gate of the PDO (Petroleum Development Oman Ltd.), Tel. 24677834; closed during Ramadan, otherwise open from Saturday to Wednesday from 07:00-12:00 and from 13:00-15:45. Drive in the direction of Al Qurm from the Al Qurm roundabout, under the Al Qurm Heights Road and take the first road on the right (Seih Al Maleh Street.) There are no signs! This road leads directly to the main gate of the PDO. The museum is located to the right of the gate. The history of oil production in the Sultanate of Oman and its technical processes are explained by means of multimedia displays.

Omani-French Museum, Muscat, in **Bayt Fransa,** Tel. 24736613; open Saturday to Wednesday 08:00–13.30, October 1-March 31 also 16:00-18:00. Go through the large city gate (*bab kabir*), then on the right, in the restored former French embassy building. A collection of historical material relating to the common Omani-French past. Especially worth seeing from an architectural point of view.

Sayyid Faisal Bin Ali Museum is located on the grounds of the Natural History Museum in a former theater building (tel. 24641650), open Saturday to Wednesday 08:00-14:00. In this compact space the development of weapons in the country from the Stone Age to the 20th century is shown, as well as an overview of the main clay fortresses.

The Sultan's Armed Forces Museum (Military history Museum), Ruwi, in Bayt al Falaj, former garrison and royal residence, Tel. 24312642; only open on Saturday and Wednesday from 08:30–12:30. Coming from Al Qurm it is to be reached by taking the last exit on the right from the Mutrah roundabout. Collection of historic weapons and uniforms; documentation about the Imamate uprising and the Dhofar War. As in all military establishments it is forbidden to take photographs here.

Museums outside of Muscat and the Capital Area

The lovingly renovated and furnished **Bayt Naman** in Barka (tel. 24641300) is open Saturday through Wednesday 09:00-13:30, In the restored **Sohar Fort** a museum dedicated to Oman's lively maritime history has been established (tel. 26844758.) The exhibition can be visited from Saturday to Thursday from 08:00-13:30, October 1-March 31, also 16:00-18:00.

A small, very interesting, private **Maritime Museum** can be visited in **Sur**. Here you can see historic photographs from the period of the East Africa trade, models of ships, household contents and woven products. The collection is housed in the club building of the local football club. Coming from Al Kamil Wa Al Wafi after passing a broadcasting tower and a small power station, you fork off to the right at the petrol station in front of a soccer pitch. Passing through the gate you come to a walled-in area with two houses. The collection is in the left hand building. If the door is closed, the warden, who lives at the rear, will be happy to open up for you.

The **Land of Frankincense Museum** is located in the **Archeaological Park of Al Balid** in Salalah (Tel. 23202566); both are open Saturday to Wednesday 8:00-14:00 and 16:00-20:00. Thursday and Friday only 16:00-20:00. In two exhibition halls, the development of Oman is documented as a seafaring nation with a summary of the development of the country from the Stone Age to the present.

Nature and Environmental Protection

A high value is placed on environmental protection in Oman. It is forbidden to disturb or to hunt animals and birds in their natural habitat. This goes for all of the various nature reserves such as the Al Qurm Nature Reserve in the Capital Area, the island of Mahawt near the island of Masirah, the protected area for the oryx antelopes in the Jiddat al Harassis region to the north of Dhofar, and above all the protected areas for sea turtles at Ras Al Jinz.

Collecting shells, coral and starfish along the coast is also forbidden (as is their purchase and export). Various species of sea snails leave their shells temporarily; a shell being empty does not mean that it is uninhabited. Along the Omani coast rare species of cone snails can be found – *Conus pennaceus* and *Conus textile* – which grow up to eight centimeters in length. When touched it shoots a 1.5 to 2 centimeter long spike out of its shell which can inject a strong nerve poison. This poison can be fatal to people; to date there is no known antidote. Fishing with hook and line is only permitted with a special license from the Directorate of Fisheries. In southern Oman fishing is permitted in the area between Mughsayl and Taqah; spear fishing and harpooning is strictly forbidden throughout Oman - partly to protect corals and certain fish species and partly as a way to avoid sharks which are attracted by the blood and could turn the hunter into the victim.

If you don't clear up after yourself and simply leave rubbish in the country (of any sort, including plastic bags and drink cans) you can reckon with a significant fine.

Nightlife

In Oman you may be dismayed if you are on the lookout for discotheques, bars, nightclubs, theaters, cinemas or other such leisure facilities, although each year more such options become available. Spending an evening in such pursuits was relatively foreign to Omanis until recently, and even now the preferred pastimes are evening picnics on any spot of grass, walks along the beach or corniche, or meeting friends at the suq, cafe or juice bar. European expatriates gather and meet at various events put on at the international hotels, such as the Intercontinental, Grand Hyatt, Sheraton, Al Bustan Palace and others. These events repeat themselves with monotonous regularity and are characterized by homesickness. Apart from the *Omani Nights* at the Al Bustan Palace every Wednesday, there are so-called theme evenings dedicated to countries such as Spain, France, England, Italy, China or Korea. Here people dine on that country's national dishes accompanied by national music against a national backdrop - and reminisce about the original. The Muscat Intercontinental even offers *Country and Western Music Evening* in the "corral" behind the hotel. And once a week you can have your fill of seafood: this is known as *Neptune's Night* or *Seafood Selection*. After dining you can have a drink in the hotel's nightclub with its obligatory live music.

Off-road

see Driving, Tour Operators

Excursions with a four-wheel drive vehicle in the wild mountain valleys and the wide deserts of Oman are certainly a great experience but should, according to the route, only be made with a good driver and, best of all, a guide who knows the locale. Recommended companies can be found under the heading Tour Operators. They can organize trips at short notice for small groups of interested tourists with competent and qualified guides according to the special interests of the group (e.g. wadis, geology, archaeology, handicrafts). The relation between cost and the quality of services is fairly balanced, and considering the time you save and level of expertise you experience, well worth it.

Tours and destinations you should see, in addition to Muscat and the Capital Area, and depending on the amount of time you have at your disposal, include the summit plateau of the Jabal Shams with its deep canyon landscape; the geologically very interesting Wadi Sahtan and Wadi Bani Awf near Ar Rustaq; the Plateau Sayq on Jabal Akhdar, with its terraced fields; the coast between Qurayyat and Sur with Qalhat, Tiwi and Wadi Shab; the tower tombs at Al Jaylah in the Eastern Hajar Mountains; the sand desert of the Wihibah in the north; the dunes of the Rub al Khali in the south; the Frankincense Trail and other UNESCO world heritage sites near Salalah; and the mountain world of Dhofar. Good suggestions for possible off-road excursions can be found in the off-road guides by Jenny Walker and Sam Owen or Explorer Publishing (*see reference section* Literature)

Opening Times

see also Museums

The **Islamic weekend** falls on Thursday and Friday; Saturday and Sunday are normal workdays in Oman.

Shops and private companies: Saturday-Wednesday mostly from 08:00-13:00 and 16:00-19:00, Thursday 08:00-14:00. On Fridays shops are closed. During Ramadan work usually begins an hour later and shops are then open longer in the evenings.

Ministries: Saturday-Wednesday 07.30-14:30; Thursday/Friday closed. During the fasting month of Ramadan service hours are 08:00-13:30.

Banks: Saturday-Wednesday 08:00-12:00, Thursday 08:00-11.30. During Ramadan work begins at 09:00. The bank branches in the departure and arrival halls at As Seeb airport are open 24 hours every day.

Markets, suqs and shopping centers: Sat-

urday-Thursday 08:00–13:00 and 16:00–21:00. The suq at Mutrah closes at 19:30. Shopping centers are closed on Friday morning whereas in suqs in the countryside this is the busy time. During Ramadan they are nearly all closed in the morning but often open until midnight.
Post offices: Saturday-Wednesday 07:30–13:00 and 15:30–19:30. The post office in Ruwi is normally open from 07:30–17:30, while during Ramadan it opens later, at 08:30, and closes earlier.
Restaurants: Many restaurants are open Saturday-Thursday from 11:00–15:00 and from 18:00–24:00, Fridays from 13:00–15:00 and from 18:00–24:00, while during Ramadan they only open after sunset (with the exception of a few restaurants in the large international hotels). The exact times of the sunrise and sunset can be found in the daily papers.

Pharmacies

see Medical Care

Photography

With the exception of installations belonging to the military or oil companies, and the airports and ports which are marked with "No Photography" signs, there are hardly any official restrictions on photography in Oman. Be careful at the airport! Although you may not notice the signs, photography here is strictly forbidden. If you break this rule you can reckon with having the film removed from your camera.
Generally it is best to try and capture the beauty and variety of the country with the senses and impress them on the memory; photography has only a limited ability to convincingly capture the magic of the country. The fleeting moment, the wealth of scents and sounds in the air, the vast dimensions of the landscape can be better captured by the memory than with a camera. If you want to photograph people, especially women, or their property, please ensure that you ask their permission in advance. If an Omani expressly forbids photography, this wish must be respected and it can easily escalate to disputes which can quickly end in police intervention.
Good **film material** can be found in the Fuji Photo Centers at Muscat and Salalah. The film best suited to the extreme light conditions in Oman are the less sensitive films (for example 18 DIN/50 ASA) with a large range of contrast. Film material is often cheaper in Oman than in Europe.

Pollen

As a rule the Omani air is free of pollen and particulates. In the desert country vegetation is sparse and during the winter months a light sea breeze sweeps the coastal areas. If you have trouble with pollen allergies here it is recommended putting a clove in the mouth, keeping it in your cheek pouch and every now and then chewing on it. The clove oil thus exuded quickly reduces any swelling of the mucous membrane and reduces the danger of inflammation in the pharyngeal space. Some Omanis are in the habit of chewing cloves every day.

Post

see also Telephone
The old letter boxes are sparsely scattered around the Capital Area, are mounted to walls, and are not at all visually prominent. The new generation, on the other hand, are bright orange pillar boxes in the form of dagger handles. Easy to find letter boxes can be found at the main entrance to the Oman Center (previously known as the O.K. Center) at the Ruwi roundabout (on the 1st

floor there is also a small post office); at the bus station at Ruwi/Plaza (opposite there is also a small post office), and at Mutrah's taxi stand near the upper entrance of the suq. Another small post office can be found in the Business District at the GTO Tower. There are more post offices in Muscat, Mutrah, Ruwi, Mina al Fahl, at the airport and in As Seeb. Here the Omanis have their post boxes, since there is no house-to-house delivery in Oman. Tourists are advised to use the postal services provided in the better hotels. Delivery of a letter from Oman to Europe takes around one week by air and three months by sea. The cost of posting a standard 10 gram letter is currently 200 baisas. Express deliveries can be made by international courier services (UPS, DHL, Fedex, etc.) which all have branches in the Capital Area.

Public Transport

Buses run between the central bus station in Ruwi/Plaza (near the Ruwi roundabout) in the Capital Area and all the larger towns. An express line runs twice a day to Salalah and another to Dubai in the United Arab Emirates. Departure times can be found in the daily papers and on the timetables at the bus station. The buses halt only at designated stops; it is not possible to get off between these stops. For destinations outside the Capital Area it is best to buy tickets in advance at the kiosk of the Oman National Transport Company, Tel. 24708522 (Salalah, Tel. 23292773), at the northern end of the row of bus stops. The possible destinations and the exact departure times can be found written on a large blue board on the outer wall of this hut. Most routes run only two or three times a day and the bus connections over long distances are not well suited to tourists.

The **service taxis**, white minibuses, are much more flexible and run non-stop along the main roads of greater Muscat as far as Barka. They all have orange taxi signs on the roof. The service taxis stop on request along the major roads - simply put out your hand. If the driver still has free seats and is not on his way to eat or pray, he will stop. You should then state your destination. If it is on his route the driver will tell you to get in with a wave or a quick welcome greeting "t-fadl." In order to be certain that you are in the right taxi it is worth repeating your destination several times, as every taxi driver has his own special route. When you want to get out you should knock audibly (loudly!) on the roof of the vehicle. The driver then stops immediately. You pay when getting out; within the Capital Area price varies according to distance between 100 and 300 *baisa* per person and is laid down by law. Haggling is senseless. The service taxis for the country's interior going to Nizwa and Sur all leave from the Burj al Sahwah roundabout at the exit in this direction.

Taxis are normally white cars with large, orange badges on the door, a taxi sign on the roof and orange painted wings. They are the only possibility to get to places away from the main roads. In the capital there is now a **taxi telephone service**. City Taxi can be telephoned round the clock on 24602211. and Hello taxis on 24607012. Mostly you stop one of the many taxis driving around by signaling them or you go direct to the taxi stands at the airport in As Seeb, at the fish market in Mutrah, at the loop at the upper exit of the suq in Mutrah in front of the large hotel. You should agree on the price with the driver before taking the ride. The taxi fares are not regulated in the way they are with the service taxis and none of the taxis has a meter. The usual fares, according to distance are between 200 *baisas* and 5 rials within greater Muscat; taxis with a designated stand in front of the large hotels have a fixed fare which is roughly double that. Drivers of normal taxis will, when possible, stop and pick up more fares while underway in order to increase their profit. This does not change the price agreed with each person. And if you leave a taxi driver waiting, for example for the time it takes to run a few quick errands, you need to arrange a fixed price for the wait.

Ramadan

see also Festivals & Holidays, Opening Times
During the Muslim month of Ramadan it is forbidden to eat, drink or smoke in public between the hours of sunrise and sunset. People who are ill, children under twelve years old and travellers are exempt and not required to fast. The exact times of the sunrise and sunset can be found in the daily papers.

Religion

see Mosques, Churches and Ramadan

Rental Cars

see Driving

Restaurants

see also Opening Times
A bit of advice: most restaurants, especially those outside of the Capital Area are very simple and small; they typically offer menues with Indian and Arabic cuisine. Normally one eats with the fingers of the right hand, although tourists are almost always automatically provided with cutlery. (If you are not provided with cutlery or wish to use your fingers in the local fashion, please take care that you only use your right hand, as using the left hand is considered unclean. If you are left-handed you should make this clear to people around you.) These small restaurants are inexpensive; the food is simple, good and plentiful. Water, soup and fresh salad are the standard accompaniments which will be served with the main dish without having to be ordered. If you want to ensure that the dish is not too spicy or will not cause a stomach upset, it is best to rely on the judgment of Omanis whose notions of food hygiene and quality are comparable to Europeans'. If you wish to seek out a restaurant frequented by Omanis there is no need to worry: you can easily recognize them by the men frequenting the establishment who are dressed in dishdashas and Omani headwear.
Typical **Omani cuisine** served in authentic surroundings is rare and hard to locate; all such restaurants take care to have their dining rooms set apart from the public gaze.
A new restaurant offering Omani specialties with a nouvelle twist in an avant garde atmosphere is **Ukhbar** (Tel 24699826, 9-12 OMR) in Bareeq Al Shatti. Traditional foods are presented in new ways, some dishes tend toward fusion cuisine, and the "mocktails" appeal to a younger crowd. Furnishings and decorations are also a blend of modern and tradtional Omani design. Local cuisine is also offered by the **Bin Atique Restaurants**, two of which are in Salalah (see below) and one can be found in Muscat on Sultan Qaboos Street behind the MacDonalds in Al Khuwayr. The **Omani Night** at the **Al Bustan Palace Hotel** (Tel. 24799666, 20 OMR) in Muscat will also win you over with excellent local dishes. It takes place every Wednesday at 19:30 during the tourist season on a piece of ground next to the hotel. Apart from culinary delights the visitor can look forward to country folk entertainment and camels.
Fish restaurants are unfortunately rare. For friends of all kinds of seafood the **theme evenings** in some of the larger hotels are heaven on earth. For about ten Omani rials

you can eat seafood until you drop. These are offered at, among others, the **Oman Sheraton** (Wednesday) and the **Sawadi Beach Resort** (Thursday) near Barka. Fish dishes are served every evening at the **Beach Restaurant** of The Chedi Hotel. A simple but very commendable seafood restaurant is the **Fisherman's Lodge Restaurant** (Tel 24568790, OMR. 4-5) next to the mosque on the hill on the road from the highway to the Crowne Plaza Hotel in Muscat. In the ground floor market fresh fish is sold, and on the first floor the same is deliciously prepared and served. Centrally located but tucked out of sight is the Sai Seas Restaurant (tel. 2471 3949, OMR. 5-6) on the first floor next to the Al Sur Lawatiyah on the Corniche in Mutrah.

There are branches of a Persian Omani chain which are a cut above average and which offer a wide selection with menus that combine the culinary worlds of Arabia, India and China. In Ruwi there is the **Omar Khayyam r**estaurant (Tel. 2470335, near the Ruwi roundabout, behind the Getco building), in As Seeb the **Golden Spoon** Restaurant (Tel. 24624214, set back from the main road on the inland side, near the main market and the Commercial Bank of Oman). Another branch of this chain can be found in a small pavilion west of the Al Harthy Complex (Tel. 24561619) in Al Qurm. In all branches a set meal costs 4-5 OMR.

The Automatic Restaurant in Muscat (Tel. 24561500, 3-5 OMR) is a very good Lebanese restaurant; it is situated behind the SABCO center in Al Qurm. The **Arabian Garden Restaurant** (Tel. 24538932, 3–4 OMR) is hidden behind a wall along the main road, a few kilometers before As Seeb, between the Al Mawaleh roundabout (with the fort in its middle) and the Al Khawd roundabout. It is on the service road which runs parallel and east of the highway and at night it is colorfully illuminated. It is especially pleasant on warm evenings – as the name suggests it is a garden restaurant. You enter through a round opening in the wall. The seating areas are separated by large aviaries with doves, peacocks and other birds.

Spread over the **Capital Area** there are more than 100 restaurants which offer almost everything in the way of international cuisine and invite you to take a culinary journey around the world. The quality of food is generally high, the prices varying as much as the contents of the menu. The top restaurant in Oman is still the **Al Marjan** (in the Al Bustan Palace Hotel, Tel. 24799666, 20–25 OMR) with its refined **French** cuisine. Outstanding Italian food and the best pizzas in Oman at affordable prices can be had at the **Tuscany** (Tel. 24602888, 3–10 OMR) in the Muscat Grand Hyatt; very good Persian food is on offer at the **Shiraz** (Tel. 24560100, 5–10 OMR) in the Muscat Crowne Plaza Hotel; for refined Indian cuisine and a varied **vegetarian** menu go to the **Mumtaz Mahal** (Tel. 24605255, 5–10 OMR), above the waterfall in Al Qurm Park, or the **Copper Chimney** (Tel. 24780207, 5–10 OMR), opposite the HSBC Bank near the GTO Tower in Ruwi; sound Asian cooking can be had at the tiny **Princes Restaurant** (Tel. 24602213, 3–5 OMR) in Al Khuwayr, next to the Zawawi mosque.

In September 1994 the **Al Bustan Bakery** opened its first outlet. This was a memorable moment for all Europeans in the country, who had tired of the usual Indian unleavened bread, and since then it is possible to get "proper" European **bread and biscuits** in Oman. The range of goods on offer and the number of outlets is constantly being extended; every six months a different European master baker or confectioner is flown in and gives the local employees a two-week course in the secrets of his regional art of baking. European-style bakery produce is on sale in the **Muscat Intercontinental** as well as on the bread shelves of all the **Al Fair supermarkets**.

Many small restaurants offer freshly pressed fruit juices, although they are often a bit out of the way. Fruit juice shops are situated at the lower entrance of the suq in Mutrah.

Branches of the **Arab World Restaurants** chain are very simple and as a rule are to be recommended. They are distributed throughout the country and always offer fresh grilled fish, which you hardly find anywhere else. You can find one, for example, in Ruwi (main road, 1st floor with balcony overlooking the shopping boulevard), in Barka (main road), Fanja (main road), Ibri (suq), Izki (old main road), al Khaburah (main road), and in Nizwa (main road/entrance to town.) The Persian-Omani **Omar Khayyam** Restaurant in Sohar (Tel. 26842606, Al Hambar Street, opposite the hospital) offers tastes of Arabia, India and China. A small selection of other restaurants that can be recommended throughout the country are the **Arab Sea Restaurant** at the back of the Sur Hotel by the suq in **Sur**, the **al Qabil Rest-House**, the **Falaj Daris Hotel** in **Nizwa**, the **Sohar Beach Hotel** and the **Sawadi Beach Resort**.

IN SALALAH

Local Omani cuisine is offered by both of the **Bin Atique Restaurants** in **Salalah** (23rd July Street to the West on the right hand side after the asphalt surface runs out, Tel. 23292384 and on the Sultan Qaboos Road to the east, directly at the roadside as the road curves to the left, Tel. 23292380, 3–5 OMR). Both restaurants are hard to recognize from the outside and the sign is only in Arabic; however they have a unique wooden boarded frontage with no windows. Each dining party is served in an individual dining room. The **Hassan bin Thabit Restaurant** (23rd July Street on a level with the new suq, but on the other side of the road) which has very good Indian cuisine. A bit further down the street heading out of the town you can eat excellent Lebanese fare at the **Baalbeck Restaurant** (Tel. 23298834). A set meal in this simple restaurant costs about 5 OMR. For fish, try the **Al Muhit** (Tel. 23211243, 5 OMR), at the western edge of town on the road to Raysut. If you want to sample camel meat, the Asser Restaurant (Tel. 23297734) is to be recommended. It is a simple restaurant situated at the end of As Salam Street in Salalah.

■ Sharks

The waters around Oman with their abundance of fish provide an excellent habitat for various species of shark. As the supply of food along the coast is plentiful and the depth of the water near the sandy beaches of the north is shallow, sharks are seldom encountered here. Up until now no incidents with sharks are known. Nevertheless to be on the safe side you should avoid swimming with open cuts. To avoid cuts to bare feet while walking on the beaches with their sharp shells and rocks it is advisable to wear flip flops or sandals.

■ Shopping

Because of the relatively small numbers of tourists, the souvenir industry is small and under-developed in Oman. However this is no cause for regret as genuine mementos that are original and very typical of the land can be found among the goods on offer in the suqs. Among these are the embroidered caps – *kummar* – worn by the men, silver jewelry and textiles as well as various incense burners and of course frankincense. Spices

make particularly good acquisitions, their excellent quality allows you to treasure your holiday long after it is over.
If you wish to buy original Omani handicrafts and at the same time would like to help local craftsmen, try the Omani Heritage Gallery (Tel. 24696974, open daily except Friday from 9:30 to 13:00 and 16:00 to 20:00) in the Jawharat Al Shatti Complex in Shatti Al Qurm. The shop is special in that it is a non-profit enterprise and the proceeds go to supporting local craft industries. Here you can buy beautifully woven textiles from all over Oman, as well as silver jewelry and pottery from Bahla and Dhofar.
For extensive and detailed information on shopping throughout the country look for *The Complete Residents' Guide* to Oman from Explorer Publishing.

Smoking

Omanis have cultivated a refined sense of smell and love all kinds of aromas. However cigarette and cigar smoke are not generally considered pleasant stimulants of the olfactory senses. Smoking is rare and never practiced in the homes of non-smokers or as an accompaniment to a meal. In Ibadhi households smoking is forbidden, as also in all of the small restaurants throughout the country.

Soft Tourism

Tourism in Oman has grown out of its infancy but is still in a juvenile stage. The first tourists were only allowed into the country in small groups in 1990, and the numbers have been increasing dramatically year after year.
Great care is being taken that the unique culture and identity of the country with its ancient customs should not be sacrificed to Mammon. So far there is no catering to mass tourism; preferred are the small study groups and the "FITs" (foreign individual travellers) who are interested in the culture and who wish to get to know the country's customs – and are prepared to adapt to them. In this way the country should be spared the culture shock which comes from unbridled development. The number of hotels has steadily increased, from only one in 1970 to over 100 in 2009, the majority of which are of the highest standards.
While Oman's oil reserves have not yet been fully exploited, it is clear that they are not inexhaustible. The unique countryside and the coast are increasingly being seen as a potential resource for the country. A trend is already recognizable: in 1991 when Oman presented itself for the first time at the tourism fair in London, in 1992 at the Expo in Seville and in 1993 at the international tourism fair in Berlin. Since then the Sultanate of Oman has been participating annually in tourism trade fairs, encouraging inbound tourism, and expanding its tourism infrastructure. Many big new resorts have appeared in the country and many others are in planning or already under construction. With careful planning both the overcrowding found along the shores of the Mediterranean and the overextension of the infrastructure as in the UAE can be avoided, while providing a sustainable source of income, new employment opportunities, an enjoyable and enlightening experience for tourists, and at the same time protecting the environment and natural resources. Whether the concept of sustainable tourism will be maintained in the next Five Year Plan remains to be seen.

Souvenirs

see Shopping, see Markets

Special Permits

Fishing licenses are given out by the Directorate General of Fisheries, Al Khuwayr, Tel. 24696300.
Permits for **turtle watching** at the sea turtles' protected reserve at the Ras Al Jinz Scientific and Visitor Center (Tel. 96550606)

Sports

Golf

Passionate golfers can finally indulge in their favorite sport with the opening of the first green golf course (there are some places to play on sand) in the form of the Muscat Hills Golf & Country Club, in As Seeb. This 18-hole tournament course was designed by David Thomas. (www.muscathills.com, tel. 24510065).

Ice skating

Believe it or not, the temptation to add frivolous amusements even in Oman was too great to resist, as shown by the introduction of ice skating in Oman at the Al Khuwayr Center (Tel. 24696492) near the Zawawi mosque in Al Khuwayr.

Swimming & sunbathing

Tourists are requested to use only the specially designated public beaches. These stretches of coastline are not used by the fishermen as are many of the others. Here you will not cause any public annoyance when wearing bathing costumes. These beaches are found along the coast of the Capital Area and are equipped by the local authorities with sunshades made out of palm branches, or concrete gazebos, a service providing welcome relief from the sun, which you will soon learn to appreciate. On the beach you may occasionally be reminded that this is the central region for oil transport; rarely, but inevitably, the otherwise glass-clear sea carries small lumps of tar, which can wind up where tourists tread, and are easiest to remove from the soles of the feet with baby oil. If you are a beach bunny ....

Beaches from North to South:

Al Qurm beach in Al Qurm stretches from the Muscat Intercontinental to the Gulf Hotel. Because of its central location it is the most popular and most frequented beach. Small coffeeshops at the beach road offer snacks and something to drink.

Bander Jissah beach near Qantab: Undoubtedly one of the most beautiful of beaches, in a unique landscape setting with rock formations and offshore islands framed within a bay.

The beach in the next bay south of Bander Jissah is reserved for members and guests of the **Oman Dive center** situated there. It can be visited for a small fee also by guests not staying there..

Surfers can hire equipment in Muscat at the Intercontinental, the Grand Hyatt and the Al Bustan Palace hotels which are all directly by the sea.

Scuba Diving

Oman's coastal waters are considered the cleanest in the Indian Ocean, with varied and astonishing life under water, and you don't need to be a diving professional to explore them. If you snorkel along the rocks at the edge of the beaches you will immediately discover a breathtaking world of corals and fabulously colored fish of all species. This is especially true of the bays south of Bander Jissah. For people who really want to dive, or would like to learn during their holiday, some of the diving clubs offer various courses and trips for all skill levels, from beginner to professional.

Oman Dive Center,
Extra Divers, Muscat, Bander Jissah,

Tel. 24824240, Fax 24824241
info@omandivecenter.com
Beautifully situated with own lodges.

Euro-Divers-Oman,
Muscat,
Shangri-La Barr Al Jissah Resort&Spa,
Tel. 662843038, Fax 662848438
oman@euro-divers.com

Blu Zone Diving,
Marine harbor Bander ar Rowdah,
Tel/Fax 24737293
bluzone@omantel.net.om

Extra Divers Al Sawadi,
Sawadi Beach Resort,
Tel. 97259099, Fax 26795535
alsawadi@extradivers.info

Extra Divers Salalah,
Crowne Plaza Resort Salalah,
Tel. 23235333 Ext. 8328
salalah@extradivers.info

Extra Divers Musandam,
Golden Tulip Khasab
Tel./Fax 26730501
info@musandam-diving.com

Trekking & Hiking

Currently marked trekking paths are being laid throughout the entire region of the Hajar Mountains. These often run along wadis with enchanting landscapes or follow hill ranges and canyons. Hiking these paths requires that you be in good condition and have the right equipment. At the beginning of the paths there is an information board. As a rule these are not circular routes and they are often intended as a day's trek, so you should reckon on spending a night in the open, returning the next day by the way you have come, or arrange to be picked up by a friend or tour operator at the end of the trek.
Maps of the marked paths were published in the collection "Oman Trekking Explorer" by Explorer Publishing Dubai and the Ministry of Tourism, Oman. Paths that are easy to find run from Misfat Al Abriyyin to Bilad Sayt (Trekking Path W9, ca. 7 hours), from Mutrah to Riyam (Trekking Path C38, ca. 2 hours), along the Jabal Shams canyon (Trekking Path W4, 6 hours) and from Ghul through Wadi Nakhar (Trekking Path W6a, 3 hours.)
A young, very enthusiastic and good guide for trekking in the Jabal Al Akhdar massive is Mohamad Rashid Al Fahdi (Tel. 99034345, aljebelakhdar@gmail.com), who grew up in these mountains and still lives there. Having a guide not only assures that you will not lose your way, it will also facilitate contact with the people living in the mountains and provide insight to their culture.

Telephone

The international code for the Sultanate of Oman is +968. (From Europe 00968 plus the local number, from North America 011968 plus the number.) There are no local area codes within Oman, all phone numbers consist of eight digits, and you may notice that those beginning with <9> are mobile phone numbers. The telephone network is continually being modernized and extended, which has resulted in several changes in the telephone numbering system. Older publications having phone numbers of 5 or 6 digits need to be updated.
Calling abroad can be done from every public telephone without any problem. The quality of the connection is excellent thanks to the latest digital technology. The public telephones are operated with telephone cards which can be bought in many shops, in post offices and even in some restaurants. Basically you can buy a telephone card everywhere where you see a rectangular sticker the size of a sheet of paper, with a telephone symbol and saying "Pay Phone Cards." These notices are not always displayed as such and there may be only a piece of cardboard with a notice in felt tip pen. The cards are in the following amounts: 1.5, 3, 5, 10 and 12 OMR.

Calls are cheaper from 20:00-06:00 for national calls and from 21:00-06:00 for international calls. These cheaper tariffs are also valid the whole of Friday. Not all mobile telephones from abroad function in Oman despite the high technical standards. Before your journey ask your mobile operator if they have a roaming agreement with Oman.

Time Difference

The time zone is UTC +4. Add three hours to local time to determine Central European Time, or just two during European summertime. In New York it is nine hours earlier than in Muscat; with Daylight Saving Time eight hours' difference.

Tipping

As a rule restaurant and hotel bills contain a 17 percent service charge and tax. An additional tip of between 200 Baisa and 1 Omani rial is usual throughout the service sector; exceptions are bus and taxi drivers, not however the tour guide.

Toilets

In Oman there are two types of toilet: the western-type WC and the Arabic squat toilets, which you also find in southern regions of Europe. In hotels and shopping centers there is usually a choice of both. The use of toilet paper is not the norm. Cleaning is done with water and the left hand - if you are not happy with this you may want to carry paper or disposable wipes with you. The left hand is thus regarded as unclean and should never be used for eating; if you are left-handed exceptions will be made, but you should make it clear to everyone that you are left-handed, since it is usual in domestic circles for everybody to eat from a common plate! While in Oman not every restaurant has a toilet, most petrol stations do, and the government has implemented a program of installing public facilities along the roadside throughout the land.

Tour Operators

An increasing number of tour operators now have the Sultanate of Oman in their program and offer package deals. A well-maintained list of approved British tour operators specializing in various tours of Oman can be found in the Internet under **www.travel-lists.co.uk**. The author of this book has his own agency **ARABIA FELIX**, which specializes in arranging individually tailored holidays and can be found under **www.oman-tours.com**.

Apart from the big tour companies Bahwan und Sahara Tours (former Zubair Tours), in recent years a number of small travel companies have sprung up in Oman, offering standard tours and also individually tailored tours. The staff, however, are often insufficiently trained in English or about Oman itself and the offices are often staffed by guest workers from abroad rather than Omanis, as they may be paid less. Such companies are more interested in turning a quick profit from tourism than in introducing visitors to what this country has to offer. In contrast there are some young companies, led personally by competent Omanis or by foreigners who have long been resident in Oman and who love the country.

Some of them engage in the tourism business as a sideline and do not operate as smoothly as the large tourist firms, but they make up for it by giving you genuine contact with the country and its people and often provide that little something extra.

The following companies are recommended for excursions into the country's interior:

Musandam Sea Adventure Tourism
Abdulfatah Al Shuhee
P.O. Box 388 Khasab P.C. 811
Tel. 26730424, Fax 26730069
Mobile: 99346321
www.msaoman.com
Specializes in tours, boat safaris to the Shim fjord, expeditions up the Jabal Harim and to archaeological sites, fishing trips and individually-tailored tours.

Oman Geo Tours & Tourism
Salim Al Maskiry
Muscat, P.O.Box 194,
P.C. 134 Shatti Al-Al Qurm
Tel. 24600914, Fax 24600917
omangeo@omantel.net.om
The experienced field geologist Salim Al Maskiry leads expeditions into the interior. The cost for such excursions is based on expenditure, duration and amount of equipment; only three passengers can be carried in each 4WD.

MARK Tours
P.O. Box 311, Ruwi P.C. 112
Tel.: 24562444, Fax: 24565434
http://www.marktoursoman.com
The internationally-staffed agency focuses on customer service and tries to fulfill even the most difficult requests. They provide many services for the incoming tour operator ARABIA FELIX (www.oman-tours.com) and in 2004 were awarded the Oman Award of Excellence for services in the field of tourism.

Golden Sands Tours
P.O. Box 1181, CPO As Seeb, P.C. 111
Tel. 79320813 or 99386966
Fax 24685637
E-mail: sma1190@omantel.net.om
This ambitious, purely Omani travel agency is run by an Omani cartographer who puts his profound knowledge of the country at the service of small groups (at least four people) for individually tailored tours in remote regions. For example desert crossings in Wihibah and The Empty Quarter for both, experienced and non experienced drivers. The special skill to drive in the sand can be provided to non experienced drivers. Standard tours are also offered.

Arabian Sands Tours
P.O. Box 2403, P.C. 211 Salalah
Tel. 99495175, Fax 23296110
E-mail: seavllas@omantel.net.om

The owner, a Bedouin, named Mussalim Hassan Qahour Al Mahri, speaks Arabic and English, as is usual, but also Mahri and Jabali, languages found in southern Oman plus German, French and a little Russian. He is an excellent guide through the Rub al Khali desert ("the Empty Quarter") and the mountains of Dhofar.

Vaccinations

see Health, Medical Care

Water

Tap water in the Capital Area is of drinking quality and tastes alright although up to 80 percent comes from the large seawater desalination plant at Al Ghubbrah. Most people drink Omani mineral water from the two large companies Masafi and Tanuf. The desalinated service water is used for watering green areas and private gardens. Houses that are not yet connected to the water mains are supplied by tankers. Blue tanker trucks transport drinking water, green ones transport service water and yellow for is sewage water.

Weights and Measures

correspond to the European SI norm – i.e., the metric system – although on occasion you may encounter an historical imperial measure, such as gallons or feet.

Glossary

Abassid – caliphate dynasty of Baghdad (750–1258), named after Abbas, the uncle of Mohammed (ca. 565 – ca. 653.)

Abu – name prefix, "father of..."

Abu Bakr – first Caliph from 632–634 (571–634), who was supported by followers of the Sunna.

Ali – fourth Caliph from 656–658 or 661 (murdered around 660–661), when his position was attacked during the last three years by the Ummayid Muawiya; Mohammed's son in law.

Azd – Arab tribe who migrated to Oman from the Yemen.

Bayt – Arabic: house.

bani – prefix to tribal name, "sons of..."

barasti – historic type of house made from palm branches, especially in coastal areas.

Al Batinah – name of the fertile coastal region between the Hajar Mountains and the Gulf of Oman, between As Seeb and Sohar.

bin – name prefix, in Arabic script the shortened form of ibn, "son of..."

bint – name prefix, "daughter of..."

Caliph – generally used for a successor of Mohammed, although only the first four caliphs, Abu Bakr, Umar, Uthman und Ali were really recognized. The dispute over whether this successor was only to have authority over the temporal realm or should also be the spiritual leader and whether he must be from the family of the Prophet, led to the split between Sunni and Shi'a. According to the historical circumstances and the language then current, the concept of caliph has differing meanings. As a rule "caliph" describes a temporal potentate. Under the rule of the Abbasids and the Ummayids the "Caliph" was also the ruler of the Islamic realm.

Capital Area – name for the area around greater Muscat.

Corniche – name of the coastal road from Mutrah to Muscat and the coastal road in Salalah.

dhow – collective term for traditional Arab sailing ships used for transport and trade.

dishdasha – long, tunic-like mostly white or bright blue, traditional clothing for Omani men, with a collar decorated with tasselled cord.

Diwan – administration of the royal court.

jabal – Arabic: mountain.

falaj – ancient, man-made water distribution channels, plural "aflaj".

Five Pillars of Islam – the five ritual duties of every Muslim, the fulfilling of which keeps the believer on the right path. These duties are: the belief in the one true God (*shahada*); the daily prayers (*salat*); fasting (*saum*); giving alms (*zakat*); and the pilgrimage to Mecca (*hajj*).

Ghafiriy – Omani confederation of tribes, originally emigrated from the Najd region; political faction.

Hajj – pilgrimage to Mecca.

Hadith – the delivered words and deeds of the Prophet Mohammed, providing the guiding principle of Islamic law (*Shariah*.)

Hinawiy – Omani confederation of tribes, originally of Yemeni origin; political faction.

Ibadhis – followers of the Islamic teachings of the Ibadhiya, the predominant form in Oman.

Ibadhiya – Islamic teachings, which stand for a recollection of the fundamental values handed down by the Prophet Mohammed. They believe the Imam should be elected by the *umma*. In contrast to the

Kharijites, Ibadhis do not wish to propound their ideals through violence. The Ibadhiya stands rather more for tolerance and dialogue.

ibn - name prefix, "son of..."

Imam - literally: prayer leader; in common parlance often a leader in both the spiritual and temporal senses. Among Ibadhis in Oman the elected head of the religious community had the rank of a king, and often in opposition to the Sultan, the temporal ruler of Oman. On occasion this conflict led to division and civil war between the Imamate in the country's interior and the Sultanate on the coast of Muscat.

Khanjar - traditional Omani curved dagger.

Kharijites - Islamic sect, for which the highest ideal is following the prescriptions of the Quran. This led to a confrontation over the office of caliph in the early Islamic period with the Ummayid rulers. They believed that the Imam, the spiritual and temporal leader, should be elected by the community of believers, the *umma*. Because the Kharijites wanted to enforce their views through violent means, they were persecuted by the caliphs.

Khawr - lagoon, often spelled Khor

Majlis - reception room for guests of the head of the household, wali's assembly room

Mihrab - prayer niche in a mosque in the direction of Mecca.

Mina - Arabic: port.

Muawiya - first Ummayid caliph (ca. 605–680) from 661–680, opponent of Ali, the last "legitimate" caliph.

Mohammed - founder of the Islamic religion (ca. 570–632); according to Muslim belief he is the last prophet, in whom the revelation of the one God is finally made manifest. His message was directed above all against contemporary belief in many gods.

Nestorians - followers of Nestorius (381–451), the patriarch of Constantinople (428–431); Nestorian teaching denied monophysitism (the union in Christ of the human and the divine) and preached that the divine word ("Logos") as Son of God and the man Jesus were closely connected but were not one (the dual nature teaching.)

Nizari - tribe which migrated to Oman from central Arabia.

Omanization - gradual replacement of foreign workers by qualified Omanis.

PDO - Petroleum Development Oman Ltd., largest employer in the country.

Qadi - Islamic legal scholar, judge.

Qanat - subterranean water channel (type of *falaj*.)

Qibla - direction to be faced during prayer, towards Mecca. A mosque's Qibla wall accordingly contains the mihrab, the prayer niche.

Ramadan - Islamic month of fasting, when no one may smoke, eat or drink in public during daylight.

Sabkha - Arabic for salt flat or salt sea.

Sharia - the codified will of God, Islamic law.

Sheikh - oldest man of a tribe, also a respectful term of address for an old man or scholar.

Shi'a - literally: party (of Ali); collective term for numerous schools of thought and law with some theological features that divide it from the Sunna.

Sultan - widely used term for a leader, but with no precise definition. Generally a sultan is a political ruler of an Islamic state. Sultan is also a common first name for men.

Sunna - literally: tradition (of the Prophet); collective term for schools of law, which base legal judgments solely on the Quran and the word of the Prophet. This school holds that the caliphs should be elected in contrast to the Shia which states that the caliph derives his authority through being nominated by the previous caliph.

Suq - Arabic for market area, consisting of fixed rows of shops; in contrast to a bazaar, which is only partially held in the open air.

Sur - Arabic: enclosed space, fort.

Umar - second caliph from 634-644 (about 592-644, murdered); introduced the Islamic calendar.

Ummayid - ruling dynasty of a family of the Quraish clan stemming from Mecca, which held the Caliphate from 661-750, as well as ruling over the Islamic empire (capital Damascus.)

Umma - Islamic world congregation, community of believers; formerly just the community of Mohammed.

Uthman - third caliph from 644-656 (about 574-656, murdered); responsible for one of the first official versions of the Quran.

Wadi Crossing - where a road crosses a wadi on the same level; motorists should be aware of the dangers of flooding after rain.

Wahhabites - followers of Mohammed ibn Abdul Wahhab (1703/04-1792), who called for a return to the roots of Islam. In the region of central Arabian Najd this branch of belief with its requirements for proselytizing became a political force, which soon dominated the whole of the Arabian peninsula.

Wali - governor of a district (*wilaya*.)

Wesir - Minister.

Wilaya - district, administrative region; the main town is the residence of the *wali*; Oman is divided up into 49 *wilayat* (majority.)

Zakat - self-restraint of Islamic believers in the form of giving to the needy; an alms tax, one of the Five Pillars of Islam.

Literature

From summer 2010 you will be able to find a selection of literature and other interesting media about Oman in the web portal **www.oman-shop.com**.

Allen, Calvin, *Oman - The Modernization of the Sultanate*, Boulder 1987
Observations on the modernisation of Oman.

Al Maamiry, Ahmad Hamoud, *Oman and Ibadhism*, New Delhi 1989.
The emergence and development of Ibadhism in Oman.

Akehurst, John, *We won a war*, Salisbury 1982.
Description of the Dhofar War from the viewpoint of a British commander.

Albright, Frank, *The American Expedition in Dhofar*, Washington 1982.
Archaeological report on the excavations at Samharam during the Fifties.

Archive Editions, *Ruling Families of Arabia, The Royal Family of Al-Bu-Said*, London 1991
Collection of all the internal British documents on the rulers of the Al-Bu-Said dynasty until 1959.

Arkless, David, *The Secret War*, London 1988.
Account of the Dhofar War as seen by a British officer.

Bennett, Norman, *The Arab State of Zanzibar*, Boston 1984, and *Arab versus European*, New York 1986.
Bibliography on Zanzibar and a historical outline of power conflicts in the Indian Ocean.

Bhacker, Mohamad, *Trade and Empire in Muscat and Zanzibar*, London 1992.
The rise of Zanzibar as a trading center and the roots of British dominance in Oman.

Bierschenk, Thomas, *Weltmarkt, Stammesgesellschaft und Staatinformation in Südostarabien (Sultanat Oman)*, Saarbrücken 1984.
Analysis of the current structure of Omani society.

Bulliet, Richard, *The camel and the wheel*, Harvard 1975.
About the domestication and use of camels in Arabia.

Carter, John, *Tribes in Oman*, London 1982.
Most detailed descriptions of the formation of different tribes in Oman.

Costa, P. / Tosi, M., *Oman Studies*, Rome 1989.
Collection of essays on archaeology in Oman.

Defremery / Charles / Gibb / Hamilton, *The Travels of Muhammed Ibn-Abdallah Ibn-Battuta*, Cambridge 1962, 2 volumes.
Account of the famous 14th century traveller.

Dodge, Bertha, *Quests for spices and new worlds*, Hamden 1988.
About the Portuguese voyages of discovery.

Düster, J. / Scholz, E., *Bibliographie über das Sultanat Oman*, Hamburg 1980.
Bibliography on the Sultanate of Oman.

El-Mallah, Issam, *Die Rolle der Frau in der im Musikleben Omans*, Tutzing 1997.
Interesting documentation on the role of women in the musical life of Oman; with accompanying video.
Obtainable from info@oman-shop.com

El-Mallah, Issam, *Omani Traditional Music*, Part1+2, Tutzing 1998.
Comprehensive documentation in 2 volumes with accompanying video.
Obtainable from info@oman-shop.com

Fiennes, Ranulph, *Where soldiers fear to tread*, London 1983.
Another report of experiences of a British fighter during the Dhofar War. The explorer later led an expedition to discover the lost city of Ubar.

Graz, Liesl, *The Omanis. Sentinels of the Gulf*, London 1982.
Country, people and customs in Oman in the Seventies.

Hauptmann, Andreas, *5000 Jahre Kupfer in Oman*, Bochum 1985.
Account of the researches into copper mining by the Mining Museum in Bochum.

Hawkings, Clifford, *The Dhow*, Lymington 1977.
Portrayal of the traditional Arabic sailing ship.

Historical Summary of Events in the Persian Gulf Shaikdoms and the Sultanate of Muscat and Oman, Archive Ed., Gerrards Cross 1987.
Collection of official reports to the British government concerning events in the Gulf region, 1920–1953.

Hourani, G. E, *Arab Seafaring in Ancient and Early Medieval Times*, Princeton 1950.

Ibn Battuta, *The Travels of Ibn Battuta*, Picador

2003.
Ibn Ishaq, *The Life of Muhammad*, translated by Professor A. Guillaume, OUP Pakistan 1967.
Jaeckli, R., *Rock art in Oman*, 1980.
Kaster, Heinrich, *Die Weihrauchstraße*, Frankfurt 1986.
Kelly, J. B., *Sultanate and Imamate in Oman*, London 1959.
Krause, Friedrich, *Die Bedeutungsverschiebung omanischer Hafenstädte und Wandlungstendenzen im omanischen Seehandel in den letzten 1500 Jahren*, Diss. Würzburg 1983.
Martinetz / Lohs / Janzen, *Weihrauch und Myrrhe*, Berlin 1989.
Maurizi, Vincenzo, *History of Sayd Said Sultan of Muscat*, Cambridge 1984.
The life of the Sultan as seen by a Frenchman, probably a spy, in his court.
Mernissi, F., *The Veil and the Male Elite: A Feminist Interpretation of Women's Rights in Islam*, Addison Wesley 1991.
Portrayal of Mohammed, his liberal attitude towards women and the restriction of their rights after his death.
Off-Road Oman, Explorer, Dubai 2008. Description of 26 off-road tours through Oman based on very detailed satellite maps.
Popp, Georg / Al-Maskari, Juma, *Oman - das andere Arabien*, Augsburg 1995.
Photograph book in German, Arabic and English. Obtainable from info@oman-shop.com
Price, Stanley, *Animal Re-Introductions, the Arabian oryx in Oman*, Cambridge 1989.
Account of the project to reintroduce the Oryx antelope into the wild in Oman.
Pridham, B. R., *Oman: Economic, Social and Strategic Developments*, London 1987
Risso, Patricia, *Oman & Muscat, an early modern history*, New York 1986
Ruete, Emilie Said, *Memoirs of an Arabian Princess*, ed. G.S.P. Freeman Grenville, East West Publications 1996.
The memoirs of Princess Salme, the daughter of the Sultan of Zanzibar who emigrated to Germany in the 19th century.
Scholz, Fred, *Muscat*, Berlin 1990.
Detailed study of the development after 1970 of the Capital Area and other towns.
Scholz, Fred (Ed.), *Die kleinen Golfstaaten. Reichtum und Unterentwicklung - ein Widerspruch?* Klett Verlag 1999.
Economic development, economic and social change in the Gulf states.
Sella, Wanda / Watt, Martin, *Frankincense and Myrrh through the Ages and a Complete Guide to Their Use in Herbalism and Aromatherapy Today*, C.W. Daniel 2004.
Severin, Timothy, *The Sinbad Voyage*, Hutchinson 1982.
Account of the construction of a traditional dhow and a journey to Canton/ China.
Sheriff, Abdul, *Slaves, Spices and Ivory in Zanzibar*, London 1987 and *Zanzibar under Colonial Rule*, London 1991.
Studies of the economy, society and politics of Zanzibar.
Sinbad the Sailor: Seven Voyages of Sinbad the Sailor, Penguin 1995
Skeet, Ian, *Oman: Politics and Development*, New York 1992.
Modern Omani history.
Stacey International (Ed.), *The wildlife of Oman and its neighbors,* London 1981.
Depiction of Omani fauna.
Thesiger, Wilfred, *Arabian Sands*, Penguin 1984.
Account of his illegal crossings of the "Empty Quarter" between 1945 and 1950.
Thomas, R. H., *Arabian Gulf Intelligence*, Cambridge 1985.
Collection of official reports to the British Government in the 18th and 19th centuries.
Tibbets, Gerald, *Arab Navigation in the Indian Ocean before the Coming of the Portuguese*, London 1971.
Translation with commentary of Ahmad bin Majid's 15th century navigation book.
Ward, Philip, *Travels in Oman*, Cambridge/New York 1987.
Regional studies combined with description of historic journeys.
Wikan, Unni, *Behind the Veil in Arabia. Women in Oman*, University of Chicago Press 1992.
Study of the role of women in Oman 1976–1978.
Wilkinson, John, *The Imamate Tradition of Oman*, Cambridge 1987, and *Water and tribal settlement in South-East Arabia, A study of the Aflaj of Oman*, Oxford 1977.
Historic development until 1970 and a study of the water distribution system.

Literature obtainable in Oman

Al Hinai, Saif bin Nasser, *Oman*, Masqat 2007.
Wunderful black and white inpressions of the actual best Omani photographer.

Al Zubair, Mohammad, *Oman - My* Beautiful Country, Muscat 2003.
Excellent, opulently produced picture book.

Böttiger, Wilhelm, *The wildlife of Oman and its neighbors*, London 1990.
The fauna of Oman and its neighbors.

Bosch, Donald, *Seashells of Oman*, London 1982.

Costa, Paolo, *Musandam*, London 1991.
Study of Musandam made in the 1970s.

Crocker Jones, Gigi, *Traditional Spinning and Weaving in the Sultanate of Oman*, HistoricAl-Association of Oman. Ruwi 1989.
Documentation of ancient spinning and weaving techniques in Oman.

Dale / Hadwin, *Adventure Trekking in Oman*, Aberdeen 2001.
Detailed guide with maps for extreme trekkers.

Dinteman, Walter, *Forts of Oman*, London 1993.
On Oman fortress architecture.

Dorr/Richardson, *The Craft Heritage of Oman*, Motivate Publishing 2004.
Comprehensive, two-volume documentation.

Dort, Stegath, *A Taste of Oman*, Muscat
A short introduction to the country's cuisine.

Gallagher, Michael / Woodcock, Martin, *The Birds of Oman,* Muscat 1980.
Ornithological study.

Gallagher, Michael, *Snakes of the Arabian Gulf and Oman,* Muscat 1990.
An important book about the snakes of Oman and how to treat snake bites.

Haj, Maulid, *A Jail Tale,* Muscat 2004.
Autobiography of an Omani in Zanzibar before and after the revolution.

Hanna, Samir, *Field Guide to the Geology of Oman*, Muscat 1995.
Tours through the unique world of Oman's geology, the most competent book on this subject.

Hanna, S./Al-Belushi M., *Introduction to the Caves of Oman*, Muscat 1996.
Comprehensive guide to the country's fascinating but not very accessible caves.

Hawley, Donald, *Oman and its Renaissance*, London 1980, *Oman* London 2003.
Large picture book about Oman in the 1970s and its historical background.

Jayakar, A.S.G., *Omani proverbs*, Cambridge 1987
Proverbs and idioms.

Klein, H. / Brickson, R., *Off-Road in Oman*, London 1992.
A little outdated but still the best guide to off-road touring.

Malallah bin Ali bin Habib, *Outline of the History of Oman*, Muscat
Brief outline of the history of Oman.

McBrierty, Vincent / Al Zubair, Mohammad, *Oman, Ancient Civilisation: Modern Nation*, Muscat 2004.
Account of the country's history, the present and the possible future from an economic standpoint.

Miller / Morris, *Plants of Dhofar*, Muscat 1988.

Ministry of Information, Sultanate of Oman, *Journal of Oman Studies*, Volumes 1-10, Muscat 1975-1989.
Resume of the latest archaeological and biological discoveries in the form of a collection of expert articles.

Ministry of Information / Facey, Will, *Oman, a seafaring Nation*, Muscat 1979.
Comprehensive study of the trading and shipbuilding tradition in Oman.

Ministry of Tourism / Explorer, *Oman Trekking*, 12 trekking maps, Muscat 2005

Novell, John, *A Day Above Oman*, London 1992.
Bird's eye view of Oman..

Novell, John, *Now & Then - Oman*, Dubai 2001.
Very interesting picture book with photographs of Oman then and now juxtaposed together with statements from travellers in Oman from various periods.

Peyton, W.D., *Old Oman*.
Oman in historical photographs.

Salm / Baldwin, *Snorkeling and Diving in Oman*, London 1992.
Small guide for divers.

Walker, J. / Owen, S., *Off-Road in the Sultanate of Oman*, Dubai 2007.
Description of 15 Off-road tours through Oman.

Useful Phrases

In Oman, as in other Arab countries, so-called "high Arabic" is used for writing and official language, and as a spoken language only in the sermon in the mosque, in official addresses or in news broadcasts. Otherwise a variety of dialects are used in everyday life, to such an extent that speakers of different dialects often cannot understand one another. The following "useful phrases" are close to the dialect spoken in Muscat. An aid to Arabic pronunciation is also included here, as the transliteration of Arabic to English will vary depending on the source.:

Pronunciation:

Vowels written double are long: *raas "head."* Consonants that are written double are also long as in Italian rosso "red" (= *ros-so*); *ham-maam* "bath" (if it were pronounced with only one *m* it means "pigeon"!.) With consonants which are to be pronounced double but are made up of two characters only the first is written double, e.g.: *faddha* "silver" (pronounced *fadh-dha)*

': glottal stop, formed in the throat: *'Abdulla* (first name.)

dh: pronounced like *th* in *the: haadha* "the, this."

dh: more muted, generated by pressing the front end of the tongue between the upper and lower front teeth, While pressing against the upper front teeth. pronounced like *th* in *there: faddha* "silver."

dj: prononced like *j* in *John,* as in *jebel* "mountain."

gh: The nearest sound for this is that of the French *r*: *ghurfa* "room" with an uvular *r* at the beginning and a rolled *r* as medial sound.

h: The sound of this letter resembles the sound of 'strong, breathy' *h* and is always pronounced: *ahlan* is pronounced *ah-lan* and not *aalan*!

h: a sharp *h* (sound a panting dog makes): *lahma "meat."*

kh: pronounced like the *ch* in Scottish *loch: khair "happiness," shaikh "sheikh"* etc.

q: a short and sharp version of the letter 'gh' or the French *r.* According to the egion it is alos pronounced like *g* in some parts of Oman, e.g. *nagiil* or *naqiil "pass."*

r: is always an *r* rolled on the tip of the tongue: *Ramadan*.

s: is always voiceless as in *ass,* aeven at the beginning of a word: *salaam "peace."*

s: is a muted s as in the name of the town *Sohar*.

sh: is pronounced as in shoe: *shukran "thank you."*

t: is a muted *t,* in which the back of the tongue is raised to the middle of the palate: *tabiib "doctor."*

th: is pronounsed like the voiveless *th* in *thing*: *thalaatha "three."*

w: is pronounced like the *wh* in *what* auszusprechen: *wadi "valley."*

y: pronounced like the *y* in *yacht*: *yaum "day."*

z: a voiced s as in *sun*: *ruzz "rice."*

Greetings and common phrases

ألسلام عليكم	**Peace be with you!**	as-salaamu 'alaikum!
وعليكم السلام	**And with you! (answer)**	a 'alaikum as-salaam!
أهلاً	**Welcome!**	ahlan! (NOT: aalan!)
مرحباً	**Welcome! (answer)**	marhaba!
كيف حالك؟	**How are you? (to a man)**	kaif haalak?
كيف حالش؟	**How are you? (to a woman)**	kaif haalish?
بخير الحمد لله	**Very well, thank you!**	bi-khair al-hamdulillah!
صباح الخير	**Good morning!**	sabaah al-khair!
مساء الخير	**Good evening!**	masaa al-khair!
تصبح على خير	**Good night! (to a man)**	tisbah 'ala khair!
تصبحي على خير	**Good night! (to a woman)**	tisbahi 'ala khair!
تصبحوا على خير	**Good night! (to a group)**	tisbahu 'ala khair!
مع السلامة	**Goodbye!**	maa 'as-salaama!
أيوه	**yes**	aiwa
لا	**no**	la
يمكن	**perhaps**	yimkin
من فضلك	**please (to a man)**	min fadhlak
من فضلش	**please (to a woman)**	min fadhlish
من فضلكم	**please (to a group)**	min fadhlakum
شكراً	**thank you**	shukran
بكل سرور	**with pleasure**	bi kulli suruur
عفواً	**Excuse me!**	'afwan!
أنا	**I**	ana

أنتَ	**you (to a man)**	anta
أنتِ	**you (to a woman)**	anti
هو	**he**	huu, huwwa
هي	**she**	hii, hiyya
نحن	**we**	nahnu
أنتم	**you** (to a group of men)	antum
أنتُنَّ	**you** (to a group of women)	antunna
هم	**they** (about a group of men)	hum
هنَّ	**they** (about a group of women)	hinna
حقي	**my**	haqqi
حقك	**your** (to a man)	haqqak
حقش	**your** (to a woman)	haqqish
حقه	**his**	haqqeh, haqqu
حقها	**her**	haqqaha
حقنا	**our**	haqqana
حقكم	**your** (to a group of men)	haqqakum
حقكن	**your** (to a group of women)	haqqakin
حقهم	**their** (about a group of men)	haqqahum
حقكن	**their** (about a group of women)	haqqahin
إيش إسَمك ؟	**What's your name?** (to a man)	aish isma
إيش إسمِك ؟	**What's your name?** (to a woman)	aish ismish?
أناإسمي	**My name is**	(ana) ismi
أنا من	**I come from**	ana min
من أين أنتَ ؟	**Where do you come from?** (to a man)	min ain anta?

من أين أنتِ ؟	**Where do you come from?** (to a woman)	min ain anti?
أنا لا أتكلم عربي	**I don't speak Arabic**	(ana) la atkallam 'arabi
أليوم	**today**	al-yaum
بكره ،غدوة	**tomorrow**	bukra OR ghudwa
أمس	**yesterday**	ams
صباح	**morning**	sabaah OR subh
ظهر	**midday**	dhur
مساء	**evening**	masa
يوم	**day**	yaum
ليلة ، ليل	**night, darkness**	laila, lail
أسبوع	**week**	usbuu'
سنة	**year**	sana
متى	**when?**	matta
ساعة	**hour**	saa'a
كم الساعة الآن؟	**What's the time?**	kam as-saa'a a al-'aan?
الساعة الآن	**It's ...**	as-saa'a a al-'aan ...
بعد ساعتين	**In two hours**	ba'ad saa'atain
بعد... ساعات	**In ... hours** (3-10)	ba'ad ... saa'aat
بعد... ساعة	**In ... hours** (more than 10)	ba'ad ... saa'a
بعد...يومين	**In two days**	ba'ad yaumain
بعد...أيام	**In ... days** (3-10)	ba'ad ... ayyaam
بعد...يوم	**In ... days** (more than 10)	ba'ad ... yaum
بعد أسبوعين	**In two weeks**	ba'ad usbuu'ain
بعد أسابيع	**In ... weeks** (3-10)	ba'ad ... asaabii'

بعد أسبوع	**In ... weeks** (more than 10)	ba'ad ... usbuu'
في الساعة ...	**At ... o'clock**	fii as-saa'a
نلتقي في الساعة ...	**We'll meet at ...**	niltaqi as-saa'a
نلتقي في ...	**We'll meet in ...**	niltaqi fii
أين يوجد؟	**Where is ...?**	ain judjad ...?
هل يوجد ؟	**Is there ...?**	hal judjad ...?, hal fii ...?
لايوجد ،ما في	**No, there isn't one**	la judjad, maa fii
كم ؟	**How much?**	kam?
بكم ؟	**What does it cost?**	bikam ...?
أين ؟	**Where?**	ain?
هنا	**here**	huna OR hina
هناك	**there**	hunaak OR hinaak

Hotel and Restaurant

فندق	**hotel**	funduq
غرفة	**room**	ghurfa
في غرفة فاضية ؟	**Do you have a room available?**	fii ghurfa faadhiya?
غرفة بسرير واحد	**single room**	ghurfa bi sariir waahid
غرفة بعدة أسرة	**room with more than one bed**	ghurfa bi 'iddat saraayir
أنا أقيمُ... ليالى	**I'm staying ... nights**	(ana) oqim ... layaali
أين الحمام ؟	**Where is the bathroom/toilet?**	ain al-hammam?
مطعم	**restaurant**	mat'am
ماء	**water**	maa
مياه معدنية	**mineral water**	mia maadiniya
ماء للشرب	**drinking water**	maa ash-shurb

ممكن أشرب هذا الماء	**Can I drink this water?**	mumkin ashrab haadha l-maa?
شاي	**tea**	shaahi OR shai
قهوة	**coffee**	qahwa
مشروب	**cold soft drink**	mashrub baarid
دجاج	**chicken**	didjaadj
لحمة	**meat**	lahma
سمك	**fish**	samak
كبدة	**liver**	kibda
رز	**rice**	ruzz
طبيخ	**vegetables**	tabiikh
بطاطا	**potatoes**	bataata
طماطم	**tomatoes**	tamaatim
بيض مع الطماطم	**eggs with tomatoes**	aidh ma' tamaatim
لبن،زبادي	**yoghurt, drinking yoghurt**	zabaadi, laban
عصير ليمون	**lemon juice**	asir limun
خبز أبيض	**white bread**	khubz abiadh
خبز	**unleavened bread**	khubz
حلوى	**omani sweet**	halwa

Travelling

سيارة	**car**	sayyara
تكسي	**collective taxi**	taksi
باص	**bus**	baas
طيارة	**aeroplane**	tayyaara

مطار	**airfield**	mataar
أين محطة ألباص،تكسي ؟	**Where is the bus stop/taxi stand?**	ain mahtahat al-baas/at-taksi?
كم تستغرق الرحلة من ...إلى... ؟	**How long does the journey from ... to ... last?**	kam tastaghriq ar-rihla min ... ila ...?
ألطريق مسفلت ؟	**Is the road asphalted?**	at-tariiq musaflat?
كم كيلومتر من ... إلى...؟	**How many km from ... to ...?**	kam kilumetr min ... ila ...?
في فندق ،مطعم ؟	**Is there a hotel/restaurant?**	hal judjad fundu mat'am?
أين أقرب محطة بترول ؟	**Where is the next petrol station?**	ain aqrab mahattat bitruul?
يسار	**left**	yasaar
يمين	**right**	yamiin
طوالي	**straight ahead**	tawaali
فوق	**above**	fauq
تحت	**below**	taht
قدام	**in front**	quddaam
في الخلف	**behind**	fil-khalf
على مهلك !	**slow down!**	'ala mahlak!
بسرعة	**fast**	bi-sur'a
قف	**stop!**	qif!
أين المدينة القديمة ،ألآثار ؟	**Where is/are the old town/ ruins?**	ain al-madiina l-qadiima/ al-athaar?
أين ألمطعم،ألفندق ؟	**Where is there a restaurant/hotel?**	ain al-mat'am/ al-funduq?

Emergency

أىن أجد طبيب،ألبوليس ؟	**Where can I find a doctor/ policeman?**	ain adjid tabiib (duktuur)/ al-buliis?
أحتاج طبيب	**I need a doctor!**	ahtadj tabiib!

عندي ألم	**I'm in pain!**	'andi alam!
رأس	**head**	raas
ذراع	**arm**	dhiraa
رجل	**leg**	ridjl
بطن	**stomach**	batn
خفيف	**mild**	khafiif
قوي،شديد	**strong**	qawi, shadiid
حمى	**fever**	humma
صداع	**headache**	suddaa'
زكام،زكمة	**cold/headache**	zakma, zukaam
إسهال	**diarrhoea**	is-hall
آلام في البطن	**upset stomach**	alam fil-batn
دوخة	**sickness, dizziness**	daukha
إلتهاب العيون	**eye inflammation**	iltihaab al'uyuun

In the souk

أين سوق ألحوائج ؟	**Where is the spice souk?**	ain suuq al-hawaayidj?
فلفل	**pepper, chillies**	filfil
قرفة	**cinnamon**	qirfa
هيل	**cardamom**	hail
ملح	**salt**	milh
سكر	**sugar**	sukkar
بخور	**frankincense, incense mix**	bukhuur
بن	**coffee beans**	bunn
ماهذا ،إيش هذا ؟	**What is that?**	maa hadha? OR aish hadha?

زبيب	**raisins**	zabiib
عنب	**grapes**	'inab, (enab)
تفاح	**apples**	tuffah
موز	**bananas**	mauz
بطيخ	**watermelons**	batidkh
برتقال	**oranges**	burtuqaal
بصل	**onions**	basal
جزر	**carrots**	djazar
أين سوق الفضة ؟	**Where is the silver souk ?**	ain suuq al-faddha?
خنجر	**dagger**	khandjar
عقد	**chain**	'iqd
علبة تحف	**jewellery box**	'ilbat tuhaf
حجاب	**amulet**	hidjaab
فضة	**silver**	faddha
ذهب	**gold**	dhahab
قديم	**old**	qadiim
جديد	**new**	djadiid
غالي	**expensive**	ghaali
غالي كثير	**too expensive**	ghaali kathiir
أنا أخذ هذا	**I'll take that one**	(ana) aakhud haadha
بكم هذا كله ؟	**How much does that make?**	bikam haadha kulle?
عندك شيء ثاني ؟	**Have you other ...?**	aaindaka shai' thaani?
أرني هذا من فضلك	**Please show me that one!**	arini haadha min fadhlak!

Numbers

واحد ١	**one**	waahid
إثنين ٢	**two**	ithnain
ثلاثة ٣	**three**	thalaatha
أربعة ٤	**four**	arba'a
خمسة ٥	**five**	khamsa
ستة ٦	**six**	sitta
سبعة ٧	**seven**	sab'a
ثمانية ٨	**eight**	thamaaniya
تسعة ٩	**nine**	tis'a
عشرة ١٠	**ten**	'ashara
عشرين ٢٠	**twenty**	'ishriin
ثلاثين ٣٠	**thirty**	thalaathiin
أربعين ٤٠	**forty**	arba'iin
خمسين ٥٠	**fifty**	khamsiin
ستين ٦٠	**sixty**	sittiin
سبعين ٧٠	**seventy**	sab'iin
ثمانين ٨٠	**eighty**	thmaaniin
تسعين ٩٠	**ninety**	tis'iin
مئة ١٠٠	**one hundred**	miyya
مئتين ٢٠٠	**two hundred**	miyyatain
ثلاثة مئة ٣٠٠	**three hundred**	thalaathmiyya
ألف ١٠٠٠	**one thousand**	alf

Days of the week

يوم السبت	**Saturday**	yaum as-sabt
يوم الأحد	**Sunday**	yaum al-ahad
يوم الإثنين	**Monday**	yaum al-ithnain
يوم الثلاثاء	**Tuesday**	yaum ath-thulathaa'
يوم الأربعاء	**Wednesday**	yaum al-arbiaa'
يوم الخميس	**Thursday**	yaum al-khamiis
يوم الجمعة	**Friday**	yaum al-djum'a

Months

يناير	**January**	yanaayir
فبراير	**February**	fibraayir
مارس	**March**	maaris
أبريل	**April**	abriil
مايو	**May**	maayu
يونيو	**June**	yunyu
يوليو	**July**	yulyu
أغسطس	**August**	aghustus
سبتمبر	**September**	sibtambar
أكتوبر	**October**	uktuubar
نوفمبر	**November**	nufambar
ديسمبر	**December**	disambar

Index

R

S

T

U

W

Odyssey Books & Guides is a division of Airphoto International Ltd.
1401 Chung Ying Building, 20–20A Connaught Road West, Sheung Wan, Hong Kong
Tel: (852) 2856 3896; Fax: (852) 3012 1825
E-mail: magnus@odysseypublications.com; www.odysseypublications.com

Distribution in the USA by W.W. Norton & Company, Inc., 500 Fifth Avenue, New York, NY 10110, USA; Tel: 800-233-4830; Fax: 800-458-6515; www.wwnorton.com

Distribution in the UK and Europe by Cordee Ltd., 11 Jacknell Road, Dodwells Bridge Industrial Estate, Hinckley, Leicestershire LE10 3BS, UK. Tel: 01455 611185; info@cordee.co.uk; www.cordee.co.uk

Distribution in Australia by Tower Books Pty Ltd., a member of the Scribo Group. Unit 18 Rodborough Road, Frenchs Forest, NSW 2086, Australia; www.towerbooks.com.au

***Oman: Jewel of the Arabian Gulf,* First Edition**
ISBN: 978-962-217-813-7
Library of Congress Catalog Card Number has been requested.

Photography/illustrations courtesy of Georg Popp and Juma Al-Maskari with the exception of: Edition Temmen Archive, pp 36, 41, 48–51, 62, 71, 86, 104, 194, 236, 248, 267 top, 285; Paul Yule, pp 341, 345; Dorothea Zeeb pp 19, 235

Translation: Russell Patien
Proof reading: Michael Dickinson
Cartography: Kartographie Huber, Arabia Felix, Edition Temmen
Layout: ARABIA FELIX Synform GmbH, Munich, Germany
Production: Edition Temmen, Bremen, Germany